Praise for *Spiritual Literacy*

"*Spiritual Literacy* will have you being more aware of the simplest object in your life to the most profound one. . . . I love that it is a collection of thoughts and feelings from many different people who all have different ideas about acknowledging the sacred in our lives. *Spiritual Literacy* is inspirational, educational, and challenging. It is easy to lose yourself in it and suddenly discover an hour has slipped by without your being aware of it. I call that a good book!"
—Rhonda Dicksion, *The New Times, Seattle*

"A gem of a book. . . . Therapeutic as well as thoroughly enjoyable to read. . . . Underneath the prodigious output of the Brussats is a core spirituality about the meaning of contemporary life that can come only from a lifetime of reading and interpreting the best that culture has to offer. . . . *Spiritual Literacy* is like a life raft to those on the verge of going under—persons with an unfulfilled hunger for more meaning and substance to their existence."
—Joseph C. Farah, *The Indianapolis Star*

"This book is a remarkable resource to begin (or continue) a rich and rewarding journey. . . . A vibrant hymn to seeing life in a different more attuned way. . . . It would be a perfect gift, a wonderful nightstand companion, and a worthwhile addition to anyone's library."
—Deborah McCann, *Religion Teacher's Journal*

"An encyclopedic single volume of spiritual nuggets. . . . When you need something to chew on, open to any page."
—Donna Schaper, *St. Anthony Messenger*

"Here is an excellent book to pick up and read a few quotations before bed, or as part of a morning ritual . . . . [It] includes a list of sources for the quotation, so that readers may follow their interests in certain areas, plus an extensive index of both subjects and writers."
—Gordon Houser, *The Mennonite*

"For those seeking messages of inspiration and tools to implement their faith, this book is an excellent beginning. It moves far beyond . . . feel-good prose . . . to provide practical suggestions for making the world better."
—Janet Silver Ghent, *Jewish Bulletin*

"This is an anthology you will find yourself going back to again and again, a real help in the great adventure that is a spiritual life."
—Rich Heffern, *Praying*

"Guide[s] the reader, in prose, poetry, and prayers, to consideration of the many aspects of life experience. . . . The reader can dip at random into the Brussats' book and sharpen the senses—of sight, sound, smell, touch—as well as find much food for thought."
—William Metzger, *The Quest*

"Because spiritual literacy requires practice, the authors include numerous journal exercises, activities (including watching particular videos), and rituals. This is a book I'll keep handy on the nightstand or on the table next to my favorite reading chair, to dip into again and again."
—Lynn Murray Willeford, *New Age Journal*

"This imaginative collation of stories, sayings, and observations drawn from a variety of traditions positions spirituality exactly where it should be, enmeshed in the web of everyday life. . . . *Spiritual Literacy* could help millions of people who might feel uncomfortable with standard piety to recover a sense of the sacred in the ordinary."
—Harvey Cox, author of *Fire from Heaven*

"Skewering shish kebab is an art. Mary Ann and Frederic Brussat are cordon bleu chefs in the art of literary shish kebab: the morsel you savor is precisely the one for which the previous one has primed your taste buds. Such magic would whet our appetite for almost any topic. No need for that. Here the topic is one for which we are famished: the sacred in everyday life. Here skewing shish kebab becomes a sacred art."
—Brother David Steindl-Rast, author of *The Music of Silence*

"*Spiritual Literacy* is a rare mixture of philosophic wisdom, humor, and plain good sense, three ingredients that, when taken together, inevitably create a sense of the sacred."
—Jacob Needleman, author of *A Little Book on Love*

"How do we find the sacred in the ordinary? By opening our eyes and delighting in Frederic and Mary Ann Brussat's extraordinary book *Spiritual Literacy*. This rich, evocative celebration of the Mystery in the mundane is a generous gift of grace!"
—Sarah Ban Breathnach, author of *Simple Abundance*

SPIRITUAL LITERACY

LITERACY

Reading the Sacred in Everyday Life

FREDERIC AND MARY ANN BRUSSAT

A TOUCHSTONE BOOK
PUBLISHED BY SIMON & SCHUSTER

TOUCHSTONE
Rockefeller Center
1230 Avenue of the Americas
New York, NY 10020

First Touchstone Edition 1998
TOUCHSTONE and colophon are registered trademarks of Simon & Schuster Inc.

DESIGNED BY ERICH HOBBING

Text set in Aldus

Manufactured in the United States of America

7 9 10 8 6

The Library of Congress has cataloged the Scribner edition as follows:
Brussat, Frederic.
Spiritual literacy: reading the sacred in everyday life/
Frederic and Mary Ann Brussat.
p.   cm.
Includes index.
1. Spiritual life.   2. Literacy.   I. Brussat, Mary Ann.
II. Title
BL624.B75   1996
291.4—dc20
96–21272
CIP

ISBN 0-684-81533-8
ISBN 0-684-83534-7 (Pbk)

Permissions and Sources start on page 549.

To all our teachers:
animate and inanimate,
direct and indirect,
visible and invisible.

ALSO EDITED BY FREDERIC AND MARY ANN BRUSSAT

100 WAYS TO KEEP YOUR SOUL ALIVE:
Living Deeply and Fully Every Day

100 MORE WAYS TO KEEP YOUR SOUL ALIVE

CONTENTS

CONTENTS

FOREWORD

BY THOMAS MOORE

It's odd that after thousands of years of great spiritual example and lit-erature we have to remind ourselves that spirituality is to be found in everyday life. The world's sacred poetry, ritual, prayer, and art are filled with images of incarnated divinity, or the eternity that lies, admittedly sometimes hidden, in the temporal, or the transpersonal that animates our personal lives. Hundreds of times painters have taken up the theme of the "Annunciation" and have pictured that moment, that eternal moment that is in all our lives, when the angel says: "You, mortal person, have divinity in you." Similar teachings are evident in Tibetan tangkas and in Indian sculptures and when William Blake says, "Eternity is in love with the productions of time."

Caught up in the immediate and the temporal, we forget the great vision and the eternal truths, or we divide one from the other, giving intense attention to the eternal on Sunday or Saturday or some other special day, while thinking that every other day is somehow unrelated to our death, the whole of our lives, and to the cosmos that is its setting.

The problem, of course, is not only a personal one. Culture has pro-gressed to a point where we imagine the human body as a machine, as a chemical apparatus, or as a computerized system, where the soul has been reduced to human behavior and genetic determinants, the whole gamut of meaning, values, purpose, and character given over to the clev-erness of philosophers or the experts in psychology who present them-selves as the secular priests of a self-improving congregation.

In the best of worlds, we can thoroughly enjoy our secularity pre-cisely because we cultivate a spiritual vision. But in the worst of worlds, these two dimensions become split, one turning into egotistic secular-ism and the other into jealous and defensive religious demagoguery. Our current effort, of which this book is an excellent example, is aimed at restoring lost bonds of spirit and matter, body and mind, church and home, work and prayer.

For years, I have been persuaded by Neoplatonists, Christian poet theologians, Greek drama, Jungian psychology, archetypal psychology, and Romantic poets that the missing third element in our divided life is the soul. It isn't sufficient to find oneself living in a materialistic world and determine to restore its lost spirituality. That response easily becomes what psychologists might call a compensatory reaction that for the best of motives might maintain the destructive divisions and paint too literal and simple a picture of the recovered spirituality. We need a fresh perspective, one that reimagines both the secular life and spiritual activity so they can be naturally in alignment with each other.

Our spiritual life needs the soul-stuff of ritual, story, image, sensation, memory, and quotidian happenstance. Our secular lives need the vision, reverence, piety, values, reflection, service, and commitments offered by a spiritual sensibility. When each side of this split is essentially affected and reconfigured by the other, then we might see a reconciliation of the two, and both our spirituality and our secularity might enjoy qualities of the soul, which, according to many ancient teachings, is the factor that makes us human.

Here I see the importance of the work done so devotedly by Fred and Mary Ann Brussat. For years, they have engaged in extraordinary projects that dig deep into the popular culture and deep into the spiritual resources found around the globe. They have recognized ties and relationships that are invisible to ordinary eyes. They have enjoyed the fourfold vision espoused by William Blake, transcending a materialistic view of culture, finding values and visions in the ordinary arts of film, video, television, books, and spoken-word audios.

Further, they have presented their insights in new forms, such as the Alphabet of Spiritual Literacy in this book or the reviews, lists, quotations, aphorisms, anecdotes, and encouragements that lace their work as a whole. They have found creative alternatives to the usual tendency of making spirituality superior, bodiless, and far removed from popular culture.

It has become painfully clear that a remote spirituality has little or no impact on the way we live as a society. People go to religious services and yet continue to pollute, take excessive profits, encourage wars, oppress, foment political division, maintain racial injustice, and promote their own moralistic agendas at the expense of a deeply moral responsiveness to a world in trouble. It's time to bring spirituality home, close to the heart and essentially connected to ordinary life.

Call it incarnational theology. Call it the reconciliation of nirvana and samsara. Call it natural spirituality. Whatever words we use, the important thing is finally to deal with the self-destructive split between the holy and the ordinary that has plagued us for centuries. I would go so far as to say that a spirituality that doesn't touch every single aspect of daily, personal, and commercial life is bogus. It's a defense and an escape from the real challenge of life, the divine call within being itself, as the theologian Paul Tillich might say.

In this volume, Fred and Mary Ann Brussat have given us their kaleidoscopic view, full of color and fun, of the wisdom of the ages, including our own. We need this wisdom desperately in a time when information and data have taken the place of insight. We need opportunities such as the one presented in this book to meditate and reflect, not just to learn and act. And it doesn't hurt to discover how many different people of our own time are hard at work sorting through the obstacles so often associated with spiritual endeavors.

As a parent, I see an additional value of this book in the way it encourages adults and children to explore the spiritual life together. One thing readers of all ages might do in response is to make their own collection of spiritual insights. We need our ancestors, guides, and fellow travelers in this work of the spirit, a community of the imagination gathered between the endpapers of a precious book. We might learn from the Brussats how to reimagine literacy for ourselves, aiming not for information and skill, but for wisdom and pleasure.

SPIRITUAL
LITERACY

INTRODUCTION

Life is a sacred adventure. Every day we encounter signs that point to the active presence of Spirit in the world around us. Spiritual literacy is the ability to read the signs written in the texts of our own experiences. Whether viewed as a gift from God or a skill to be cultivated, this facility enables us to discern and decipher a world full of meaning.

Spiritual literacy is practiced in all the world's wisdom traditions. Medieval Catholic monks called it "reading the book of the world." Muslims suggest that everything that happens outside and inside us is a letter to be read. Native Americans find their way through the wilderness by "reading sign." From ancient times to today, spiritually literate people have been able to locate within their daily life points of connection with the sacred.

For us, the signs have come most often from books and popular culture. Even as a young boy, I was an avid reader. A life organized around books began in earnest when I was in high school and started collecting my own library. Each new book meant the beginning of a treasure hunt for meaning as I underlined significant passages. By the time I attended theological seminary to study for the Christian ministry, my small village of books had grown into a city. I filled binders with notes on the collection, along with reviews of the films I was seeing.

Meanwhile, as a young woman, I was more interested in the new medium of television. But I did love quotations. When I was in college, I copied into blank books my favorite poems, prayers, and passages from letters, novels, and nonfiction works. In a very real sense, these were my holy books filled with the wisdom I found most useful.

When we decided to get married in 1969, we realized that books and quotations truly had been lifeshaping for us. In order to honor this during the ceremony, we had our wedding party read us meaningful quotations before we took our vows. This ritual expressed what we had long felt but not really articulated: that reading itself is a spiritual practice

15

which defines us, unites us, and helps us discover the sacred in our everyday life.

After our wedding, we moved to New York City and created a review magazine for Christian ministers and youth workers. In our brochure, we acknowledged that we felt called "to relate the living Word of God to the happening world," and this meant being attentive to the times in which we lived.

The 1960s, then coming to a close, had made clear to us that reading books was not enough. Other texts demanded interpretation as meaning bearers. Feature films spoke to a whole generation of baby boomers in ways that books did not, and rock music had become the underground newspaper of the airwaves. It was mood, myth, and message, exploring issues from personal values questions to larger social concerns such as peace, ecology, and racism. By reviewing movies and popular music for our magazine, we expanded our spiritual practice to incorporate these cultural texts.

We also began to look for meanings in that most pervasive of contemporary life situations—watching television. In 1978, we started a decade-long career, writing values-oriented discussion guides to TV programs for schools, community groups, and churches and synagogues. During the period we still regard as the golden age of TV movies and miniseries, we organized community awareness campaigns around dozens of dramas on such historical events and social issues as the Holocaust, nuclear proliferation, battered women, incest, AIDS, and homelessness. We discovered that television is a powerful storyteller which constantly creates occasions for us to identify, test, and exercise our values. These projects taught us that even the most commercial entertainment medium can provide spiritual nourishment by encouraging us to learn more about ourselves and our neighbors.

Often throughout our career, we have been asked why we devote so much energy to the popular culture. At those times, we recall a statement by Protestant theologian Samuel H. Miller: "In the muddled mess of this world, in the confusion and the boredom, we ought to be able to spot something—an event, a person, a memory, an act, a turning of the soul, a flash of bright wings, the surprise of sweet compassion—somewhere we ought to pick out a glory to celebrate." For more than twenty-five years, we have been reading books, viewing movies and videos, watching television, and listening to records and tapes, and we have picked out many glories to celebrate.

CONTEMPORARY READINGS
OF UNIVERSAL EXPERIENCES

The reviews, meditations, and discussion guides we have published in our magazines and newsletters, as well as those we have written for other publications, have focused on the values and visions in contemporary culture. We have assumed that the spiritual dimension of life is evident everywhere, not just in holy places and exceptional deeds.

Since 1990, we have devoted ourselves to identifying materials that would be good companions for those on a spiritual journey. We have sought out cultural resources which are expressive of the quest for meaning and purpose, wholeness and healing, commitment and community, contemplation and social activism. In other words, we have wanted to be tutored by spiritually literate contemporaries. It is their words and observations we have collected in this book.

Some of these writers you will recognize as spiritual teachers. Others are poets, playwrights, screenwriters, nature writers, novelists, and essayists. Some of our sources are very obvious; others are unlikely or unexpected. What they share, and what we admire in them, is their ability to find and describe Spirit near at hand.

The readings in this book reflect the wide variety of approaches to and experiences of the sacred in everyday life. Many of us recognize the presence of Spirit moving in our lives through encounters with things, places, nature, and animals. Chapters two, three, four, and five include selections on these common catalysts of spirituality.

Our activities also put us on a spiritual path. Everything from cooking, eating, chores, hobbies, the creative arts, and work can be important steps toward a life of spiritual meaning, as the readings in chapters six and seven attest. When we see the world with a spiritually literate focus, we frequently find ourselves moved to service; chapter eight is a guide to this path.

A spiritual perspective is perhaps most evident in our relationships. We use this term broadly to refer to the many connections in our lives. For example, we are intimately attached to our bodies, as is clear through our sexuality and our approaches to health, illness, and death. We obviously have close ties to partners, family, and friends, but we are also part of layers and layers of communities. Chapters nine, ten, and eleven bring together illustrations of these relational paths.

We come full circle in the final chapter to the most concrete experiences of daily life. Beginning with waking up in the morning and ending with a late-night snack, these readings show us how Spirit moves through our ordinary activities and becomes known to us.

Throughout the book, we have added spiritual readings of our personal experiences. In many instances, we were prompted to practice spiritual literacy in this way by one of the passages we have quoted. It is our hope that, as you read through this book, you will be inspired to do the same.

A SKILL WITH NO PREREQUISITES

Is spiritual literacy difficult? Are there any prerequisites? Do you need to have reached some state of enlightenment to be able to decode the world? Some traditions do see such understanding as a gift or "awakening," but we believe it is a skill that can be developed.

Spiritual literacy is integral to the practice of the world's religions, and we will present evidence of this from a number of sources. Although our own background is Christian, and Jesus is a great exemplar of spiritual literacy, we certainly do not believe that finding the sacred in the everyday is limited to any one religious tradition.

In any case, we are talking about spiritual literacy, not religious literacy. Many people today describe themselves as spiritual but not religious, and we honor this distinction. A useful image was offered by Bede Griffiths, a Christian who spent most of his life in India. During a video interview made shortly before his death in 1993, Griffiths spread out his hand. The religions are like the separate fingers, he said, and are quite distinct from each other. But if you trace them to their source, the palm of the hand, you see that they all come together in their depths. Thirteenth-century German mystic Meister Eckhart put it another way, calling God an underground river of wisdom with many wells tapping into it.

The readings and our commentaries in this book are fed by that river of universal wisdom. Spiritual literacy is not concerned with sorting out religious dogmas and beliefs. To be spiritually literate does not require you to master certain texts or to climb to a high rung on the ladder of enlightenment. It is not an esoteric and mysterious practice for the initiated few; indeed, spiritual literacy is the very opposite of such elitism. Some of the most spiritually literate people are children and indigenous people who cannot even read letters on a page. For them and for us, literacy means being able to find sacred meaning in all aspects of life.

The more adept we become at reading the world spiritually, the more comfortable we will be with different images of God. For example, in the Hebrew Bible, Yahweh is described as a potter, a weaver, an eagle, a midwife, and more. In the New Testament, Jesus concocts images of God as a woman who diligently searches her house for a lost coin, as a shepherd who risks all to find one last straggler, and as a father who welcomes his prodigal son back with open arms.

All the world's religions have contributed images to a vast collection of titles and metaphors for God. Throughout this book, we freely use different designations, capitalizing them to indicate their reference to the holy and always keeping in mind that while a certain image may contain elements of the truth, no one image can capture the whole Truth.

THE BASICS:
THE ALPHABET OF SPIRITUAL LITERACY

Most of us started reading lessons by learning the alphabet. We have borrowed that bit of pedagogy and created an Alphabet of Spiritual Literacy, a collage of wisdom from the world's religions and from spiritual teachers of all eras. Spread throughout the book, these letters elaborate on the practices of spirituality which show up repeatedly in the chapters of readings.

Following is a summary of the Alphabet of Spiritual Literacy, with pointers on how the practices can spell meaning in your daily life. If ever you are tempted to ask why a particular passage in this book is spiritual, check the alphabet, and you will find that it demonstrates one of these practices.

A
ATTENTION

Pay attention. Stay awake and totally alert. See with receptive eyes and discover a world of ceaseless wonders.

B
BEAUTY

Walk the path of beauty. Relish and encourage its inward and outward expressions. Acknowledge the radiance of the creation.

BEING PRESENT

Live in the present moment. Don't obsess about the past or worry about the future. All you need is right here now.

C
COMPASSION

Open your heart, mind, and soul to the pain and suffering in the world. Reach out to others and discover the rewards and obligations of deep feeling.

CONNECTIONS

Cultivate the art of making connections. See how your life is intimately related to all life on the planet.

D
DEVOTION

Express your feelings of praise and adoration through devotional practices. Pray with words and pray through your actions.

E
ENTHUSIASM

Celebrate life with this intoxicating passion. It adds zest to everything and helps build community. Hold nothing back.

F
FAITH

Recognize and accept that there is another dimension to life than what is obvious to us. Live with obstacles, doubt, and paradox, knowing that God is always present in the world.

FORGIVENESS

In both your private and public lives, discover the sweet release that comes from forgiving others. Feel the healing balm of being forgiven and of forgiving yourself.

G
GRACE

Accept grace and your world will be larger, deeper, richer, and fuller. Look for its intimations everywhere. Let this seed of the Giver of Life bloom in your words and deeds.

GRATITUDE

Spell out your days with a grammar of gratitude. Be thankful for all the blessings in your life.

H
HOPE

Let this positive and potent emotion fuel your dreams and support your service of others. Through your attitudes and actions, encourage others never to lose hope.

HOSPITALITY

Practice hospitality in a world where too often strangers are feared, enemies are hated, and the "other" is shunned. Welcome guests and alien ideas with graciousness.

I
IMAGINATION

Give imagination free rein in your life. Explore its images and ponder its meaning-making moments, and it will always present you with something new to be seen, felt, or made known.

J
JOY

Rejoice and be exceedingly glad. Find this divine energy in your daily life and share it with others.

JUSTICE

Seek liberty and justice for all. Work for a free and fair world where oppression and inequality no longer exist.

K
KINDNESS

Let Spirit flow through you in little acts of kindness, brief words of encouragement, and manifold expressions of courtesy. These deeds will add to the planet's fund of good will.

L
LISTENING

Cultivate the art of deep listening in which you lean toward the world in love. All things in the universe want to be heard, as do the many voices inside us.

LOVE

Fall in love over and over again every day. Love your family, your neighbors, your enemies, and yourself. And don't stop with humans. Love animals, plants, stones, even the galaxies.

M
MEANING

Constantly try to discover the significance of your experiences. Seek further understandings from sacred texts and spiritual teachers.

N
NURTURING

Take good care of the best that is within you. Self-exploration and personal growth continue throughout our lifetimes and equip us to tend to the needs of others.

O
OPENNESS

Hold an open house in your heart for all people and all things. Practice empathy with others and receptiveness toward the universe.

P
PEACE

Protect the earth's future by promoting peace every day. Your small steps will link you with others who are combating violence in the world.

PLAY

Be playful. Express your creative spirit in spontaneity. Hurrah the pleasures of being, and let loose your laughter.

Q
QUESTING

Savor questions and thrill to the quest. See your life as a journey that quickens your faith and deepens your soul.

R
REVERENCE

Practice reverence for life. The sacred is in, with, and under all the things of the world. Respond with appropriate respect and awe.

S
SHADOW

Give up trying to hide, deny, or escape from your imperfections. Listen to what your demons have to say to you.

SILENCE

Slow down. Be calm. Find a place where you can regularly practice silence. There you will find the resources to revitalize your body, mind, and soul.

T
TEACHERS

Be willing to learn from the spiritual teachers all around you, however unlikely or unlike you they may be. Always be a sensitive student.

TRANSFORMATION

Welcome the positive changes that are taking place in your life. Open up the windows and let in some fresh air. Wholeness and healing are waiting in the wings.

U
UNITY

In this age of global spirituality, respect differences but affirm commonalities. Work together with those who are trying to make the world a better place.

V
VISION

Practice the art of seeing the invisible. Use the wisdom of your personal visions to renew yourself and your community.

W
WONDER

Cultivate a vibrant curiosity and welcome the reports of your senses. The world is alive and moving toward you with rare epiphanies and wonderful surprises. Remember you are standing on holy ground.

X
THE MYSTERY

Accept the unknown as part of life. Don't try to unravel the profound mysteries of God, human nature, and the natural world. Love the ineffable.

Y
YEARNING

Follow your heart's boundless desire. It takes you out of yourself and fosters an appreciation for the multidimensional pleasures of life.

You

Accept that you are a child of God. Sing your own song with gusto. Fulfill your mission as a copartner with the Holy One in the unfolding drama of the universe.

Z
ZEAL

Be passionately aroused by life. Cherish every moment, honor your commitments, and treasure your kinship with all.

POINTS OF ENTRY

Once you are familiar with the letters of spiritual literacy and begin reading, you will discover that you have favorite types of books. Do you like novels, mysteries, biographies, or wisdom literature? Just as you have a preferred genre of reading material, you will have favorite ways of reading the world. Perhaps you feel closest to Spirit in nature or through your service in your community. Perhaps your family is your greatest source of spiritual nourishment. Readings on many different avenues to Spirit are included in this book, so that you can start with your favorites and then work through the chapters in any order you please.

The term literacy, in its most general usage, means being able to read and *write*, and we do not want to ignore the latter skill. At the end of each chapter, we suggest ways you can practice spiritual literacy through writing—not writing as in putting pen to paper, although there are some suggestions for journal work, but writing as acting in a way that makes spiritual literacy concrete and practical in your life.

THE BOUNTY OF LITERACY

As we have gathered material for this volume, we have tried to imagine what it would be like to be illiterate, unable to read a book, a sign on the highway, a menu at a restaurant, or a story to a child. We would have to engage in tricks and evasions just to get through many everyday activities that require reading skills. We would know that books open the door to the information and inspiration we need for personal independence and fulfillment, but we would not have access to them.

Being spiritually illiterate would put us in a similarly dim and shallow world. If we could not read the signs of Spirit in daily life, we would not see the web which connects us with other people and the natural world. We would miss those intimations of "something more" that are possible in our work, our leisure, and our relationships. Like other illiterates, we would find ourselves trying to compensate and cover up for what we sense is a real void in our lives. We would know that everything around us contains signs and wisdom, but we just wouldn't get it.

Spiritually literate people from our time and earlier eras assure us that this need not be our reality. As you explore the readings in this book, you will see how spiritual literacy changes your perspective on life. Your body is a temple of God, and your home is holy ground. Your encounters with others reveal your connection with the Oneness, and your activities put you in touch with Spirit and enable Spirit to work through you.

In the pages to come, you are invited to join others who have found that spirituality is played out through the ordinary and the everyday. For when we are spiritually literate, we discover that the whole world is charged with sacred meaning.

READING THE SACRED
IN EVERYDAY LIFE

In the 1995 film *Smoke*, Auggie Wren manages a cigar store on the corner of Third Street and Seventh Avenue in Brooklyn. Every morning at exactly eight o'clock, no matter what the weather, he takes a picture of the store from across the street. He has four thousand consecutive daily photographs of his corner all labeled by date and mounted in albums. He calls this project his "life's work."

One day Auggie shows the photos to Paul, a blocked writer who is mourning the death of his wife, a victim of random street violence. Paul doesn't know what to say about the photos; he admits he has never seen anything like them. Flipping page after page of the albums, he observes with some amazement, "They're all the same." Auggie watches him, then replies: "You'll never get it if you don't slow down, my friend."

The pictures are all of the same spot, Auggie points out, "but each one is different from every other one." The differences are in the details: in the way people's clothes change according to season and weather, in the way the light hits the street. Some days the corner is almost empty; other times it is filled with people, bikes, cars, and trucks. "It's just one little part of the world but things take place there too just like everywhere else," Auggie explains. And sure enough, when Paul looks carefully at the by now remarkably unique photographs, he notices a detail in one of them that makes all the difference in the world to him.

We see Auggie as a model of a spiritually literate person. He reads the world—in his case, one corner in Brooklyn—for meaning. By its very nature, his project is rooted in the everyday. He knows how closely we may need to look to see the significance of seemingly ordinary and insignificant events. He understands that some of the most rewarding spiritual journeys are those we take on our own block.

As Taoist philosopher Chuang Tzu puts it, "One has to be in the same place every day, watch the dawn from the same house, hear the same birds awake each morning, to realize how inexhaustibly rich and different is sameness." That is the challenge of *everyday spirituality*—no star bursts, no skies opening, no mountaintop experiences. Just today and today and today. Just Auggie standing at the corner with his camera every morning.

Such searches for the sacred within the precincts of the ordinary are part of an honorable and diverse tradition. Many primal and goddess religions invest nature and the body with spiritual meaning and value. Celtic Christians sought to glorify God through their household duties, work in the fields, and lilt of a song. They invited God to join them in their daily deeds, believing that anywhere could become the place for an encounter with the Holy One. Within the Christian monastic traditions, everyday acts are hallowed and considered to be as important as devotional rituals and community worship.

Judaism, which calls itself a way of life, emphasizes taking ordinary experiences and making them holy. Islam urges believers to look for signs of God's activity in everything going on around them. Hinduism encourages recognizing manifestations of the divine in an enlightened person, a cow, a plant, or even a small object. Buddhist masters the world over have helped practitioners regard the routines of daily life, from walking to cooking, as essential spiritual practices.

What do we mean when we talk about everyday spirituality? There are numerous definitions. "The spiritual life is, at root, a matter of seeing," John Shea, a contemporary Catholic theologian, reminds us. "It is all of life seen from a certain perspective. It is waking, sleeping, dreaming, eating, drinking, working, loving, relaxing, recreating, walking, sitting, standing, and breathing. . . . spirit suffuses everything; and so the spiritual life is simply life, wherever and whatever, seen from the vantage point of spirit."

Jungian therapist Jeremiah Abrams defines spirituality as a "holy longing, a yearning to know the meaning of our lives, to have a connection with the transpersonal." Two simple but profound definitions are offered by Alan Jones, dean of Grace Cathedral in San Francisco, who regards spirituality as "the art of making connections," and by Jewish scholar David Ariel, who calls it "heart knowledge."

Catholic educator Regina Coll suggests that spirituality is an "awareness of the 'more than meets the eye' in our daily lives . . . it refers to our hopes and dreams, our patterns of thought, our emotions, feelings, and behaviors." Gerald May, a psychiatrist and director of spiritual guidance, seconds that view, linking the term to "our deepest values and desires, the very core of our being."

Many define spirituality as a way of being in the world. According to Catholic Bishop Pedro Casaldaliga, poet of the Amazon Indians, "spirituality is a measure of our humanity—personal depth, conscience, deep will." Another Catholic, Sister Joan Puls, locates it "in our human responses to the brokenness of our world, the threats to our planet home, the crisis points in our own lives, and the pleas and plight of human beings around us." Latin American liberation theologian Leonardo Boff calls spirituality "that attitude which puts life at the center, and defends and promotes life against all the mechanisms of death, desiccation, or stagnation."

The journey toward wholeness is a common motif in some definitions of spirituality. Psychotherapist Molly Young Brown writes: "When we expand our awareness, strengthen our center, clarify our purpose, transform our inner demons, develop our will and make conscious choices, we are moving toward deeper connection with our spiritual self." Marsha Sinetar, who has written extensively about self-actualization, notes that "everyone is spiritual to one degree or another, although many people don't admit it."

Many definitions, subtle differences in emphasis. All of them allow for spirituality to be an everyday adventure that can touch more and more areas of our lives. Brother David Steindl-Rast, a Benedictine monk, has one of the clearest explanations we have encountered.

> Sometimes people get the mistaken notion that spirituality is a separate department of life, the penthouse of our existence. But rightly understood, it is a vital awareness that pervades all realms of our being. Someone will say, "I come alive when I listen to music," or "I come to life when I garden," or "I come alive when I play golf." Wherever we come alive, that is the area in which we are spiritual. And then we can say, "I know at least how one is spiritual in that area." To be vital, awake, aware, in all areas of our lives, is the task that is never accomplished, but it remains the goal.
> —BROTHER DAVID STEINDL-RAST
> in *The Music of Silence*

A SLICE
OF THE SPIRITUAL RENAISSANCE

Using these definitions, we can see that spirituality is evident everywhere today. There are as many expressions of it as there are individuals with different longings, convictions, interests, values, beliefs, traditions, and rituals. Consider these examples.

A group of women gets together once a month to take turns answering one question. They share their deepest concerns and the stories of their lives.

A retired couple comes to the beach every day with their dogs. They carry garbage bags and pick up litter as they walk. They love the beach and make a habit of caring for it.

A jogger runs in the park every morning, come rain or shine. At a certain point, she switches to glide and her movement seems almost effortless.

A woman teaches in the Sunday School and serves as an officer of the women's group at her church. Through her daily demonstrations of enthusiasm for church work, she inspires others to become involved.

A wise and creative entrepreneur, who occasionally expresses an aversion to religious matters, has pioneered the field of informal life-long learning with innovative seminars, speeches, and articles. Learning is his spiritual practice, and it enables him to give full expression to his gifts and skills.

A young couple has just had their first child and decides to return to the synagogue. They want their boy to relish his ethnic roots and to experience the practice of Judaism.

A group of therapists gathers on a weekday afternoon to talk about their night dreams and to do mental imagery exercises as a way of getting in touch with their inner lives.

A woman in a stress-filled job attends yoga class every other day. This combination of bodywork and meditation relaxes and revitalizes her.

A woman has two close encounters with death in as many years. She accepts them as wake-up calls and reorders her life, giving herself more time for self-nurturing. She sees a spiritual director and makes room in her busy schedule for daily devotional reading and prayer.

A small circle of people meets each month to talk about the story of a movie in relation to the stories of their own lives; they call the process they are going through together "soul making."

Our list could go on and you, no doubt, could add more examples to the mix. There is a spiritual renaissance happening throughout the world, and the evidence is all around us.

*   *   *

Spirituality is alive and well in many religious congregations where individuals have expressed the desire to deepen their relationships to God. Programs in spiritual formation are attracting those interested in exploring their own traditions and learning about other approaches to the life of Spirit. Men and women are joining prayer groups to lift their concerns as a community, and adult education classes study everything from sacred texts to the roots of their rituals.

People regularly go on retreats where silence and solitude help them get in touch with the sacred. Others attend workshops and conferences with spiritual themes. In many communities, spiritual directors are available to offer guidance to seekers in one-to-one relationships.

Bookstores are brimming with titles on every spiritual subject imaginable. Computer online services enable individuals to dialogue with others thousands of miles away about critical religious, political, and social issues; they also provide ways to keep up with the ever-expanding field of spiritual resources.

Even popular culture is beginning to reflect the spiritual renaissance. Movie story lines focus on how life-threatening illnesses, moral dilemmas, or challenges to love and friendship can become the impetus for spiritual journeys. Characters on television series grapple with ethical issues as they raise their families and cope with crises on the job.

Many people come to spirituality through transformational psychology and therapy. Their quest is to take responsibility for their lives and to become all they were meant to be. Individuals on this path may use the psychospiritual resources of mythology, dreams, and storytelling in their search for wholeness. By living purposefully, they are able to transmute adversity, suffering, and pain into insights about love, healing, and renewal.

Recovery programs for substance or relationship addictions are also roads to spirituality. Alcoholics Anonymous and other Twelve-Step programs help men and women square off with their compulsions and with their feelings of worthlessness and hopelessness. By meeting regularly with others, talking about their situations, and sharing their stories, many participants learn to appreciate the spiritual dynamics of community, tolerance, forgiveness, and gratitude.

Ecology and love of the Earth bring others to spirituality. People on this path feel a kinship with the planet and seek to live in harmony with the natural world. They take environmental problems seriously and believe that a spiritual perspective is needed to propel a global environmental movement of true power and presence.

Women's spirituality has been in bloom for several decades. By gathering in groups, engaging in rituals, and comparing experiences, women are following their inner lights, reconceptualizing God, and reinterpreting sacred stories. Many come to a new appreciation of overlooked and undervalued feminine qualities. Some discover meaning in goddess religions, others in neo-paganism, and still others in the wisdom of Sophia.

Men, meanwhile, have been on their own spiritual journeys. Having realized the value of intimacy and male bonding, they gather on weekend retreats or at regular meetings to honor their feelings and discuss their relationships. By tending to their wounds and wrestling with their fears, many men discover new pathways to the sacred in their lives.

New Age spirituality is a multifaceted phenomenon that defies all attempts to pin it down. This freelance form of spirituality can be seen in every segment of society and is discussed in magazines, books, workshops, and seminars. The repeated emphasis is upon both personal and planetary transformation. New Age spirituality provides a variety of avenues to seekers who are looking for a more holy and holistic vision of life.

Another outburst of spirituality is evident in the volunteer work and political activism of men, women, and children seeking to make a better world. These people find meaning and purpose in banding together with others to serve a cause—whether feeding the homeless, helping people with HIV and AIDS, saving the whales, calling for the cleanup of toxic dump sites, supporting victims of domestic violence, or combating economic exploitation of workers in global industries.

Finally, the spiritual renaissance is characterized by an unprecedented amount of sharing of resources among peoples of the world, enabling individuals to widen and deepen their spiritual journeys. The nineteenth-century American abolitionist William Lloyd Garrison coined the term "citizens of the world," and that moniker has been eagerly assumed by spiritually literate individuals from all the traditions.

With a remarkably broad sampling of sacred literature in print in many languages, and with worldwide communication taking giant steps through computer technology, seekers today have access to a wealth of material on the world's religions. "It may well be," Ewart Cousins states, "that the meeting of spiritual paths—the assimilation not only of one's own personal spiritual heritage but that of the human community as a whole—is the distinctive spiritual journey of our time."

According to Protestant theologian Harvey Cox, spiritual seekers can move in and out of different religions without losing their psyches in the process. In a profound recent book, *Encountering God*, Diane Eck, who grew up a Christian in Bozeman, Montana, writes about how her encounters with Hindus in Banaras, India, help her come to a richer appreciation of God and everyday spirituality. Eck's experience of inter-religious dialogue bolsters her belief in pluralism, which, she explains, does not mean giving up our commitments but opening them up to the challenges of mutual discovery, understanding, and transformation.

In the Alphabet of Spiritual Literacy, we have included a crosscut of spiritual teachers from different traditions and all parts of the globe. They bring to us diverse images of God, ethical purviews, and devotional prac-tices. A world-encompassing spirituality is not only a challenge but a necessity. As the venerable thirteenth-century monk Thomas Aquinas reminds us, "diversity is the perfection of the universe."

BLOCKS TO LITERACY

Despite this current activity and all the testimony from the world reli-gions on the way of the everyday, many people are still not convinced that spirituality is integral to and not separate from daily life. There are reasons for this—strong influences that can be hard to shake. A chief block is worldview.

To be spiritually literate, we need to embrace the world, believing that it is full of meanings which we can discover. But we cannot experi-ence the full wonder, mystery, and healing power of the world if we hold a totally negative image of it. Physicist Albert Einstein was once asked, "What's the most important question you can ask in life?" He replied, "Is the universe a friendly place or not?"

We all know people who would answer no to that question; they view the world as a bleak and terrible place. In some religious circles, for example, the world is regarded mainly as a playground for the Devil. We have met individuals who are so obsessed with apocalyptic visions of the end of the world that they keep looking for signs of the imminent deba-cle. Others are so terrified of violent crime that their chief image of the world is that of a dangerous place.

As antidotes to these images of the world as Devil-ridden, doomed, and dangerous, we can suggest more positive ones. The poet Mary Oliver offers a counterpoint to Einstein's question when she says, "There is only one question: How to love this world." Here are a few ways to do so that we have come across in our readings.

The world as a friend summons up a relationship that is intimate, car-ing, and based on mutual respect. As writer Robert Sardello points out, "Seeing the world as friend is like seeing the world for the first time."

The world as a sensuous being is an image that grows out of James Lovelace's Gaia Hypothesis. It views the earth as a living, breathing being. This image encourages us to appreciate the physical beauty of the world.

The world as the body of God is the radical image of Christian theologian Sallie McFague. This reimagining of the world emphasizes God's glory and mystery in the here-and-now.

The world as lover has been suggested by deep ecologist and Buddhist Joanna Macy. This image gives free play to a passion for life, erotic energy, and soulful living.

Perhaps the most vivid image of all is *the world as self.* This one goes all the way back to ancient China.

> See the world as your self.
> Have faith in the way things are.
> Love the world as your self;
> then you can care for all things.
> —LAO-TZU
>   in the *Tao Te Ching*
>   translated by Stephen Mitchell

A story points to the second major block to spiritual literacy, the inability to embrace our own experiences.

"Where shall I look for Enlightenment?" the disciple asked.

"Here," the elder said.

"When will it happen?" the disciple asked.

"It is happening right now," the elder answered.

"Then why don't I experience it?" the disciple persisted.

"Because you do not look," the elder said.

"But what should I look for?" the disciple continued.

"Nothing. Just look," the elder said.

"But at what?" the disciple asked again.

"At anything your eyes alight upon," the elder answered.

"But must I look in a special kind of way?" the disciple went on.

"No. The ordinary way will do," the elder said.

"But don't I always look the ordinary way?" the disciple said.

"No, you don't," the elder said.

"But why ever not?" the disciple asked.

"Because to look you must be here. You're mostly somewhere else," the elder said.

—JOAN CHITTISTER
in *There Is a Season*

A whole series of habits and attitudes can prevent us from discovering the meaning of our lives. One is our tendency to escape the present by fleeing into busyness, boredom, or distraction. Busyness often takes us away from relationships and actions that matter; boredom imprisons us in the blahs or puts us on automatic pilot; and distraction kidnaps our consciousness and holds us hostage to trivial pursuits.

Another problem is shallowness or the refusal to plumb the depths of our experiences. By skimming the surface, we miss what lies beneath. "Your soul suffers if you live superficially," Nobel Peace Prize–winner Albert Schweitzer cautions.

A peculiarly postmodern block to everyday spirituality is cynicism, which is reflected in phrases like "Lighten up, this isn't brain surgery!" This statement implies that very little, indeed only matters of life and death, should be taken seriously. It indicates an attitude that condones gliding through life without being touched or moved by anything.

A final block to spiritual literacy is the frequent assumption that spirituality is somehow complicated and requires special training or a calling. Not so, assert spiritual teachers through the ages. For those with ears to hear and eyes to see, Spirit is as near as your breath.

Psychologist Ken Wilber had an epiphany on this point one day when he was considering the meaning of enlightenment.

Spirit, and enlightenment, has to be something that you are fully aware of right now. *Something you are already looking at right now.* As I was receiving these teachings, I thought of the old puzzles in the Sunday supplement section of the newspaper, where there is a landscape and the caption says, "The faces of twenty famous people are hidden in this landscape. Can you spot them?" The faces were maybe Walter Cronkite, John Kennedy, that kind of thing. The point is that you are looking right at the faces. You don't need to see *anything* more in order to be looking at the faces. They are completely entering your visual field already, you just don't recognize them. If you still can't find them, then somebody comes along and simply points them out.

It's the same way with Spirit or enlightenment, I thought. We are all already looking directly at Spirit, we just don't recognize it. We have all the necessary cognition, but not the recognition.

—KEN WILBER
in *Grace and Grit*

SPIRITUAL LITERACY FILTERS

Let's explore one other important aspect of spiritual literacy—the different filters commonly used in spiritual readings. Just as photographers use filters on their lenses to remove haze from a scene or to enhance the brightness of a certain color, the traditions use filters to emphasize particular understandings of the sacred. Filters do not change the scene as much as they change the perception. The spiritually literate passages collected in this book include examples of writers using four different filters.

The first, and perhaps the most familiar, is *sacramentalism*, in which the creation is seen as a sign pointing to God. Objects, places, events, and relationships can be reminders, reflections, metaphors, analogies, symbols, or samples of the divine reality. Catholic Bishop Fulton Sheen uses the image of the universe as a windowpane; you see through the visible to the Invisible God. This understanding is evident in the primal religions that regard the world as being infused with Spirit, and in the wisdom traditions that encourage believers to look for hints of God in the world around them. The following story captures the essence of this filter.

God decided to become visible to a king and a peasant and sent an angel to inform them of the blessed event. "O king," the angel announced, "God has deigned to be revealed to you in whatever manner you wish. In what form do you want God to appear?"

Seated pompously on his throne and surrounded by awestruck subjects, the king royally proclaimed: "How else would I wish to see God, save in majesty and power? Show God to us in the full glory of power."

God granted his wish and appeared as a bolt of lightning that instantly pulverized the king and his court. Nothing, not even a cinder, remained.

The angel then manifested herself to a peasant saying: "God deigns to be revealed to you in whatever manner you desire. How do you wish to see God?"

Scratching his head and puzzling a long while, the peasant finally said: "I am a poor man and not worthy to see God face to face. But if it is God's will to be revealed to me, let it be in those things with which I am familiar. Let me see God in the earth I plough, the water I drink, and the food I eat. Let me see the presence of God in the faces of my family, neighbors, and—if God deems it as good for myself and others—even in my own reflection as well."

God granted the peasant his wish, and he lived a long and happy life.

—STORY
quoted in *Peacemaking Day by Day*

According to sacramentalism, anything can become a disclosure of grace. We experience intimations of the divine in a lover's embrace, a rainbow, a baby's smile, a bird's flight overhead, a friend's forgiveness, a dolphin's leap, or the selfless service of a volunteer.

Another important filter used to explain the relationship between God and the world is *panentheism*, which means "everything in God, and God in everything." Panentheism is not the same as pantheism, which identifies God with nature, or dualism, which emphasizes the gulf between God and creation. It stresses immanence—God within the world—over transcendence—God above and separate from the world. This poem from an ancient Welsh text reveals that panentheism is certainly not a new idea.

I am the wind that breathes upon the sea,
I am the wave on the ocean,
I am the murmur of leaves rustling,
I am the rays of the sun,
I am the beam of the moon and stars,
I am the power of trees growing,
I am the bud breaking into blossom,
I am the movement of the salmon swimming,
I am the courage of the wild boar fighting,
I am the speed of the stag running,
I am the strength of the ox pulling the plough,
I am the size of the mighty oak,
And I am the thoughts of all people,
Who praise my beauty and grace.

—*The Black Book of Camarthan*
quoted in *Celtic Fire*
edited by Robert Van de Weyer

Panentheism enables us to see all of life as sacred. Matthew Fox, one of the most prolific contemporary proponents of this understanding, uses the image of the universe as the divine womb containing us all; the way we treat things, nature, animals, places, and people is the way we treat God.

A third filter used to put the sacred and the world in better focus is divinization or sanctification.

A little girl was standing with her grandfather by an old-fashioned open well. They had just lowered a bucket to draw some water to drink. "Grandfather," asked the little girl, "where does God live?"

The old man picked up the little girl and held her over the open well. "Look down into the water," he said, "and tell me what you see." "I see myself," said the little girl. "That's where God lives," said the old man. "He lives in you."

—MARK LINK
in *Challenge*

Judaism and Christianity emphasize that humans are made in the image of God. The Quakers believe "There is that of God in everyone." In his book *The Orthodox Church*, Timothy Ware points out how this belief is reflected in that tradition: "This respect for every human being is visibly expressed in Orthodox worship when the priest censes not only the icons but the members of the congregation, saluting the image of God in each person." Divinization does not mean that we are God or are becoming God, but it does mean that we are vessels containing the Holy One.

A fourth filter is demonstrated in this passage.

Whenever I touch a flower, I touch the sun and yet I do not get burned. When I touch the flower, I touch a cloud without flying to the sky. When I touch the flower, I touch my consciousness, your consciousness, and the great planet Earth at the same time. . . . The miracle is possible because of insight into the nature of interbeing. If you really touch one flower deeply, you touch the whole cosmos. The cosmos is neither one nor many. When you touch one, you touch many, and when you touch many, you touch one. Like Shakyamuni Buddha, you can be everywhere at the same time. Think of your child or your beloved touching you now. Look more deeply, and you will see yourself as multitudes, penetrating everywhere, interbeing with everyone and everything.

—THICH NHAT HANH
in *Cultivating the Mind of Love*

This view of the interconnection of all creation is an example of a filter that is nontheistic. Thich Nhat Hanh, a Vietnamese Buddhist monk and peace activist, calls this filter "interbeing." It engenders within us a sense of unity and harmony with the world and its abundant wonders. And as anyone who has felt a mystical sense of at-oneness with nature or with other people knows, this experience can lead to a transformed respect for everyday life and its mysteries.

DIFFERENT WAYS TO READ

The word "read" shares a root with such words as art, skill, ordain, adorn, and ordinary. Reading is a skill that addresses the ordinary. The root of the word "read" actually means "to fit together" and this is the natural enterprise of the spiritual life. When we read the world spiritually, we make connections between obvious and not-so-obvious things, places, events, feelings, and thoughts.

As you peruse these pages, you will see that there are three different ways to read the world spiritually. In the next four chapters, the readings are grouped according to these three ways; in later chapters, where the selections are organized by subject, you will still find examples of all of them.

First, we read the world for what it teaches us about Spirit. Sometimes these lessons are expressed in analogies, metaphors, symbols, and stories. Through this kind of reading, we gain a new understanding of our place in the universe and learn to recognize the many movements of Spirit.

Second, we read the world to see what it can show us about the meaningful life. Everything that happens to us and everything we encounter contribute to our journey toward wholeness. By reading the texts of our experiences in this way, we pick up clues as to who we are and what we need to deal with. Here is where we discover ways to get in touch with the depth of our souls and the breadth of our connections with others.

Third, we read the world for what it is. Not as a symbol; not as a teaching; not as a mirror; simply for what it is. This involves a basic respect for the intrinsic value of everything apart from its utility to us. It also acknowledges that no matter how honed our reading skills are, there are some things we cannot possess with our reason or envision in our imagination. There are mysteries in life that reflect the Great Mystery.

On the way to our favorite restaurant, we often pass an empty lot. It lies there untended and mostly unloved, and yet to us it is never a worthless piece of property. Turning our attention to it, we discover the many ways it can be read spiritually.

In one reading, we see this lot as a symbol of the truth that the Creator can bring life out of anything. One month, it is bare from the ravages of winter. The next month, it's spring, and the lot comes to life. Stumps branch off into saplings and turn into major trees incredibly quickly. Birds come to join squirrels, grasshoppers, bees, mice, and probably a few rats. The lot is a seed bed for an amazing variety of wild and hearty plants that are determined to survive. Everything and anything is possible in this world.

Surrounded by a wire fence, sandwiched between a movie cineplex and a building that looks like it might fall down at any second, the lot is also a garbage dump. It is littered with junk: the usual assortment of soda cans, newspapers, and paper bags, but also car fenders and old chairs. Now the lot becomes an analogy of the Mother God, taking the rejected of the earth into her comforting arms.

On another day, we find ourselves identifying with the lot as an aspect of ourselves—the parts which we abandon, neglect, or abhor. We would just as soon walk right by without noticing it. But what we resist persists, and the empty lot by summer has become a wet and green overgrown tangle of roots, flowers, and leaves. Some parts of us are grounded, some are in bloom, and some are reaching to feel the wind.

We stop and look closely at the lot on a late summer afternoon. It seems to be humming. Birds are flitting about. The insects are swarming. Everything seems to be happening at once and it is hard to tell which activity has priority, much as in our own lives.

One day we pass to see that the lot is empty again, all the trees pushed over and the weeds mowed down. Why, we will never know. Now our reading has to recognize that this is simply an empty lot on Thirty-fourth Street between Second and Third Avenues. And that is enough. It is a place of mystery and beauty, and it has our respect.

Like Auggie's corner in Brooklyn, this lot in the heart of Manhattan is just one little part of the world, but meanings are evident there all the time. Gazing through the wire fence, we recall the words of the Christian journalist Malcolm Muggeridge: "Every happening great and small is a parable whereby God speaks to us, and the art of life is to get the message."

THINGS

Know, O my son that each thing in the universe is a vessel full to the brim with wisdom and beauty.

—RUMI

Even the common articles made for daily use become endowed with beauty when they are loved.

—SOETSU YANAGI

Take, for example, a pencil, ashtray, anything, and holding it before you in both hands, regard it for a while. Forgetting its use and name, yet continuing to regard it, ask yourself seriously, "What is it?" . . . Its dimension of wonder opens; for the mystery of the being of that being is identical with the mystery of the being of the universe—and yourself.

—JOSEPH CAMPBELL

If you love it enough, anything will talk with you.

—GEORGE WASHINGTON CARVER

The value of a personal relationship to things is that it creates intimacy and intimacy creates understanding and understanding creates love.

—ANAIS NIN

Never was anything in this world loved too much, but many things have been loved in false ways and in all too short a measure.

—THOMAS TRAHERNE

To grasp God in all things—this is the sign of your new birth.

—MEISTER ECKHART

Begin with loving a small and inconspicuous thing—a pot, a nail, or a toothbrush—and you have taken the first step on the path of everyday spirituality. There are many who have preceded you.

Christians, for example, hold everyday objects in high regard as vessels with which they can serve God. Jewish mystics teach that every created thing contains sparks of the divine. Hindus take great pleasure in ordinary things as manifestations of Brahman. And Sufi poets find the fingerprints of the Beloved on everything.

Despite this broad and holy tradition, many of us still have a hard time loving, honoring, and caring for things. We have many possessions but regard them superficially, value them slightly, and treat them shabbily. Our materialism lacks depth. Yet, as French priest Pierre Teilhard de Chardin reminds us, "things have their within."

Our exploration of spiritual literacy, then, starts with the familiar, ordinary things in our lives. Our tutors in this area include spiritual masters, poets, artists, craftspersons, and children.

Many religious teachers comment on the layers of meaning that can be uncovered through the contemplation of things. Poets are often connoisseurs of the commonplace, directing our attention to how things add richness to our lives. William Wordsworth writes: "With an eye made quiet by the power/of harmony, and the deep power of joy/we see into the life of things." Gerard Manley Hopkins, in one well-known poem, reminds us "there lives the dearest freshness deep down things."

Artists and craftspersons illuminate the beauty of the things around us. Through his paintings, Vincent van Gogh teaches us to see the extraordinary in a coffeepot, a pair of worn-out shoes, or a pipe and pouch. Sculptor Louise Nevelson uses discarded objects as parts of her complicated and beautiful sculptures.

Children model an easy and natural closeness to things. "Children with the freshness of their senses come directly to the intimacy of this world," observes Rabindranath Tagore, the great Indian poet. "This is the first great gift they have."

Like these tutors, we come to know things only when we enter into partnership with them. How different we might feel about our world after making a practice of saying hello and thank you to the refrigerator that hums while it keeps our food cool, to the slippers that warm our feet on cold winter nights, and to the pen that expends all its ink so that we can express ourselves. Things also deserve our care, even something as simple as polishing the coffee table until it shines.

We need to establish what Jewish theologian Martin Buber called an "I-Thou" relationship with the objects we choose to have as companions in our lives. When we cherish our things, they reciprocate; when we ignore them, they can turn toxic.

In this chapter, we explore how things can be pathways to spirituality. The spiritual practices of love, beauty, gratitude, imagination, and compassion all get a workout when we live consciously with things. We have included readings about things as carriers of meaning, devotional aids, and teachers. Other passages reveal how things put us in touch with our past and our loved ones. In the final set of readings, we discover how things challenge us on our spiritual journey. For they have lives of their own and are often tinged with mystery.

THINGS AS REFLECTIONS OF SPIRIT

Our first group of readings illustrate how things reflect the presence of Spirit in the world. Spiritual literacy enables the writers here to see a thing for what it is and as something more.

[There is a] late nineteenth century Hasidic tale about a rebbe who told his followers, "Everything that has been created in God's world has a lesson to teach us."

Thinking that the rebbe was engaging in hyperbole, one of his followers called out, "And what can we learn from the train?"

"That because of being one minute late," the rebbe answered, "you can lose everything."

"And from the telegraph?"

"That for every word you pay."

"And from the telephone?"

"That what we say *here,* is heard *there.*"

—Rabbi Joseph Telushkin
in *Jewish Wisdom*

Things make connections between everyday experiences and the world of deep meaning. They can point beyond themselves to the profound.

An engagement ring is a messenger that tells the story of a pledge of love. Beyond the material value of the ring is the invisible and unseen assurance of being loved; that is why the ring is placed on the finger that the ancients believed had a vein that led directly to the heart.

—FULTON J. SHEEN
in *From the Angel's Blackboard*

In many cultures and religious traditions, certain things are perceived to have power and miraculous properties. For Catholics, holy relics are things that draw our attention and adoration to God. In the next passage, Presbyterian minister and writer Frederick Buechner helps us to see that even seemingly mundane or commercial objects can serve as spiritual facilitators.

I remember sitting parked by the roadside once, terribly depressed and afraid about my daughter's illness and what was going on in our family, when out of nowhere a car came along down the highway with a license plate that bore on it the one word out of all the words in the dictionary that I needed most to see exactly then. The word was TRUST. What do you call a moment like that? Something to laugh off as the kind of joke life plays on us every once in a while? The word of God? I am willing to believe that maybe it was something of both, but for me it was an epiphany. The owner of the car turned out to be, as I'd suspected, a trust officer in a bank, and not long ago, having read an account I wrote of the incident somewhere, he found out where I lived and one afternoon brought me the license plate itself, which sits propped up on a bookshelf in my house to this day. It is rusty around the edges and a little battered, and it is also as holy a relic as I have ever seen.

—FREDERICK BUECHNER
in *Telling Secrets*

Bells, candles, and incense are objects traditionally used in religious rituals, but really anything can be a spur to a richer spiritual life. Brother David Steindl-Rast, a Benedictine monk, shows us how.

I use devotional objects to foster patience, just as the beads of a rosary are devotional tools to foster mindfulness. My tools to cultivate patience are fossils that friends have given me. I have a small trilobite, an ancient marine animal, and another that may be an early form of the nautilus, and recently I received a tiny fish that's six hundred million years old. I look at those and handle them, and that's helpful to me.

—Brother David Steindl-Rast
in *The Ground We Share*

Things can encourage such spiritual practices as being present, openness, and wonder. They are also constant reminders of the Mystery of Love among us.

Picasso was right when he said that we do not know what a tree or a window really is. All things are very mysterious and strange (like Picasso's paintings), and we overlook their strangeness and their mystery only because we are so used to them. Only dimly do we understand the nature of things. What are things? They are God's love become things.

God also communicates with us by way of all things. They are messages of love. When I read a book, God is speaking to me through this book. I raise my eyes to look at the countryside: God created it for me to see. The picture I look at today was inspired by God in the painter, for me to see. Everything I enjoy was given lovingly by God for me to enjoy, and even my pain is God's loving gift.

—Ernesto Cardenal
in *Abide in Love*

Spiritual literacy encourages us to permit a wide variety of things to touch our inner life, to renew and revivify us. In this entry from his prayer journal written to God, Catholic novelist and sociologist Andrew Greeley describes the sacramental power of trains and train noises.

[Louis] MacNeice has a lovely poem about the sound of a railroad train at night when he was young, how soothing and reassuring it was. I know the exact feeling. I have experienced it many times here at Grand Beach in the summer time, but that experience also recalls something much deeper in my own past. I would not have heard the train on Augusta Boulevard or Mayfield Avenue, so it must go back to my earliest years on Austin Boulevard before I was six years old. But the experience was the same as his—the soft rumble waking me in the night and the feeling that somehow I was reassured by the sound, perhaps by the presence of the outside world beyond my dreams, perhaps also by my romantic identification with trains as the gateway to adventure. Anyway trains and train noises are a sacrament to me, a sign of grace and transcendent presence in the world, this time in benign sounds and power and a hint of adventure. A love sign of Your presence in the world.

—ANDREW GREELEY
in *Sacraments of Love*

In his parables, Jesus of Nazareth uses things to comment on the "big picture." When he refers to a lost coin and a needle, he illuminates larger truths about the Kingdom of God. In the next reading, Catholic writer Henri J. M. Nouwen sees wagon wheels as sacred symbols.

In my home country, the Netherlands, you still see many large wagon wheels, not on wagons, but as decorations at the entrances of farms or on the walls of restaurants. I have always been fascinated by these wagon wheels: with their wide rims, strong wooden spokes, and big hubs. These wheels help me to understand the importance of a life lived from the center. When I move along the rim, I can reach one spoke after the other, but when I stay at the hub, I am in touch with all the spokes at once.

To pray is to move to the center of all life and all love. The closer I come to the hub of life, the closer I come to all that receives its strength and energy from there. My tendency is to get so distracted by the diversity of the many spokes of life, that I am busy but not truly life-giving, all over the place but not focused. By directing my attention to the heart of life, I am connected with its rich variety while remaining centered. What does the hub represent? I think of it as my own heart, the heart of God, and the heart of the world. When I pray, I enter into the depth of my own heart and find there the heart of God, who speaks to me of love. And I recognize, right there, the place where all of my sisters and brothers are in communion with one another. The great paradox of the spiritual life is, indeed, that the most personal is most universal, that the most intimate, is most communal, and that the most contemplative is most active.

The wagon wheel shows that the hub is the center of all energy and movement, even when it often seems not to be moving at all. In God all action and all rest are one. So too prayer!

—HENRI J. M. NOUWEN
in *Here and Now*

Mexican writer Octavio Paz contemplates the spiritual lessons that handmade objects can teach us.

The thing that is handmade has no desire to last for thousands upon thousands of years, nor is it possessed by a frantic drive to die an early death. It follows the appointed round of days, it drifts with us as the current carries us along together, it wears away little by little, it neither seeks death nor denies it: it accepts it. Between the timeless time of the museum and the speeded-up time of technology, craftsmanship is the heartbeat of human time. A thing that is handmade is a useful object but also one that is beautiful; an object that lasts a long time but also one that slowly ages away and is resigned to so doing; an object that is not unique like the work of art and can be replaced by another object that is similar but not identical. The craftsman's handiwork teaches us to die and hence teaches us to live.

—OCTAVIO PAZ
in *In Praise of Hands*

The more we look at the things around us with spiritually literate eyes, the more meanings we begin to find in them. It is no wonder that, in ancient and modern rituals, everyday things are used to signify important ideas. We can make our own readings of ceremonial objects through the spiritual practices of imagination, listening, and meaning.

A ceremonial object holds skan. It holds power. It holds the love and energy of the one who makes it. It holds the intentions and prayers of its maker. It is a teacher as it assists in the process of its creation. It is an object of meditation. It is a symbol for those who still need symbols to "wake up." It is the toy of a cosmic child who is heaven-bent on contributing to peace and dignity on our planet. It is a tattletale about the recipient of its gift. It is a prophet about events about to happen. It is a stunning prop on stage. It is a microphone, sky to earth and earth to sky. It is a needle that weaves together all living things. It is the focal point of attention and, by capturing attention, it is a co-creator in life. A ceremonial object is held in high regard by all children, young and old. It is a central topic of conversation. It is a piece of art. It is part of the collection in a museum. It is a history marker. It is an artifact of people who live and breathe and procreate. A ceremonial object is not necessary for worship, but it certainly makes it more fun.

—SCOUT CLOUD LEE
in *The Circle Is Sacred*

My first eagle feather, one light and innocent, was given to me by a traditional healer I'd gone to see when I was sick. He told me a story about feathers. When he was a child his home had burned down. All that survived the fire were eagle feathers. They remained in the smoking ruins of their home, floating on top of black ash and water. The feather he gave me was one of those. I still keep it safe in a cedar box in my home. . . .

There is something alive in a feather. The power of it is perhaps in its dream of sky, currents of air, and the silence of its creation. It knows the insides of clouds. It carries our needs and desires, the stories of our brokenness. It rises and falls down elemental space, one part of the elaborate world of life where fish swim against gravity, where eels turn silver as moon to breed.

—LINDA HOGAN
in *Dwellings*

Pilar and Daniel Weinberg's son was baptized on the coast. The baptism taught him what was sacred.

They gave him a sea shell: "So you'll learn to love the water."

They opened a cage and let a bird go free: "So you'll learn to love the air."

They gave him a geranium: "So you'll learn to love the earth."
And they gave him a little bottle sealed up tight: "Don't ever, ever open it. So you'll learn to love mystery."

—EDUARDO GALEANO
in *Walking Words*

THINGS AS MIRRORS OF PERSONAL DEPTH

We tend to think of things as outside and separate from ourselves. But when we read the world spiritually, we discover that things often set us on pathways which lead us back to the meaningfulness of our lives. Things house our feelings, memories, and connections with others, both living and dead.

When we regard things this way, our interactions with them become spiritual exercises. For example, the young boy in the next reading discovers the spiritual practice of transformation by ringing a sterling silver dinner bell.

One dreary afternoon in my fourth year, when I was sick and weak, Grandma Clara, wanting to cheer me, reached to the top of the credenza and took down a forbidden object: the sterling silver dinner bell. She said I could ring it all I wanted "whenever you like." Then she left me alone in my room. When I held the bell up to my ear and rang it quietly it sounded exactly like the thin, gleaming roundness it was made of. This bell had always been ceremonial and mute, meant for calling servants who didn't exist. But thanks to my condition, permission had arrived. The forbidden sound was airborne, and I would be safe and whole forever. I wanted the sound to stay soft and private, and be so close to my ear that it would last forever. Ringing the bell again and again put me in a bright swoon. No one said no.

—W. A. MATHIEU
in *The Musical Life*

Some things have personal significance for us because they have been given to us, or because they once belonged to someone we loved. One of my most cherished possessions is a painting I inherited from my grandfather Brussat.

ATTENTION

Spiritual literacy is about paying attention. All kinds of wonderful and important things are going on directly in front of us but we miss most of them because we are not awake.

Buddha says everything comes down to one thing—staying awake. And remember Jesus in the Garden of Gethsemane? "Remain here and stay awake with me," he tells his disciples. They cannot do it.

God is in the details. Paying attention requires discipline and practice.

People who meditate are on the right track, according to writer Catherine Bateson: "They are seeking therapy for a wounded capacity to attend."

Two detectives on popular television programs are good role models for those of us who want to become more attentive. Over and over again Jessica Fletcher on *Murder She Wrote* creates the big picture out of a series of small observations. And Columbo, of course, follows up on every detail when he is trying to solve a puzzle.

"Attention," clinical psychologist Timothy Miller observes, "is the intention to live without reservation in the here-and-now."

To be attentive we must put ourselves in a place where we are open and receptive and totally present.

"For lack of attention," writes the English mystic Evelyn Underhill, "a thousand forms of loveliness elude us every day." Yes, and much more.

Moments of grace, epiphanies, and great insights are lost to us because we are in too much of a hurry to notice them. Slow down or you'll miss the good stuff.

It is reported that the poet and doctor William Carlos Williams used to carry a notepad around with him. On it was written: "Things I noticed today that I've missed until today."

Ask yourself in the morning—what will my attention bring me today? By evening's end, you will have an answer.

Be prepared to look long and steadily at things. They will speak to you and reveal themselves.

"Boredom," notes gestalt therapist Fritz Perls, "is lack of attention." Take yourself off automatic pilot and you enter a whole new world of wonders.

"The moment one gives close attention to anything, even a blade of grass," writer Henry Miller observes, "it becomes a mysterious, awesome, indescribably magnificent world in itself."

Pay attention. Stay awake. Jelaluddin Rumi, the thirteenth-century Sufi poet, knows what is required:

> No more words. In the name of this place we drink in
> with our breathing, stay quiet like a flower.
> So the nightbirds will start singing.

After he died in his eighties, my parents were quite taken aback when I installed in my bedroom the grim, dark, and ominous painting of a shipwreck that had hung in Grandpa's living room. But I felt that a part of me was smashed and dashed on the shore when my greatest male advocate died. I remember looking at the painting and recalling the medieval prayer, "Lord, help me, because my boat is so small and your sea is so immense." The painting was also precious to me because the image of the beached vessel mirrored the plight of my grandfather, who was marooned by illness for the last thirty years of his life in a chair in his living room.

The painting now hangs above my desk. Recently I noticed within the dark overall impression of the scene a rather amazing array of subtle but bright colors. Now when I look at it, I think of my ship-wrecked grandfather and the brightness his love brought into my life.

Many years ago, my aunt gave me a glass ball filled with water, and a snowman the size of my thumb. If you turned the sphere upside down, it would begin to "snow" around the little man in the stovepipe hat.

It has been on my desk for over thirty years. When I am stuck on a word, or when I lean back against my chair in exhaustion, I reach over sometimes and shake the glass and watch the snowman disappear in the blizzard.

Am I the lost snowman sometimes being shaken into nothingness?

—CHRISTOPHER DE VINCK
in *Songs of Innocence and Experience*

Things serve not only as mirrors of our inner quests and questions, but also as agents of change.

We give special consideration to the arrangement of personal arti-facts in bathrooms and on dresser tops. When visiting another person's house, I tend to get my strongest sense of shrine-making in these spaces. If I came from an aboriginal community and did not know the contents or functions of things in the cosmetic con-tainers, jewelry displays, grooming tools, shaving equipment, and other items laid out in personal rooms, I might think they were shrines and collections of talismans. We use these tools of trans-formation to influence events in the future and endow ourselves with good fortune, and the presence of benevolent and protecting spirits.

—SHAUN MCNIFF
in *Earth Angels*

I am not a good shopper; never have been; even as a girl with my parents' money. The act of selecting and buying things, especially something I plan to have for some time, seems to bring out my shadow side. I get my purchase home and immediately have second thoughts, which begin a cycle of judgment. Did I look around enough? Was this the best buy? Should I have saved my money for something more sensible? Once when I was in the grip of such a litany of doubts, Fred said, "Stop, you are hurting its feelings. Nothing is perfect."

The two readings that follow suggest that imperfection can even be cause for wonder and delight.

Once upon a time there was a king who ruled a small kingdom. It wasn't great, and it wasn't really known for any of its resources or people. But the king did have a diamond, a great perfect diamond that had been in his family for generations. He kept it on display for all to see and appreciate. People came from all over the country to admire it and gaze at it. . . .

. . . Then one day a soldier came to the king with the news that, although no one had touched the diamond, for it was guarded night and day, the diamond was cracked. The king ran to see, and sure enough there was a crack right through the middle of the diamond.

Immediately he summoned all the jewelers of the land and had them look at the diamond. One after another they examined the diamond and gave the bad news to the king: the diamond was useless; it was irredeemably flawed. The king was crushed, so were the people. Somehow they felt they had lost everything.

Then out of nowhere came an old man who claimed to be a jeweler. He asked to see the diamond. After examining it, he looked up and confidently told the king, "I can fix it. In fact, I can make it better than it was before." The king was shocked and a bit leery. The old man said, "Give me the jewel, and in a week I'll bring it back fixed." Now the king was not about to let the stone out of his sight, even if it *was* ruined, so he gave the old man a room, all the tools and food and drink he needed and he waited. The whole kingdom waited. It was a long week.

At the end of the week the old man appeared with the stone in his hand and gave it to the king. The king couldn't believe his eyes. It was magnificent. The old man had fixed it, and he had made it even better than it was before! He had used the crack that ran through the middle of the stone as a stem and carved an intricate, full-blown rose, leaves, and thorns into the diamond. It was exquisite.

The king was overjoyed and offered the old man half his kingdom. He had taken something beautiful and perfect and improved upon it! But the old man refused in front of everyone, saying, "I didn't do that at all. What I did was to take something flawed and cracked at its heart and turn it into something beautiful."

—Megan McKenna
in *Parables*

ANTHEM

Ring the bells that still can ring,
Forget your perfect offering.
There is a crack in everything.
That's how the light gets in.
—Leonard Cohen
in *Stranger Music*

In addition to their roles as mirrors of the present, things can provide entry points into the past, and so support the spiritual practice of connections.

Jean Cocteau described what happened to him when he was walking down the street on which a large part of his youth had been spent. . . .

. . . Thinking of the past, he trailed his hand along the wall. But he was not satisfied with the result: he felt something was missing. . . . He decided to repeat the experiment, but this time . . . he bent down, closed his eyes, and let his hand trace the wall at a height which had been natural in the days he went to school. And immediately appeared what he had vaguely been expecting. "Just as the needle picks up the melody from the record, I obtained the melody of the past with my hand. I found everything: my cape, the leather of my satchel, the names of my friends and of my teachers, certain expressions I had used, the sound of my grandfather's voice, the smell of his beard, the smell of my sister's dresses and of my mother's gown."

Cocteau's notes oblige us to ask: where did his memories come from? . . . First they were not there—Cocteau searched for them in vain—and then they were. Where did they come from, and where were they at the moment of their reappearance? . . . The [memories] were in the wall.

—J. H. VAN DEN BERG
in *The Changing Nature of Man*

The sentimental value of things often exceeds their practical uses. They become old friends who share our lives.

The battered old chair in which I am sitting. I have owned this chair for more than twenty years, ever since I found it abandoned in an alley. At that time I was a college student so poor that I could not afford to buy a chair at a secondhand store. Perhaps seventy years ago a talented person sat down at a drafting table and worked hard to create its durable, elegant design. That person's effort and talent lives on in this chair, long after he or she has died. This chair has supported me through the writing of a senior thesis, a master's thesis, a doctoral dissertation, and three versions of this book, not to mention hundreds of professional reports. It has supported me while I've read countless books and magazines. I have sat comfortably in it while I laughed, cried, and rocked my babies to sleep. It has never required a repair, never frustrated me in any way.

—TIMOTHY MILLER
in *How to Want What You Have*

I have a rocking chair that, like Cocteau's wall and Miller's chair, contains pieces of my personal history. I don't know its full story, but I remember clearly when it became a vital part of my life. At twelve, I

had the interests of other girls my age: riding my bike, swimming, music lessons. But some of my most precious moments I spent in that chair, rocking and listening over and over to the same record. My chair and my music were companions on the journeys of my imagination. I daydreamed about women who could do anything and traveled the world meeting extraordinary people. At times, I simply engaged in a rocking meditation, my body and mind relaxed and in sync.

The chair now lives in our loft. When I rest my head on its cushioned back and begin to rock, I can transport myself to nearly every period of my life. Many things emit this sense of history.

Any table of virgin fir, any maple chair, any oak floor is a bundle of stories. At a lull in the conversation, move your napkin aside. There are centuries under one hand's span, and the timbre of a long, spirited life for the rap of a knuckle.

—Kim R. Stafford
in *Having Everything Right*

I've had a heap of comfort all my life making quilts, and now in my old age I wouldn't take a fortune for them. Sit down here, child, where you can see out of the window and smell the lilacs, and we'll look at them all. You see, some folks have albums to put folks' pictures in to remember them by, and some folks have a book to write down the things that happen everyday so they won't forget them; but, honey, these quilts are my albums and my diaries, and whenever the weather's bad and I can't get out to see folks, I just spread out my quilts and look at them and study over them, and it's just like going back fifty or sixty years and living my life over again.

—Eliza Calvert Hall
in *A Quilter's Wisdom*

Things punctuate the key moments in our lives and serve as reminders of what we value.

Countless couples tell me about simple things they gave each other when they were first married and poor as church mice that have more meaning in their lives than the many more and costlier things they have since given one another. One man keeps in his medicine cabinet, in spite of innumerable moves, the shaving mug and brush his wife gave him when they first got married even though he now shaves only electrically. "I would sooner leave my right hand behind," he told me when I discovered the relic in his bathroom cabinet. These are those special gifts we give one another that reach deep into our hearts and are forever memorable. That's what the song means when it asks for something to remember you by.

—JOHN R. AURELIO
in *Returnings*

We do not take our disappearance lightly. It hurts to realize that most of what we cherish will someday be treated as garbage. Throwing away the memento of a loved one feels like we are consigning that person's memory to trash. A daughter describes the conflict she faces each time she comes upon her deceased mother's umbrella in storage:

"I don't know why I'm saving it. It's old and dirty and torn, and yet I've taken it with me each time I've moved. It's been over twenty years since my mother died, yet I can't seem to throw it out. A few times already, I've held it over the dumpster, ready to drop it in, but I wasn't able to. It's crazy, because I never look at it, except when I go to get something else out of storage and there it is. Then I pick it up and look at it, and I can see my mother walking along with it like it was yesterday. She was never without it. I go through the same debate over and over again: should I keep it or throw it away? I always end up putting it back."

—WENDY LUSTBADER
in *Counting on Kindness*

Things can be angels, bringing the spirit of our ancestors into our hearts, or they can be tuning forks and teachers reminding us of who we are and why we are here. Terry Tempest Williams, one of our favorite essayists, captures these dimensions of things in the following reminiscence.

"It's important to have a hobby," Mimi said, "something to possess you in your private hours."

My grandmother's hobby was spending time at the ocean, walking along the beach, picking up shells.

For a desert child, there was nothing more beautiful than shells. I loved their shapes, their colors. I cherished the way they felt in the palm of my hand—and they held the voice of the sea, a primal sound imprinted on me as a baby.

"Your mother and I took you to the beach shortly after you were born," Mimi said. "As you got older, you played in the sand by the hour."

I played with these shells in the bathtub. . . .

Mimi would knock on the bathroom door.

"Come in," I would say.

She surveyed my watery world. I handed her the puffer, wet.

"When I die," she said smiling, "these shells will be your inheritance."

Thirty years later, these shells—the same shells my grandmother collected on her solitary walks along the beach, the shells we spread out on the turquoise carpet of her study, the shells we catalogued, the shells I bathed with—now rest in a basket on a shelf in my study. They remind me of my natural history, that I was tutored by a woman who courted solitude and made pilgrimages to the edges of our continent in the name of her own pleasure, that beauty, awe, and curiosity were values illuminated in our own home.

My grandmother's contemplation of shells has become my own. Each shell is a whorl of creative expression, an architecture of a soul. I can hold *Melongena corona* to my ear and hear not only the ocean's voice, but the whisperings of my beloved teacher.

—TERRY TEMPEST WILLIAMS
in *An Unspoken Hunger*

THINGS AS THINGS

In May 1995, Bob McNamara of CBS News reported the unusual story of Judy Daniel's little yellow duck. The duck was part of a set of plastic ornaments on her lawn in the small town of Grapevine, Texas. One day it disappeared and Mrs. Daniel assumed that it had been carried away by an animal; but a year later, the plastic duck returned with a photograph album showing where it had been.

"The World Quack Tour '94–'95" album contains forty-three pictures of the duck's travels: the duck with a park ranger in St. Louis, by the Rhine, in the Alps, across from Parliament in London, in front of the Eiffel Tower in Paris, at Niagara Falls, and on the beach in Hawaii. "He's been a lot more places than I've been," said Judy Daniel.

The Daniels have no idea how the little yellow plastic duck managed all this travel; they have not been able to figure out who might have accompanied it. Reporter McNamara speculated: "Somewhere, someone is enjoying this mystery as much as the Daniels, but the only witness isn't saying a word." "Well, the world is full of mystery," added Dan Rather of CBS News.

For whatever reason, some forms and icons acquire a life of their own, and not necessarily only holy images. When I was married, my husband and I hung in our bedroom a photograph of the beautiful, coquettish Evelyn Nesbitt, an infamous flapper from the Twenties. Our Evelyn had the uncanny habit of talking animatedly during the evening. As if engaged in parlor conversation, Evelyn batted her eyes, glanced around the room, lowered her head, moved her lips murmuringly and shockingly smiled on occasion to reveal her teeth, despite the fact that the photograph portrayed her with her lips together. After a night or two of this, I said to my husband, "Isn't that funny? That photograph always seems to be talking."

He looked at me shocked. "I thought I was the only one who could see it," he said. Then we proceeded to describe to each other her every wink, nod, mutter and mannerism. Unfortunately, neither of us could hear a word she ever said, and the photograph was still talking when we shut out the light.

—NORMANDI ELLIS
in *Dreams of Isis*

The great Sufi teacher, musician, and poet Hazrat Inayat Khan writes: "Everything in life is speaking, is audible, is communicating, in spite of its apparent silence." As a character in a recent novel by Lynne Sharon Schwartz points out, once we have a relationship with a thing, it begins to speak intimately to us.

My bed, a modest double, nothing kingly or queenly, has become more than a haven or refuge. It's a lover. At my most exhausted moments I sense it reaching toward me like the vibrations of the universe, for the Tai Chi teacher says the universe is a great system of vibrations we draw to us by our feelings: fear draws fear, love draws love. I almost hear the bed whispering to me to come, the way you might feel a lover longing for you miles away, and I come readily, falling onto the waiting mattress, firm but yielding as an accomplished lover, the strong coils beneath the stuffing like reliable bones beneath the flesh. I lie down as eagerly as did the princess worn out from her wanderings, except under this mattress is no irritating pea. No, the bed is a perfect and perfectly welcoming lover. The pillow sinks benignly under the weight of my head and rises mildly around my hair. I pull the sheet over me to be utterly surrounded, voluptuously embraced. It folds coolly around my legs as a lover's skin may be cool at first touch, but it quickly warms up from my body's heat, creating a tube of warmth. As the bed presses gently along the length of me, I let go. Every cell yields to the embrace which of late I find satisfying like no other. Totally understanding, the bed accepts that I have nothing to offer but warmth, which I have in abundance. I need not respond or embrace in return. The bed seeks nothing for itself—its pleasure is to wrap me in pleasure.

—LYNNE SHARON SCHWARTZ
in *The Fatigue Artist*

Even things that don't talk or touch us have palpable energy. We have discovered this through books. Over the years we have reviewed thousands of books which are now housed in free-standing bookcases demarcating areas of our loft. The guest room is set apart by bookcases containing novels. Some friends tell us that while sleeping there, they have had incredibly complex dreams, which we can attribute to the fact that books are magical and potent things emanating great energy.

This sensitivity about books is fueled, I believe, by an intuition that they are variations of the emotional fingerprint. They carry with them, even as multiples, something of the author or designer. It helps that they are largely organic, made of paper and leather, which seems to help them "speak." It is the common experience of anyone who owns or uses a library, or spends any length of time in the company of books, that you pick up something even from unopened volumes, almost by osmosis. The shelves seem to communicate in ways that racks of tapes or microfilm never can or will. And long familiarity with a collection eventually produces what Arthur Koestler called intervention by the "Library Angel" who causes volumes to leap from the shelf and open at the precise page that contains the reference you require, even if you are not yet consciously aware of such a need.

—LYALL WATSON
in *The Nature of Things*

Despite their mysterious powers, our usual attitude toward things, especially seemingly inconsequential ones, is to ignore or casually discard them. A more spiritual approach is to practice gratitude and love toward them.

Dental floss gets used and thrown away without a thought. How is it different from your toothbrush? Why do you reuse your toothbrush and throw away dental floss? The smallest, cheapest of objects serve us every day. They deserve our attention, proper use (or reuse), and thanks. It isn't foolish to thank your dental floss.

—DAVID K. REYNOLDS
in *Pools of Lodging for the Moon*

My grandmother didn't believe in wasting anything. She used to tell me to kiss my tin foil gum wrappers before I threw them away, so I would think about the value of things before I got rid of them.

—DAWNA MARKOVA
in *No Enemies Within*

Grandmothers seem to understand these truths intuitively. My grandmother Cutting used to unwrap her birthday or Christmas presents very slowly. She wanted to take home the ribbons and wrapping paper. As a little boy I never knew why she was as excited about those things as she was about what was inside the package, but now I do. Grandmother was a great lover of small things that everyone else overlooked.

BEAUTY

"One of the most important—and most neglected—elements in the beginnings of the interior life is the ability to respond to reality, to see the value and the beauty in ordinary things, to come alive to the splendor that is all around us," writes Trappist monk Thomas Merton.

We miss so much of the beauty that emanates from the people, places, and things around us. We just don't see it.

"Looking for and enjoying beauty is a way to nourish the soul," observes Matthew Fox, an Episcopal priest and modern mystic. "The universe is in the habit of making beauty. There are flowers and songs, snowflakes and smiles, acts of great courage, laughter between friends, a job well done, the smell of fresh-baked bread. Beauty is everywhere."

To walk this path is to acknowledge the goodness of creation. Then with the twelfth-century German mystic Hildegard of Bingen, we can feel the radiance of things.

According to writer Deena Metzger, "Beauty is the Navajo designation for the alliance with the spirits and nature. Beauty, or *Tepheret*, is the very heart of the Kabbalistic tree of life, the place where spirit and form meet, the site of the connection between the divine and the earthly."

Thus, whether we are moved by the beauty of a Beethoven symphony, the paintings of Georgia O'Keeffe, or the singing of Barbra Streisand, there is spiritual refreshment to be had. Or as the English novelist and poet D. H. Lawrence puts it, "The human soul needs beauty even more than it needs bread."

In some cultures, this need for beauty is honored in rituals and the arts. The Japanese reverence this virtue in the tea ceremony, flower arrangements, calligraphy, and other activities. The Balinese have found a way to integrate beauty into everyday life where it belongs.

Buddha taught that morality is the true beauty of a human being and that it is revealed in relationships. Professor of geography Yi-Fu Tuan writes: "A spontaneous act of generosity, performed with unselfish grace is an example of moral beauty, as are certain acts of courage; genuine modesty is a possible example, as is selfless love. Although moral beauty is a natural gift, it is nevertheless more likely to emerge and flourish in societies that appreciate and encourage it."

Beauty in all its forms should be encouraged in our homes. It is what best-selling spirituality author Marianne Williamson celebrates as "spiritual radiance."

Drink deep of the shining and ephemeral glories that surround you. Drink deep of the beauty which nourishes your soul. Drink deep of the grace notes that accompany your experiences of the sublime. Then you will never have to utter the lament of the third-century philosopher St. Augustine: "Too late have I loved you O Beauty, so ancient and so new, too late have I loved you!"

BEING PRESENT

"Now or never! You must live in the present, launch yourself on every wave, find eternity in the moment," urges Henry David Thoreau, the nineteenth-century American philosopher.

Leave the past to God's mercy. Leave the future to God's discretion. This moment is all there is.

The Chinese philosopher Lao-tzu counsels, "The Master gives himself up/to whatever the moment brings." The Hasidic teacher Rebbe Nachman of Breslov advises, "Each day has its own set of thoughts, words and deeds. Live in tune." The Sufi mystic Jelaluddin Rumi says, "Stay here, quivering with each moment/like a drop of mercury."

Be here in the moment, as an artist is here with focused attention, whether you are cooking, cleaning, praying, playing, or reading. Be here in the moment, as an athlete is here in that sweet spot of time when everything is effortless, fluid, and free.

"No moment is trivial since each one contains a divine kingdom and heavenly sustenance," explains the eighteenth-century Jesuit spiritual director Jean Pierre de Caussade.

The banquet is spread out before us, and it is the wish of the Divine Host that we partake of the present moment without regrets for the past or fears of the future.

Catholic teacher and preacher Fulton J. Sheen puts it this way: "The University of the Moment has been built uniquely for each of us. This wisdom distilled from intimate experience is never forgotten; it becomes part of our character, our merit, our eternity."

Pledge yourself to the moment and let it teach you. Surrender yourself to the moment and let it preach you.

Episcopal priest Robert Farrar Capon warns, "We spend a long time wishing we were elsewhere and otherwise." We are like the character in the movie *Postcards from the Edge* who sends a card home from vacation, "Having a wonderful time. Wish I were here." Buddhist teacher Jack Kornfield comments, "The quality of presence determines the quality of life."

We devote too much of our energy trying to avoid being present. Better to follow the example of Teresa of Avila, a sixteenth-century Spanish Carmelite mystic. She told the nuns of her convent that if she began to levitate during Mass, they should grab hold of her so she wouldn't fly off.

Equally disheartening are our attempts to label certain activities as worthless. Jungian therapist Helen M. Luke delineates this problem: "We hurry through the so-called boring things in order to attend to that which we deem more important, interesting. Perhaps the final freedom will be a recognition that every thing in every moment is 'essential' and that nothing at all is 'important.'"

Spanish cellist Pablo Casals says, "Each second we live is a new and unique moment of the universe, a moment that never was before and never will be again."

Stay in the moment. That is where the Invisible Lover is, close as your breath.

My wife just gave me a new pair of slippers. I said to her, "I guess this means that it's time to throw the old ones out." They were moccasins lined with wool. I had worn them for two decades. The soles were sound, but the seams were coming apart. I reluctantly put them in the trash.

An hour later I went into the kitchen and saw that my wife had taken them out. They were sitting on the floor like old friends. I reflected on how their shape and aging had been formed through daily life with my feet. They served me well for many years. And now at the end of their useful life, they cannot adapt to another person. I am the only one who can fully appreciate their being and their history. They depend upon me for this.

My wife said, "I couldn't bear to see them in there with the milk cartons and food scraps."

"I'll find a use for them," I said.

—SHAUN McNIFF
in *Earth Angels*

Sometimes the best way to empathize with the life of things is to animate them, an exercise in sympathy which comes naturally to children. The always imaginative James Hillman, elder statesman of contemporary depth psychology, shows us the way.

If things are ensouled, then they too require rituals of disposal which we are beginning to find again in our recycling projects, appropriately called Redemption Centers. Instead of the old punishing puritanical moralisms about dropping litter on the street, we need a new and enjoyable animism that children would be the first to understand. "Don't throw that candy wrapper on the street"— not because it's dirty or bad manners; not because it's wrong; not because "what if everybody did that?"—but instead "because your candy wrapper doesn't want to lie around in the gutter or be stepped on; it wants to be in the trash basket along with all its friends."

—JAMES HILLMAN
in *Kinds of Power*

Over the years they have lived together, Andy and Shelly have nick-named much of their furniture and household appliances. For exam-ple, they have a sprawling red sofa, which they call Big Red. . . .

In their living room they also have a worn Oriental rug which is threadbare in several places, earning it the nickname "Treadia." Shelly says she apologizes to the rug when she vacuums it and "wears it down a bit more." The vacuum, too, has a nickname— "J. Edgar"—since it is a large, old, sputtering Hoover.

Among their kitchen appliances are a Cuisinart called Oscar, an electric mixer called Lady Sunbeam, and an iron called Miss Proctor.

"Of course," says Shelly, "we've nicknamed the car. It's a dilapi-dated station wagon that my father gave us years ago when he bought a new car. I keep telling Andy that it once was a fancy fam-ily car, but it now has all the signs of old age—a faded paint job, rust, and tears in the upholstery, so we call it Faded Glory."

—WILLIAM BETCHER
in *Intimate Play*

After nearly eighteen years of uninterrupted service, our freezer one day failed to cool its contents. A serviceman made the repair and then asked to use our vacuum, explaining that a key part of the freezer had over-heated because of all the dust and cat fur under it. Fred and I nodded; pulling the freezer out of its built-in closet was not part of our cleaning routine.

"Could you vacuum under the refrigerator too?" I asked.

Later, coming to sign the service slip, we were greeted with this news: "Your refrigerator breathed a huge sigh of relief when I vacuumed."

"You talk to the machines?"

"Talk and listen; in my line of work, you have to."

The first time Davy saw Ernestina, she was boiling water for tea and talking to Aunt Helen's teakettle. She was polite and persuasive. She told it the advantages of boiling; she told it about the other pots wait-ing to take its place. She put her hands on her hips and said, "Pot, what is your determination in this matter?" and the pot boiled.

—NANCY WILLARD
in *Things Invisible to See*

This kind of respect for things puts a whole new slant on the meaning of service.

Not only persons call for service; their things do, too—the oil changed, the VCR cleaned, the dryer repaired, the message transmitted. Ceremonies of the repairman. Objects have their own personalities that ask for attention, just as the ads show the smiling bathtub that enjoys the new cleanser or the wood siding that likes the fresh stain which protects it from decay. Treating things as if they had souls, carefully, with good manners—that's quality service. . . .

This idea of service demands surrender, a continuous attention to the Other. It feels like humiliation and servitude only when we identify with a ruling willful ego as mirror of a single dominating god. But what if a God is in each thing, the other world distributed within this world?

Theology calls this distribution of the divine within all things the theory of immanence, and, sometimes, pantheism. . . .

A theology of immanence means treating each thing, animate and inanimate (perhaps the distinction no longer clearly obtains), natural and man-made, as if it were alive, requiring what each living thing requires above all else: careful attention to its properties, their specific qualities. This plant needs little water; this wood won't bear great weight and burns with a smoky fire. Look at me carefully: I am an aspen, not an oak. Notice differences, pay attention, give respect (re-spect = look again). Notice what is right under your nose, at your fingertips, and attend to it as it asks, according to its needs.

—JAMES HILLMAN
in *Kinds of Power*

Hillman is justifiably critical of busy individuals who look with derision on the tasks of washing windows, sweeping trash, and making beds, and who view the maintenance of things as meaningless. They would do well to listen to Eileen Caddy, one of the founders of the Findhorn community in Scotland, who says: "When you take a dirty floor. . . and make it spotlessly clean, and then polish it until it shines, it radiates back to you the love which you poured into it; the divinity of that floor has been drawn forth."

Our inability to deal with things sometimes means we just let them accumulate and not neatly at that. This can be viewed as a spiritual problem.

Moreover, a close inspection of our countryside would reveal, strewn over it from one end to the other, thousands of derelict and worthless automobiles, house trailers, refrigerators, stoves, freezers, washing machines, and dryers; as well as thousands of unregulated dumps in hollows and sink holes, on streambanks and roadsides, filled not only with "disposable" containers but also with broken toasters, television sets, toys of all kinds, furniture, lamps, stereos, radios, scales, coffee makers, mixers, blenders, corn poppers, hair dryers, and microwave ovens. Much of our waste problem is to be accounted for by the intentional flimsiness and unrepairability of the labor-savers and gadgets that we have become addicted to.

Of course, my sometime impression that I live on the receiving end of this problem is false, for country people contribute their full share. The truth is that we Americans, all of us, have become a kind of human trash, living our lives in the midst of a ubiquitous damned mess of which we are at once the victims and the perpetrators.

—WENDELL BERRY
in *What Are People For?*

When we renovated our loft, we planned lots of storage space. We wanted to put things away—out of sight and out of mind. But we did that so successfully that now we live among many things and live with few of them. Recently, knowing that everything in life has a purpose, we realized that too many of our things have not had an opportunity to fulfill theirs. They sit frustrated in cabinets behind closed doors waiting for the moment when we will use them. It must be a sin to so restrain them. We don't need to throw them away as much as we need to give them their freedom, even if all that happens is that they go to the recycling center or a thrift shop.

Neglected and ignored things may turn toxic. Art therapist Shaun McNiff points out: "Many ancient tribal societies have created elaborate rituals to deal with the angry spirits of things that have not been cared for and become destructive."

The spirits of things are not always saccharine. Many of us have probably kicked the tires of our cars and uttered savory expletives when the machine refuses to start. As soon as the thing does not submit to our will, it becomes a "being" in its own right, something to whom we address aggression or a plea for cooperation.

Whenever "a thing" acts, or does not act, in ways contrary to a person's will, it is immediately animated. We howl and plead, "Why are you doing this to me?" I take the car for granted until it fails me, and then I become absorbed by its being. People who scoff at the idea of talking to trees and stones have no trouble speaking passionately at a mechanical device with a mind of its own.

—SHAUN MCNIFF
in *Earth Angels*

For years, the loud shrieking car alarms on the streets below my office window nearly drove me up the wall. Mary Ann could not believe my reaction to this noise pollution. Then one day I realized that the cars might just be venting all the anger they felt for being left alone so often. In the event that the alarm was actually signaling trouble, it was conveying the car's fear of real harm. Now whenever I hear a car alarm go off, I gently whisper, "Calm down, everything is going to be okay."

Our relationships with things are complicated by society's uneasiness with assigning meaning to what many consider to be lifeless and expendable. In contrast, spiritually literate craftspersons, poets, artists, and children open our eyes to the value of things both in relationship to and apart from humans.

It is as if the honorable craftsman in his journey of exploration of the material asks, "What can this wood, this clay, this glass, do?" instead of "What can I do with it?" For that he has to listen to the material, entreat it, support it where it needs support and be tough and demanding with himself, even more demanding than he is with the material. This listening requires his most exacting attention. If his mind wanders, his hands holding the tool will stray. He will hit the wood too hard, or gouge too deeply or at the wrong angle. The wood, abandoned, without the support of human mind, will become "discouraged" and the product will fail. Most carvers do make use of a glue pot, to glue back parts cut off by mistake, but attention is a stronger glue.

—CARLA NEEDLEMAN
in *The Work of Craft*

Poets often give us unusual perspectives on things. Naomi Shihab Nye, a Palestinian-American poet, read the following poem on the Bill Moyers television series "The Language of Life."

FAMOUS

The river is famous to the fish.

The loud voice is famous to silence,
which knew it would inherit the earth
before anybody said so.

The cat sleeping on the fence is famous to the birds
watching him from the birdhouse.

The tear is famous, briefly, to the cheek.

The idea you carry close to your bosom
is famous to your bosom.

The boot is famous to the earth,
more famous than the dress shoe,
which is famous only to floors.

The bent photograph is famous to the one who carries it
and not at all famous to the one who is pictured.

I want to be famous to shuffling men
who smile while crossing streets,
sticky children in grocery lines,
famous as the one who smiled back.

I want to be famous in the way a pulley is famous,
or a buttonhole, not because it did anything spectacular,
but because it never forgot what it could do.
—NAOMI SHIHAB NYE
in *Hugging the Jukebox*

The recognition that everything has its own place, integrity, and happiness leads naturally to the spiritual practices of attention and wonder. Consider the work of artist Claes Oldenburg. His larger than life sculptures of common things teach about imagination and reverence. Behold the clothespin! Poet Mary Oliver stops us with a vivid image of a thing experiencing the spiritual practice of joy.

The shriek, then the happiness of the drawn nail. How it blinks again, in the sunlight.

—MARY OLIVER
in *Blue Pastures*

Children also help us hone our spiritual literacy skills through the practices of love, compassion, and play.

When a little boy finds an old electric motor on a junk heap, he is pierced to the heart by the weight, the windings and the silent turning of it. When he gets it home, his mother tells him to throw it out. Most likely he will cry. It is his first and truest reaction to the affluent society. He usually forgets it, but we shouldn't. He is sane; society isn't. He possesses because he cares. We don't.

—ROBERT FARRAR CAPON
in *Bed & Board*

My son once found the hip-bone of a large cow. He wore it as a stately garment or as armor; he played the bone like a guitar or played himself in the bone like a dinosaur. He circulated his interest upon the bone back into his discovery of it in the woods, to the being who had walked it before abandoning it, to the shape and feel of it, to hanging it on the wall and looking at it and the shadows it cast. And the bone was transformed—quite beyond the original fragment of decay in the woods—into images of everything from death to art.

—LYNDA SEXSON
in *Ordinarily Sacred*

Finally, children, as little beings themselves, know what it feels like to want to be seen for themselves and celebrated for their uniqueness. To see the meaning of things as they do, says Rabbi David J. Wolpe, we need a spiritual perspective.

Children do not study shoeboxes to manufacture better boxes. They study them because they *are*. That is a rare but wonderful devotion. It is important and necessary to study things for some purpose. It is holy to study them for no purpose. Each moment is precious not because of what it can be used for, but simply because it is. Creation is only one use of time. Another is appreciation.
—DAVID J. WOLPE
in *Teaching Your Children About God*

PRACTICING SPIRITUAL LITERACY: THINGS

Every skill, including spiritual literacy, improves with practice. We get better at reading the world when we do it regularly and when we run our readings past others. At the end of every chapter in this book, you will find some suggestions for practicing spiritual literacy.

The first set of suggestions includes questions you might use to spark conversations with family and friends or reflections in your journal. The second section covers activities and projects for individuals, groups, or families, including several that involve children. Finally, you are invited to sample some spiritual exercises and rituals, based on different traditions, that honor the presence of the sacred in everyday life.

CONVERSATIONS/JOURNAL ENTRIES

- In the story at the beginning of this chapter, a rabbi identifies the lessons of a train, a telegraph, and a telephone. Make similar readings of a computer, a shaken soda can, a backpack, or a kite.
- Talk or write about a thing that is a symbol of Spirit for you.
- Name the most treasured objects of your childhood. Why were they important to you? Do you still have any of them? What objects have comparable meaning for you today?
- What are a few of your prized possessions that were handmade for you, given to you by someone else, or once belonged to another person? Identify any special feelings they elicit. What things do you want people to have as remembrances of you?
- What do your things say about you to others? What things have you recently dispensed with, or could easily give away, because they no longer reflect either you or your interests? What things are part and parcel of the current you?
- Which of your possessions have you named? How did you choose each name? How else do you pay respect to the things in your life?

ACTIVITIES/PROJECTS

- Have a party for your things. Gather all the electronic gadgets in your house and give them a good dusting and cleaning. Check to see that cords are in good shape and any filters are changed. As part of your party fun, give out "Exceptional Service Awards" to signify your gratitude for what these things do for you.

- Rent the video movie *The Object of Beauty*. The film revolves around a couple living above their means in a London hotel. Her most prized possession is a Henry Moore bronze figurine. When it disappears, she is devastated, feeling she has lost a friend. Her boyfriend is upset because he regards the statue as a commodity that can be sold. The chambermaid who takes the figurine views it as a treasure—something to light up her life. This video film is a thought-provoking meditation on objects of desire.

- "A true poet is a friendly person," writes William Wordsworth. "He takes into his arms even cold and inanimate things and rejoices in his heart." Go to the library or bookstore and find poems that celebrate ordinary things. Here are two volumes to start with: Pablo Neruda's *Ode to Things* and Francis Ponge's *The Voice of Things*.

- Louise Nevelson and other artists have shown us that a piece of metal can be as numinous as a cathedral window if only we have eyes to appreciate its divine qualities. Go on a treasure hunt and collect materials to make a junk sculpture. Neighborhood children can be especially resourceful in finding unusual objects. Title your sculpture "Sacred Things," and see how your creativity responds.

SPIRITUAL EXERCISES/RITUALS

- Find or make an object to use as an aid during meditation or ceremonies. The wisdom traditions suggest many possibilities: candles, beads, flags, stones, fetishes.

- Short blessing prayers are part of many religious traditions. They express gratitude for a thing and also convey an awareness that the Creator of the Universe is present in or through it. Write blessing prayers for the objects on your desk, in your kitchen, or in your recreation room.

- On February 8, Japanese Buddhists observe "Needle Memorial Day" to honor all the needles which have been killed in action over the previous year. Plan an annual observation for things that have worn out.

- Create a welcoming ritual for a new possession, beginning with a blessing prayer. Express your understanding of the special gifts this thing now brings into your life. Some people may want to speak on behalf of other things in your household, welcoming them to their community. Then all vow to honor and cherish these new companions.

PLACES

Wherever you live is your temple
if you treat it like one.

—Buddha

It is essential to experience all the things and moods of one
good place.

—Thomas Merton

This world, this palpable world, which we are wont to treat
with the boredom and disrespect with which we habitually
regard places with no sacred association for us, is in truth a
holy place, and we did not know it. Venite adoremus.

—Pierre Teilhard de Chardin

A place will express itself through the human being just as it
does through its wild flowers.

—Lawrence Durrell

Perhaps the most radical thing we can do is to stay home, so
we can learn the names of the plants and animals around us;
so that we can begin to know what tradition we're part of.

—Terry Tempest Williams

I want to remind myself and others that our homes can become sacred places, filled with life and meaning. We do not need cathedrals to remind ourselves to experience the sacred.

—GUNILLA NORRIS

There is nothing like staying at home for real comfort.

—JANE AUSTEN

From the things in our daily lives, we move out a step to the places that have spiritual significance. Whereas things bear the fingerprints of the Beloved, places reveal footsteps. The Ground of Being is one of the names given to God, and with spiritual literacy we locate the Holy Presence concretely on the Earth. "The place where you are standing," Yahweh says in Exodus, "is holy."

People throughout history have gravitated to geographical power points seeking personal transformation: Stonehenge in England, the river Ganges in India, the Western Wall in Jerusalem, Ayers Rock in Australia, the Temple at Delphi in Greece, St. Peter's Basilica in Rome, Mecca in Saudi Arabia, and other sites. In some religious traditions, pilgrimage to sacred places is both a duty and a privilege.

Certain kinds of earthly places have traditionally had spiritual meanings attached to them, notably deserts. The Jews traveled in the desert and became a community; Jesus went there to pray and to prepare for his ministry; and Muhammad received his commission in a desert cave.

Places affect us, says the Hebrew psalmist. The Lord's green pastures and still waters restore the soul. The Chinese have observed that an individual's well-being is influenced by location and have devised a system of reading the energy or *chi* of places to find beneficial positions for buildings and rooms.

In the ancient goddess tradition and the more recent Gaia hypothesis, the Earth is seen as the body of the Divine Mother. The primal or first religions on the planet, which are still practiced today by tribal communities in Australia, Africa, Asia, and the Americas, have a particularly acute sense of place. World religions expert Huston Smith calls this an "embeddedness in place." Referring to observations made by anthropologist Claude Levi-Strauss, Smith explains that for tribal peoples, "location in place—not any place, but in each and every instance the exact and rightful place—is a feature of sanctity." For example, the Kogi, a tribal people living in the mountains of Colombia, perform elaborate rituals to make sure that everything in their physical environment is in its proper place, and they believe that by doing so they are healing the universe.

In this chapter, we look at spiritual geographies and sacred places, from the Earth seen from space to distinctive landscapes that shape a person's character. Any place can have spiritual meaning, especially our own homes. Many of the writers represented in the following pages are essayists who have focused on the multiple meanings of home, finding evidence there of the spiritual practices of connections, nurturing, transformation, and mystery.

Steeping ourselves in a place, simmering in its bounties, celebrating its wonders, and loving its peculiarities are necessary steps on a spiritual journey. We often take for granted the places where we work and play. To get to know them again, or perhaps for the first time, involves acts of consecration and imagination. Or as Wendell Berry puts it: "My most inspiring thought is that this place, if I am to live well in it, requires and deserves a lifetime of the most careful attention."

SPIRITUAL GEOGRAPHIES

The Earth and its features—the subject of the field of geography—can be read for spiritual significance. Whether we regard the Earth as a sacrament which reminds us of the Creator, as the body of the Great Spirit, or as another link in the great Chain of Being, our spiritual journeys have to take place here. Devotional writer Edward Hays, calling himself a planetary pilgrim, sees the Earth as "a living spaceship, a conscious interlocking organism on a voyage." The supreme achievement of the Apollo space missions may be that those explorers brought us a new sacred image of unity.

Leafing idly through *The Home Planet*, I stop at a picture of Earth floating against the black velvet of space. Africa and Europe are visible under swirling white clouds, but the predominant color is blue. This was the one picture from the Apollo missions that told the whole story—how small the planet is in the vast sprawl of space, how fragile its environments are. Seen from space, Earth has no national borders, no military zones, no visible fences. Quite the opposite. You can see how storm systems swirling above a continent may well affect the grain yield half a world away. The entire atmosphere of the planet—all the air we breathe, all the sky we fly through, even the ozone layer—is visible as the thinnest rind. The picture eloquently reminds one that Earth is a single organism.

—DIANE ACKERMAN
in *The Rarest of the Rare*

83

The entire planet is holy ground, but traditionally some places are regarded as being more special than others. Spiritually literate writers often contemplate the meaning of landscapes.

It's strange how deserts turn us into believers. I believe in walking in a landscape of mirages, because you learn humility. I believe in living in a land of little water because life is drawn together. And I believe in the gathering of bones as a testament to spirits that have moved on.

If the desert is holy, it is because it is a forgotten place that allows us to remember the sacred. Perhaps that is why every pilgrimage to the desert is a pilgrimage to the self. There is no place to hide, and so we are found.

—TERRY TEMPEST WILLIAMS
in *Refuge*

Mountains have long been a geography for pilgrimage, places where peoples have been humbled and strengthened. They are symbols of the Sacred Center. Many have traveled to them in order to find the concentrated energy of Earth and to realize the strength of unimpeded space. Viewing a mountain at a distance or walking around its body, we can see its shape, know its profile, survey its surrounds. The closer you come to the mountain, the more it disappears. The mountain begins to lose its shape as you near it. Its body begins to spread out over the landscape, losing itself to itself. On climbing the mountain, the mountain continues to vanish. It vanishes in the detail of each step. Its crown is buried in space. Its body is buried in the breath.

—JOAN HALIFAX
in *The Fruitful Darkness*

How wonderful are islands! Islands in space, like this one I have come to, ringed about by miles of water, linked by no bridges, no cables, no telephones. An island from the world and the world's life. Islands in time, like this short vacation of mine. The past and the future are cut off; only the present remains. Existence in the present gives island living an extreme vividness and purity. One lives like a child or a saint in the immediacy of here and now. Every day, every act, is an island, washed by time and space, and has an island's completion. People, too, become like islands in such an atmosphere, self-contained, whole and serene; respecting other people's solitude, not intruding on their shores, standing back in reverence before the miracle of another individual.

—ANNE MORROW LINDBERGH
in *Gift from the Sea*

Some sacred places seem filled with great power and enchantment. Visitors feel a connection to a deeper wisdom and may experience breakthroughs into alternate realities.

The early Celts believed in "thin places": geographical locations scattered throughout Ireland and the British Isles where a person experiences only a very thin divide between past, present, and future times; places where a person is somehow able, possibly only for a moment, to encounter a more ancient reality within present time; or places where perhaps only in a glance we are somehow transported into the future. Some of the stories here that associate the saints with intuitive and psychic powers attest to these "thin places."

—EDWARD C. SELLNER
in *Wisdom of the Celtic Saints*

The waterfall tumbling over the escarpment before me is like no other: a trembling pillar of white water descending from the sky into the valley with all the aplomb of some lustral fluid bent upon purification. The spray drifts towards me with the slow elegance we associate with a large flag in the wind. . . . No wonder my nomad friends regard Jim Jim falls with a certain awe. They consider the place to be *maraiin,* or sacred, since it embodies a spirit of its own. . . .

. . . In principle, they have little interest in the new, except where it is eminently practical. Thus they look upon a place like Jim Jim falls as being a spiritual warehouse where age-old intuitions are permanently stored. They come here to stock up on those invisible perceptions the waterfall constantly echoes. In the presence of tiny, black-striped fish and larger cobalt-coloured ones, they too are able to drift under submerged stones, feeling the glory of weightlessness as it pertains to their own soul.

—James G. Cowan
in *Letters from a Wild State*

Wild and distant places speak to many who find in them opportunities to engage in the spiritual practices of wonder and gratitude.

. . . we need something more than rigorously protected forests and pristine parklands to keep us whole. We need not dispense with the formalities of parks and refuges, but we must recognize something else that is vital: the essential *forms* of nature, the underlying variety, are more complex than our capability to appreciate or circumscribe, and are fundamental to our welfare. . . . We need land where we can be truant and not have to pay to get in or be inspected on the way out. Each of us needs to sneak into country still unvisited by the masses, even if that means waking up at five before most people roll out of bed.

If you cannot find terrain magnificent enough to take your breath away, gravitate to places that can at least increase your heartbeat.

—Gary Nabhan
in *Songbirds, Truffles & Wolves*

The point of going somewhere like the Napo River in Ecuador is not to see the most spectacular anything. It is simply to see what is there. We are here on the planet only once, and might as well get a feel for the place. We might as well get a feel for the fringes and hollows in which life is lived, for the Amazon basin, which covers half a continent, and for the life that—there, like anywhere else— is always and necessarily lived in detail: on the tributaries, in the riverside villages, sucking this particular white-fleshed guava in this particular pattern of shade.

—Annie Dillard
in *Teaching a Stone to Talk*

Mythologist Joseph Campbell reports that in India a sacred place might consist of a red circle drawn around a stone so that the environment becomes metaphoric. "When you look at that stone, you see it as a manifestation of Brahman, a manifestation of the mystery." Any place where the Mystery breaks through into our consciousness is holy.

A hospital corridor can be a mysterious place, a terrible and holy threshold upon the boundary of the soul. Here you will find an opening through which you might apprehend and embrace unexperienced aspects of God. Uprooted from your ordinary days, the hospital confounds the peaceful soul with the realization that the God of daily living is also the God of sudden dying. The God of the comforting parish sanctuary is also the God of the Intensive Care Unit. The God of beeswax candle and incense is the God of vomit and pus; the God of white linen and embroidered chasuble is the God of plastic curtain and sweaty sheet; the God of organ and flute is the God of squeaky gurney wheels and crying children; the God of deep port wine and delicately embossed communion bread is the God of infected blood and wounded flesh.

—SUZANNE GUTHRIE
in *Grace's Window*

Poet and essayist Kathleen Norris has coined the term "spiritual geography" to get at the peculiar and important ways a specific region can speak to our souls and transform us. For more than twenty years, she and her husband have resided in a house built by her grandparents in Lemmon, a small town near the border of North and South Dakota.

The High Plains, the beginning of the desert West, often act as a crucible for those who inhabit them. Like Jacob's angel, the region requires that you wrestle with it before it bestows a blessing. This can mean driving through a snowstorm on icy roads, wondering whether you'll have to pull over and spend the night in your car, only to emerge under tag ends of clouds into a clear sky blazing with stars. . . .

Or a vivid double rainbow marches to the east, following the wild summer storm that nearly blew you off the road. The storm sky is gunmetal gray, but to the west the sky is peach streaked with crimson. The land and sky of the West often fill what Thoreau terms our "need to witness our limits transgressed." Nature, in Dakota, can indeed be an experience of the holy. . . .

Where I am is a place where the human fabric is worn thin, farms and ranches and little towns scattered over miles of seemingly endless, empty grassland. On a clear night you can see not only thousands of stars but the lights of towns fifty miles away. Scattered between you and the horizon, the lights of farmhouses look like ships at sea. The naturalist Loren Eiseley once commented on the way Plains people "have been strung out at nighttime under a vast solitude rather than linked to the old-world village with its adjoining plots. We were mad to settle the West in [this] fashion," he says. "You cannot fight the sky." But some have come to love living under its winds and storms. Some have come to prefer the treelessness and isolation, becoming monks of the land, knowing that its loneliness is an honest reflection of the essential human loneliness. The willingly embraced desert fosters realism, not despair.

—KATHLEEN NORRIS
in *Dakota*

The place closest to our hearts and minds is often the one where we grew up. In his memoir, novelist John Updike describes a visit to his hometown.

Toward the end of Philadelphia Avenue, beside the park that surrounds the town hall, I turned and looked back up the straight sidewalk in the soft evening gloom, looking for what the superstitious old people of the county used to call a "sign." The pavement squares, the housefronts, the remaining trees receded in silence and shadow. I loved this plain street, where for thirteen years no great harm had been allowed to befall me. I loved Shillington not as one loves Capri or New York, because they are special, but as one loves one's own body and consciousness, because they are synonymous with being. It was exciting for me to be in Shillington, as if my life, like the expanding universe, when projected backwards gained heat and intensity. If there was a meaning to existence, I was closest to it here.

—JOHN UPDIKE
in *Self-Consciousness*

My home, until I was fourteen, was a small town of six thousand in South Dakota on the edge of the Great Plains. As a girl I marked out my territory on roller skates and homemade stilts. I could get anywhere else I wanted to be on my bicycle. Years later, the family drove back to South Dakota after we had lived in Karachi, a crowded Asian city on the sea, and in Indianapolis, a midsize metropolis in the heart of Midwest farmlands. We headed west through Illinois, Iowa, and a corner of Minnesota, all with similar landscapes. But almost as soon as we crossed the Minnesota–South Dakota border, we went down a steep bluff and the land just leveled out. I was surprised by an enormous sense of relief. I took a deep breath and let it out. I looked over at my sister. Cora had the same look on her face, the one that spelled "Home!"

There is something very comforting about the flat terrain imprinted on me as a child. I used to think it might be the monotony of the scenery that appealed, enabling me to relax and drift, never to worry about a surprise over the next hill or around the bend. But now I know it is Dakota's openness that I love and need. Look straight ahead in any direction on the prairie and Heaven touches Earth. South Dakota, with its long views, taught me the very important spiritual lesson that it is not necessary to look up to find the sky.

And who hasn't leaned west, at least once? Caught in the longing for something far off, over a hill, around a bend—something just glimpsed in the falling sunlight of evening and tinted gold. . . . William Wordsworth said it best, describing a simple walk at twilight. He is asked: "What, you are stepping westward?" And answers with a pilgrim's excess: "Yea. 'Twould be a wildish destiny. . . ."

This multilobed landscape, gentle and harsh by turns, has hold of me; here I stay, a free woman, unable to move. I feel the land with my eyes, with my sense of balance, with all the details of how a breeze picks up perfumes off a hillside, the way a cloud is caught on the needles of a pine tree and torn into mist, how wheat is grown in crescents along the slope of an ancient ash mound. . . . I wonder sometimes at the *me* that never grew because I grew here and not somewhere else, the *me* that would have grown elsewhere in place of the self I became. A given landscape permits and prohibits how one perceives, what one is literally able to experience.

—SALLIE TISDALE
in *Stepping Westward*

C

COMPASSION

"Compassion is a foundation for sharing our aliveness and building a more human world," according to writer Martin Lowenthal. It is a way of relating to people, places, and things. And it is a key to transforming ourselves and others.

The world's religions provide us with images that help put this spiritual practice in focus. The Buddha of Compassion, explains Buddhist writer Sogyal Rinpoche, is represented in Tibetan iconography as having "a thousand eyes that see the pain in all corners of the universe and a thousand arms to reach out to all corners of the universe to extend his help."

The Christian mystic Mechtild of Magdeburg describes the Holy Spirit as "a compassionate outpouring of the Creator and the Son." Of course, one of the best known parables of Jesus focuses on the compassion demonstrated by the Good Samaritan who helps the injured man on the road to Jericho.

Ryokan, the Zen monk who writes such wonderful poetry, puts forward his own image of compassion: "Oh, that my monk's robes were wide enough to gather up all the people in this floating world."

And Protestant Jim Wallis, founding editor of *Sojourners* magazine, writes: "At times I think the truest image of God today is a black inner-city grandmother in the U.S. or a mother of the disappeared in Argentina or the women who wake up early to make tortillas in refuge camps. They all weep for their children and in their compassionate tears arises the political action that changes the world. The mothers show us that it is the experience of touching the pain of others that is the key to change."

Teacher of mythology Joseph Campbell notes: "Compassion for me is just what the word says; it is 'suffering with.' It is an immediate participation in the suffering of another to such a degree that you forget yourself and your own safety and spontaneously do what is necessary."

This means reaching out with caring to others. It means identifying with the homeless person on the street, with the depressed teenager who is about to commit suicide, with the helpless trees in the Amazon rain forest, with the frightened animals in a laboratory, and with the tortured feelings of anger and hate that we harbor in our own psyches.

Buddhist teacher Jack Kornfield calls compassion "the quivering of the pure heart—when we have allowed ourselves to be touched by the pain of life." Under this rubric, even the idea of the enemy vanishes and is replaced by the notion of someone who needs our understanding and love. Through compassion, we conquer the numbness and the daze which keeps us closed off from the messes and miseries of the world.

This path is available to us. Protestant minister and writer Frederick Buechner sums it up: "Compassion is the sometimes fatal capacity for feeling what it is like inside somebody else's skin. It is the knowledge that there can never really be any peace and joy for me until there is peace and joy finally for you too."

CONNECTIONS

"All of us are born mystics," writer Ann Gordon tells us, "for the capacity to experience wonder and a primal sense of connectedness with all life is our birthright."

And what mystics have always known has been confirmed by physics and ecology—all things are interconnected. What happens in one place affects all places.

We are finally settling into a period when the dueling dualisms of the past are giving way to holistic thinking. The separations between mind and body, human nature and the natural world, are being scrapped for a new project—the reenchantment of the world. We are learning what Christian theologian Richard Niebuhr knows: "Passage into larger, more encompassing life takes place in our acts of connecting with living beings whom we, in our casual unmindfulness, treat as separate from ourselves."

Spiritual literacy clarifies and intensifies the connections in our lives. "When you look inside yourself, you see the universe and all its stars in infinity," writes Swiss psychologist C. G. Jung. The result is "an infinite mystery within yourself as great as the one without."

Self and world are linked in ever-expanding circles. "When we plant a tree, we are planting ourselves," Buddhist ecologist Joan Halifax observes. "Releasing dolphins back to the wild, we are ourselves returning home. Composting leftovers, we are being reborn as irises and apples. . . . we can know the activity of the world as not separate from who we are but rather of what we are."

We are kith and kin of stones, trees, groupers, and galaxies. Zen master and poet Thich Nhat Hanh uses the term "interbeing" to express this connectedness. "Looking at anything, we can see the nature of interbeing. A self is not possible without non-self elements. Looking deeply at any one thing, we see the whole cosmos. The one is made of the many."

Theologian Catherine Keller vividly demonstrates what this means: "I cannot exist without in some sense taking part in you, in the child I once was, in the breeze stirring the down on my arm, in the child starving far away, in the flashing round of the spiral nebula."

This concept of interbeing transforms our understanding of ethics. Writer Brian Patrick asks, "Who is our neighbor? The Samaritan? The outcast? The enemy? Yes, yes, of course. But it is also the whale, the dolphin and the rainforest. Our neighbor is the entire community of life, the entire universe. We must love it all as our self."

Freelance writer Mark Collins brings it even closer to home: "Every drop of blood that falls in Tibet or Cambodia or Gallipoli or Iraq lands on our shoes and spatters the hem of our best suit."

To solve the problems of spaceship Earth we must all work together now. Starhawk, a peace activist, sets out the challenge: "The Hopis say that we all began together; that each race went on a journey to learn its own road to power, and changed; that now is the time for us to return, to put the pieces of the puzzle back together, to make the circle whole."

What is significant about sacred places turns out *not* to be the places themselves.

Their power lies within their role in marshaling our inner resources and binding us to our beliefs.

Our act of "holding sacred" is the root, not the place where we choose to carry out that act.

It is in that act that we give places power to affect our lives.

In holding a place sacred, we grant power to a place and acknowledge that power of the place. As an ikon or through its own inherent patterns, we acknowledge its ability to impact our awareness of certain relationships and their value to us.

Sacred places thus forge and strengthen bonds between us and the universe in which we believe.

They empower us by affirming the wholeness of the universe we see revealed about us, and by reflecting our chosen place and role in that universe.

—THOMAS BENDER
in *The Power of Place*
edited by James A. Swan

HOME

Our second set of spiritual readings focuses on how a deep sense of place contributes to a meaningful life. "Every man, every woman," suggests nature writer Edward Abbey, "carries in heart and mind the image of the ideal place, the right place, the one true home, known or unknown, actual or visionary." The thirteenth-century Sufi mystic Jelaluddin Rumi tells a story on just this point. This version of it comes from Jungian therapist Helen Luke.

A caravan of men and camels crossed a desert and reached a place where they expected to find water. Instead they found only a hole going deep into the earth. They lowered bucket after bucket into the hole, but the rope each time came back empty—no bucket and no water. They then began to lower men into the hole, but the men, too, disappeared off the end of the rope. Finally a wise man among the party volunteered to go down into the hole in search of water.

When the wise man reached the bottom of the hole, he found

himself face to face with a horrible monster. The wise man thought to himself, "I can't hope to escape from this place, but I can at least remain aware of everything I am experiencing." The monster said to him, "I will let you go only if you answer my question." He answered, "Ask your question."

The monster said, "Where is the best place to be?"

The wise man thought to himself, "I don't want to hurt his feelings. If I name some beautiful city, he may think I'm disparaging his hometown. Or maybe this hole is the place he thinks is best." So to the monster he said, "The best place to be is wherever you feel at home—even if it's a hole in the ground."

The monster said, "You are so wise that I will not only let you go, but I will also free the foolish men who came down before you. And I will release the water in this well."

—HELEN M. LUKE
in The Way of Woman

In the next readings, essayists Scott Russell Sanders and Linda Weltner answer the question: How does a house become a home?

The short answer is that these walls and floors and scruffy flower beds are saturated with our memories and sweat. Everywhere I look I see the imprint of hands, everywhere I turn I hear the babble of voices, I smell sawdust or bread, I recall bruises and laughter. After nearly two decades of intimacy, the house dwells in us as surely as we dwell in the house. . . .

Our rooms will only be as generous and nurturing as the spirit we invest in them. The Bible gives us the same warning, more sternly: Unless God builds the house, it will not stand. The one I live in has been standing for just over sixty years, a mere eyeblink, not long enough to prove there was divinity in the mortar. I do know, however, that mortar and nails alone would not have held the house together even for sixty years. It has also needed the work of many hands, the wishes of many hearts, vision upon vision, through a succession of families.

Real estate ads offer houses for sale, not homes. A house is a garment, easily put off or on, casually bought and sold; a home is skin. Merely change houses and you will be disoriented; change homes and you bleed. When the shell you live in has taken on the savor of your love, when your dwelling has become a taproot, then your house is a home.

—SCOTT RUSSELL SANDERS
in *Staying Put*

These four walls provide a safe perch from which I can contemplate all sorts of possibilities, knowing that on my inner compass, true north will always point me home.

A house absorbs caretaking like a sponge, storing it up in the softness of comfortable couches and the soothing tones of a muted wallpaper, then returning all that love to the original giver. All the hours spent arranging the furniture, choosing colors, even washing the floors, turn out not to have been in vain. Everything we have given we have given to ourselves. The home upon which we have lavished so much attention is the embodiment of our own self-love.

I'm not surprised that many of us experience uneasiness when cut off from this source of emotional nourishment for too long, but to tell the truth, it's not the comforts of home I'm counting on to ease my journey into the future.

It's the comforting.

—LINDA WELTNER
in *No Place Like Home*

Home is not only a refuge and a sanctuary. It can also be a workshop for the creation of our identity.

This is my home. This is where I was born. This is the bayou that runs in my dreams, this is the bayou bank that taught me to love water, where I spent endless summer hours alone or with my cousins. This is where I learned to swim, where mud first oozed up between my toes. . . .

This is my world, where I was formed, where I came from, who I am. This is where my sandpile was. I have spent a thousand hours alone beneath this tree making forts for the fairies to dance on in the moonlight. At night, after I was asleep, my mother would come out here and dance her fingers all over my sand forts so that in the morning I would see the prints and believe that fairies danced at night in the sand.

—ELLEN GILCHRIST
in *Falling Through Space*

Home is a place where you can catch a dream and ride it to the end of the line and back. Where you can watch shadow and light doing a tight little tango on a wooden floor or an intoxicated moon rising through an empty window. Home is a place to become yourself. It's the right spot, the bright spot, or just the spot where you can land on your feet or recline in a tub of sparkling brew if you're so inclined. It's a place of silence where harmony and chaos are shuffled like a deck of cards and it's your draw. It's somewhere you can close a door and open your heart.

—THEO PELLETIER
quoted in *Where the Heart Is*
edited by Julienne Bennett
and Mimi Luebbermann

Many people today are saying blessings and performing rituals to emphasize their connections to their homes and all they stand for. The ceremonies themselves are spiritual readings of the meaning of place, often signaling gratitude and hospitality.

WELCOME MORNING

There is joy
in all:
in the hair I brush each morning,
in the Cannon towel, newly washed,
that I rub my body with each morning,
in the chapel of eggs I cook
each morning,
in the outcry from the kettle
that heats my coffee
each morning,
in the spoon and the chair

that cry "hello there, Anne"
each morning,
in the godhead of the table
that I set my silver, plate, cup upon
each morning.

All this is God,
right here in my pea-green house
each morning
and I mean,
though often forget,
to give thanks,
to faint down by the kitchen table
in a prayer of rejoicing
as the holy birds at the kitchen window
peck into their marriage of seeds.

So while I think of it,
let me paint a thank-you on my palm
for this God, this laughter of the morning,
lest it go unspoken.

The Joy that isn't shared, I've heard,
dies young.
—ANNE SEXTON
in *The Awful Rowing Toward God*

We are here today to create our home. This dwelling, this collection of wood and nails and plaster and paint, possesses a spirit which today becomes part of our family. We welcome this home, embrace it, and trust it with our bodies and our hearts for as long as we live under this roof. We are grateful for the shelter and warmth it provides.

For as long as we live here, our cares will be as light as this feather. Our worries will float gently out of the window and away. (Open the window and let the feather drift away in the breeze.)

For as long as we live here, our path will be lit like the flame of this candle. Our home will shelter and protect us so the flame will burn ever bright and warm. (Light the candle.)

For as long as we live here, our lives will be full of flavor like this salt. Our home will hold it in unexpected places, offering it for our continuous delight. (Sprinkle the salt in the nooks and crannies of every room of your home.)

For as long as we live here, our souls will be nourished as we are nourished by this bread. We shall never hunger in body or spirit. (Take a few bites of the bread.)

For as long as we live here, our lives shall be filled with love as this smoke fills our home. Like this smoke, our love shall expand and permeate all of the rooms of this house. (Light the smudge stick and make a full circuit of the house with it.)

Our heartbeats, our breath, and our dreams join those of our home and of all the others who lived here before us. When one day we leave this home, we will leave a part of ourselves behind but shall carry a part of this home with us. We welcome our home into our family, and we joyfully await all of our tomorrows within its embrace.

Finally, take the still-lit smudge stick and circle around the outside of the house, laughing and singing and generally making merry.

—HOLLY L. ROSE
in *Where the Heart Is*
edited by Julienne Bennett
and Mimi Luebbermann

*The stage of my life has changed; old doors are
closed and new ones now stand open.*

Though I may have seen this space before, I now come to make it mine, to call it home.
Hello and greetings to the heart and soul of this new setting.

*I honor this place that will shelter me, and I embrace
the changes and opportunities that this move invites
into my life.*

—NOELA N. EVANS
in *Meditations for the Passages
and Celebrations of Life*

When you move into your first home, plant a tree at the front of the house to act as a welcome to all the people who will come to your door in the years to come. Choose it carefully so that it will be a showpiece. Type out a short piece explaining what the tree is, the event it symbolizes, the date and perhaps a short verse. Add a photograph and put it in an album. Add photos of the tree as it grows. But this is not the end. Make every event in your life the reason to plant a living memory, a shrub, another tree, a climbing rose over an archway. The album then becomes the record of a living ritual of your life throughout the years. If you choose wisely they will grow and give beauty and character to the whole garden.

—Dolores Ashcroft-Nowicki
in *Daughters of Eve*

We have never been able to move without saying good-bye to all the rooms of the apartment. Houses are full of soul and so are rooms.

Attics mutely speak the truth that a family is more than the individuals who inhabit a structure at a specific moment. Families are a complex web of lives stretched across years and generations as well as vast geographical and cultural distances. . . .

An attic's contents—forgotten treasures, souvenirs from long-ago times, belongings once possessed by a deceased aunt or grandparent or cousin—serve to remind us that we are part of a larger organic whole. They tease us into the mystery that our lives are not bounded but extensive, that our identity does not end at the outline of our silhouette but is in fact much larger, much more generous and more expansive than our present vision would allow.

—Wendy Wright
in *Sacred Dwelling*

Every other Sunday during my childhood, my sister and I would accompany our parents on a visit to Grandfather Brussat's house. It was a gigantic three-story place with five bedrooms, a mysterious passageway between floors, and a musty basement. While our parents talked with Grandfather, Carol and I would sneak up to the attic, which was forbidden territory. It was ten times the size of our attic and even included a bedroom.

I can still remember the enchantment of touching the ancient dusty

*furniture, looking at the old suits and dresses in the wardrobe, and
reading some of the books and papers which were stacked there. I felt
great energy pulsating through this place, unlike anything I knew in
my own home.*

*We usually spent only ten or fifteen minutes on these secret excur-
sions. But they were well worth the risk. By the time I got downstairs, I
was breathless, as if I had just seen some ghosts or touched the hem of
Father Time.*

*Our homes often demonstrate what the mystics know: that life con-
sists of connections—with nature, our past, and other people.*

> I leave the bedroom . . . I begin walking
> through my house. I will traverse it
> many times today like a creature
> covering her turf. It is a journey
> that zigzags and returns upon itself . . .
> a circumambulation . . . a re-remembering of "place."
>
> I know this is the way many ancients prayed—
> circling a holy site to deepen their devotion. . . .
> The floor in this house is wood . . . wide, old boards.
> When I walk I am walking on the wood and in the woods.
> I am walking on the life of these trees.
> They have been cut and planed . . . offered up
> for this sheltering.
>
> —Gunilla Norris
> in *Being Home*

Let me describe my grateful center to you. I was seven years old,
and my parents were trying to move to the West Coast. Our relative poverty, however, caught up with us, and we were forced
to winter in the cabin of an uncle in the Rocky Mountains. The
time was difficult for my parents, I am sure, but for me it was
glory. . . .

But my most vivid memory is of the fireplace. (I had never been
around a fireplace before, all our heat heretofore having come from
the coal furnace in our Nebraska home.) Every night I would pull
out the bed that hid in the couch by day and climb under the heavy
quilts, my head less than ten feet away from the crackling warmth.

Night after night I would fall asleep, watching this strange yellow blaze that warmed us all. I was in my grateful center.

—RICHARD J. FOSTER
in *Prayer*

I used to laugh at my Italian relatives who always wanted to sit in the kitchen. They even built houses without dining rooms. Big kitchens were all they wanted. They lived their whole lives in those kitchens, around the stove, eating, talking, playing cards, reading newspapers, drinking coffee. When they weren't around the stove, they were in church, in God's home, but that's another story.

Home is where the stove is. When I think of all the places I've lived, I think of what I cooked in the kitchen: cheese tarts in Cambridge, beet soup in Berkeley, and shrimp curry in Singapore. Home is where I saute the garlic and chop the onions, where the frying pan makes music.

An old Russian proverb says, "The oven is the mother." Food, warmth, acceptance, I can find it all at the stove.

—JO ANN PASSARIELLO DECK
in *Where the Heart Is*
edited by Julienne Bennett
and Mimi Luebbermann

There has always been something soulful about kitchens to me. Perhaps it is because I spent so much of my boyhood in this room talking with my mother, Harriett Brussat. I was an outsider at school because I was so skinny. My mother was a great cook and was always trying to fatten me up, but I burned off calories with incredible speed.

Each night after school, I met her in the kitchen. She gave me a plate of cookies to munch on while she prepared the evening meal and I reviewed the events of my day. I still didn't gain any weight but I always knew that I could count on Mother to listen patiently to my laments and make me feel loved. In doing so, she provided nourishment for my body and my soul. To this day, the kitchen remains for me a place of comfort, reverie, and communion, a source of strength.

Private places often invoke the spiritual practices of imagination and transformation.

As a child I had a secret place. Every day at sunset I visited a grove of birch trees surrounded by a hedge of sweet-smelling privet. At the center was a mound where I would lie down and listen to the steady rhythmic heartbeat of the earth. For seven years I performed this daily ritual; even in winter I could feel this pulse as though I were connected by a rootlike umbilicus to the dark core of the land.

The grove faced west and formed a kind of *kiva* or womblike container. This enclosure had all the power of an ancient shrine; it was a place of dying and becoming. As the light intensified and left the sky awash in crimson flames, I learned a way of being in the world and in transition. Something within me changed as the earth underwent its own transfiguration and as the day's activity gave way to the long, slow respiration of the night.

—VALERIE ANDREWS
in *A Passion for This Earth*

I now realize that the sacred space I created for myself, the room in which I do my writing, is really a reconstruction—a reactivation, if you will—of my boyhood space. When I go in there to write, I'm surrounded by books that have helped me to find my way, and I recall moments of reading certain works that were particularly insightful. When I sit down to do the writing, I pay close attention to little ritual details—where the notepads and pencils are placed, that sort of thing—so that everything is exactly as I remember it having been before. It's all a sort of "set-up" that releases me. And since that space is associated with a certain kind of performance, it evokes that performance again. But the performance is play.

—JOSEPH CAMPBELL
in *Reflections on the Art of Living*
selected and edited by Diane K. Osbon

My studio, a cabin on the bank of the creek, is both my place of work and a retreat. Within it I have gathered objects that have special meaning for me. Three volumes of photographs help me recollect various chapters in my autobiography. Several semiprecious stones catch and diffuse the light into a kaleidoscope of colors. A gnarled tree root that looks vaguely like an old man, found on a hike with my father in 1938, stands in the corner and keeps guard over sacred memories. Several masks on the wall remind me of certain demons, jokers, wild animals, and green-eyed old men I have glimpsed in the thickets of my soul. There is a wood stove for warmth, a bed for sleeping and dreaming, a spare chair for a friend, rugs and blankets I have collected from journeys to places where women still weave by hand, and candles for soft light. When I need solitude, I turn off the phone and fax and sit until my breath comes slow and gentle, and I am able to enter into the sanctuary that always awaits me at the center of my being.

—SAM KEEN
in *Hymns to an Unknown God*

Everyone has a spot where they feel comfortable and safe. My octogenarian mother called the end of the green velvet Empire couch in the living room her perch. No one else in the family encroached upon it, for it was her sole spot, at the end of two footpaths across the carpet: one from the bedroom to the living room, and the other from the couch to the kitchen and back. Each day she settled at the end of the couch, and it served as her base of operation for twenty years.

As she grew older and walking became more difficult, she spent more time at her perch. Through the three large windows across the room, she could see the front yard and street and the weeping willow tree and the sky. From her perch she watched for the postman, noticed the neighbors, and filled her days with reading and an occasional television program. She loved to have a fire in the grate on cold, cloudy days and shared her perch with the family cat that lay beside her and slept, often in unison with her.

No other place in the house had such profound meaning for her. A lamp on the rosewood table provided light and a wristwatch lay face up to help keep track of time. The perch was constant and she felt safe there.

—TOM ADAMS
quoted in *Where the Heart Is*
edited by Julienne Bennett
and Mimi Luebbermann

My favorite perch on the world is no more. It was a white, weather-beaten, four-posted cabana on the most beautiful beach in Antigua. It stood tall and survived Hurricane Hugo in 1989, but Hurricane Luis was too formidable a foe and the cabana was blown to bits in 1995. I'm glad that I kissed her four corners when I last left her, a month before the hurricane. This is the blessing I gave my cabana a few years earlier.

Blessed are you, o Cabana: for watching over me when I needed rest, for hosting countless conversations with Mary Ann and friends, for framing the beauty of the turquoise ocean, for giving shade from the noonday sun, for providing shelter from the rain. I'm grateful to you for seeding so many of my memories about the past, for housing so many of my dreams about the future, and for being such a reliable and loving friend in the present. Thank you for those times when it was just you and me in the dark of the night savoring the breeze and the mesmerizing sound of the waves. Thank you, Cabana, for doing what you do best with such unstinting faithfulness and simple elegance.

RESPECT FOR PLACE

As we saw in our exploration of things in the last chapter, some spiritual readings of the world require an attitude of respect that is not derived from something's value to us. We love it because it is. This is certainly true of places. The Earth was here before humans and may well outlast us.

But what is involved in respect for a place? Wendell Berry, one of the best writers on this subject, suggests that to begin, we must truly dwell in a landscape.

Seen as belonging there with other native things, my own nativeness began a renewal of meaning. The sense of belonging began to turn around. I saw that if I belonged here, which I felt I did, it was not because anything here belonged to me. A man might own a whole county and be a stranger in it. If I belonged in this place it was because I belonged to it. And I began to understand that so long as I did not know the place fully, or even adequately, I belonged to it only partially. That summer I began to see, however dimly, that one of my ambitions, perhaps my governing ambition, was to belong fully to this place, to belong as the thrushes and the herons and the muskrats belonged, to be altogether at home here. That is still my ambition. But now I have come to see that it proposes an enormous labor. It is a spiritual ambition, like goodness.

The wild creatures belong to the place by nature, but as a man I can belong to it only by understanding and by virtue. It is an ambition I cannot hope to succeed in wholly, but I have come to believe that it is the most worthy of all.

—WENDELL BERRY
in *Recollected Essays 1965–1980*

Respect for a place also involves acknowledging its mystery and wildness. Naturalist Gary Snyder reminds us what grand forces shape our landscapes.

Our place is part of what we are. Yet even a "place" has a kind of fluidity: it passed through space and time—"ceremonial time" in John Hanson Mitchell's phrase. A place will have been grasslands, then conifers, then beech and elm. It will have been half riverbed, it will have been scratched and plowed by ice. And then it will be cultivated, paved, sprayed, dammed, graded, built up. But each is only for a while, and that will be just another set of lines on the palimpsest. The whole earth is a great tablet holding the multiple overlaid new and ancient traces of the swirl of forces. Each place is its own place, forever (eventually) wild. A place on earth is a mosaic within larger mosaics—the land is all small places, all precise tiny realms replicating larger and smaller patterns.

—GARY SNYDER
in *The Practice of the Wild*

One of the best ways to get to know a place is to read—or write—its biography. John Hanson Mitchell investigated what had happened on one square mile in Massachusetts over a period of fifteen thousand years.

It occurred to me, after I came to know Nompenekit, that if I were to thoroughly understand Scratch Flat, genuinely dig out the story of the things that happened here, I could not rely solely on the maps, town records, and other official documents; I would have to get all the sources. And so I began asking everyone I could think of who might know something about the place or its past—archeologists, historians, old farmers, local eccentrics, Indian shamans, developers, newer residents, and local farmhands. I began to take on all comers, so to speak, all views of the past, present and future, and all the official and unofficial histories. And from these various sources, all of which I set down here without prejudice, I think I have uncovered the mystery; I think I have discovered what it is that I sensed in the woods and fields on my first walk over this insignificant little patch of the planet.

—JOHN HANSON MITCHELL
in *Ceremonial Time*

On a small scale, we can make many marvelous discoveries in our own backyards.

Digging in the garden, cutting worms and centipedes in two, finding glass shards and tin cans, chips of tile, medicine bottles, cold-cream jars—their mouths crammed with dirt—a chair from a child's dollhouse, the rim of a china cup. Deeper: a Seneca arrowhead, a strip of berry-colored cloth. My yard is a patch of history I dig up, push seeds into, and then stand back from with hubris when it erupts in neat rows of green. I am, more than anywhere else in the landscape, a creature of the garden, happy to invest my sweat here, to watch daily for nearly invisible increments of growth in our lettuce or green beans and breathe the mingled scents of herbs. Here I can feel the active love of attachment, the work of place making.

—DEBORAH TALL
in *From Where We Stand*

When I was twelve, my family moved from the country to the crowded suburbs of New Jersey, and I felt we had done the unforgiveable—we had left behind the place that supported us and gave us everlasting life. There were no more rose bushes or rows of irises and hollyhocks. I could no longer pick apples from our yard or run down the road to get fresh eggs from the neighbor's farm.

Years later, I realized that the land is always with us. The world as we first knew it remains imprinted on the body and the brain

D

DEVOTION

Devotion is a word derived from the Latin *devitio* for "vow" or "total dedication." St. Francis de Sales, a seventeenth-century French ecclesiastic, amplifies the term: "Devotion is simply the promptitude, fervor, affection and agility which we have in service of God."

The great spiritual traditions suggest a veritable treasure trove of devotional acts. There are morning and evening prayers, graces said over meals, and reverent physical gestures.

Consider, for example, all the ways people pray. Christians bow their heads and fold their hands. Native Americans dance and Sufis whirl. Buddhists sit quietly and Hindus offer sacrifices. Orthodox Jews bob their heads back and forth.

"Everything that one turns in the direction of God is prayer," said Ignatius Loyola, founder of the Society of Jesus. Richard Foster, a Quaker who has written wisely on different kinds of prayer, calls one type "Praying the Ordinary." It is seeing God in the ordinary experiences of life.

Douglas V. Steere, another Quaker, observes: "Devotion is not a thing which passes, which comes and goes as it were, but is something habitual, fixed, permanent, which extends our every instant of life and regulates all our conduct."

In our times, individuals are expressing a yearning for more informal devotional styles. David A. Cooper, a Jewish mystic and retreat leader, speaks to this need: "The Sufis believe that every aspect of daily life has potential as a devotional practice. Every bodily movement has its source in the divine. Everything we do, everything seen or heard, tasted or touched, can be undertaken as a devotional practice."

That way of putting it opens many doors. Episcopal priest Matthew Fox walks through one of them and establishes that tai chi, yoga, aikido, and making love are all examples of prayer.

We can express our devotion with our bodies in political protest, in dance, on pilgrimages, and in action for others. Dorothy Day, cofounder of the Catholic Worker Movement and a dedicated social reformer, says, "I believe some people— lots of people—pray through the witness of their lives. Through the work they do, the friendships they have, the love they offer people and receive from people."

We begin to see the possibilities: a quiet time in the early morning hours when we look out the window in wonder; a weekly call to a special friend during which we share our deepest feelings; a reflective pause before we leave work and go out to lunch; a meditative period on the commuter train home; some quiet time with our children at bedtime. All these are devotional practices which feed the soul and spur spiritual growth.

Whether our devotional practices are traditionally formal or in the modern spirit of informality, what is important is truthful self-expression and heartfelt worship.

"Adoration is nothing less than the oxygen of survival," says Andrew Harvey, a modern-day mystic. "The happiest life of all is one which is burning away consciously in the fire of divine love and devotion."

like tiny fossils embedded in a piece of shale. As a child, one has that magical capacity to move among the many eras of the earth; to see the land as an animal does; to experience the sky from the perspective of a flower or a bee; to feel the earth quiver and breathe beneath us; to know a hundred different smells of mud and listen unself-consciously to the sloughing of the trees. We are continually articulating the intelligence of the planet, which has grown up through all the species. The whole earth lives within us, and in every moment, we are both its creators and discoverers. We only need to reawaken all these early memories.

—Valerie Andrews
in *A Passion for This Earth*

No matter how much we honor the integrity of place, from time to time, we are bound to have mixed feelings about where we live.

Some days I think this one place isn't enough. That's when nothing is enough, when I want to live multiple lives and have the know-how and guts to love without limits. Those days, like today, I walk with a purpose but no destination. Only then do I see, at least momentarily, that most everything is here. To my left a towering cottonwood is lunatic with bird song. Under it, I'm a listening post while its great, gray trunk—like a baton—heaves its green symphony into the air.

I walk and walk, from the falls, over Grouse Hill, to the dry wash. Today it is enough to make a shadow.

—Gretel Ehrlich
in *Islands, the Universe, Home*

Sometimes the simple pleasures of place are nearly impossible to put into words. They are encompassed in the spiritual practices of love and devotion. In this passage from a novel, an elderly man surveys his farm.

From the rise, he looks out over his place. This is it. This is all there is in the world—it contains everything there is to know or possess, yet everywhere people are knocking their brains out trying to find something different, something better. His kids all scattered, looking for it. Everyone always wants a way out of something like this, but what he has here is the main thing there is—just the way things grow and die, the way the sun comes up and goes down every day. These are the facts of life. They are so simple they are almost impossible to grasp.

—BOBBIE ANN MASON
in *Spence + Lila*

Scott Russell Sanders reframes this key relationship to the land in spiritual terms.

"The man who is often thinking that it is better to be somewhere else than where he is excommunicates himself," we are cautioned by Thoreau, that notorious stay-at-home. The metaphor is religious: to withhold yourself from where you are is to be cut off from communion with the source. It has taken me half a lifetime of searching to realize that the likeliest path to the ultimate ground leads through my local ground. I mean the land itself, with its creeks and rivers, its weather, seasons, stone outcroppings, and all the plants and animals that share it. I cannot have a spiritual center without having a geographical one; I cannot live a grounded life without being grounded in a *place*.

In belonging to a landscape, one feels a rightness, at-homeness, a knitting of self and world. This condition of clarity and focus, this being fully present, is akin to what the Buddhists call mindfulness, what Christian contemplatives refer to as recollection, what Quakers call centering down. I am suspicious of any philosophy that would separate this-worldly from other-worldly commitment. There is only one world, and we participate in it here and now, in our flesh and our place.

—SCOTT RUSSELL SANDERS
in *Staying Put*

Every place is a vortex of energy, some locations more so than others. Practitioners of feng shui take readings of the energy of places, and the forces they describe are both positive and negative.

It is difficult to describe the difference between "good" and "bad" places in scientific terms. The nearest anyone has yet come to a system of such knowledge is the Chinese practice of *feng shui*. This translates literally as "wind and water" and embodies an ancient belief that we are linked to our environment by natural forces which make some places more harmonious and auspicious than others. It is part art, part science, combining intuition with a compass and a set of rules on where and how to build, worship, give birth or bury your dead. And it works to the extent that the result of such geomancy in rural China is a pattern of house, farm and village design that wonderfully reconciles man and nature. I know few places where landscaping has been so consistently successful, setting buildings into the environment with what looks like effortless ease.

—LYALL WATSON
in *The Nature of Things*

Call it energy, vibes, or the spirit of a place—its mystery is very inviting. During a stay at a mountain hermitage, David Cooper, a student of Jewish mysticism discovered how a place can also make demands.

Everything seems to have its own spirit. Plants, insects, rocks, even the firewood. This hut also has a spirit, a different kind, one that has been nourished by the thoughts of previous hermits. This hut-spirit tends the local mice and chipmunks. It sets tasks for the human beings who spend their time here. I was moved to repair the table, fix a window, and mend other odds and ends. This spirit also has a splendid sense of humor; I like it very much.

—DAVID A. COOPER
in *Entering the Sacred Mountain*

Robert Sardello has done pioneer work on ways to ensoul a place by recognizing its value in the scheme of life. Here is a good example:

Some time ago I was asked to speak to a group of city managers on the topic of architecture and the quality of life in the city. The meeting took place in a small room in the city's convention center. The room itself was sick. It had no windows, and the drab acoustic ceilings pressed in from above, sandwiching the room with oppression. The door was without a handle. It had only a steel plate for the hand and was indistinguishable from a public restroom entry. No molding marked a difference between ceiling and walls, and between walls and floor. Painted institutional gray, its floor covered with rough carpet, the space was filled with ugly brown folding chairs. The conversation in that space was interesting. It all gravitated toward power. A group of fairly ordinary people, city workers, all began talking about how they would change the architecture of the city. But no one noticed the suffering of this room. So how would it be possible to trust how they would reshape the city? . . . A great deal could be done to care for the soul of the room, starting with the recognition that it is hurting. What could be done? Simple things. A small table with a flower placed on it would honor the room. Anything given to the room that indicates through its presence a linking between this place and the larger world honors the room by saying that it is part of the world and not a space capsule. Anything that gives sensory experience to the room retrieves the soul from abstraction. A flower, a wooden table, a ceramic vase, a little earth, the necessary watering of a plant—with such gestures we have located this room on earth.

—ROBERT SARDELLO
in *Facing the World with Soul*

Spiritual literacy leads naturally to place etiquette. Apologies are often in order, and so is gratitude.

If you slam a door you must return to it, open it, and close it properly, and apologize to it for your insensitivity. If you leave a faucet dripping, you must shut it properly and apologize to it. If you leave a light or appliance on unnecessarily or break a pencil lead or drop a coin or kick up the corner of a rug or otherwise behave thoughtlessly, particularly if you are in haste or angry or otherwise upset at the time, you must correct the behavior and apologize to the offended object.

—DAVID K. REYNOLDS
in *Thirsty, Swimming in the Lake*

My first Zen teacher, Soen-roshi, always made a little bow of gratitude to the world around him, and I learned that from him. It's a wonderful habit. Even if I'm leaving some neutral or lifeless place, like a motel room, it feels right to thank the room for its hospitality. In Zen practice, one bows to the buddha principle, the imminence of awakening, within oneself. I love that idea. A bow is a wonderful way to appreciate this moment, pay respectful attention to the world around you.

—PETER MATTHIESSEN
quoted in *Talking on the Water*
by Jonathan White

In the 1992 screen adaptation of E. M. Forster's novel Howards End, *Mrs. Wilcox is madly in love with her ancestral home. In an early scene, she walks around the house slowly, taking in every inch of it with wonder and appreciation. Just before her death, she decides to leave this sacred place to Margaret, who is not a relative but a kindred spirit. Her family does not understand. In the novel, Forster gives a spiritually literate explanation for Mrs. Wilcox's action. "To them, Howards End was a house: they could not know that to her it had been a spirit, for which she sought a spiritual heir." When Margaret visits the house in the film, she follows in her benefactor's footsteps, slowly circling the house, her attention doing justice to Mrs. Wilcox's trust in her.*

Another 1992 movie, Enchanted April, *shows how a place can be a bearer of spiritual nourishment. In this story, four women from London vacation together for a month in a medieval castle in Italy. They need some time away from the alternating currents of social pressure and boredom in their lives. From the first morning when they throw open the shutters and look out onto this Italian paradise, they are revitalized by the sun, the sea, and the fragrance of the flowers. The place encourages them to count their blessings and live in the present moment. And it literally sets each one of them on the path of heart.*

Native Americans have much to teach us about walking in beauty on the Earth. The author of the next passage wanders through his village and discovers the special vibrations of place.

Living and walking in the village each day was like walking into myself, as a loving plane of existence. I used to jog, run, or walk through the village every morning just so I could get my loving pats from the village sites. There were the weathered pathways which wound their way among the adobe style structures, the open space in the center of the village, and the mountains in the distance. On early morning walks I used to enjoy breathing the familiar air. The fresh air, like a resonating intelligence hanging as a cover on the surfaces of the village, was delightful to drink into my lungs. Yet, each day the experiences were interestingly different and spatially new. It was not uncommon for me to walk into alternate realities unexpectedly. . . . The energy was always shifting, was always different. The resonating vibrations in the sacred sites were always changing so that the people in the village were always alive with energy. These sacred spaces, generating life sustaining powers, maintained our integrity as a group, orienting each individual toward the community's highest ideals.

—Joseph Rael
in *Being & Vibration*

To belong to a place, we need to have respect and stay alert. About the time we were finishing the Alphabet of Spiritual Literacy, Mary Ann brought home an alphabet book she had found in the children's department of our local bookstore. Alphabet City is a tribute to the urban environment and a paean to the spiritual practices of attention and wonder. In a remarkable collection of twenty-six paintings, artist Stephen T. Johnson locates all the letters of the alphabet in ordinary city sights. The end of a construction sawhorse is revealed to be the letter A. Viewed from the side, a streetlight is the letter E. The crisscrossing walkways in a park form an H. The steel beams on a bridge make an N. Johnson writes that he hopes his paintings "will inspire children and adults to look at their surroundings in a fresh and playful way."

We have discovered that the city—any place really—can yield wonders when we stay open to them. When Mary Ann lived in Pakistan, her family used to say that every time they left the house, they could expect to see something they had never seen before in their lives. This practice of openness to new experiences and teachings is valuable in any setting. So is the regular use of the active imagination to find meaning in place.

Recently, I went out for a walk and jotted down my impressions of how the city touches me and I touch the city. Call this my spiritual reading of New York.

I got my shoes polished today, and I did it for the city. The streets are all decked out for the Christmas holidays, and I want to be part of the celebration. As my shining shoes hit the pavement, the street responds, "Yes! Yes!"

I'm anonymous as I push my way through the crowds. There is a certain freedom I can enjoy here—the freedom to try on different selves by wearing a cape, a cowboy hat, or an outlandish ring. No one can say I am acting out of character. Looking at the people I'm passing, I wonder how many of them are costumed to explore a new self.

Paradoxically, my anonymous self is forced to be social here. I have to deal with groups in the city with whom I might otherwise never come in contact. Hundreds of languages are spoken in New York; if I were to stand on this corner for an hour, I could hear many of them.

Within just a few blocks I pass several ethnic enclaves. I decide to eat in a restaurant in one of them just to do my small bit to keep the homogenization of America at bay. I'm all for diversity within unity.

Passing a bench and a bus stop, I realize I will never look at them the same after seeing the movie Forrest Gump. *How many storytellers have rested there and talked about the meaningful moments and people in their lives?*

Most ledges around town are eminently sitable too. Except for the one on that building over there. I wonder if the management asked the ledge's permission before it imbedded jagged spikes in its skin so that people cannot rest there.

My eyes drift upward. I stretch my neck and drink in the ornate designs at the tops of buildings. Too often I forget to notice the gargoyles, flowered carvings, and gracious columns.

All sizes of buildings fascinate me. I love it when the exterior of an old building is cleaned and put under a spotlight at night. This gesture proves that one can be ancient and beautiful at the same time.

I'm also glad to see some buildings are dark at night. Everything needs a rest.

Buildings going up and coming down remind me that the city mirrors our yearning to constantly reinvent ourselves. But is personal renewal, like urban renewal, sometimes ruthless?

I need to have compassion for that mournful building over there that has seen better days. I also want to welcome the new building on the block. It has suffered resentful looks from people in the neighborhood during its often noisy construction.

Stores with open doors like the vegetable stand on the corner are said to do very well. I take it as a metaphor for my need to keep an open heart and an open mind.

I walk into the lobby of a building. Does it ever get tired of putting on a happy, cheerful face? Meanwhile, the potholes in the street outside signify that constant stress takes its toll. How do we lessen the demands we make on others, including this street?

The city seems to be very accommodating to my small needs. Whenever I need to tie my shoelaces, I am able to find a fire standpipe of suitable height for the task. Thanks, pipe.

We rely on the kindness of strangers in the city. It's holy work when building superintendents sweep the sidewalks every day. Each time we safely ascend to our offices or descend to the street, we are the beneficiaries of the ministrations of countless maintenance people and elevator inspectors.

There are so many little blessings in the city.

The stop sign at the corner makes me slow down and savor the scenery.

The fire hydrant I pass now is a little St. Christopher just waiting to be of assistance in an emergency.

The fire escape on that building is its silent protector; it is always on guard, and it doesn't carry a gun.

The trash container is my blood brother of conscience, always beckoning us to keep the city clean.

The snow from last week's storm is white and crisp in the park. The pile by the sidewalk is more typical. Dirty snow is a lesson about city life. It is tempting to look for only the positive, the fresh and the new. But there are all kinds of pollution here too. We are assaulted by daily doses of grime. I can't ignore the shadow side of the city.

I look up at an impressive church on a busy corner and try to discern what it is telling me. It has a simple but clear message: there is no separating the sacred and the secular. God is at the intersection.

I like heights and the city is full of them. Going to the top of a tall building is a spiritual experience. Above, around, and below me is a happening world. Buildings, streets, parks, traffic, people, all blend into one vision. From this perspective, everything fits together. The city makes mystics of us all.

PRACTICING SPIRITUAL LITERACY: PLACES

CONVERSATIONS/JOURNAL ENTRIES

- Identify a landscape which you would call your "spiritual geography." In your journal, write about its special meaning to you.
- Share a story about a particular place that comforted you or transformed your perspective on yourself.
- Recall memorable dreams set in the locations where you have lived. Which appear the most often? Why do you think this happens?
- In Europe, it is customary to name one's home. What would you name your home?
- Try this journal exercise. Each day for the next week, identify a blessing coming to you from your home. During the next weeks do the same for blessings from your neighborhood, your city/town/area, your country, and the planet.
- Where is the spiritual center of your home? Why did you choose it?
- Who has tutored you in the pleasures of place? When did you first become aware of feelings of affection or wonder for your home?
- Have you ever been in a place that you felt was "sick"? Describe its symptoms. How could you help to heal it?
- If you are living with other people, talk about how you have created your environment. Through its furniture, decorations, and arrangement, is your home a reflection of everyone's interests? How have you provided for privacy and community? How do you respect each other's space? How do you show respect to the place itself?

ACTIVITIES/PROJECTS

- Make a map of the neighborhood where you grew up. Include details such as the location of your house, school, park, place of worship, library, secret hiding place, best friend's home. Take an imaginary walk through your neighborhood and get in touch with your early feelings about place.
- Become a local historian. Create a scrapbook with pictures or drawings representing the different developments in your area. Who first lived on this land? Who settled here? What lifestyles flourished? What imprint have those who lived here left upon this place?

- Accompany a child on a visit to a historical site in your area. Together, try to imagine what it was like living there years ago.

- Look into the folklore, fictions, essays, poems, and art connected to your region. Think about how landscape has influenced customs, language, and tradition. Stage a reading of literature about your place at the local coffee shop, library, church, synagogue, or other community center.

- Rent the two French movies by director Yves Robert, *My Father's Glory* and *My Mother's Castle,* adapted from the memoirs of Marcel Pagnol. These beautifully photographed films will encourage you to consider the embrace of place upon your consciousness. Other recommended movies about place: *The Milagro Beanfield War, The Trip to Bountiful, Local Hero, A River Runs Through It, The Secret of Roan Inish.*

- Walk around the perimeter of your property. Explore it as if seeing it for the first time. What do you notice, feel, hear, smell? Continue this process as you move further out into your community. Make a list of things you notice that you have never seen before in your life.

- Spend some time making your home a more soulful place. For example, you might make changes so that it is more reflective of your attachments, commitments, and interests. Books on the Chinese art of feng shui explain this system of gauging energy flow in an area and making corrections using plants, arrangement of furniture, mirrors, wind chimes, flowing water, and other elements.

SPIRITUAL EXERCISES/RITUALS

- Locate spiritual markers or power points in your town. If you can't find any, create your own sacred spot with piles of stones or sculpted mounds.

- Make a pilgrimage to a site considered to be sacred in your spiritual tradition. Stay open to the possibility of a breakthrough experience while there.

- Hold a ritual to honor a special place in your life. Examples: the place where you have been most creative; the place where you began, or ended, a significant relationship; the place where you discovered something new about yourself; the place where you brought life out of death.

- Create prayers of thanksgiving for the different rooms of your house. When you bless the food that you eat, remember to also thank the room where it was prepared and the place where you are eating.

- Set up a home shrine consisting of objects, writings, or pictures which have spiritual meaning for you. Make it a place for reading, prayer, and contemplation.

NATURE

My profession is always to be alert, to find God in nature, to know God's lurking places, to attend all the oratorios and the operas in nature.

—HENRY DAVID THOREAU

My book . . . is the nature of created things, and any time I wish to read the words of God, the book is before me.

—ANTHONY OF THE DESERT

There is only one sacred manuscript, the sacred manuscript of Nature, which alone can enlighten the reader.

—HAZRAT INAYAT KHAN

If you wish to know the Divine, feel the wind on your face and the warm sun on your hand.

—BUDDHA

As often as you can, take a trip
out to the fields to pray.
All the grasses will join you.
They will enter your prayers
and give you strength to sing praises to God.

—RABBI NACHMAN OF BRESLOV

The Great Spirit is the life that is in all things—all creatures and plants and even rocks and the minerals. All things—and I mean all things—have their own will and their own way and their own purpose.

—ROLLING THUNDER

Whenever a person breaks a stick in the forest, let him consider what it would feel like if it were himself that was thus broken.

—NIGERIAN PROVERB

Nature provides a theater for some of our most dramatic experiences of the sacred. Most people can tell you about a time when they were soothed, inspired, or awed while contemplating the natural world.

The settings may vary but the feelings are universal. Communion with nature may take place while walking through the woods, watching a sunset, fishing in a mountain stream, looking at the waves of the ocean, observing the ripples on a lake, or sitting under a tree in a park.

Often these occasions turn into mystical moments when we sense that all the inhabitants of the world—the trees, flowers, fields, streams, hills, rocks, dolphins, bears, birds, and babies—are our relations, as Native Americans express it. When this happens, we have started to read the book of nature.

Both the historical and the primal religions emphasize the importance of the natural world as a reservoir of spiritual meaning. For Jews, Christians, and Muslims, the Earth reflects the glories of God. Buddhists, Hindus, and Taoists look for the connections between nature and human nature.

For the aboriginal peoples of the Americas, Africa, Asia, and Australia, the land and all the creatures upon it are spiritual teachers who must be listened to and taken seriously. The shamans of these groups are those who understand the languages of stones, plants, trees, and animals.

In this chapter, we turn to nature writers, ecologists, and naturalists to help us combat what ecologist and philosopher Thomas Berry calls the disease of autism—our inability to communicate with anybody but our own kind. Like playwright William Shakespeare, they find "sermons in stone." Like nature writer Edward Abbey, they "try to write prose psalms which praise the divine beauty of the natural world."

Spiritual literacy enables all of us to reenchant the world. With this perspective, we come to a new appreciation of the wonders of nature, and we rejoice in the spiritual nourishment she so often provides. We may also find ourselves identifying with nature and feeling her pain. "Healing people and healing the planet are part of the same enterprise," asserts cultural analyst Theodore Roszak.

The readings on the following pages explore how nature abounds with images which direct us toward Spirit and personal wholeness, how she leads us to a deeper respect for the mysteries of life, and how she reminds us of our small role in the long stretch of time.

Finally, our spiritual practices get plenty of exercise outdoors. Spiritual literacy in nature requires that we be attentive, open, playful, and reverent. Our care for the creation leads us naturally to compassion and Earth etiquette. These attitudes and actions are essential elements of everyday spirituality.

NATURE AS SPIRITUAL DIRECTOR

In Barbara Kingsolver's novel Animal Dreams, *Codi returns to her hometown of Grace, Arizona, to take care of her father. She begins a job teaching at the high school and resumes a relationship with Loyd, a Native American she dated as a teenager. Codi is trying to figure out what to do with her life and she suspects that what she does, especially in regard to her surroundings, will determine who she is. One day she is talking with Loyd about the Indians' corn dance.*

"So you make this deal with the gods. You do these dances and they'll send rain and good crops and the whole works? And nothing bad will ever happen. Right. . . ."

. . . After a minute he said, "No, it's not like that. It's not making a deal, bad things can still happen, but you want to try not to *cause* them to happen. It has to do with keeping things in balance."

"In balance."

"Really, it's like the spirits have made a deal with *us*."

"And what is the deal?" I asked.

"We're on our own. The spirits have been good enough to let us live here and use the utilities, and we're saying: We know how nice you're being. We appreciate the rain, we appreciate the sun, we appreciate the deer we took. Sorry if we messed up anything. You've gone to a lot of trouble, and we'll try to be good guests."

"Like a note you'd send somebody after you stayed in their house?"

"Exactly like that. 'Thanks for letting me sleep on your couch. I took some beer out of the refrigerator, and I broke a coffee cup. Sorry, I hope it wasn't your favorite one.'"

I laughed because I understood "in balance." I would have called it "keeping the peace," or maybe "remembering your place," but I liked it. "It's a good idea," I said. "Especially since we're still here sleeping on God's couch. We're permanent houseguests."

"Yep, we are. Better remember how to put everything back how we found it."

—BARBARA KINGSOLVER
in *Animal Dreams*

There are two major spiritual models used to describe humanity's relationship to nature. The stewardship model has people striving to be good houseguests by protecting nature. Environmentalist Helen Caldicott puts it well: "Each of us must accept total responsibility for the earth's survival. We are curators of life on earth, standing at the crossroads of time."

The other model, the mystical one, emphasizes that everything is part of God. We are not here just to care for and sleep on God's couch. God is the couch.

In the following pages, we mix examples of both approaches to nature, for they share one assumption: that nature is our spiritual director helping us discover and respond to the presence of the Holy in our lives. And like any good director, she encourages us to try new spiritual practices.

> The beauty of the trees,
> the softness of the air,
> the fragrance of the grass,
>   speaks to me.
>
> The summit of the mountain,
> the thunder of the sky,
> the rhythm of the sea,
>   speaks to me.
>
> The faintness of the stars,
> the freshness of the morning,
> the dewdrop on the flower,
>   speaks to me.
>
> The strength of fire,
> the taste of salmon,
> the trail of the sun,

and the life that never goes away,
they speak to me.

And my heart soars.
—Chief Dan George
and Helmet Hirnschall
in *My Heart Soars*

Many people find that nature is a conduit to the sacred. Dan Wakefield describes his childhood experiences in his spiritual autobiography.

Though I still attended Sunday school sporadically, I began to feel more spiritual refreshment out of doors than in church. In the fields and woods not far from my house, in the burning leaves of autumn and the running streams of spring, I felt close to the source and mystery of things. The perfume of wet clover, the rough hide feel of the bark of oaks, rushes of wind lifting curled red maple leaves off the hard autumn ground in swirling eddies—these and all the million sights, sounds, and smells of nature, from the sweet taste of foxtail grass I chewed as I strolled, to the quick flash of a perch below the surface of a brook, all were revelations and messages of some great creating force, which of course was God.

Sometimes I felt a frustration that I couldn't decipher the message, that I couldn't learn the meaning of it all, of life and earth, simply by trying to communicate with nature: staring, for instance, as hard as I could at a rock with layers of colors, or feeling its smooth cool surface with my fingers and pressing it in my palm as if I could squeeze out an answer. I knew there were secrets in the woods and sometimes I felt I was very close to them, close to understanding, and there was a thrill in sensing such knowledge was *there* if only I could look close enough or be still enough or attuned enough.

—Dan Wakefield
in *Returning*

Experiences in nature do seem to put us in a reflective mood. As the next readings illustrate, nature is simply providing the impetus for our spiritual discoveries.

There is a wonderful Chasidic story about the child of a rabbi who used to wander in the woods. At first his father let him wander, but over time he became concerned. The woods were dangerous. The father did not know what lurked there.

He decided to discuss the matter with his child. One day he took him aside and said, "You know, I have noticed that each day you walk into the woods. I wonder, why do you go there?"

The boy said to his father, "I go there to find God."

"That is a very good thing," the father replied gently. "I am glad you are searching for God. But, my child, don't you know that God is the same everywhere?"

"Yes," the boy answered, "but I'm not."

—DAVID J. WOLPE
in *Teaching Your Children About God*

In South India there is a pilgrimage to a place called Sabarimala. It is a pilgrimage to the forest and hundreds of thousands of people go there every year. The deep meaning of this is that people need to go back from time to time to the forest, to the wilds, where they were before they belonged to a settled civilization with a home and a city. We need to recall the freedom of the forest. Some time each year, at least, we should go out from our fixed abode, leaving our possessions and everything to which we are attached, and become free to wander or to settle in some very quiet place, to be free for some time like the *sannyasi*.

—BEDE GRIFFITHS
in *River of Compassion*

SLEEPING IN THE FOREST

I thought the earth
remembered me, she
took me back so tenderly, arranging
her dark skirts, her pockets
full of lichens and seeds. I slept
as never before, a stone

on the riverbed, nothing
between me and the white fire of the stars
but my thoughts, and they floated
light as moths among the branches
of the perfect trees. All night
I heard the small kingdoms breathing
around me, the insects, and the birds
who do their work in the darkness. All night
I rose and fell, as if in water, grappling
with a luminous doom. By morning
I had vanished at least a dozen times
into something better.
—MARY OLIVER
in *Twelve Moons*

"Consider the lilies of the field," Jesus says in the Bible, and it's reported that the nineteenth-century poet Emily Dickinson claimed that was the only commandment she never broke.

I don't think it is enough appreciated how much an outdoor book the Bible is. It is a "hypaethral book," such as Thoreau talked about—a book open to the sky. It is best read and understood outdoors, and the farther outdoors the better. Or that has been my experience of it. Passages that within walls seem improbable or incredible, outdoors seem merely natural. This is because outdoors we are confronted everywhere with wonders; we see that the miraculous is not extraordinary but the common mode of existence. It is our daily bread. Whoever really has considered the lilies of the field or the birds of the air and pondered the improbability of their existence in this warm world within the cold and empty stellar distances will hardly balk at the turning of water into wine—which was, after all, a very small miracle. We forget the greater and still continuing miracle by which water (with soil and sunlight) is turned into grapes.
—WENDELL BERRY
in *Sex, Economy, Freedom & Community*

According to the Jewish Midrash, a heathen asked Rabbi Joshua ben Karhah, "Why did God speak to Moses from a thornbush?" Realizing that no matter where God spoke from, a question might arise, Rabbi Joshua replied, "God spoke from the thornbush to teach that there is no place where the Divine presence is not, even in a lowly thornbush." Here is another spiritual reading of that biblical event.

Recently I have been reading Exodus, wondering about Moses and the burning bush. Moses, it is written, "turns aside to see a wonder," a bush that burns but is not consumed. Throughout my life, I had thought this a ridiculous passage. Why should God get Moses' attention by such outlandish means? I mean, why couldn't He just have boomed, "Hey, Moses!" the way He would later call to the great king, "Hey, Samuel!"

Now I know why. The truth, when really perceived and not simply described, is always a wonder. Moses does not see a technicolor fantasy. He sees the bush as it really is. He sees the bush as all bushes *actually* are. . . .

All that is living burns. This is the fundamental fact of nature. And Moses saw it with his two eyes, directly. That glimpse of the real world—of the world as it is known to God—is not a world of isolate things, but of processes in concert.

God tells Moses, "Take off your shoes, because the ground where you are standing is holy ground." He is asking Moses to experience in his own body what the burning bush experiences: a living connection between heaven and earth, the life that stretches out like taffy between our father the sun and our mother the earth. If you do not believe this, take off your shoes and stand in the grass or in the sand or in the dirt.

—WILLIAM BRYANT LOGAN
in *Dirt*

For Nicaraguan poet and priest Ernesto Cardenal, observations of nature give rise to the spiritual practice of wonder.

Everything in nature has a trademark, God's trademark: the stripes on a shell and the stripes on a zebra; the grain of the wood and the veins of the dry leaf; the markings on the dragonfly's wings and the pattern of stars on a photographic plate; the panther's coat and the epidermal cells of the lily petal; the structure of atoms and galaxies. All bear God's fingerprints.

There is a style, a divine style in everything that exists, which shows that it was created by the same artist. Everything is multiplicity within unity. Everything is both like other things and unique. Every individual thing has its own manner of being; it is that thing and not anything else. At the same time there are millions and millions of others like it, both minute creatures and immense stars. Everything has its own stripes, speckles, spots, dapples, veins, or grain—the caterpillar, the clay pot, the chameleon, the Klee painting and the Persian carpet, sea spray, stalactites, white agate veins in pebbles, the carpet of autumn leaves, wood, marble, sea shells, and the skeleton of the reptile....

In the image of God who created them, all beings are at once one and many, from the galaxy to the electron.

No two caterpillars are alike, no two atoms, no two stars, even though they look the same in the sky at night. But all things also have something in common. The poet seeks to discover this pattern, this design running throughout creation, and tries to see how even the most different things have an underlying likeness. The mountains skip like rams and the hills like young lambs.... Your hair is like a flock of goats winding through the mountains of Gilead.

—Ernesto Cardenal
in *Abide in Love*

Cardenal's view of nature is representative of sacramentalism, one of our spiritual literacy filters, in which nature is seen as a reflection of the divine reality. The Buddhist approach puts the emphasis on what nature can show us about life. There are eighty-four thousand different dharma doors for teaching, and many of them can be found in the natural world.

You should entreat trees and rocks
to preach the Dharma, and you
should ask rice fields and gardens
for the truth. Ask pillars for the
Dharma and learn from hedges
and walls. Long ago the great god

Indra honored a wild fox as his
own master and sought the Dharma from him calling him
"Great Bodhisattva."

—ZEN MASTER EIHEI DOGEN
quoted in *How to Raise an Ox*
by Francis Dojun Cook

Macrina Wiederkehr is a member of Scholastica Monastery in Fort Smith, Arkansas. She is a Catholic nun who has a facility for finding the sacred in the ordinary.

I must share with you a story about a particularly barren time in my life when I used a tree for a spiritual director. I learned so much that year because I listened in silence. . . .

Because it was small I couldn't lean on it but could only sit beside it. That taught me a lot about what the role of spiritual guide should be.

Even though it was small, it had the ability to give me a certain amount of shade. You don't have to have a lot of leaves to give shade.

Because it was silent I listened deeply. You don't need a lot of words to connect with God.

When it got thirsty I watered it. The miracle of water is a little like the miracle of God's love. That little sycamore taught me a lot about foot washing. Watering it was a great joy. A soul-friend relationship never works only one way. There is a mutual giving and receiving.

I learned from my tree that being transplanted is possible. I can always put down roots again, connect with the Great Root, and grow on. . . .

I wouldn't recommend using a tree for a spiritual guide all the days of one's life, but that sycamore got me through a long stretch of barrenness. It was only a little tree, and I didn't know it was holy until I spent time with it. Truly, holiness comes wrapped in the ordinary.

—MACRINA WIEDERKEHR
in *A Tree Full of Angels*

Gunilla Norris is a psychotherapist and author of several books on everyday spirituality. In one of them, she imaginatively muses upon the saints she meets while tending her garden over the course of one year.

There are so many [leaves]. Piles of them. I take pleasure in their abundance. More saints than you could ever dream of. Each one singular. Each one itself. Yellow, red, orange, parchment. They sail down in the autumn air like fearless sky divers. They are so trusting—letting go completely. Not questioning as I do . . . Will it be safe? Will I understand? Will it hurt? . . . stalling, qualifying, questioning, instead of releasing and taking to the air. . . .

The wildflower saints provoke me to remember the steadiness of return, year after year. They tell me that one does not need to be cultivated to be beautiful. They tell me that the soul remembers its essence, if it is given room to grow. . . .

These gentle flowers remind me that we surrender to no one finally but to our own soul, to the essence of ourselves, which is hidden in God. Sweet and wild is the experience of surrender. There is nothing more intimate.

—GUNILLA NORRIS
in *Journeying in Place*

Joyce Rupp is another spiritually literate writer and retreat leader who has a knack for drawing out subtle truths from the natural world.

One winter morning I awoke to see magnificent lines of frost stretching across my window panes. They seemed to rise with the sunshine and the bitter cold outside. They looked like little miracles that had been formed in the dark of night. I watched them in sheer amazement and marveled that such beautiful forms could be born during such a winter-cold night. Yet, as I pondered them I thought of how life is so like that. We live our long, worn days in the shadows, in what often feels like barren, cold winter, so unaware of the miracles that are being created in our spirits. It takes the sudden daylight, some unexpected surprise of life, to cause our gaze to look upon a simple, stunning growth that has happened quietly inside us. Like frost designs on a winter window, they bring us beyond life's fragmentation and remind us that we are not nearly as lost as we thought we were, that all the time we thought we were dead inside, beautiful things were being born in us.

—JOYCE RUPP
in *Praying Our Goodbyes*

Nature often holds up a mirror so we can see more clearly the ongoing processes of growth, renewal, and transformation in our lives.

The most exemplary nature is that of the topsoil. It is very Christ-like in its passivity and beneficence, and in the penetrating energy that issues out of its peaceableness. It increases by experience, by the passage of seasons over it, growth rising out of it and returning to it, not by ambition or aggressiveness. It is enriched by all things that die and enter into it. It keeps the past, not as history or as memory, but as richness, new possibility. Its fertility is always building up out of death into promise. Death is the bridge or the tunnel by which its past enters its future.

—WENDELL BERRY
in *Recollected Essays 1965–1980*

For me, learning to use the self-observer has been a lesson in composting. I have always been fascinated by the compost pile just outside our garden. It contains bits of old food, thick and gnarled weed roots, rotting flowers, egg shells. It seethes with life. Over time, with moisture and heat, this decaying pile of unwanted organic matter becomes sweet-smelling, fertile, crumbly compost. And so it is with the discarded parts of ourselves that we have swept under the carpet. Under the watchful eye of the self-observer, all that we have rejected, denied, and hidden, is exactly what can nurture our growth.

—ANNE SCOTT
in *Serving Fire*

One day as I was about to step on a dry leaf, I saw the leaf in the ultimate dimension. I saw that it was not really dead, but that it was merging with the moist soil in order to appear on the tree the following spring in another form. I smiled at the leaf and said, "You are pretending." Everything is pretending to be born and pretending to die, including that leaf. The Buddha said, "When conditions are sufficient, the body reveals itself, and we say the body exists. When conditions are not sufficient, the body cannot be perceived by us, and we say the body does not exist." The day of our "death" is a day of our continuation in many other forms.

—THICH NHAT HANH
in *Living Buddha, Living Christ*

NATURE AS MODEL

Our experiences in nature can teach us much about our relationship to the universe, but sometimes our response to the astounding natural beauty around us can only be ecstatic.

Last night the moon came dropping its clothes in the street.
I took it as a sign to start singing,
falling up into the bowl of sky.
The bowl breaks. Everywhere is falling everywhere.
Nothing else to do.

—JELALUDDIN RUMI
in *The Essential Rumi*
translated by Coleman Barks
with John Moyne, A. J. Arberry,
and Reynold Nicholson

Nature also provides an unending supply of images for the stories we tell.

The old theory [of the four elements] never really told us what the universe is made of, but rather how it moves, the way and feel of things. Earth is stubborn, conservative, and slow, with a long memory. Water is elusive and humble, seeking the low places. Air is a trickster, fickle and shifty. Fire is fierce, quick, greedy, and bold.

Over the centuries, these four characters have played leading roles in stories told by countless peoples. So Earth is the dry land that God separated from the watery beginnings. It is the mud brought up from the bottom of the primal sea by muskrat or loon, to offer solid ground where creatures with legs might walk. It is the dust from which we come and the dust to which we return. Water is the formless potential out of which creation emerged. It is the ocean of unconsciousness enveloping the islands of consciousness. Water bathes us at birth and again at death, and in between it washes away sin. It is by turns the elixir of life or the renewing rain or the devastating flood. Air is the wind that blows where it wills. It is the voice sounding in the depths of matter, the word made flesh. It is breath, which the Romans called *spiritus*, a divine thread drawn through every living creature. And Fire is the transformer, cooking meat, frightening beasts, warming huts, forging tools, melting, shaping. It is cleansing and punishing, flaming up from the sacred bush and lashing out from the furnaces of hell. Fire is a power given by the gods or stolen from them for the benefit of a bare forked animal. It is cosmic energy, lighting the stars, lurking in the atom, smoldering in every cell.

. . . when you sit beside a lake—dirt or stone beneath you and waves lapping at your feet and wind blowing in your face and the sun beating down—you are still keeping company with the old quartet.

—Scott Russell Sanders
in *Writing from the Center*

The closest I come to the old quartet is our neighborhood park. People are always telling Fred and me that we need to get out in nature more, but the park is nature, I reply. This year I began a spiritual discipline of walking around its perimeter every day. I try to practice attention, hospitality, and wonder on these short walks and allow the trees, bushes, birds, and animals to speak to me. Then I record the day's experiences in my journal. Here is an example.

June 22: It rained last night and the park today looks like it has been through the wash and the colors have all come out clean. The grass is greener, the leaves darker, the flowers brighter, the soil richer, the animals friskier. Why is it that we wake up, see a dark overcast sky, and declare glumly, "It's raining." Today the rain seems a blessing, a relief, a gift—like the rain that drenches Lancelot and Gueneviere in the movie First Knight. *He tips a leaf so the rain water flows into her mouth. I could drink rain from a leaf today too.*

I loved the rain as a child. I loved the sound of it on the leaves of trees and roofs and window panes and umbrellas and the feel of it on my face and bare legs. I loved the hiss of rubber tires on rainy streets and the flip-flop of windshield wipers. I loved the smell of wet grass and raincoats and the shaggy coats of dogs. A rainy day was a special day for me in a sense that no other kind of day was— a day when the ordinariness of things was suspended with ragged skies drifting to the color of pearl and dark streets turning to dark rivers of reflected light and even people transformed somehow as the rain drew them closer by giving them something to think about together, to take common shelter from, to complain of and joke about in ways that made them more like friends than it seemed to me they were on ordinary sunny days. But more than anything, I think, I loved rain for the power it had to make indoors seem snugger and safer and a place to find refuge in from everything outdoors that was un-home, unsafe. I loved rain for making home seem home more deeply.

—FREDERICK BUECHNER
in *The Sacred Journey*

In the next passage, a photographer describes how he discovered a picture. The position of a tree leaning over a pond speaks to his situation at the time, and as he responds to the image, nature speaks back.

One hazy, chilly December morning, I walked, camera and tripod balanced on my shoulder, through a stand of oaks toward the edge of a pond. The water was silver-gray and still like a mirror hung in an empty, unlit hall. A thin mist fell, or more accurately, hung in the air. Rain had soaked the landscape during the night, and mud at the water's edge sucked at my shoes. In the yawning light, I saw an oak leaning at a precarious angle over the water. The soil had eroded over time, dissolving much of the tree's foundation, yet the oak's roots were locked tenaciously into the receding land. Against the threat of drowning, this tree survived through an elegant dance of balance, perseverance and heroism. Almost in praise, the pond mirrored the oak's profile creating a beautiful mandala-like wheel with spokes of water, leaves, earth and light.

As I set up and focused the tree on my camera's ground glass, I thought how often in my own life I have lived just on the edge of

ENTHUSIASM

Enthusiasm means "one with the energy of God." It derives from root words pointing to being inspired and possessed by the Divine. There is something awesome about people who practice this spiritual quality. They are vibrantly alive.

A story is told by writer Margaret M. Stevens. Three brick masons are busy at work. When the first is asked what he is building, he answers without looking up, "I'm just laying bricks." The second replies, "I'm building a wall." But the third responds with great enthusiasm, "I'm building a cathedral!"

Enthusiastic souls give all they've got, holding nothing back. That's why essayist Ralph Waldo Emerson concludes that "Nothing great was ever achieved without enthusiasm. The way of life is wonderful; it is by abandonment."

It is difficult to stifle the ardor or dampen the spirits of people who really believe in what they are doing. They operate on full throttle. "Enthusiasm," according to writer George Matthew Adams, "is a kind of faith that has been set on fire."

There certainly is no shortage of ideas, ideals, causes, or crusades available to enlist our allegiance or enthusiasm. But we set up roadblocks. One is lethargy—the loss of interest in life and its adventures. The other is the postmodern attitude of cynicism—a refusal to acknowledge that our existence has meaning and purpose.

It is clear from his writing and speaking that the popular American preacher Norman Vincent Peale is a big fan of enthusiasm. "There is real magic in enthusiasm," he says. "It spells the difference between mediocrity and accomplishment. . . . It gives warmth and good feeling to all your personal relationships." He especially likes its ability to bring people together. "Your enthusiasm will be infectious, stimulating and attractive to others," he tells us. "They will love you for it. They will go for you and with you."

Enthusiasm lights up your life and the lives of those around you. In an essay, newspaper columnist Linda Weltner writes: "Modern life can grow dull and predictable . . . Still there's one magic talisman left that has the power to bring freshness, novelty, and surprise into your life. Someone else's enthusiasm."

This spiritual quality gives added value to everything it touches. Enthusiasm is a catalyst for delight on the job. It enlivens any relationship. Enthusiasm pumps zest and meaning into leisure, creativity, community, and service. No wonder parents consistently single it out as the one gift they want to be sure to pass on to their children.

Let's look again at the meaning of the word, this time through scientist Louis Pasteur: "The Greeks have given us one of the most beautiful words of our language, the word 'enthusiasm'—a God within. The grandeur of the acts of men are measured by the inspiration from which they spring. Happy is he who bears a God within."

heroic acts. How I've operated within safe, comfortable boundaries that defined the limits of what I could accomplish. At this time in my life, I was considering leaving a comfortable, secure job to follow my heart's urging to photograph and write. I stood on the edge of an uncertain future, mud sucking at my shoes, and stared out through the mists across silver-gray water at this leaning oak. Through its example, I saw clearly through the mists of doubt separating me from a decision. I stood for a long moment and imagined the worst that could happen if I stretched too far over the edge of my fears. Then, in that second when I snapped the shutter recording this moment on film, I stepped across an imaginary line in my mind. In the pond's dark mirrored water I saw a face. It smiled back at me.

—WILLIAM GUION
on *Leaning Oak and Reflection*
New Orleans, 1991

One of the bounties of nature is that she is open to so many different spiritual readings. The photograph described above appears on the cover of this book. When we first saw it, we were struck by the image of the mirrored universe: as above, so below. The tree and its reflection are one and the same, as the Creator and the created are joined in a unity. In the Judeo-Christian tradition, we say that we are made in the image of God; the visible mirrors the invisible.

From the shore, the tree is an ambassador to the mysterious unknown beneath the surface of the pond. This motif also speaks to our understanding of the world. The tree's roots hold to the surface; its leaves scan the depths. Heaven and Earth come together in one graceful arch: a mandala for everyday spirituality.

With careful planning, we can use the features of nature to make other points about the proper relationship between humanity and the harmonies of the natural world, as did the Japanese tea master in the next reading.

The Japanese tea master Sen no Rikyu built a teahouse on the side of a hill overlooking the sea. Three guests were invited to the inaugural tea ceremony. Hearing about the beautiful site, they expected to find a structure that took advantage of the wonderful view. After arriving at the garden gate, they were perplexed to discover a grove of trees had been planted that obstructed the panorama. Before entering the teahouse, the guests followed the traditional custom of purifying their hands and mouths at the stone basin near the entry. Stooping to draw water with a bamboo ladle, they noticed an opening in the trees that provided a vision of the sparkling sea. In that humble position they awakened to the relationship between the cool liquid in the ladle and the ocean in the distance, between their individuality and the ocean of life.

—ANTHONY LAWLOR
in *The Temple in the House*

In the next passage, David K. Reynolds, a Western authority on Japanese psychotherapy, shows how nature demands that we live in the present moment.

Today, walking along the beach, I spotted a rock, slick and shiny. It attracted my attention, and I picked it up. But on closer inspection it turned out to be shiny because it was wet. As it dried, the rock became ordinary. It was just a rock. I was disappointed at first, and I almost threw it away. But the rock had been wonderfully smoothed by the sand and the waves. Although it was merely a plain rock ground smooth by the elements, it turned out to be worth keeping, even treasuring.

I found another rock as I walked the beach today. It, too, had been ground down and polished by reality. It had no sharp edges anymore. When I walk too fast I miss these small, smooth rocks that so fascinate me. They are my cousins, somehow, models of what I would like to become. But here I am now.

—DAVID K. REYNOLDS
in *Thirsty, Swimming in the Lake*

The key phrase is "But here I am now." The realization that nature keeps us in the eternal now is echoed in an interesting interpretation of Jesus' term "kingdom of God" by Stephen Mitchell, a poet who has prepared new translations of biblical texts. He writes: "[Jesus] was talking about a state of being, a way of living at ease among the joys and sorrows of our world. It is possible, he said, to be as simple and beautiful as the birds

of the sky or the lilies of the field, who are always within the eternal now."

The Japanese haiku form is perfectly suited to showcase this kind of presence. It focuses on one image but from it arises a multitude of associations.

> The end of spring
> lingers
> in the cherry blossoms.

> The spring sea rising
> and falling, rising
> and falling all day.
> —BUSON
> in *The Essential Haiku*
> edited by Robert Hass

> Summer night—
> even the stars
> are whispering to each other.
> —ISSA
> in *The Essential Haiku*
> edited by Robert Hass

To know the blessings of nature, we often have to set aside the concerns of our ego. There is an element of grace in nature experiences. The spiritual practices of openness and silence help us remain receptive to them.

The temple was built on an island and it held a thousand bells. Bells big and small, fashioned by the finest craftsmen in the world. When the wind blew or a storm raged, all the bells would peal out in a symphony that would send the heart of the hearer into raptures.

But over the centuries the island sank into the sea and, with it, the temple bells. An ancient legend said that the bells continued to peal out, ceaselessly, and could be heard by anyone who would listen. Inspired by this legend, a young man traveled thousands of miles, determined to hear those bells. He sat for days on the shore, facing the vanished island, and listened with all his might. But all he could hear was the sound of the sea. He made every effort to block it out. But to no avail; the sound of the sea seemed to flood the world.

He kept at his task for weeks. Each time he got disheartened he would listen to the village pundits, who spoke with unction of the mysterious legend.

Then his heart would be aflame . . . only to become discouraged again when weeks of further effort yielded no results.

Finally he decided to give up the attempt. Perhaps he was not destined to hear the bells. Perhaps the legend was not true. It was his final day, and he went to the shore to say goodbye to the sea and the sky and the wind and the coconut trees. He lay on the sand, and for the first time, listened to the sound of the sea. Soon he was so lost in the sound that he was barely conscious of himself, so deep was the silence that the sound produced.

In the depth of that silence, he heard it! The tinkle of a tiny bell followed by another, and another and another . . . and soon every one of the thousand temple bells was peeling out in harmony, and his heart was rapt in joyous ecstasy.

—ANTHONY DE MELLO
in *The Song of the Bird*

The heightened sense of connection we feel in nature has consequences. A spiritually literate person not only identifies with the delights of trees and rocks and rivers, but also empathizes with their pain and feels compassion for them when they are violated.

As I gazed at the brown silt-choked waters absorbing a black plume of industrial and municipal sewage from Memphis and followed bits of some unknown beige froth floating continually down from Cincinnati, Louisville, or St. Louis, I experienced a palpable pain. It was not distinctly located in any of my extremities, nor was it like a headache or nausea. Still, it was very real. I had no plans to swim in the river, no need to drink from it, no intention of buying real estate on its shores. My narrowly personal interests were not affected, and yet somehow I was personally injured. It occurred to me then, in a flash of self-discovery, that the river was part of me.

—J. Baird Callicott
in *Environmental Ethics*

Reb Nachman was once traveling with his Hasidim by carriage, and as it grew dark they came to an inn, where they spent the night. During the night Reb Nachman began to cry out loudly in his sleep, waking up everyone in the inn, all of whom came running to see what had happened.

When he awoke, the first thing Reb Nachman did was to take out a book he had brought with him. Then he closed his eyes and opened the book and pointed to a passage. And there it was written "Cutting down a tree before its time is like killing a soul."

Then Reb Nachman asked the innkeeper if the walls of that inn had been built out of saplings cut down before their time. The innkeeper admitted that this was true, but how did the rabbi know?

And Reb Nachman said: "All night I dreamed I was surrounded by the bodies of those who had been murdered. I was very frightened. Now I know that it was the souls of the trees that cried out to me."

—Hasidic tale
in *Gabriel's Palace*
selected and retold by Howard Schwartz

EARTH ETIQUETTE

Our third set of readings examines what is involved in an intimate and caring relationship with the natural world. We can learn some of the answers from indigenous people.

When the Apache woman gave birth to her child she did so under a tree. The placenta was placed in the tree, for it was regarded as the child's double. Whenever the tree's leaves were renewed in the spring the life of the person born there would also be renewed. If the individual at some point in his or her life felt the need for renewed strength and purpose, that person could make a pilgrimage back to the birth spot and there perform a ceremony; this would renew his or her strength. The Apache Chief Geronimo said of the Apaches who were dying on the reservations that they died because they were not allowed to visit the spot where they were born to be renewed.

—JOHN A. SANFORD
in *Soul Journey*

Only men whose wives were with child were permitted to cut into the tree. When a giant tree is felled, the jungle heaves; it thunders and roars. Felling a tree is like giving birth. Men with pregnant wives will give proper care and attention to this difficult task, as it is they who will damage least this jungle world in order to protect their wives and their future generations. These trees are alive, says the Lacandon. When a mahogany is transformed into a canoe, it must be fed because it still lives, though in another form. To lose such a living being by cutting it improperly would indeed be unfortunate. So it was that this tree was felled by six men with pregnant wives.

—JOAN HALIFAX
in *The Fruitful Darkness*

Everything in creation possesses energy. Through the Zen practice of shikan-taza—just sitting, Stephanie Kaza, a professor of environmental studies, feels the energy of trees. She notes that Richard St. Barbe Baker, the great tree-planting saint of England, used to spend at least ten minutes each day with his hand on the trunk of a tree. He said this recharged his energy by connecting him with the tree's powerful circuitry. According to Kaza, "He was quite serious about this; he recommended it as a natural cure for malaise, stress, and other degenerations of the body and mind." In the passage below, Anne Scott makes a similar discovery.

Years ago I had read that it was a tradition among some California Native Americans to go into the redwood forests when they needed strength. Standing with their backs against a tree they would remain there until they were quite literally recharged. I remembered this brief description the day I took my husband to a hospital emergency room and watched him struggle for his life with asthma.

After leaving Stephen in the hospital, I returned home, drained of hope, and exhausted. I went to the redwoods nearby and leaned against one of the trees. Feeling soothed and calmed, I remained in this position with my eyes closed for several minutes. As I moved away from the tree, ready to go home, I noticed that my palms tingled. At about six inches from the tree, the tingling intensified, but any further away it weakened. I repeated this motion many times to convince myself that I wasn't imagining that I could feel what the Chinese refer to as *ch'i*. In Japan they call it *ki*, and in India, *prana;* we know it as the life force.

This glimpse into the unseen, which for me had previously been the unreal, gave me great comfort. I was no longer alone. I knew that I was held, a single thread within the intricate lacework connecting all living things. Before this awareness, I would have only entered into the darkness of matter, seen only the pain that is held in the body. But now I had experienced in my body the joy that is hidden in matter. It was safe for me to listen to my own rhythms.

—ANNE SCOTT
in *Serving Fire*

I loved climbing trees as a boy. Each time I pulled myself up to a new branch, I felt I was rising above the pressures of school. The trick was to find a crook in the tree where I could sit and lean against the trunk. I would put my head close to the bark to hear the tree breathing. When there was a strong wind, I imagined that the tree and I were moving together in a slow dance. For me, trees were always feminine. They accepted me, made a place for my presence, and tolerated my silent meditations. They never questioned me about my moods. I enjoyed being held in the embrace of the tree and, by extension, the natural world.

Treetops, I discovered as a child, were made for praying. Time seemed to stop. Close to the sky and the movement of the clouds, I knew I was connected to something greater than myself. Best of all, I could survey the whole horizon. Trees taught me to look for the big picture, to seek a bird's-eye view of things.

It takes practice to be present with a tree. Hospitality, openness, and reverence are all important. Here Stephanie Kaza says hello to an alder.

Now in your presence, I see how straight and elegant you stand, especially next to the gangly willows. Your gray-white dappled trunks are tall and smooth, as if you shot up fast before any injurious forces could do you harm. Your trunks are barely scarred except for the knots from past years' branches. I extend a shy hand, meeting your body, firm and cool against my skin.

I wonder if a tree knows when someone's hand is on its body. Does it feel a little warm, like an exchange of electricity? This act of reaching out is a small gesture, but it is filled with great intention. I am simply trying to say hello across the barriers of form and language. I believe the hands communicate this intention most honestly. The voice and mind are not direct enough. Or perhaps they are too complex for the first step of making contact. Besides, the tree and I have such different minds and voices. I don't know the language of these alders at all. I can only guess at the shape of a tree's mind and what it knows about life on the edge of a pond. How does this water taste to an alder? How does the morning sun feel on its new leaves? How does the wind feel moving through its branches?

—STEPHANIE KAZA
in *The Attentive Heart*

One of our favorite scenes in the television version of The Autobiography of Miss Jane Pittman *is when this elderly woman explains why she talks to a tree: "When you talk to an old oak tree that's been here for all these years, and knows more than you'll ever know, it's not craziness; it's just the nobility you respect."*

On the Caribbean island of Antigua where we sometimes vacation, there is a very noble tree. As trees go on this dry island, it is grand, its branches spreading out in a distinctive shape that seems to form a mattress for the clouds. It is at least 100 years old and once provided shelter for sugarcane workers in the surrounding fields. Now it stands like a sentry on the road, an invitation to stop.

We did stop one day and walked around its huge trunk, trying to imagine what this tree had witnessed in its history and what it could tell us. On the far side from the road, we discovered a makeshift seat, a few boards nailed into a place where the roots branch off before diving into the ground. We realized that others before us had felt close to this tree. Were they simply taking their ease in its shade or were they, like us, coming to visit with a spiritual elder?

Several autumns ago, I walked up to the pine tree in my backyard and asked it one question: "What is institutional violence?" The tree did not answer right away. So I sat at its roots and waited. The backyard was covered with brilliantly colored leaves, the air was fresh, and suddenly I forgot that I was waiting for an answer. The tree and I were just there, enjoying ourselves and each other. After sitting for a long time, I turned to the tree, smiled, and said, "I no longer need an answer." Then I thanked it and awarded it the Grand Transnational Peace Prize.

—THICH NHAT HANH
in *Love in Action*

Many people can claim to have rescued an animal from the streets, but I'm happy to say that I rescued four trees. One day in New York's Soho district, I noticed four long curly willow vines leaning against a wall. Figuring they had been part of a store display, I stuck my head into the nearest doorway and inquired about them. "You can have them if you want them, lady," the clerk replied.

I maneuvered the willows into a taxi and took them home. I called my neighbor Rick, who has created a garden on the roof of our building. Together, we planted the trees in large flower pots on a sunny part of the roof. Within a week new shoots had appeared along the greenest one. Within two weeks all four showed signs of life. By summer's end, they were full of thin green leaves which caught every whisper of wind moving across the roof. How much heart they have, I think, every time I see those four trees holding on, making new leaves and creating branches. Willows like to grow on the edges of rivers, I recall from my childhood books. But these four are thriving on a tar roof. Nature is persistent, and every day there is a new miracle to behold.

For example, take stones. Many people regard rocks with indifference, considering them worthless, lifeless objects. But in the following passages, the authors have different points of view.

On second thought, I decided to show the old man one more thing. Digging around in my car, I reached for the large rock I had found by the side of the road. It had markings that looked exactly like ancient pictographs. I went back to the trailer and showed him the rock. He touched it quickly with both hands as if to read it and said, "Where did you find this rock?" I told him, "By the side of the road." And he said, "Well, then you better read it since it came to you." I drove home that night, back to the cities, hundreds of miles, thinking that I carried the journal of the earth with me.

—Burghild Nina Holzer
in *A Walk Between Heaven and Earth*

I take my children to the beach. On the north shore of Long Island it is a pretty stony proposition. The mills of the gods grind coarsely here; but, in exchange for bruised feet and a sore coccyx, they provide gravel for the foundation of the arts. Every year we hunt for perfect stones: ovals, spheroids, lozenges, eggs. By the end of the summer there are pebbles all over the house. They have no apparent use other than the delight that they provide to us, but that is the whole point of the collection. The very act of hunting them is an introduction to the oblation of things. Look at this one! Do you think it will split evenly enough for arrowheads? What color is that one when it's wet? Lick it and see. Daddy wants a big flat round one to hold the sauerkraut under the brine. Will this one do? We walk down the beach lifting stones into our history: we are collectors, ingatherers of being. Humankind is the lover of textures, colors, and shapes—the only creature in the whole world that knows a good pickling stone when it sees one.

—Robert Farrar Capon
in *The Romance of the Word*

A man, walking on a beach, reaches down and picks up a pebble. Looking at the small stone in his hand, he feels very powerful and thinks of how with one stroke he has taken control of the stone. "How many years have you been here, and now I place you in my hand." The pebble speaks to him, "Though to you, I am only a grain of sand in your hand, you, to me, are but a passing breeze."

—Martin Lowenthal and Lar Short
in *Opening the Heart of Compassion*

Moving from rocks on the beach, we come to the ocean. She entices us with her beauty and the mysteries which lie in her depths.

Seen from a great height, the ocean appears flat, silent, and blue—a blue so turbulent and dark. The sea looks blue because it reflects the sky, but it's always a deeper blue than the sky itself because it doesn't reflect all the light. Some of its color also comes from the seabed. In the ocean, light falls from above as "downwelling light." Some fish, squid, firefleas, and other creatures make their own glow. But mainly light cascades over them. You need to be under the skin of the ocean, part of its gelatinous fathoms, to find illumination. When we look down on the ocean, it appears opaque. All its fascinating life-forms and geography are hidden, which leave a mental void that quickly fills with imagined terrors. Therefore many people perceive the ocean as another form of night. And yet we are also drawn to the ocean; we like to vacation beside it, staring for countless hours at its hypnotic pour and sweep. It's both mesmerizing and narcotic. An impulse ancient and osmotic connects our fluids with the ocean's. I suppose we feel drawn to it because we ourselves are small marine environments on the move.

—DIANE ACKERMAN
in *The Rarest of the Rare*

We are both drawn to the ocean—I for its sights, Fred for its depths—but we haven't had many opportunities to truly experience the sea's underwater wonders. Then we vacationed on Grand Cayman island, known for its spectacular coral wall, and we went for a ride in a small research submarine.

We descended quickly, 800 feet, to the dark ocean floor. Illuminated only by the submarine's lights, it reminded us of pictures of the lunar surface. The deepwater corals looked like bonsai trees arranged as accents on a large monochrome painting. But then we began to ascend—600 feet, 400 feet, 350 feet—and the scene changed.

"Colors!" Fred exclaimed.

Colors indeed! Before us was a veritable artist's palette. After the stark whiteness and pristine clarity of the depths, we were amazed by the coral wall's range of colors: reds, lavenders, pinks, creams, peaches, oranges. "As far as we know," the submarine's pilot, a marine biologist, said with authority, "fish do not see color." But then, for whom is this riotous gift of color? Divers cannot go down this far without ships.

Perhaps the bright colors splashed so profusely on the coral wall in that dark deep are indicators of the Great Artist's love of beauty and the wild extravagance of the created world. And reminders that we need to be appropriately grateful and awed.

Ecophilosopher Thomas Berry warns us that, "If the Earth does grow inhospitable toward human presence, it is primarily because we have lost our sense of courtesy toward the Earth and its inhabitants, our sense of gratitude, our willingness to recognize the sacred character of habitat, our capacity for the awesome, for the numinous quality of every earthly reality." The next readings illustrate how respect of nature can be acted out using the spiritual practices of hospitality, love, nurturing, and listening.

I once lived near a mansion where only one of the many gardeners employed had succeeded with every one of the roses. I asked him the secret of his success. He told me that the other gardeners treated all the roses not unwisely, but too generally. They treated them all in precisely the same way; whereas he himself watched each rosebush separately, and followed out for each plant its special need for soil, manure, sun, air, water, support and shelter.

—WILLIAM MCNAMARA
in *Christian Mysticism*

Even as a small child George Washington Carver revealed an uncanny knowledge of all living things. The farmers in the small Missouri town of Diamond Grove noticed the fragile black boy wandering for hours over the land, examining various plants and bringing back varieties with which he healed sick animals. Entirely on his own, the boy established a garden in a remote piece of bottom land. Using salvage lumber and other materials he built a secluded greenhouse in the woods. Once asked what he was doing alone so many hours, Carver replied, "I go to my garden hospital and take care of hundreds of sick plants."

His special talent did not go unnoticed by farmers' wives, who brought him their sick house plants, asking him to make them bloom. Carver sang to the plants as he placed them gently in tin cans filled with soil of his own concoction. He covered them care-

FAITH

"Faith is the touching of a mystery," writes Alexander Schmemann, a Russian Orthodox priest. "It is to perceive another dimension to absolutely everything in the world. In faith, the mysterious meaning of life comes through. . . . To speak in the simplest possible terms: faith sees, knows, senses the presence of God in the world."

Faith is a relationship with the Ancient of Days that grounds one's life. Or as Protestant theologian Paul Tillich puts it, "Faith means being grasped by a power that is greater than we are, a power that shakes us and turns us, and transforms and heals us."

Jews, Christians, and Muslims all hold to the catalytic power of faith. It enables believers to walk in the dark without fear.

Bakole wa Ilunga, a Catholic archbishop in Zaire, assures us, "Faith is not a momentary feeling but a struggle against the discouragement that threatens us every time we meet with resistance."

There is no guarantee of an easy or smooth ride for believers. "Faith," according to Protestant minister Samuel H. Miller, "faces everything that makes the world uncomfortable—pain, fear, loneliness, shame, death—and acts with a compassion by which these things are transformed, even exalted."

Every new experience is a challenge to faith since the way is never clear and the obstacles are many. "To choose what is difficult all one's days as if it were easy," notes English poet W. H. Auden, "that is faith."

Although certitude about God is a temptation to believers, it is an illusion. "True faith," Anglican priest Kenneth Leech suggests, "can only grow and mature if it includes the elements of paradox and creative doubt. Such doubt is not the enemy of faith but an essential element of it. For faith in God does not bring the false peace of answered questions and resolved paradoxes."

We must be content to live with mysteries that cannot be explained or solved. Our task is to stay human.

Another part of our task, according to Rabbi Abraham Joshua Heschel is "to bring God back into the world, into our lives. . . . To have faith in God is to reveal what is concealed."

Faith is a path of heart that enables us to perceive the mysterious meaning of life, to confront and overcome obstacles, to live with doubt and paradox, and to be at home in a world where the Ground of Being is always present.

Although faith is usually spoken of in somber or sober terms, we prefer the more buoyant note of a hymn written by Protestant minister and composer Al Carmines: "Faith is such a simple thing. It can't talk, but only sing. It can't reason, but can dance. Take a chance. Take a chance. Life is full of ways to go. Sun, rain, wind, snow. All unknowingly we trace a geography of grace. From breath to breath and blink to blink, it's never quite the way we think."

FORGIVENESS

"Life is an adventure in forgiveness," declares writer and editor Norman Cousins. This spiritual practice is manifested in our relationship to the Source of Peace, in our perception of self, and in our dealings with others.

"If you want to see the brave, look at those who can forgive," we read in the Hindu sacred poem *The Bhagavad Gita*. "If you want to see the heroic, look at those who can love in return for hatred."

Jesus, a very brave man, prays while hanging on the cross of death, "Father, forgive them, for they know not what they do."

Love of enemies is a crucial part of Indian freedom fighter Mahatma Gandhi's philosophy of nonviolence. And Dr. Martin Luther King Jr., the African-American civil rights leader, adds, "Forgiveness is not an occasional act; it is a permanent attitude."

More recently, black South Africans, many of whom are Christians, have tried to follow in King's footsteps. "We witness," Anglican Bishop Desmond Tutu proclaims, "by being a community of reconciliation, a forgiving community of the forgiven." Those who have felt the liberation of being touched by the grace of the One Who Embraces All can take that feeling to the streets.

"When you forgive somebody who has wronged you, you're spared the dismal corrosion of bitterness and wounded pride," Protestant minister Frederick Buechner writes. "For both parties, forgiveness means the freedom again to be at peace inside their own skins and to be glad in each other's presence."

What sweet release it is to let go of the burden of a nettlesome grievance or a long-lived grudge. Forgiveness is an invitation to start over again. And receiving forgiveness from someone we have wronged is equally uplifting.

Then there is the issue of self-inquisition. D. Patrick Miller, senior writer for *Yoga Journal,* offers this thought: "Never forget that to forgive yourself is to release trapped energy that could be doing good in the world." To make amends with ourselves is no small matter.

"The practice of forgiveness is our most important contribution to the healing of the world," says popular speaker Marianne Williamson. This practice covers all of our relationships and is an indispensable step in the renewal of both our public and private lives.

Writer David Augsburger concludes: "Since nothing we intend is ever faultless, and nothing we attempt ever without error, and nothing we achieve without some measure of finitude and fallibility we call humanness, we are saved by forgiveness."

fully at night and took them out to "play" in the sun during the day. Returning the thriving and blooming plants to their owners, he was often asked how he could work such miracles. Carver replied modestly: "All flowers talk to me, and so do hundreds of living things in the wood. I learn what I know by watching and loving everything."

—BILL SCHUL
in *Life Song*

According to Francis Kilvert, crops have different "voices," depending on whether it is day or night. In his diary for July 16, 1873, he wrote: "As I walked along the field path I stopped to listen to the rustle and solemn whisper of the wheat, so different in its voice by day. The corn seemed to be praising God and whispering its evening prayer."

—RONALD BLYTHE
in *The Pleasures of Diaries*

Whenever parents teach their children good manners, Earth etiquette should be part of the lesson.

I was four years old when I first remember learning Earth manners. I had gathered a small bouquet of periwinkles for my mother. The periwinkles came from the church yard. Mama explained to me that the small flowers belonged to the Mother Earth and our preacher man was the gardener at the church. It was wrong for me to take flowers from the mother without first asking the preacher. It was wrong to take the flowers without first paying the mother. She said it was like someone cutting off my hair without asking me. She made me take the flowers back to the church and explain to the preacher what I had done. She helped me plant new seeds to replace what I had taken. At the time, it seemed like a very big thing.

—SCOUT CLOUD LEE
in *The Circle Is Sacred*

I was taught as a boy that while I should not pick other people's flowers, they would be happy if I helped them pull weeds. I was too young to protest that a weed, in the words of philosopher Ralph Waldo Emerson, is just "a plant whose virtues have never been discovered."

Consider the dandelion. I was encouraged to regard these plants as difficult weeds that spoil the green grass beauty of suburban lawns. "Be sure you get all the roots," I was instructed, "or they will just grow back. And don't let them go to seed, or you'll have even more weeds to deal with."

Now I have a different attitude toward dandelions. I drink a tea made from those hearty roots to cleanse my system. And I regret those times when I sprayed them with poison to stop them from blooming. Catholic Bishop Fulton Sheen speaks of plants in general, but I think particularly of dandelions, when he says: "Plants tell us that life must live not only for itself, but also for others. The trunk and the branches are for self, but the blossoms are for a generation yet unborn. The lesson of altruism is hidden in every blossom."

Nature, of course, does have its downsides. Floods, hurricanes, blizzards, and tornadoes wreak havoc on humans, animals, plants, and landscapes. Rather than ignore these realities by romanticizing nature, spiritual literacy acknowledges them through the practice of shadow.

Rick Bass, who lives in one of the most beautiful areas of the United States, Montana, knows all about shadow.

If it is snowing when you go out to get wood for your fireplace, tie one end of a rope around your waist and tie the other end to the cabin door. The snow can start coming down so fast and hard that in the short time it takes you to get to the woodshed, you can get lost in a whiteout on your way back. It doesn't sound like it's possible, but it happened to me once. A light snow turned heavy in just seconds, and then became a blizzard. I ended up staying in the woodshed all night waiting for daylight. I felt ridiculous, but not as ridiculous as I would have felt dying within a mile of my cabin, when all I had wanted to do was get a few sticks of wood.

There is some compass in all of us that does not want us to walk a straight line. I respect this, and do not try to challenge it in blizzards.

Sometimes people run out of gas (visitors, not locals) up on the pass, where during the winter traffic can go by only every second or third day, and some of them freeze to death in their cars—traveling without heavy clothes, without sleeping bags in the back—and others freeze in the woods when they get out of their cars and try to walk for help. Everyone up here has CB and shortwave radios in their trucks. You can live in a dangerous place quite easily, but to visit it is another thing.

—RICK BASS
in *In the Loyal Mountains*

The spiritual practice of shadow involves our recognizing and naming the demons in our midst, and nature may actually issue the alarm.

In a time of such destruction, our lives depend on this listening. It may be that the earth speaks its symptoms to us. With the nuclear reactor accident in Chernobyl, Russia, it was not the authorities who told us that the accident had taken place. It was the wind. The wind told the story. It carried a tale of splitting, of atomic fission, to other countries and revealed the truth of the situation. The wind is a prophet, a scientist, a talker.

—LINDA HOGAN
in *Dwellings*

The environment is often the victim of the shadow elements of human nature—greed, disconnection, and carelessness, for example—as these spiritual readings illustrate.

One of the worst ecological disasters in history—a huge 10,080,000-gallon oil spill in Valdez, Alaska, in 1989—dramatized our urgent need to move beyond dependence on fossil fuels and all their problems. The Exxon oil tanker that ran aground symbolized some of the major problems in our economic system today. The drunken captain of the ship was symbolic of the drunken captains of industry who let their own addiction to power and greed destroy companies through huge debts and corporate takeovers. The heavy black oil spilling from the ship symbolized uncontrolled industrial growth polluting the pristine waters, the symbol of Spirit. Not only humans were affected; the creatures of the wild—fish, birds, and otters—became stuck in the heavy, sticky oil and died.

Our disconnection from the beauty and purity of the natural

world gave us a big message—miles wide. If our obsession with consumption and materialistic pursuits continues unchecked, we too will be coated in a heavy, black muck, unable to free ourselves to the flow of the Spirit. Through the eyes of love, we can feel a deep compassion for the pain of the wildlife and natural world affected by the oil spill. But seen from an evolutionary perspective of significance, this great disaster may have been the shock needed to wake up humanity to the vast destruction of the environment occurring everywhere today.

—CORINNE MCLAUGHLIN and GORDON DAVIDSON
in Spiritual Politics

I went out walking on the beach today. It was fresh and breezy and my hair kept being blown annoyingly across my face. For some reason, my thoughts were full of Amilcar and his mad moral certainties. I was distracted from them, fairly ruthlessly, when I trod on a fat blob of tar the size of a plum. It squashed between three toes of my left foot, clotted and viscous like treacle.

The next hour was spent in a frustrating search for some petrol or alcohol to clean it off. There was none in the house so I had to hobble through the palm grove to the village. I bought a beer bottle full of pink kerosene from one of the old trading women and eventually, with some effort and enough cotton wool to stuff a cushion. I managed to remove all traces of tar from my foot.

Now I sit on my deck, feeling stupid and exhausted, looking dully out at the ocean, a strong smell of kerosene emanating from my left foot, my toes raw red and stinging from the crude and astringent fuel.

The weight of the sense world overpowers me some days, today clearly being one of them.

—HOPE CLEARWATER
in Brazzaville Beach
by William Boyd

In a time when there is so much death and destruction in nature, we need more last rites for living beings. Stephanie Kaza incorporates the spiritual practices of forgiveness, compassion, and imagination into a ceremony that soulfully touches the heart.

Now we were together for the winter holidays in my mother's home; facing the loss of the elm. Experts had been consulted, the matter discussed, a decision made. The tree would come down. I stood outside in the gray dawn light and gazed at the tree, rain falling gently on my face and shoulders. What could I possibly do? I felt obliged to mark this tree's passage from life to death; something inside was crying for the tree. My brothers stayed inside, leaving me alone with my uncertainty.

It was almost eight a.m.; the tree crew would arrive soon. I looked through my suitcase for miscellaneous tools of ceremony. What is the proper ritual for a tree death? I didn't know. I had never seen one done before. Tree removal is something arborists do, a specialty trade like being a mortician. Most people don't pay close attention to this kind of work. Today I would. The sadness was gaining momentum. I thought a ceremony might at least deflect my grief.

With three sounds from a small bell, I began. I walked slowly around the tree nine times, breathing deeply, calling the tree people to listen. I knew almost nothing of the tree's history. I had barely begun a conversation with this tree. It felt like giving communion to a total stranger before death. Last rites, these were last rites. I lit a small candle and offered four sticks of incense to the four directions, placing them at the base of the tree. The tree was the centerpiece of its own altar, the altar of its death.

The tree workers arrived with their gear—chain saws, ropes, belts, and harnesses. They had heard I wanted to do a ceremony— what were they imagining? They pulled on their climbing boots and checked the chain saws. Only a few minutes remained before the first cut. It looked like they were preparing for surgery, only this was not going to be a healing operation. My brother used the word *murder.* Yes, why not call it that? It was a premeditated choice to destroy another living being. I chanted a dedication under the dripping rain, a request for forgiveness for those who plant trees too close to homes. I asked for compassion for those who are uncertain about how to care for tree beings and for those who suffer the consequences of loss of tree friends. I felt unprepared with tree prayers. I had never learned anything of this sort in Sunday school.

Three last bells and the short ceremony was over. It was a quiet act of intention that did little to reverse the fate of the tree. But at least the elm did not die alone. I brought the lit candle inside to symbolize the life of the tree. We could watch it burn down as the tree was dismantled. My nieces and nephews were awake now and wanted to know what I was doing. My brother thought it better for them not to participate in the ceremony. They wouldn't understand, he said. They would ask, "Why are you killing the tree?" Children are too young to understand, he said. I wondered. Maybe children are the *only* ones who understand. It made sense to them that the candle was the tree.

Chunk by chunk the tree workers handed down the limbs of the tree. They worked carefully and skillfully, drawing on years of experience with tree morphology. Even in the rain they placed the branches precisely, never hitting the roof or fence during the three-hour process. When the last big section of trunk fell to the ground, it shook the house with a solemn thump. My nephew came running in. "Aunt Steph, Aunt Steph, the candle fell over!" The children explained the obvious: "Of course," they said, "the candle fell over because the tree died."

—STEPHANIE KAZA
in *The Attentive Heart*

Here is another ritual, this one celebrating the unity of all life. We begin with the senses and arrive eventually at a point of total identification—feeling the flower garden inside us. This is a model of sympathetic appreciation of nature leading to a mystical experience.

Spend time in a flower garden. Stay there as long as you wish, but make sure your visit is long enough to take in the various charms that the world of blossoms and petals provides. You can sit in a chair or on the grass, lie down looking up at the flowers from below, or walk around. However you choose to spend your time, be aware that you are a guest in someone else's home—nature's—so act accordingly.

If the day is warm and sunny, savor the rays and imagine how the flowers must feel at this very moment. Look closely at the variety of blooms, at the different shapes and colors, at the way the individual blossoms grow out of their leafy sheaths. Now use your sense of smell to take in the stunning array of fragrance, all of which can be divinely overpowering.

Keep an eye out for the various animal life that also lives in the garden, the birds and squirrels, the insects that fly, the ones that crawl. Notice how intently they go about their business, how they move from place to place trying not to notice you but in fact finding that task difficult. Close your eyes and listen to the sounds of the garden, the chirping and humming, and the movement of the stems and leaves in the mild breeze.

Now see if you can transcend your individual senses and feel the presence of the garden inside you. Try to become just another flower, at home in the garden as if you were in your own house or place of worship.

—ALAN EPSTEIN
in *How to Have More Love in Your Life*

The life force of nature is unstoppable. And that, too, is a sign of Spirit.

SEED. There are so many beginnings. In Japan, I recall, there were wildflowers that grew in the far, cool region of mountains. The bricks of Hiroshima, down below, were formed of clay from these mountains, and so the walls of houses and shops held the dormant trumpet flower seeds. But after one group of humans killed another with the explosive power of life's smallest elements split wide apart, the mountain flowers began to grow. Out of the crumbled, burned buildings they sprouted. Out of destruction and bomb heat and the falling of walls, the seeds opened up and grew. What a horrible beauty, the world going its own way, growing without us. But perhaps this, too, speaks of survival, of hope beyond our time.

—LINDA HOGAN
in *Dwellings*

Going on with or without us, nature remains part grace, part mystery, and part tutor. Spiritual literacy enables us to read the natural world as a book about our sacred community, and the lessons it contains become the focus of our prayers.

Earth teach me stillness
   as the grasses are stilled with light.
Earth teach me suffering

as old stones suffer with memory.
Earth teach me humility
as blossoms are humble with beginning.
Earth teach me caring
as the mother who secures her young.
Earth teach me courage
as the tree which stands all alone.
Earth teach me limitation
as the ant which crawls on the ground.
Earth teach me freedom
as the eagle which soars in the sky.
Earth teach me resignation
as the leaves which die in the fall.
Earth teach me regeneration
as the seed which rises in the spring.
Earth teach me to forget myself
as melted snow forgets its life.
Earth teach me to remember kindness
as dry fields weep with rain.

    —UTE PRAYER

      quoted in *Earth Prayers from Around the World*
      edited by Elizabeth Roberts and Elias Amidon

PRACTICING SPIRITUAL LITERACY: NATURE

CONVERSATIONS/JOURNAL ENTRIES

- Study the geography of the Earth close to where you live. What soils are predominant? What plants are indigenous to the area? What is the average rainfall in your area? Where does the sun rise and set throughout the year?
- Share a story with family or friends, or write in your journal, about a time when you were humbled, soothed, or awed by something in the natural world. How did you feel connected to nature?
- When was the last time you communed with nature in silence? What did you learn about the Earth? About yourself?
- What is your reaction to people who claim that plants respond positively to their ministrations of care and their talking to them? Have you ever known anyone with "a green thumb"? What impressed you about the person's treatment of plants?
- What practices of Earth etiquette do you think will prove most helpful in the fight against environmental degradation?
- Describe a scary or negative experience you have had in nature—i.e., an example of its shadow elements.
- What spiritual teachers have given you the most insight into the languages of nature?

ACTIVITIES/PROJECTS

- Pick a tree that is very special to you. Express your thanks for what it has given and taught you. Or adopt a tree and look out for its welfare.
- On your next trip, take only pictures of nature: trees, rocks, shrubs, hills, flowers. Then caption them in your album with the appropriate messages they gave to you, or the feelings they aroused in you.
- "Nobody sees a flower—really—it is so small—we haven't time—and to see takes time like to have a friend takes time," artist Georgia O'Keeffe writes. Spend some quality time with a flower and note your responses. Then look at some of O'Keeffe's flower paintings.
- The next time you have a picnic in a park, go to the beach, or visit a tourist stop along the highway, take a trash bag along and spend a few minutes picking up litter.

- Join with others in your community on an Earth-cherishing reclamation project, such as seeding wildflowers along a drab patch of road.
- Get down and dirty in your backyard. Sense the Earth as an animal senses it. Hang out with nature.
- Organize a rock hunting expedition with neighborhood children. Look for stones in a park, along a riverbank, or near a building site. Pick out only those stones that speak to you with their shapes, sizes, or faces. Remember it is always a good idea before removing a rock from its home to ask its permission.
- Rent two French films written and directed by Eric Rohmer which contain magic moments created by nature. In *Summer*, a young woman's new lease on life comes through a ray of the setting sun—a green flash. And in *Four Adventures of Reinette and Mirabelle*, a country girl and a city girl get up in the early hours to witness a silent point in time between the night and the dawn.

SPIRITUAL EXERCISES/RITUALS

- Use the following passage by Natalie Goldberg as a spiritual meditation on nature as a teacher: "Be tough the way a blade of grass is; rooted, willing to lean, and at peace with what is around it."
- Choose some appropriate passages from the Bible and follow the suggestion of Wendell Berry and read them outdoors.
- Use items collected in nature—stones, acorns, leaves—as devotional aids. Edward Hays suggests using small stones as prayer pebbles, dedicating each one to a specific intention or person in need. In the morning, arrange the pebbles in a pattern on your personal altar; as you pass them during the rest of the day, you will be reminded of your commitments, concerns, and hopes.
- Create a ritual for Earth Day, the summer and winter solstices, or another seasonal holiday. Many ritual books have suggestions for these observances. Conduct your ritual in nature. Or bring some of nature into your worship space.
- Include in your daily prayers petitions to alleviate the sufferings of polluted streams, dying plants and trees, contaminated drinking water, and toxic lands, beaches, and seas.

ANIMALS

Every creature is full of God and is a book about God.

—MEISTER ECKHART

One should pay attention to even the smallest crawling creature, for these too may have a valuable lesson to teach us, and even the smallest ant may wish to communicate with a man.

—BLACK ELK

God nourishes everything, from the horned buffalo to nits, disdaining no creature—for if he disdained creatures due to their insignificance, they could not endure for even a moment. Rather he gazes and emanates compassion upon them all. So should you be good to all creatures, disdaining none.

—THE KABBALAH

The truly wise person kneels at the feet of all creatures.

—MECHTILD OF MAGDEBURG

As a small child, I could not understand why I should pray for human beings only. When my mother first had kissed me good night, I used to add a silent prayer that I had composed for all creatures.

—ALBERT SCHWEITZER

The animal shall not be measured by man. In a world older and more complete than ours, they move finished and complete, gifted with extensions of the senses we have lost or never attained, living by voices we shall never hear. They are not brethren, they are not underlings; they are other nations, caught with ourselves in the net of life, fellow prisoners of the splendor and travail of the earth.

—HENRY BESTON

Spiritual readings of animals start with one important understanding: animals are our teachers. Through our encounters with them, we learn about Spirit and about ways to exist on the Earth. In countless stories, myths, and dreams, animals are wise elders, imparting wisdom about the world and hinting at the great mysteries of life.

Some people minimize the value of entering into relationships with animals, regarding them as inferior beings put on Earth to serve humans as food, tools, entertainment, and transportation. But to be spiritually literate means to recognize that animals are much more than what humans might do with them. The word "animal" actually comes from the Latin *animalis*—having a soul—and is closely linked to the noun *animus* or breath.

Anyone who has lived with animals on a day-to-day basis knows intuitively that they do indeed have souls. And they are great mentors. They are curious about the world and very much alive to the report of their senses. They have a full repertoire of emotions including joy, disappointment, guilt, fear, anger, contentment, embarrassment, gratitude, and grief. They evidence loyalty, and they certainly care for their families. Sometimes they display an altruism which touches the heart.

St. Francis of Assisi, a thirteenth-century Catholic monk, held animals in such high regard that he addressed them as brothers and sisters. Today, many people are trying to kindle that kind of connection with animals. The important role of pets as friends and healers is widely accepted, and research documents that pets can literally help lower a person's blood pressure and reduce stress. Cats, dogs, and birds have made a big difference in the lives of emotionally disturbed children, withdrawn patients with mental illnesses, lonely nursing home residents, and isolated prisoners.

Another sign of a transformed view of animals is public support for animal rights organizations. These groups are trying to stem the tide of violence perpetrated against animals in the name of medical progress and business success. People are also working to maintain and extend the protection offered threatened and endangered species. The ardor and energy of those involved in these projects attest to the renewed interest in the spiritual ties between humans and animals.

Meanwhile, naturalists open our eyes to the value of encounters with creatures in the wild. In these situations, the wolf, the eagle, or the whale set the terms for the meeting and we, like supplicants, must wait with hospitality, openness, and wonder. Writer Catherine Bateson gives an example: "The singing of whales has become for many people a paradigmatic experience of the sacred, an encounter with another species living in a totally different medium, suddenly known as a kin rather than as stranger." Naturalist writer Barry Lopez adds that "to encounter a truly wild animal on its own ground is to know the defeat of thought, to feel reason overpowered."

What are animals? Are they alien creatures—unknown and unknowable, "other nations" with whom humans merely share the planet? Or are they our companions and teachers, exemplars of qualities we would do well to imitate? Included in this chapter are readings covering all of these possibilities. Animals, as you will see, are some of the best spiritual literacy tutors around.

ANIMALS AS SYMBOLS

One day, as Fred and I approached our neighborhood park, we were greeted by a heart of pigeons. They were flocked on the grass around a young woman with a shopping bag full of bird seed. She had walked a circle on the lawn, spreading the seed behind her, and the pigeons had followed her, some lingering in the formation to feast on her gifts. Where she stood, there must have been fifty birds spread out in front of and beside her in two directions, making the top of a large heart shape.

We make such signs on the Earth with our relationships to animals. Spiritual literacy enables us to look at a scene like this one, and to see it as an analogy of a larger reality. We are given what we need, and we respond with a trusting heart.

Outside the Cathedral holding ancient relics in Valencia, a woman kissed pigeons. She saw these birds as symbols of God. Gray and white and black as discarded shells, these were creatures I'd been taught to think of as "filthy." They *seemed* filthy, in fact, with their staring orange eyes and patchy feathers. But now, while I looked, they turned into doves. Of course they always were doves, or rather, of course doves always really were a type of pigeon. But I never really believed it until this woman showed me her belief. Her kiss transformed ugliness to beauty.

So it was like a fairy tale after all. It was the old story: what is loved reveals its loveliness. Here she squatted, radiant, smiling, enrobed in life, in a dozen pairs of folded wings, in a dozen pairs of pearl gray and, as I looked, yes, even lavender, even royal purple wings—a woman in an ordinary black cotton dress who smiled as if she knew she was the luckiest person on earth, swathed in blessing.

—BONNIE FRIEDMAN
in *Writing Past Dark*

Jesus, Buddha, Zen masters, Sufi seers, and Hasidic sages all talk about animals in their stories. Any animal can be a symbol or a messenger of the Divine, and animals also may remind us of our spiritual needs.

THE BAT

I was reading about rationalism,
the kind of thing we do up north
in early winter, where the sun
leaves work for the day at 4:15.

Maybe the world is intelligible
to the rational mind:
and maybe we light the lamps at dusk
for nothing. . . .

Then I heard wings overhead.

The cats and I chased the bat
in circles—living room, kitchen,
pantry, kitchen, living room. . . .
At every turn it evaded us

like the identity of the third person
in the Trinity: the one
who spoke through the prophets,
the one who astounded Mary
by suddenly coming near.
　　　　　—JANE KENYON
　　　　　　in *The Boat of Quiet Hours*

It was the deer, fleeting gracefully along the rims of the ridges, that most clearly epitomized my yearnings for union with a God I occasionally glimpsed at the edges of my awareness. Despite their abundant numbers in the surrounding hills, I seldom saw deer near my house during the daylight hours. But I would hear them in the night and, come morning, would find hoofprints in my lawn.

Following deer trails through the woods, I would feel a secret communion with these shy, gentle creatures, so defenseless, so hunted. Yet one day I realized that I too was hunting them in my own way. I recognized that I wanted to exercise a subtle kind of dominion over the deer, that I desired to see them when and where and how I pleased. That is not the way with deer.

Deer appear or they don't. If you are in the right place at the right moment, you will see them, perhaps even very close at hand. But once you try to touch them, they flee. So, I discovered, it is with the comings and goings of the Spirit of God. If I wait, quietly going about the tasks of my day, I might glimpse a trace of His activity in my life, a subtle sign that He is just beyond the edge of my vision.

—KAREN KARPER
in *Where God Begins to Be*

Birdsong brings relief
to my longing.

I am just as ecstatic as they are,
but with nothing to say!

Please, universal soul, practice
some song, or something, through me!
—JELALUDDIN RUMI
in *The Essential Rumi*
translated by Coleman Barks
with John Moyne, A. J. Arberry,
and Reynold Nicholson

An animal's behavior shows us ways of bringing meaning into our lives.

I am looking at a great blue heron who is building a nest in the pine tree next to my father's home. Every once in a while she stretches her long neck and points her head toward the heavens, and I feel the stretch in my throat. She stands immobile for long periods staring into the eastern horizon and then floats to the canal below for some food. I have seen this heron mother for years in the same pine tree. Winter is her season to nest. She stands like a blue-gray guardian of the past, not seeming to take notice of the flow of traffic on the highway to her south. . . .

This great heron reminds me that storying is a kind of root

medicine, a way for us to enter our depths and derive nourishment from the fruitful darkness. For her life to succeed, this big mother heron needs her old pine tree and her dark inland water. She needs continuity, heights, and depths for her life to be complete. It is this way with tellings, with stories, with myths, with prayer, prophecy, and song. They call forth the firmness of the tree and the yielding of deep water in moments of transmitted inspiration.

—JOAN HALIFAX
in *The Fruitful Darkness*

Ever since I first began to hear a hermit thrush singing out of a hillside, hidden from view, I have tried to stop, look, and listen for the qualities of things unseen. The songs of the white-throat or of the hermit thrush rise out of the true proportions of space. The birds sing of an imperishable forest. They inherit the memories of their race, and I believe the land itself has a memory. Intellectual and material ascendancy is not for them.

—JOHN HAY
in *A Beginner's Faith in Things Unseen*

What I learned is that of all the creatures that I can see in this landscape, the geese best represent the communion of saints. They depend on one another. The lead goose does the most work, but when it is tired, it falls back and another takes its place. To be able to rely on others is a deep trust that does not come easily.

The geese fly in the wake of one another's wings. They literally get a lift from one another. I want to be with others this way. Geese tell me that it is, indeed, possible to fly with equals.

—GUNILLA NORRIS
in *Journeying in Place*

Indigo buntings are small but emphatic birds. They believe that they own the place, and it is hard to ignore their claim. The male birds—brilliant, shimmering blue—perch on the garden posts or on top of the cedar trees that have taken over the pasture. From there they survey their holdings and belt out their songs, complicated tangles of couplets that waken me first thing in the morning; they keep it up all day, even at noon, after the other birds have quieted. The indigo buntings have several important facts to tell us, especially about who's in charge around here.

—Sue Hubbell
in *A Country Year*

Not only do animals make us question who is in charge, they help us discover our place in the universe.

We can learn a lesson from the little spider. Watch a spider as she patiently rebuilds her web each time it is broken or removed. Seldom will she move its location but chooses to rebuild it with patience. She reweaves its broken strands each time they are broken. She waits, in patience, for dinner to come into her white cosmos of tiny threads. . . .

Like the spider, we must return again and again to rebuild our webs by bringing together the threads of our lives and uniting them to the divine center within. Without such work, our lives become disconnected, unpeaceful and broken. Perhaps the next time we see a spider's web, we can see it as a spiritual classroom and not simply something to be swept away. . . . The Hopi Tribe of the Southwest has in its holy books a holy woman. She is the Divine Mother, but her name isn't Mary, it is Spider Woman. She brings together the idea of patience and the Holy Mother as intercessor between God and the people.

—Edward Hays
in *Pray All Ways*

. . . I once received an unexpected lesson from a spider.

It happened far away on a rainy morning in the West. I had come up a long gulch looking for fossils, and there, just at eye level, lurked a huge yellow-and-black orb spider, whose web was moored to the tall spears of buffalo grass at the edge of the arroyo. It was her universe, and her senses did not extend beyond the lines and spokes of the great wheel she inhabited. Her extended claws could feel every vibration throughout that delicate structure. She knew the tug of wind, the fall of a raindrop, the flutter of a trapped moth's wing. Down one spoke of the web ran a stout ribbon of gossamer on which she could hurry out to investigate her prey.

Curious, I took a pencil from my pocket and touched a strand of the web. Immediately there was a response. The web, plucked by its menacing occupant, began to vibrate until it was a blur. Anything that had brushed claw or wing against that amazing snare would be thoroughly entrapped. As the vibrations slowed, I could see the owner fingering her guidelines for signs of struggle. A pencil point was an intrusion into this universe for which no precedent existed. Spider was circumscribed by spider ideas; its universe was spider universe. All outside was irrational, extraneous, at best raw material for spider. As I proceeded on my way along the gully, like a vast impossible shadow, I realized that in the world of spider I did not exist.

—LOREN EISELEY
in *The Unexpected Universe*

Lulu herself would never, after her first long absence from the house, come so near to any of us that we could touch her. In other ways she was friendly, she understood that we wanted to look at her fawn, and she would take a piece of sugar-cane from an outstretched hand. She walked up to the open dining-room door, and gazed thoughtfully into the twilight of the rooms, but she never again crossed the threshold. She had by this time lost her bell, and came and went away in silence.

My houseboys suggested that I should let them catch Lulu's fawn, and keep him as we had once kept Lulu. But I thought it would make a boorish return to Lulu's elegant confidence in us.

It also seemed to me that the free union between my house and the antelope was a rare, honourable thing. Lulu came in from the wild world to show that we were on good terms with it, and she made my house one with the African landscape, so that nobody could tell where the one stopped and the other began.

—ISAK DINESEN
in *Out of Africa*

Thomas Aquinas, a thirteenth-century Catholic theologian, is impressed by the diversity within the animal kingdom. And he has an explanation for it. "Because the divine goodness could not adequately be represented by one creature alone, God produced many and diverse creatures, that what was wanting in one in the representation of the divine goodness might be supplied by another." Take, for example, the alien world of the bee.

My bees cover one thousand square miles of land that I do not own in their foraging flights, flying from flower to flower for which I pay no rent, stealing nectar but pollinating plants in return. It is an unruly, benign kind of agriculture, and making a living by it has such a wild, anarchistic, raffish appeal that it unsuits me for any other, except possibly robbing banks.

Then there is that other appeal, the stronger one, of spending, during certain parts of the year, a ten- or twelve-hour working day with bees, which are, when all is said and done, simply a bunch of bugs. But spending my days in close and intimate contact with creatures who are structured so differently from humans, and who get on with life in such a different way, is like being a visitor in an alien but ineffably engaging world.

—SUE HUBBELL
in *A Country Year*

By being with animals, we may learn how to expand the repertoire of our devotional practices.

While Hasidim believed in the importance of observing the *mitzvot*, learning Torah, and praying with devotion, they believed that there was a deeper spiritual realm of listening to the world as the song of God. The disciples of the Maggid of Mezritch, for example, noted that their teacher went to the pond every day at dawn and stayed there for a little while before returning home again. One of his students explained that he was learning the song with which the frogs praise God.

—DAVID S. ARIEL
in *What Do Jews Believe?*

Once a man went to visit a certain saintly man. When the visitor arrived he found the holy man in prayer. He sat so still that not even a hair of his head moved. When the holy man had finished his prayer, the visitor asked where he had learned such stillness. He replied, "From my cat. She was watching a mouse hole with even greater concentration than you have seen in me." The holy man's cat was seeking something with all her heart and soul. Such seeking gives power. The intensity of desire gives one the power to return, day after day, to the "hot-seat" of sitting still. If we are making little headway on our spiritual quest, perhaps we should ask ourselves if we are seeking our goal with the same passion that a cat seeks a mouse.

—EDWARD HAYS
in *Secular Sanctity*

In fables going all the way back to Aesop in ancient Greece, animals have been bearers of truths. Here's a story from India.

There lived a pious man in Bengal, India. Every day a Sanskrit scholar would come to his house and read aloud a few soul-stirring spiritual teachings from the Gita, the Upanishads and the Vedas. The master of the house listened devotedly to these discourses. The family had a bird called Krishna. It was kept in a cage in the room where the discourses were given and also listened to these talks.

One day the bird spoke to its master and said, "Could you please tell me what benefit you derive from these spiritual talks?"

The master answered, "Krishna, you don't seem to understand that these spiritual talks will liberate me, free me from bondage!"

The bird said, "You have been listening to these discourses for the last few years, but I don't see any changes in you. Would you kindly ask your teacher what will actually happen to you?"

On the following day the master of the house said to his teacher, "Guru, I have been listening to your spiritual talks for the last ten years. Is it true that I will get liberation and freedom?"

The teacher was still. He scratched his head, pondered the question, but found no reply. He remained silent for about an hour and then left the house.

The master of the house was stunned. His guru could not give an answer to the bird's question, but the bird found an answer.

From that day on, the bird stopped eating. It stopped singing. It

178

became absolutely silent. The master and his family placed food inside the cage every day, but the bird would not touch anything.

One day the master looked at the bird and, seeing no sign of life in it, took it gently out of the cage. With a sad heart, he placed his Krishna on the floor. In a twinkling the bird flew away into the infinite freedom of the sky!

The bird taught. Its master and his guru learned: silence liberates.

—SRI CHINMOY
in *Garden of the Soul*

Poet Coleman Barks notes that all the mystical traditions love birds and their singing: "Birds represent our longings for purity and freedom and they carry messages of ineffable joy." In the next poem, birds demonstrate the spiritual practice of grace.

Birds make great sky-circles
of their freedom.
How do they learn it?

They fall, and falling,
they're given wings.

—JELALUDDIN RUMI
in *The Essential Rumi*
translated by Coleman Barks
with John Moyne, A .J. Arberry,
and Reynold Nicholson

ANIMALS AS TEACHERS

As a bee seeks nectar
from all kinds of flowers,
seek teachings everywhere;
like a deer that finds
a quiet place to graze,
seek seclusion to digest

all you have gathered.
Like a madman
beyond all limits,
go wherever you please,
and live like a lion,
completely free of all fear.
　　—NAMKHAI NORBU
　　　in *The Crystal and the Way of Light*
　　　edited by John Shane

Animals are teachers in most cultures. They showed the earliest humans what foods to eat, which plants to use for medicine, and how to build lasting homes. To this day, they alert us to areas that have become too dangerously polluted to sustain life. Reports abound of animals guiding people to safety over dangerous terrain and through rough seas.

Folk tales, fables, teaching stories, children's books, and popular movies prove that there are lessons in animal antics, morals in their social structures, and virtues evident in their behavior. From the Three Little Pigs to White Fang, Charlotte the spider, the Lion King, and Babe, the pig who learns the vocation of sheepdog, we watch animals to find out how to make our lives better.

Native American nations have an amazing array of stories about animals which reflect their deep respect for the wisdom of many-legged, winged, and finned creatures. Individuals and tribes may take an animal as a guide or totem, drawing upon its strengths and applying them to daily experiences. Here is a Native American meditation on the medicine— defined as "anything that improves one's connection to the Great Mystery and to all of life"—of one animal guide, the buffalo.

All animals are sacred, but in many traditions White Buffalo is the most sacred. The appearance of White Buffalo is a sign that prayers are being heard, that the sacred pipe is being honored, and that the promises of prophesy are being fulfilled. White Buffalo signals a time of abundance and plenty.

Buffalo was the major source of sustenance for the Plains Indians. It gave meat for food, hides for clothing, warm and soft buffalo robes for long winters, and hooves for glue. The medicine of Buffalo is prayer, gratitude and praise for that which has been received. Buffalo medicine is also knowing that *abundance* is present when all relations are honored as sacred, and when gratitude is expressed to every living part of creation.

Because of its desire to give the gifts that its body provided, and because of its willingness to be used on Earth for the highest good before entering the hunting grounds of Spirit, Buffalo did not readily stampede and run from hunters. . . .

Buffalo medicine is a sign that you achieve nothing without the aid of the Great Spirit and that you must be humble enough to ask for that assistance and then be grateful for what you receive.

—JAMIE SAMS and DAVID CARSON
in *Medicine Cards*

Matthew Fox dedicated his book The Reinvention of Work *to his dog Tristan. In an interview, Fox praised Tristan for being good at what he does. The interviewer asked, "What's his 'work'?" "His work is to hang around the house and sniff." After Tristan's death, Fox wrote a moving eulogy to his companion.*

Don't get me wrong when I describe Tristan as person and as spirit. He was also 100% dog. Always dog. Always eager to play, to learn, to eat, to go for walks, to go for rides in the car, to visit the beach, to chase squirrels, birds, cats, ducks, geese. Once when he caught a squirrel and turned it upside down on the lawn, he just studied it. He did no harm to it whatsoever. It was as if he had played the game and won but did not really care about winning. He just wanted to know a squirrel "up close and personal" one might say.

There were uncanny things that Tristan knew and did. For example, two years before he died I bought a musical keyboard, a kind of mini-piano. A friend set it up for me in the living room. It has four legs with a bar connecting two of them. That night, when I sat down for the first time to play at the piano, Tristan came over and laid his body down across the leg of the piano for a good ten minutes. It was the one and only time he did this. It was his blessing of the instrument, his accepting of this new being into our shared world.

—MATTHEW FOX
in *Creation Spirituality*

181

GRACE

Sufi poet Jelaluddin Rumi says:

> You are so weak. Give up to grace.
> The ocean takes care of each wave
> til it gets to shore.
> You need more help than you know.

Ramakrishna declares, "The winds of grace are always blowing, but you have to raise the sail." The gifts move across the waters. We can't control or earn them, but we must be willing to receive them.

St. Paul writes in Ephesians 2:8, "For by grace you have been saved through faith, and this is not by your own doing, it is the gift of God." To accept this gift is to step into a world that is larger, deeper, richer, and fuller.

Thomas Aquinas, a thirteenth-century Italian Catholic theologian, notes, "Grace is nothing else than a beginning of glory in us." Elsewhere, he adds, "Grace renders us like God and a partaker of the divine nature." John Wesley, the founder of Methodism, agrees, as do most Greek Orthodox Christians. Through the bounty of grace, we discover the Divine Guest inside us.

Signs that the Blessed One is working within and through us are what spiritual educator Celeste Snowber Schroeder calls "gracelets" or "the moments of meaning in the mundane." Writer Charles G. Finney suggests, "A state of mind that sees God in everything is evidence of growth in grace and a thankful heart."

Eighteenth-century Jesuit priest Jean Pierre de Caussade explains this phenomenon: "Divine action has always been the source from which flows a torrent of grace which spreads over everything. Henceforth I shall no longer seek it within the narrow confines of a book or the life of a saint, or a sublime idea."

We come to realize that daily life is a theater of grace with continuous performances. The sacred is here and there and everywhere. Suddenly our lives take on a special radiance from within.

"Grace happens," Buddhist Joanna Macy observes, "when we act with others on behalf of our world." An attitude of caring is a natural outgrowth of grace and our continual partaking of the Divine.

Again, Rumi says:

> Something opens our wings. Something
> makes boredom and hurt disappear.
> Someone fills the cup in front of us.
> We taste only sacredness.

GRATITUDE

For sixty years I have been forgetful,
every minute, but not for a second
has this flowing toward me stopped or slowed.
I deserve nothing. Today I recognize
that I am the guest the mystics talk about.
I play this living music for my host.
Everything today is for the host.

Jelaluddin Rumi, Sufi seer and poet, is right. We are guests on the great, good Earth, and our every breath should be one of gratitude to the Host. The medieval Christian mystic Meister Eckhart suggests that if the only prayer we say in our lifetime is "thank you," that would suffice.

Yes, and why not every day! Let's put a song of praise on our lips in the early morning hours. For the breath that fills our lungs and for our unique bodies. For loved ones, family, and our circle of friends. For the bountiful little blessings which arrive in our lives unheralded.

"Praise God," says the Hasidic teacher Rebbe Nachman of Breslov. "It puts everything into its proper place and perspective." Gratitude rejoices with her sister joy and is always ready to light the candles and have a party. Gratitude doesn't much like the old cronies of boredom, despair, and taking-things-for-granted. But they are welcome to the party anyway because we are grateful for everything. Let's endorse British writer G. K. Chesterton's idea of "taking things with gratitude and not taking things for granted."

Sachiko Mirata, a scholar of Islam, calls gratitude the first character trait that people owe to Allah. Ingratitude is to shut our eyes to the obvious. "God is the source of all good, so we must thank him for it."

Saying thank you to the Great Provider is only one part of a life of gratitude. Another side is revealed by Protestant preacher Elton Trueblood: "I find that the one thing which I want to put into practice in my own life is the conscious and deliberate habit of finding somebody to thank." Say thank you to somebody who least expects it from you today.

Gratitude paid to all around us becomes a spiritual exercise. Show your gratitude to the music that enchants, to the winter boots that stand up to the wear and tear of the elements, to the movie that brings tears to your eyes.

"All of us have experienced times in our lives that were so precious and special that if it were possible we would have had time stand still so we might live that moment forever. A good time is a taste of God," affirms John Aurelio, a Catholic priest.

Feast on the moments that stand out in your mind as precious enough to replay again and again. Now repeat the mantra: "A good time is a taste of God."

Walk down the street of a busy city amidst the chaos of traffic, the implacable noise of vehicle and machine, the unrelenting pace of people heading to infinite destinations. Suddenly you see a blind man and his black labrador guide dog. They advance as one amid the formlessness and the indifference of our sidewalk disarray. The dog, attentive to every move, makes his way among a thousand targets. His pace is cautious but firm, neither too fast nor too slow, always aware of his master's progress. There is a wisdom in the animal's actions that goes well beyond our comprehension. His patience is inexhaustible, his caring of the utmost seriousness, his concentration on the details and nuances of his work painstakingly intense. Occasionally the dog will turn his head to read his master's intentions, to capture his need, and then resume his discipline. As dog and man turn a corner, they disappear from our view.

—EDUARDO RAUCH
in *The Parabola Book of Healing*

In addition to demonstrating the spiritual practices of play and attention, our pets can teach us about enthusiasm, joy, and love.

I wonder how different life would be for me if I could be as lacking in self-doubt and self-judgment as Putnam. His whole being demonstrates an assumption that he is a lovable creature, a deserving creature, and an enjoyable one. His fat, aged self simply squirms with the sacred knowledge that he is one of God's creatures. Such direct light makes me turn my eyes away.

To act as if one had the total endorsement of the universe behind one's particular existence would be extraordinary! I hedge my bets by offering to others what I myself want, by restricting my requests for love and help to those I know will not reject me out of hand. I am oh, so careful, whereas I could, with a Putnam-like trust, meet the world with a joyful, natural wag.

—GUNILLA NORRIS
in *Journeying in Place*

One thing I will give cats in all of this—they do love. No one can tell me cats do not in some way feel something for us that transcends the full stomach and the warm cushion. Those are what they demand, not what they feel about us. On their own level, in their own way, and certainly by their own choice, my cats think the world of me. I don't know if gratitude is involved, and I don't know if some vestigial or perhaps nascent social sense is at play, but cats seek my company, like my lap, want to be on the foot of my bed even when there are lots of other soft places around. We have a thing going, and it has been viewed by both the cats and me as good. To me, that amounts to love.

—ROGER A. CARAS
in *A Celebration of Cats*

We share our home with two cats. Boone, who is short-haired and yellow, has been a boon to our lives for more than sixteen years; he was named after the frontier explorer because during his first evening in the loft he checked out every part of it. Bebb is fourteen, long-haired, and black and white. His coloring was not the reason we named him after the outrageous preacher in Frederick Buechner's novels; it had more to do with his spunk and his big heart.

We have learned many things from living with Boone and Bebb. Some lessons are directives we would be wise to follow: Live a rhythmic life. Sit and savor the present moment. Gaze intently. Stretch often. Keep out of harm's way. Take good care of your family. Be independent, but don't be afraid of being dependent on others. Cherish your wildness, even if no one else does. When you want something, be persistent. When someone pays attention to you, respond with affection. If you are embarrassed, turn your back on the situation and get on with your life. Enjoy small treats. Keep yourself clean. Take a nap when you need one, and try to relax more.

Our cats' behavior also points to simple truths: By certain instinctive actions, you honor your ancestors. Play is an expression of personality and soul. Curiosity is a sign of the creative spirit. Everyone needs a secret space. The night holds many surprises.

Being hospitable to animals is the first step in discovering their teachings. A leap of imagination also is required when access to their kingdom is limited.

All alone, obviously the snail is very much alone. He doesn't have many friends. But he doesn't need any to be happy. He is so attached to nature, enjoys it so completely and so intimately, he is a friend of the soil he kisses with his whole body, of the leaves, and of the sky toward which he so proudly lifts his head with its sensitive eyeballs; noble, slow, wise, proud, vain, arrogant. . . .

And that is the lesson they offer us. They are saints, making their life into a work of art—a work of art of their self-perfection. Their very secretion is produced in such a way that it creates its own form. Nothing exterior to them, to their essence, to their need is of their making. Nothing disproportionate, either, about their physique. Nothing unessential to it, required for it.

—FRANCIS PONGE
in *The Voice of Things*

The gecko remains motionless for hours; with a snap of his tongue he gulps down a mosquito or a gnat every now and then; other insects, on the contrary, identical to the first, light unawares a few millimeters from his mouth, and he seems not to perceive them. Is it the vertical pupil of his eyes, separated at the sides of his head, that does not notice? Or does he have criteria of choice and rejection that we do not know? Or are his actions prompted by chance, or by whim?

The segmentation of legs and tail into rings, the speckling of tiny granulous plates on his head and belly give the gecko the appearance of a mechanical device: a highly elaborate machine, its every microscopic detail carefully studied, so that you begin to wonder if all that perfection is not squandered, in view of the limited operations it performs. Or is this perhaps the secret: content to be, does he reduce his doing to the minimum? Can this be his lesson, the opposite of the morality that, in his youth, Mr. Palomar wanted to make his: to strive always to do something a bit beyond one's means?

—ITALO CALVINO
in *Mr. Palomar*

Study any animal long enough, and it may give you an insight to carry into your own experiences. The qualities we usually associate with an animal deserve a second look. Why, for example, are cows contented?

There used to be—there still is—a motto on every can of Carnation evaporated milk. This milk is "From Contented Cows," it says. I believe it. Cows are a happy lot.

It's hard to imagine a similar motto for any other domestic animal. Wool from contented sheep? Sheep are far too fretful and anxious for that. They also dislike having their wool removed. Eggs from contented chickens? Get real. Not one American chicken in fifty—probably not one in five hundred—enjoys her life much. . . .

Cows are happy. Cows have a gift for it. There's a big dairy herd in Norwich, Vermont, that seems to me to typify the bovine ability to enjoy life. There are about eighty cows in this herd: black-and-white Holsteins plus a few tan Jerseys and red Ayrshires. Cows are sociable animals, and mostly the whole eighty will stay in the same part of whatever field they're in.

—Noel Perrin
in *Last Person Rural*

Fred gave me the first of my "allies," a collection of small animal figures which watch over me as I work at my desk. First came Bear, a perfect choice since lately I had been dreaming of bears, following a rather frisky cub through fields and deep water caves. In some Native American stories, Bear's strength is the power of introspection. I knew the dreams signaled a turn on my spiritual journey, one that included more attention to my inner life.

My second ally was Turtle. She tells me it is okay for me to move at my own pace even when I am surrounded by high energy people. I need to hold my ground to stay grounded. The turtle is a small box, and I keep a "Slow Is Beautiful" button inside.

Sometimes, however, I know I have to get going on a project and that's when I look up at Flamingo. She says "Move it!" This animal is not mentioned in most symbol books. My association comes from the scenes of running flamingos at the beginning of the 1980s' television series Miami Vice.

I also had to find my own meaning for Penguin. I read about these animals in the encyclopedia and learned that they can live on both land and sea, but are more at home in the sea. My penguin is walking, so he has become my reminder that I can stand tall even when I find myself in alien territory.

My allies encourage me to pay attention to particular features of my life. Sometimes even inconspicuous animals can open our eyes.

A prisoner lived in solitary confinement for years. He saw and spoke to no one and his meals were served through an opening in the wall.

One day an ant came into his cell. The man contemplated it in fascination as it crawled around the room. He held it in the palm of his hand the better to observe it, gave it a grain or two, and kept it under his tin cup at night.

One day it suddenly struck him that it had taken him ten long years of solitary confinement to open his eyes to the loveliness of an ant.

—ANTHONY DE MELLO
in *Taking Flight*

Essayist Scott Russell Sanders shares a wonderful example of the practices of love and kindness toward animals: "Once again this spring, the seventy-seventh of her life, my mother put out lint from her clothes dryer for the birds to use in building their nests. 'I know how hard it is to make a home from scratch,' she says, 'I've done it often enough myself.'" About his mother's actions, Sanders comments: "That is fellow feeling, the root of all kindness."

Abu Yazid made his periodic journey to purchase supplies at the bazaar in the city of Hamadhan—a distance of several hundred miles. When he returned home, he discovered a colony of ants in the cardamom seeds. He carefully packed the seeds up again and walked back across the desert to the merchant from whom he had bought them. His intent was not to exchange the seeds but to return the ants to their home.

—SUFI LEGEND
retold in *Breakfast at the Victory*
by James P. Carse

In Kenya, a man hungry for sweetness walks into a clearing and blows a few notes on a whistle. Soon a bird flutters at the edge of the clearing, chatters loudly, then flies a short distance into the woods. The man follows, carrying an ax. When the man draws near to where the bird has perched, it flies again, and the man follows. And so they move into the forest, on wing and foot, until they come to a tree the bird has chosen. If the man walks too far, the bird circles back, circles back, until at last the man discovers the right tree. He chops a hole in the hollow trunk and lifts out the dripping combs, gathering honey for tongues back home. The bird eats what the man leaves behind, honey and bee larvae and wax. So bird and man serve each other, one pointing the way and one uncovering the sweetness.

—SCOTT RUSSELL SANDERS
in *Writing from the Center*

Animals mirror back to us the love and care we have for others. They also expose the parts of ourselves we try to hide.

Parrots learn profanity more easily than common phrases since we utter our curses with so much vigor. The parrot doesn't know the meaning of these words, but he hears the energy invested in them. Even animals can pick up on the power we have hidden in the shadow!

—ROBERT A. JOHNSON
in *Owning Your Own Shadow*

In our desire to read the spiritual significance of animals, there is a tendency to ascribe to them only noble and ideal characteristics. A truer portrait recognizes the full range of animal behavior.

Last spring, our family was in Yellowstone. We were hiking along Pelican Creek, which separated us from an island of lodgepole pines. All at once, a dark form stood in front of the forest on a patch of snow. It was a grizzly, and behind her, two cubs. Suddenly, the sow turned and bolted through the trees. A female elk crashed through the timber to the other side of the clearing, stopped, and swung back toward the bear. Within seconds, the grizzly emerged with an elk calf secure in the grip of her jaws. The sow shook the yearling violently by the nape of its neck, threw it down, clamped her claws on its shoulders, and began tearing the flesh back from the bones with her teeth. The cow elk, only a few feet away, watched the sow devour her calf. She pawed the earth desperately with her front hooves, but the bear was oblivious. Blood dripped from the sow's muzzle. The cubs stood by their mother, who eventually turned the carcass over to them. Two hours passed. The sow buried the calf for a later meal, she slept on top of the mound with a paw on each cub. It was not until then that the elk crossed the river in retreat.

We are capable of harboring both these responses to life in the relentless power of our love. As women connected to the earth, we are nurturing and we are fierce, we are wicked and we are sublime. The full range is ours.

—TERRY TEMPEST WILLIAMS
in *An Unspoken Hunger*

[The great horned owls] are the pure wild hunters of our world. They are swift and merciless upon the backs of rabbits, mice, voles, snakes, even skunks, even cats sitting in dusky yards, thinking peaceful thoughts. I have found the headless bodies of rabbits and blue jays, and known it was the great horned owl that did them in, taking the head only, for the owl has an insatiable craving for the taste of brains. I have walked with prudent caution down paths at twilight when the dogs were puppies. I know this bird. If it could, it would eat the whole world.

In the night, when the owl is less than exquisitely swift and perfect, the scream of the rabbit is terrible. But the scream of the owl, which is not of pain and hopelessness and the fear of being plucked out of the world, but of the sheer rollicking glory of the death-bringer, is more terrible still. When I hear it resounding through the woods, and then the five black pellets of its song dropping like stones into the air, I know I am standing at the edge of the mystery, in which terror is naturally and abundantly part of life, part of even the most becalmed, intelligent, sunny life—as, for example, my own. The world where the owl is endlessly hungry and endlessly on the hunt is the world in which I live too. There is only one world.

—MARY OLIVER
in *Blue Pastures*

Dolphins are some of the most loved animals by humans—and that is not surprising. Throughout history, they have been known to come to the aid of stranded sailors. They are great communicators, reaching out to us, their fellow mammals, with language and actions.

As I swam, snorkel mask down, arms at my side to signal that I would wait for [the dolphins] to choose to play with me, I heard far below the familiar high-frequency dialogue. It sounded like the high-pitched whine of a jet engine right before takeoff, combined with rapid creaks and bleeps. The sounds encircled my body and then, as the dolphins came closer, there was that astonishing physical sensation of being probed by their sonar. It's as subtle as an X ray, but exhilarating. My whole body tingled, stomach gurgled, head felt pleasurable pricking as if a high-speed ping-pong game played with light was bouncing around my brain. . . .

Every time I'm sounded by a cetacean, I feel as if my cells are penetrated, seen, and—what is most remarkable—*accepted*. I've never felt judgment, even if the dolphin chose to bypass me for another playmate. Dolphin researchers report that often, whether a dolphin spends five or forty-five minutes with a swimmer, that person will say it was enough, all they needed, as much as they could receive. In fact, every time I've swum with dolphins, my human companions have admitted afterward that we each felt like the favorite. Could it be we have something to learn about parenting from dolphins?

—BRENDA PETERSON
in *Living by Water*

I learned about acceptance from a horse. For a long time I was convinced that horses and Fred Brussat just don't get along. I was not happy about this because I admire these strong and beautiful animals. On an airplane flight I met a woman who lives on a farm in Virginia where she and her parents breed and train horses. I told her about my one nightmarish experience on a riding expedition. While other members of the party made one flip of the reins and their horses sauntered off, mine would not move. When he finally did, it was only for a few yards. Then he ate some leaves off a tree while the rest of the party disappeared out of sight. After I had given him many kicks in the flank, the horse finally decided to move—at a full gallop with me holding on

H

HOPE

A teacher does her best and hopes that her enthusiasm for learning has lit a fire inside her students for reading. A woman working in a hospice hopes that the people in her care will have finely finished deaths. A human rights activist in prison hopes that he will be freed soon to resume his work.

Like us, these individuals are animated by hope, which Czechoslovakian playwright and politician Vaclav Havel maintains is "a dimension of the Spirit. It is not outside us but within us."

This potent and positive human faculty must be distinguished from its dangerous sister, expectation, which steals us from the present and pushes us down the path of disappointment when things don't go our way.

Hope, in contrast, is patient. It is willing to stay with us in the here and now, and it assures us the future is open. Protestant minister William Sloane Coffin states, "Hope arouses as nothing else can arouse, a passion for the possible."

There is a forward thrust to bold projects and schemes begun with great commitment, ardor, and idealism. Hope is the fuel which keeps them going and growing.

"What oxygen is to the lungs," Swiss theologian Emil Bruner writes, "such is hope to the meaning of life." No wonder Martin Luther, the leader of the Protestant Reformation, urges us to realize, "Everything that is done in the world is done by hope." We get up, we give it our finest effort, and then we hope for the best.

But certain common tendencies undermine this approach to life. Science fiction writer Ursula LeGuin warns: "Hopelessness can arise, I think, only from an inability to face the present, to live in the present, to live as a responsible being among other beings in this sacred world here and now, which is all we have, and all we need to found our hope upon."

What is true for one is true for many. "Hope is the strongest driving force for a people. Hope which brings about change, which provides new realities, is what opens our road to freedom," writes Oscar Arias from contemporary Latin America. For millions all over the world, hope is the daily bread that feeds the soul and breeds the courage to continue in the face of poverty, disease, unemployment, and starvation.

For the refugees, the homeless, the oppressed, the prisoners of conscience, hope is a tonic that keeps them going. Or as another Latin American, Ruben A. Alvez, puts it: "Hope is hearing the melody of the future."

One of the best melodies of the future is found in a hymn by Protestant minister Al Carmines: "I believe in a new world. I do, yes I do. And I live in this trust: that although everything I see may turn to dust, we are moving inexorably, inexorably, inexorably, toward a new world."

HOSPITALITY

"How shall we live?" asks Mechtild of Magdeburg, a thirteenth-century Christian mystic. Her answer: "Welcoming to all." Hospitality is an essential spiritual practice.

It begins with an open mind, generous and receptive to others. It means looking for the positive in people, ideas, dreams, and social schemes.

That's quite different from being cynical, hostile, and critical of everything. Judgment is a terrible swift sword, cutting the new and the unfamiliar into smithereens.

Hospitality means that in the name of the Eternal Womb we hold the world in an embrace. The biggest disgrace is turning away. As French novelist Albert Camus says wisely, "Nothing is true that forces me to exclude."

Christian monasteries have a long-standing tradition of taking in strangers as if they were Christ. These places have an open-door policy toward those in need. They are heeding the advice in Hebrews 13:2: "Do not neglect to show hospitality to strangers, for thereby some have entertained angels unawares."

This spiritual practice goes against the grain of the postmodern world where there is still great fear, distrust, and hatred of strangers.

In the biblical accounts, Jesus is the most hospitable of people, mingling with rich and poor, Jew and Gentile, and individuals of low repute. He continually crosses boundaries in the name of love. And when it is time for him to be entertained, the two sisters Mary and Martha take distinctly different approaches. Like them, we are hospitable in various ways in a variety of settings.

"Hospitality," writes Benedictine sister Joan Chittister, "is the way we come out of ourselves. It is the first step toward dismantling the barriers of the world. Hospitality is the way we turn a prejudiced world around one heart at a time."

Start with your own situation and those who are close at hand. Share who you are and what you have. Then extend the practice to your neighbors and the world.

Hospitality is an important ingredient in many of the world's religions. Tibetan Buddhist monks greet strangers in their temples with the question, "Welcome, friend, from what noble spiritual tradition do you come?"

This largesse of spirit is sorely needed in our antagonistic times. Dialogue, not dogmatism, is the key. As the English philosopher and essayist Francis Bacon notes, "If one be gracious and courteous to strangers it shows you are a citizen of the world."

We need more citizens of the world who are united by hospitality, open to new ideas, tolerant of strangers, and willing to face the mystery of the human adventure.

"Hospitality," Joan Chittister concludes, "binds the world together." Open your door.

for dear life. We caught up with the group, and he started his routine all over again. Stop, eat, and run. Stop, eat, and run. I was angry and embarrassed.

The woman listened patiently to my story and then said, "Horses are incredibly sensitive animals, able to discern exactly what kind of person is riding them. In this case, the horse realized that you are a noncon-formist, a person who does not like to be identified with a crowd. So the animal gave you a ride perfectly suited to your personality. The next time you go riding, relax. The horse knows you and what's best for you." This stranger totally reframed my experience, and I got off the plane with renewed confidence in myself as one who could relate to an animal.

One afternoon as the children watched television and I folded laundry, we heard a terrible thud against the patio door. I turned in time to see blue wings falling to the ground. A bird had flown into the glass.

None of us said a word. We looked at one another and crept to the door. The children followed me outside. I half-expected the bird to be dead, but she wasn't. She was stunned and her right wing was a little lopsided, but it didn't look broken—bruised, maybe.

The bird sat perfectly still, her eyes tiny and afraid. She looked so fragile and alone that I sat down beside her. I reached out my little finger and brushed her wing.

A voice came from behind me. "Why doesn't it fly off, Mama?"

"She's hurt," I said. "She just needs to be still."

We watched her. We watched her stillness. Finally the children wandered back to the television, satisfied that nothing was going to "happen" for a while. But I couldn't leave her.

I sat beside her, unable to resist the feeling that we shared something, the two of us. The wounds and brokenness of life. Crumpled wings. A collision with something harsh and real. I felt like crying for her. For myself. For every broken thing in the world.

That moment taught me that while the postures of stillness within the cocoon are frequently an individual experience, we also need to share our stillness. The bird taught me anew that we're all in this together, that we need to sit in one another's stillness and take up corporate postures of prayer. How wonderful it is when we can be honest and free enough to say to one another, "I need you to wait with me," or "Would you like me to wait with you?"

I studied the bird, deeply impressed that she seemed to know instinctively that in stillness is healing. I had been learning that too, learning that stillness can be the prayer that transforms us. How much more concentrated our stillness becomes, though, when it's shared.

The door opened again. "Is she finished being still yet?"

"No, not yet," I said, knowing that I was talking as much about myself as the bird. We went on waiting together. Twenty minutes. Thirty. Fifty.

Finally she was finished being still. She cocked her head to one side, lifted her wings, and flew. The sight of her flying made me catch my breath. From the corner of my eye I saw her shadow move along the ground and cross over me. Grace is everywhere, I thought. Then I picked myself up and went back to folding laundry.

—Sue Monk Kidd
in *When the Heart Waits*

ANIMALS AS AUTONOMOUS BEINGS

In Africa, two men stand at a river which they are about to cross, when they notice crocodiles looking at them. "Are you afraid?" says one to the other. "Don't you know that God is merciful and good?" "Yes, I do," says the frightened man. "But what if God suddenly chooses right now to be good to the crocodiles?"

—Elie Wiesel
in *Sages and Dreamers*

Animals are often revelations of the sacred, and they do teach us about living whole and meaningful lives. But if we limit our readings to such discoveries, we are simply using animals for our own purposes. A spiritually literate approach to animals also recognizes that they are extraordinary beings in their own right.

In the next reading, Laurens van der Post, a philosopher and conservationist, comes to a new understanding of the spiritual practice of beauty when he meets a rhinoceros in the wild.

I stood there for about two or three minutes looking at him and wondering about him. I thought with great emotion how beautiful he was . . . I found nothing that, in the context of its time and the language of life, was not dignified, honorable, and exceedingly lovely. I have not often been so moved by such a sense of discovery as he gave and this new capacity of response he evoked within myself; this resolution that once you break through into the rhinoceros's idiom, discover what a rhinoceros mother would find beautiful in a rhinoceros son, the impression animal beauty makes on you is blinding. All these emotions went through me while looking at him, until there came a moment when he turned sideways. He said a sort of "goodbye" and I too turned away.

—LAURENS VAN DER POST
in *A Walk with a White Bushman*

One of Fred's and my favorite movies is The Bear, *directed by Jean-Jacques Annaud. The story follows the adventures of an orphaned bear cub who joins up with a giant grizzly and learns from him the basics of survival in the wild.*

In a subplot, the bears are tracked by two hunters. In a key scene, one of the men is waiting at a lookout point on a rock ledge. He leans over to get a drink of water from a stream and when he looks up again, he sees the grizzly towering over him. The bear brings his head within inches of the terrified man, opens his mouth, and roars. The hunter appears to shrink. The bear looks at this weak, frightened creature for a minute, then turns and walks away.

The part of me that clutches at metaphors finds in this moment a lesson about dealing with conflict. Some opponents are not worthy; some fights are not worth the effort. I can release my anger, roar as loud as I can, but then it's best to just walk away.

But another part of me reads this scene as a reminder of the distance that remains between the human and the animal worlds. Students of bear behavior might question the whole premise of this movie. Would a territorial male bear adopt and protect a cub? Would a wounded bear walk away from a vulnerable opponent? We can't ever really know— that is the humbling aspect of it. We cannot get inside the mind of a wild animal.

One hot evening three years ago, I was standing more or less *in* a bush. . . . I was focused for depth. I had long since lost myself, lost the creek, the day, lost everything but still amber depth. All at once I couldn't see. And then I could: a young muskrat had appeared on top of the water, floating on its back. Its forelegs were folded languorously across its chest; the sun shone on its upturned belly. Its youthfulness and rodent grin, coupled with its ridiculous method of locomotion, which consisted of a lazy wag of the tail assisted by an occasional dabble of a webbed hind foot, made it an enchanting picture of decadence, dissipation, and summer sloth. I forgot all about the fish.

But in my surprise at having the light come on so suddenly, and at having my consciousness returned to me all at once and bearing an inverted muskrat, I must have moved and betrayed myself. The kit . . . righted itself so that only its head was visible above water, and swam downstream, away from me. I extricated myself from the bush and foolishly pursued it. It dove sleekly, reemerged, and glided for the opposite bank. I ran along the bankside brush, trying to keep it in sight. It kept casting an alarmed look over its shoulder at me. Once again it dove, under a floating mat of brush lodged in the bank, and disappeared. I never saw it again.

—ANNIE DILLARD
in *Pilgrim at Tinker Creek*

I don't usually like seeing wildlife from a plane very much: It's often the easiest way to see rare creatures, but it's not an intimate way to see them. With the condors, however, the experience in the plane was building into something remarkably different. I was with them in their element. In the air, they weren't cumbersome. They were at home. . . .

In the air, the condors had another culture, built on winds and air and wings. Next to us, [the condor] cruised on giant wings, body immobile, steady and strong. The feathers at the tips of his wings blew and fluttered as he glided through the air. His head swiveled, the way a modern dancer isolates and moves a single body part. I looked out of the plane window, watching his red head rotate while he flew, looking below, looking sideways. And looking straight at me.

There's nothing like being transfixed in the gaze of a spectacular wild animal. Always it's a shock to me—the sudden recognition of strangeness. In the condor's stare, I felt a disorienting self-consciousness that came with losing my role for a precious moment: I was no longer sure whether I was the seer or the seen. I got a fleeting sense of what I must look like to the condor, both of us made visible in the same light of day. The gaze also forced me to enter the picture, to occupy a place in the skies with the condor. In the look of the condor, I recognized a part of me that had existed unknown to myself.

I could also see in the look that the condor has a world and a life of its own, that it will always be strange to us. This was the condor of the skies, a magnificent soarer, looking down upon the monotonous and endless traffic of our lives.

—CHARLES BERGMAN
in *Wild Echoes*

Issa was a Japanese haiku poet who has been compared to Robert Frost because he was a farmer poet, and to Walt Whitman because he was a miniaturist who loved nature. Robert Hass, an American poet who has translated many of Issa's haikus, comments on Issa's practice of being present: "Issa's poems ask us to see the image as if it were the whole of reality. . . . he's just saying 'is,' 'is,' 'is,' over and over again."

Goes out,
comes back—
the loves of a cat.

Deer licking
first frost
from each other's coats.

The toad! It looks like
it could belch
a cloud.

The crow
walks along there
as if it were tilling the field.

That wren—
looking here, looking there.
You lose something?
——Issa
in *The Essential Haiku*
edited by Robert Hass

Issa loved all creatures and seems to have been especially fond of insects. He wrote over a thousand poems about them, some of which reveal his very accommodating nature.

Don't worry, spiders,
I keep house
casually.

I'm going to roll over,
so please move,
cricket.

Even with insects—
some can sing,
some can't.

The flies in the temple
imitate the hands
    of the people with prayer beads.

The Mosquito at my ear—
does it think
    I'm deaf?
        —ISSA
            in *The Essential Haiku*
            edited by Robert Hass

*Some animals are annoying when they venture into what we consider
to be our territory. Perhaps we would do well to adopt the hospitable
attitude of St. Rose of Lima, a seventeenth-century Peruvian recluse,
who chose mosquitoes as her favorite pets and used to have them sing
to her while she prayed. But perhaps it is easier to admire and discover
the spiritual meanings of butterflies.*

When I was little, growing up in a rural town in the heart of the
country, I used to pursue monarch butterflies across yards and gardens. Like most children, I found them magical and otherworldly, a
piece of the sun tumbling across the grass. I knew about both air-
planes and birds—they made noises and skedaddled through the
sky. And in my foolishness I thought flying insects held only
menace. But there was something special about butterflies: they
were safe, clean, colorful as Christmas wrap. They were delicate
and silent and even a little acrobatic as they grazed on flowers.
Fluttering madly—but moving slowly—from bloom to bloom,
they looked the way my heart sometimes felt. . . .

A hundred million monarchs migrate each year. Gliding, flapping,
hitching rides on thermals like any hawk or eagle, they fly as far as
four thousand miles and as high as two thousand feet, rivaling the
great animal migrations of Africa, the flocking of birds across North
America. Occasionally, one will be bamboozled by the jet stream and
wind up in Mauritius or England. They need only water and nectar
to thrive, but they are sensitive to cold and must spend the winter
somewhere warm or die. So, in the fall, those west of the Rocky

Mountains fly to the coast of California to cluster in select groves of eucalyptus and pine, while eastern monarchs migrate to Mexico. The routes aren't learned—it's straight genetics. . . .

It's easy to get mesmerized watching the monarchs glide overhead, with the sun shining through their wings, as if they were small rooms in which the light had been turned on. A cluster trembles on a branch; then, in a silent explosion, they burst into the air and fly down to a Christmas pine in the direct sun near the road. Sitting on the tips of the branches with their wings spread wide, they might be orange and gold ornaments. They are silent, beautiful, fragile; they are harmless and clean; they are determined; they are graceful; they stalk nothing; they are ingenious chemists; they are a symbol of innocence; they are the first butterfly we learn to call by name. Like the imagination, they dart from one sunlit spot to another. To the Mexicans, who call them *las palomas,* they are the souls of children who died during the past year, fluttering on their way to heaven.

—DIANE ACKERMAN
in *The Rarest of the Rare*

The spiritual practice of wonder is constantly engaged when we observe animals. Columnist Bill Schul recalls an Indian friend telling him, "Look at what the snake has to work with: no hands, no feet, and yet he does very well." Around such marvels, we need to mind our manners.

The Chewong people are one of the numerous Orang Asli, or "original peoples," who have long inhabited the now-dwindling but biologically rich tropical rainforest ecosystems of peninsular Malaysia. In their world, *all* species of animal inherently deserve profound human respect. . . .

Nowhere is this more evident than in the ancient Chewong prohibition against ridiculing animals, as embodied in the sacred laws known collectively in the Chewong language as *talaiden.* One of the major tenets of *talaiden,* concerned specifically with proper human attitudes toward other animal species, mandates that *no animal whatsoever may be teased or laughed at.*

If a group of young children in a Chewong village playfully taunt a captive bird or snake—or even if they are behaving too boisterously in the vicinity of animal flesh that is being prepared, cooked, or eaten—an adult member of the community is likely to step forward, scold them sternly, and insist that they stop it at once.

—DAVID SUZUKI and PETER KNUDTSON
in *Wisdom of the Elders*

Good manners imply the honoring of differences. But as we have lost contact with animals in the wild, and have little concept of how they live outside human influence, we often try to fit them into our narrow preconceptions about them. When you think about it, it is just as bad to stereotype snakes and wolves and hyenas as it is to stereotype races of people.

"Poisonous" plants and creatures can be invoked as protectors, protectors of place. Within a bioregion, they protect the deeper forest and are allies to their ecologies. As allies of human beings, they protect against drowsiness and insensitivity, preventing us from charging through fragile terrain with a heavy foot and blind eye. They teach alertness and respect as we interact with place. They also evoke certain qualities within humans. One can like the jaguar stalk and enjoy the night, blend with the environment and disappear into its body. Protectors teach humans to sing like wolf, to go inside like bear, and to relax like snake.

Human beings have for a long time destroyed the protectors of the wild regions. For many humans, these plants and creatures are dangerous and mean suffering or death. They represent something evil in the world, on this Earth, that should not be ignored. They excite the impulse to eradicate, to kill. Their power both fascinates and intimidates. Here is the enemy! And wolf and mountain lion are shot; coyote is poisoned. That which requires one to be more careful, more mindful, is eliminated. And with the passing of wolf and rattler, poison oak and thorn, passes the integrity of the habitats they guard.

—JOAN HALIFAX
in *The Fruitful Darkness*

Anyone who has lost a beloved pet knows that the passing of an animal can have a profound effect. Terry Tempest Williams takes that kind of caring into the wilderness.

It was a dead swan. Its body lay contorted on the beach like an abandoned lover. I looked at the bird for a long time. There was no blood on its feathers, no sight of gunshot. Most likely, a late migrant from the north slapped silly by a ravenous Great Salt Lake. The swan may have drowned.

I knelt beside the bird, took off my deerskin gloves, and began smoothing feathers. Its body was still limp—the swan had not been dead long. I lifted both wings out from under its belly and spread them on the sand. Untangling the long neck which was wrapped around itself was more difficult, but finally I was able to straighten it, resting the swan's chin flat against the shore.

The small dark eyes had sunk behind the yellow lores. It was a whistling swan. I looked for two black stones, found them, and placed them over the eyes like coins. They held. And, using my own saliva as my mother and grandmother had done to wash my face, I washed the swan's black bill and feet until they shone like patent leather.

I have no idea of the amount of time that passed in the preparation of the swan. What I remember most is lying next to its body and imagining the great white bird in flight.

I imagined the great heart that propelled the bird forward day after day, night after night. Imagined the deep breaths taken as it lifted from the arctic tundra, the camaraderie within the flock. I imagined the stars seen and recognized on clear autumn nights as they navigated south. Imagined their silhouettes passing in front of the full face of the harvest moon. And I imagined the shimmering Great Salt Lake calling the swans down like a mother, the suddenness of the storm, the anguish of its separation.

And I tried to listen to the stillness of its body.

At dusk, I left the swan like a crucifix on the sand. I did not look back.

—Terry Tempest Williams
in *Refuge*

We are all in this place together, and we can best acknowledge this truth by paying our respects to those who live here with us.

We humans think we are smart, but an orchid, for example, knows how to produce noble, symmetrical flowers, and a snail knows how to make a beautiful, well-proportioned shell. Compared with their knowledge, ours is not worth much at all. We should bow deeply before the orchid and the snail and join our palms reverently before the monarch butterfly and the magnolia tree. The feeling of respect for all species will help us recognize the noblest nature in ourselves.

—THICH NHAT HANH
in *Love in Action*

LISTENING

My father could hear a little animal step,
or a moth in the dark against the screen,
and every far sound called the listening out
into places where the rest of us had never been.

More spoke to him from the soft wild night
than came to our porch for us on the wind;
we would watch him look up and his face go keen
till the walls of the world flared, widened.

My father heard so much that we still stand
inviting the quiet by turning the face,
waiting for a time when something in the night
will touch us too from that other place.

—WILLIAM STAFFORD
in *Stories That Could Be True*

During the last year of his life, my father, Amos Michael, developed a friendship with a toad. The toad lived in the flower bed behind the house in Indianapolis. Daddy used to sit on the steps there and talk toward the flowers. My mother could see him from the kitchen window.

Before long, the toad would hop out. Daddy would speak to it in his soft gentle voice, all the while stroking its back. The toad would just sit there and absorb the attention like it was sunshine.

Hearing this story from my mother, I remembered that this was a man who always did have a way with animals. When I was a girl, he used to let our pet chicken ride on his bald head. He encouraged us to take good care of our pets, even helping me secure appropriate food for the salamander I would find each year and keep in a shoebox until Daddy told me it was time for it to return to the wild. When for high school biology class, I had to go birdwatching, Daddy was there right beside me, binoculars raised and camera ready.

After my father's death, the toad was never seen again near the house. But when my mother and I went to the cemetery a few miles away to plant two yews next to Daddy's grave, she was not surprised when a toad hopped out from behind the headstone. Either he had heard about my father or he had followed him, his presence writing an addendum to Daddy's epitaph: "Here lies a friend of toads."

BIRDFOOT'S GRAMPA

The old man
must have stopped our car
two dozen times to climb out
and gather into his hands
the small toads blinded
by our lights and leaping,
live drops of rain.

The rain was falling,
a mist about his white hair
and I kept saying
you can't save them all,
accept it, get back in
we've got places to go.

But, leathery hands full
of wet brown life,
knee deep in the summer
roadside grass,
he just smiled and said
*they have places to go to
too.*
—JOSEPH BRUCHAC
in *Entering Onondaga*

PRACTICING SPIRITUAL LITERACY: ANIMALS

CONVERSATIONS/JOURNAL ENTRIES

- Did you have a pet when you were growing up? How did it enrich your life? List some reasons why children should have pets.
- Talk or write about your most vivid encounter with a wild animal. How did you feel? What did you learn about the animal and about yourself from this experience?
- Has an animal played a part in your dreams recently? What do you think it is trying to tell you?
- Consider the many ways animals are caregivers. For example, they help children develop self-esteem, and they serve as companions to lonely people. How and when have animals helped you care for your soul?
- People see animals through different lenses. To some, a horse is a large, herbivorous quadruped of the family Equidáe. To others, it is a study of motion, beauty, strength, and intelligence. Who or what has most deeply informed your view of animals?
- If you could come back to Earth as an animal, which one would you be? Why?

ACTIVITIES/PROJECTS

- If you want to see your animal friends get a fair shake, join the ASPCA (American Society for the Prevention of Cruelty to Animals), the National Wildlife Federation, PETA (People for the Ethical Treatment of Animals), the World Wildlife Fund, or another advocacy organization for animals. Look in the phone book to locate local offices, or check in the reference section of your library for the addresses of national and international offices.
- The Endangered Species Act is like a "911" distress line for life-forms with a jeopardy status. Find out which animals from your area of the world are currently on the endangered list.
- Reread your favorite fable, story, or book about an animal, and try to figure out what first attracted you to this creature.
- Animal stories can be spurs to activities in the home. *Keepers of the Animals: Native American Stories and Wildlife Activities for Children*, by Michael J. Caduto and Joseph Bruchac, is packed with wonderful tales and related educational projects.

- Several contemporary card systems—consisting of a deck of cards depicting pictures of animals and a companion book giving the stories and myths associated with them—are designed to simulate the ways animal totems have been used in different cultures. One of the most popular, *Medicine Cards*, by Jamie Sams and David Carson, is based on Native American teachings. *Beasts of Albion*, by Miranda Gray, focuses on the animals which appear in British folklore, and *The Druid Animal Oracle* refers to the sacred animals in the Celtic tradition. Try playing with these cards to see if you can tap the wisdom of the animals, perhaps picking an animal "guide" on your birthday.

- Research and report on the lives of individuals, such as St. Francis of Assisi, Dian Fossey, and Albert Schweitzer, who qualify as patron saints of animals.

- There are hundreds of films available on video about animals—from documentaries to cartoons and television nature programs. Here are some of our favorites: *Andre; The Bear; Black Beauty; Charlotte's Web; Free Willy; Gorillas in the Mist; Homeward Bound; Lassie; Never Cry Wolf.* Hold an animal film festival and invite your friends.

SPIRITUAL EXERCISES/RITUALS

- Plan a worship service around the theme that all creatures are to be loved and accepted as signs of God's bounty. Create a banner using lyrics from the hymn by Cecil Frances Alexander: "All things bright and beautiful/All creatures great and small/All things wise and wonderful/The Lord God made them all."

- The Zuni people of New Mexico have used small stone carvings of animal figures as helpers, as conduits to another reality, and as sources of personal renewal. To better understand this devotional system, and to determine whether it could be a meaningful practice for you, read Hal Zina Bennett's book *Zuni Fetishes*.

- Many churches have a "Bless the Animals Liturgy" around the feast day of St. Francis of Assisi in the first week of October. Take your pet to be blessed, or hold a blessing ceremony in your home.

- Create a ritual for the day you bring a new animal into your household. A farewell ritual for the death of a pet is also recommended. Edward Hays's handbook for worship in the home, *Prayers for the Domestic Church*, has prayers for both situations.

LEISURE

All the qualities of a spiritual teacher can be found in a person who can cook an egg perfectly.

—Sufi teacher

Don't cook with ordinary mind and don't cook with ordinary eyes.

—Zen master Dogen

Cooking is one of the best ways for your authentic self to remind your conscious self that you are an artist. Like the union of canvas and pigment, cooking is alchemy, a work of Wholeness-in-progress.

—Sarah Ban Breathnach

When eating a fruit think of the person who planted the tree.

—Vietnamese saying

A true hobby is the achievement through play of something very close to the Creator's delight.

—Robert Farrar Capon

It does no good to think moralistically about how much time we waste. Wasted time is usually good soul time.

—Thomas Moore

Leisure makes the human more human by engaging the heart and broadening the vision, deepening the insight and stretching the soul.

—Joan Chittister

In the rush and noise of life, as you have intervals, step within yourselves and be still. Wait upon God and feel his good presence; this will carry you through your day's business.

—William Penn

Jewish theologian Martin Buber relates a Hasidic tale about a teacher who lived an unusually abundant life. After his death one of his disciples was asked, "What was most important to your teacher?" The student answered, "Whatever he happened to be doing at that moment."

We already have explored how things, places, nature, and animals can be the catalysts which precipitate spiritual experiences. They point us toward the sacred presence in the world and teach us about the lineaments of a whole and meaningful existence. But while these aspects of life may set us on a spiritual path, it is our activities that move us along it.

Every activity can be read for its spiritual meaning. When we act out of the center of our being, when we act with awareness of the ultimate value of existence, when we come alive to our deeper selves and the wider community—then everything we do is a step on our spiritual journey.

This chapter covers a wide range of leisure-time activities. In some of the readings, the authors discover a spiritual truth while engaged in a particular project, similar to what we have seen when people find meaning through time spent in nature or during an encounter with an animal. In many of the readings, however, it is the process—the doing itself—which makes the connection to the spiritual dimension of life.

Take eating, for example. As we eat, we are linked with those who have prepared the food; we are grateful to all the plants and animals who lived and died for this moment; we remember with love and compassion others throughout the world who hunger and thirst as we do; and we are graced with the presence of the Lord of the Universe at the table with us.

We also realize that there is much to value in the food itself. It has healing properties and is able to soothe our souls and lift our spirits. It arouses our senses of sight, smell, and touch. It is capable of transporting us to the past via the memory of a meal, or to another culture by the taste of an unusual dish. It creates fellowship around the table and contributes to the extension of our caring.

Of course, just getting the food to the table unleashes other spiritual impulses. Cooking is a hands-on art mixing intuition, tradition, and passion. Renowned food writer M. F. K. Fisher observes that "our three basic needs for food and security and love are so mixed and mingled and entwined that we cannot straightly think of one without the other." A cook cooks and the universe spins. Or as Native American writer Edward Epse Brown notes, "You need to put yourself into the food, and then the blessedness comes out of it."

In the common corners of our experience, other practices from the Alphabet of Spiritual Literacy are honed. Household chores are exercises in being present. Hobbies offer us opportunities to express ourselves and to nurture our growth through silence, attention, imagination, and wonder. They awaken within us deep reserves of devotion, commitment, and fascination. "We don't do anything special," philosopher Willigis Jager writes about basic activities of the spiritual life, "we try to enter the moment and become one with whatever it is we are doing just then. That's where God is closest to us."

Exercise and sports ground us in our bodies and instruct us in presence and play. Our sabbaths, days off, and vacations give us a welcome relief from our efforts, revealing the spiritual benefits of letting go. And through the celebrations and rituals we design to give meaning and structure to our days, we are able, in philosopher Sam Keen's apt phrase, to "knead the vision of the sacred into the dough of everyday life."

EATING AND COOKING

As an eater, I acknowledge the domain of the sacred. I recognize that the act of eating may be ritualized and inspired. It may be given symbolic meanings that are religious or spiritual in nature. It may even be joyous.

I further agree that eating is an activity that joins me with all humanity. I recognize that to be an eater is to be accountable for the care of the earth and its resources. I acknowledge that despite our differences, we are all ultimately nourished by the same source. As such, I agree to share.

I recognize that at its deepest level eating is an affirmation of life. Each time I eat I agree somewhere inside to continue life on earth. I acknowledge that this choice to eat is a fundamental act of love and nourishment, a true celebration of my existence. As a human being on earth, I agree to be an eater. I choose life again and again and again . . .

—MARC DAVID
in *Nourishing Wisdom*

How, when, and what we eat makes a spiritual statement, which is why this ordinary, daily act is ritualized in many cultures and traditions.

Since the beginning of time, people who trust one another, care for one another, and are deeply connected to one another have shared food as a sign of and a reaffirmation of their relationship.

When attention is paid to this sharing, it takes on a ritual character. The nurturing of the body becomes a metaphor of the mutual nourishing of lives. Every time we hold hands and say a blessing before a meal, every time we lift a glass and say fine words to one another, every time we eat in peace and grace together, we have celebrated the covenants that bind us together.

—ROBERT FULGHUM
in *From Beginning to End*

In Jewish teachings . . . it is taught that when a person eats, he should concentrate totally on the food and the experience of eating it, clearing the mind of all other thoughts. He should have in mind that the taste of the food is also an expression of the Divine in the food, and that by eating it, he is incorporating this spark of the Divine into his body. A person can also have in mind that he will dedicate the energy that he will obtain from this food to God's service. It is taught that when a person does this, it is counted as if the food he is eating is a sacrifice on the Great Altar in Jerusalem.

Therefore, eating itself can be a form of meditation as well as a means through which one can draw closer to God.

—ARYEH KAPLAN
in *Jewish Meditation*

The [Native American] way of eating is one of the best ways to understand their companionship with silence. Eating is slow, deliberately so, and is given enough space to happen. The bread is dipped with attention into the sauce, observed with appreciation, taken to the mouth with a kind of lingering anticipation. I enjoy watching those around me separate the food with care, relish the individual flavors, consider the time it took to prepare each, wonder from whose kitchen or pot it came. It is not that Indians do not speak during a meal, but conversation is not primary. Eating is. It gets full and unembarrassed attention. Usually when the people gather for a celebration or a memorial meal, there is an impressive gathering of foods. The lowly pinto bean receives its share of interest and appreciation. Soups provide ample occasion for reflection. I have found the *act* of eating with Indian peoples is usually a quiet, pleasant meditation of gifts. Feelings of gratitude come easy. Much communication goes on during the meal, but talk is not steady.

Because eating is so daily, there is a beauty in that kind of quiet, thoughtful sharing.

—MARY JOSÉ HOBDAY
in *Western Spirituality*
edited by Matthew Fox

Brother Lawrence, a seventeenth-century Christian monk, is known for viewing cooking as a way of practicing the presence of God. Of his kitchen, he writes: "The time of business does not with me differ from the time of prayer, and in the noise and clatter of my kitchen, while several persons are calling for different things, I possess God in as great tranquility as if I were upon my knees at the blessed sacrament." Cookbook author Bettina Vitell also views the kitchen as a sacred place; it is where she practices mindfulness.

The kitchen is a place that sharpens us. It's a place that wakes us up. Our sense of smell becomes keener. We taste with greater subtlety. We see with more clarity and our movements become quick and sure.

But there are times when we are not as sensitive, not as focused. We are distracted and nothing seems to go right. In the kitchen the results are easy to notice. The sauce burns, the bread doesn't rise, and dishes slip out of our hands.

Cooking requires that we be fully present. This is one of its greatest teachings.

It keeps bringing us back to what is happening in the moment and continually calls our attention to what we are doing.

We smell when the cake is ready to come out of the oven and we taste when the soup is almost done to perfection. When the water boils on the stove, we turn down the heat.

Through cooking we can become more responsive to what is happening around us. In the very same way that the Chinese cook was able to sharpen his knives just by using them, we can sharpen our lives by living them with awareness, moment by moment.

—BETTINA VITELL
in *A Taste of Heaven and Earth*

Cooking that taps our creativity, that we throw ourselves into with desire and delight, is sacred to the core.

Man . . . is the animal who cooks his food. But cooking isn't just heating things up, just as architecture isn't simply the piling of blocks one on top of another. Cooking is the expansion, by reason and skill, of flavor into art. All distinctively human activity involves a kind of priestly lifting of nature into forms that, while new to nature itself, are actually elations and perfections of it. . . .

. . . God, if we believe the Scriptures, created the world out of delight; and he runs it, not by shoving things around with main force, but by attraction—by desire for Himself as the Highest Good. . . .

. . . Likewise, all cooking is physical activity; but the cook is drawn, throughout the process, by the good of taste.

Seasoning, therefore, is a sacrament, a real presence in a specific matter, of the desire for the Highest Good.

—ROBERT FARRAR CAPON
in *Food for Thought*

"What's so original about this man?" asked a visitor. "All he gives you is a hash of stories, proverbs, and sayings from other Masters."

A woman disciple smiled. She once had a cook, she said, who made the most wonderful hash in the world.

"How on earth do you make it, my dear? You must give me the recipe."

The cook's face glowed with pride. She said, "Well, ma'am, I'll tell yer: beef's nothin'; pepper's nothin'; onion's nothin'; but when I throws *myself* into the hash—that's what makes it what it is."

—ANTHONY DE MELLO
in *More One Minute Nonsense*

Cooks often offer improvised courses in human nature while they are working.

I used to love to watch my grandmother make bread for the Sabbath. Elbow-deep in flour, she taught me kitchen psychology while braiding the dough. One morning, when I was five or six, she said, without lifting her eyes from the table, "People have energy which makes their lives yeast. Their souls get sick if they don't let it out. It gets confused. It doesn't have a way of rising so it twists and strangles instead of becoming a new pattern." Her fingers tangled in the dough as she spoke and her beautiful bread became a mass of chaos. She struggled to free her hands. In the process, the shape of the bread was destroyed.

"Then we have to go back to the beginning and start again with the kneading and the rising," she said as she began to punch the dough flat again.

—DAWNA MARKOVA
in *No Enemies Within*

Be gentle when you touch bread.
Let it not lie, uncared for,
Unwanted.
So often bread is taken for granted.
There is such beauty in bread—
Beauty of surf and soil,
Beauty of patient toil.
Wind and rain have caressed it,
Christ often blessed it.
Be gentle when you touch bread.

—CELTIC PRAYER
in *The Open Gate*
by David Adam

I was just thinking
one morning
during meditation
how much alike
hope
and baking powder are:
quietly
getting what is
best in me
to rise,

awakening
the hint of eternity
within.

I always think of that
when I eat biscuits now
and wish
that I could be
more faithful
to the hint of eternity,
the baking power
in me.
—MACRINA WIEDERKEHR
in *Seasons of Your Heart*

Soup is a reliable friend that will never let you down. Next, two readings explore the many meanings associated with a pot of soup, and then, Laurie Colwin pays tribute to this soulful treat.

What do you see here, my friend? Just an ordinary old cooking pot, black with soot and full of dents.

It is standing on the fire on top of that old wood stove, and the water bubbles and moves the lid as the white steam rises to the ceiling. Inside the pot is boiling water, chunks of meat with bone and fat, plenty of potatoes.

It doesn't seem to have a message, that old pot, and I guess you don't give it a thought. Except the soup smells good and reminds you that you are hungry. . . .

But I'm an Indian. I think about ordinary, common things like this pot. The bubbling water comes from the rain cloud. It represents the sky. The fire comes from the sun which warms us all—men, animals, trees. The meat stands for the four-legged creatures, our animal brothers, who gave of themselves so that we should live. The steam is living breath. It was water; now it goes up to the sky, becomes a cloud again. These things are sacred. Looking at that pot full of good soup, I am thinking how, in this simple manner, Wakan Tanka takes care of me. We Sioux spend a lot of time thinking about everyday things, which in our mind are mixed up with the spiritual. We see in the world around us many symbols that teach us the meaning of life. . . . You could notice if you wanted to, but you are usually too busy. We Indians live in a world of symbols and images where the spiritual and the commonplace are one. . . . To us they are part of nature, part of ourselves—the earth, the sun, the wind and the rain, stones, trees, animals, even little insects like ants and grasshoppers. We try to understand them not with the head but with the heart, and we need no more than a hint to give us the meaning.

—LAME DEER
in *Lame Deer, Seeker of Visions*

I made soup tonight
and all my ancestors danced
in the pot, with the barley
the beans, the knuckle and neck bones,
enriching this brew;
Here women joined
love and ancient wisdom, the knowledge
salt and pepper bring; secrets
that are ritual and legacy.

—ELSA GARCIA
in *Open Mind*
by Diane Mariechild

In all your life you will be hard-pressed to find something as simple, soothing, and forgiving, as consoling as lentil soup. You can take things out of it or put things into it. It can be fancy or plain . . .

Lentils are friendly—the Miss Congeniality of the bean world. They take well to almost anything. But let us start from scratch. The most minimal lentil soup calls for a cup of lentils; a quart of water or stock of any kind; one sliced carrot; one or two cloves of garlic, minced; one small diced onion; and there you are. This makes a nice plain soup to which no hungry person can object.

—LAURIE COLWIN
in *More Home Cooking*

"O taste and see that the Lord is good," goes Psalm 34:8. That verse comes to life at our dinner table whenever we eat corn on the cob. There is something very special about this food. Perhaps it's all those memories of play.

That is the magic of corn, America's most emblematic food. It evokes memories of sunburn and rowing and swimming in the lake or wandering on the beach looking for shells. It is true soul food and requires of the exhausted cook nothing more than a large pot of boiling water and some people willing to do the shucking. Furthermore, it provides entertainment for small children, who find corn silk irresistible.

—LAURIE COLWIN
in *More Home Cooking*

Now consider the lowly onion. In the next two readings, it evokes the spiritual practices of mystery and reverence.

I see God in onions. I always have. I remember when I first saw my mother slicing into an onion when I was about six. I stopped my playing, awestruck. What is this vegetable that is so pure, so watery-white, so many-layered in concentric rings that make mounds of perfect circles as they fall open onto the cutting board? I begged her to let me cut some, despite her warning that it would make my eyes burn. I can remember the concentration and reverence welling up within me as I awkwardly tried to make perfect slices. My eyes *did* burn and I had to stop after a few cuts, but I vowed that I would understand onions some day and cook with them myself.

My contemplation of the Mystery in the onion continues to this day. As an artist I have paid homage to my friend the onion by creating a stained glass window of an underground bulb that now hangs in a local food co-op. As a cook I have learned how to coax the sweetness out of an onion, and to tame its fire into mellow good humor. I can cut them now without crying, but not without pausing for a brief moment. Red onions are especially divine. I hold a slice up to the sunlight pouring in through the kitchen window, and it glows like a fine piece of antique glass. Cool watery-white with layers delicately edged with imperial purple . . . strong, humble, peaceful . . . with that fiery nub of spring green in the center, aspiring to sprout and become more . . . "Ah! Look at *this* one!" I cry to my husband and daughter nearby. They look at each other and smile at me tolerantly. "That's a really nice one." They don't "get" God in onions the way I do, but they know that we Mystics have to stick together.

—MARY HAYES-GRIECO
in *The Kitchen Mystic*

THE TRAVELING ONION

When I think how far the onion has traveled
just to enter my stew today, I could kneel and praise
all small forgotten miracles,
crackly paper peeling on the drainboard,
pearly layers in smooth agreement,
the way knife enters onion
and onion falls apart on the chopping block,
a history revealed.

And I would never scold the onion
for causing tears.
It is right that tears fall
for something small and forgotten.
How at meal, we sit to eat,
commenting on texture of meat or herbal aroma
but never on the translucence of onion,
now limp, now divided,
or its traditionally honorable career:
For the sake of others,
disappear.

—NAOMI SHIHAB NYE
in *Words Under the Words*

The kitchen is a place to exercise our imagination. Poet and novelist Nancy Willard gives us a lesson in just what this means.

HOW TO STUFF A PEPPER

Now, said the cook, I will teach you
how to stuff a pepper with rice.

Take your pepper green, and gently,
for peppers are shy. No matter which side
you approach, it's always the backside.
Perched on green buttocks, the pepper sleeps.
In its silk tights, it dreams
of somersaults and parsley,
of the days when the sexes were one.

Slash open the sleeve
as if you were cutting a paper lantern,
and enter a moon, spilled like a melon,
a fever of pearls,
a conversation of glaciers.
It is a temple built to the worship
of morning light.

I have sat under the great globe
of seeds on the roof of that chamber,
too dazzled to gather the taste I came for.
I have taken the pepper in hand,
smooth and blind, a runt in the rich
evolution of roses and ferns.
You say I have not yet taught you

to stuff a pepper?
Cooking takes time.

Next time we'll consider the rice.

—NANCY WILLARD
in *Carpenter of the Sun*

*And here, from human potential philosopher Jean Houston, is an
inspiring tutorial on the stuffed artichoke.*

For our next course, I offer the very essence of maturity, a stuffed
artichoke, prepared in the way I was taught by Nana, my Sicilian
grandmother. The artichoke is the great bulb of life. It is prickly on

the outside, a fortress of walls within walls, yet within it contains both a culture and a psychology. In this it is the mirror of yourself. You may be surrounded by walls of egotism, arrogance, and fear, a well-defended citadel of mistrust and misunderstanding, pocked by too many assailants. But inside, as with the artichoke, is a very soft heart. Because one's heart has been wounded so many times, it is shielded by tough, pointy leaves and must be opened very carefully.

Like a life, the artichoke gains richness and savor from being combined with many flavors. I slice off just the top third. Then I crush the bulb a little bit so that the leaves open up, as we've all been crushed and our layers exposed—wearing our hearts on our sleeves. Then I make a stuffing of bread crumbs, the sacred grain, the staff of life, to which I add basil for greening, oregano for piquancy, and garlic—much garlic—for pungency. I also add the bite of freshly grated aged cheese, romano or peccorino or parmesan, the kindness of olive oil, and the grounding of salt. And for spiciness, I will often put in a bit of cardamom, which I'll grind, or coriander as a strange Sicilian undercurrent. Sometimes I even throw in a little bit of pickled oregano bud in the form of chopped caper. Then I mix that up and carefully stuff each leaf, spiraling inward to the center choke.

When it has been slowly braised to just the right moment of tenderness, the stuffed artichoke becomes a hologram, each part containing the whole. It symbolizes how each aspect of a life has the potential for a full relation to the totality. The sweet does not remain simply sweet. It is set off by the sour and the bitter and the pungent. The same is true of the salty parts: even tears contain a bit of greening. Life as usual imitates cuisine, and the art of cooking is a metaphor for composing a life.

—JEAN HOUSTON
in *A Mythic Life*

Food images can be used to reflect upon the big picture, as in the passage above, and to illustrate the nature of the spiritual quest, as Coleman Barks suggests in the following introduction to Jelaluddin Rumi's poem about a chickpea.

Rumi's image of a disciple is a chickpea that sprouts and enjoys the rainy gardens of sexual pleasure. It matures to its hardened form, then gets picked and thrown in the cooking pot. The cook's tending is careful and constant and, in Rumi's case, garrulous. Gradually the disciple softens and takes on flavors the cook adds. Eventually he or she becomes tasty enough to be appealing to those who in the Sufi tradition are called the True Human Beings. So the chickpea moves from garden to cooking pot to a taste for the cook, finally to become sustenance for a mysterious community.

CHICKPEA TO COOK

A chickpea leaps almost over the rim of the pot
where it's being boiled.
"Why are you doing this to me?"

The cook knocks him down with the ladle.

"Don't you try to jump out.
You think I'm torturing you.
I'm giving you flavor,
so you can mix with spices and rice
and be the lovely vitality of a human being.

Remember when you drank rain in the garden.
That was for this."

Grace first. Sexual pleasure,
then a boiling new life begins,
and the Friend has something good to eat.

Eventually the chickpea
will say to the cook,
    "Boil me some more.
Hit me with the skimming spoon.
I can't do this by myself. . . ."
       —RUMI
          in *The Essential Rumi*
          translated by Coleman Barks
          with John Moyne, A. J. Arberry,
          and Reynold Nicholson

Megan McKenna, a prolific Catholic writer and teacher, is always on the lookout for fresh images of the Scriptures.

A good image of the scriptures is the Greek dessert pastry baklava. It is rich, about an inch thick and cut into inch squares. It is made of thin layers of philo dough, honey, nuts and butter pressed down and packed firmly together. A good pastry maker packs the dough into one hundred and twenty or more layers. And when we read the scriptures, we take one layer at a time and savor it. Each time we eat a layer and incorporate it into our flesh and blood, we can discover another layer and eat more. But not to swallow, digest, and incorporate it into our bodies and lives means that we may just keep eating the same layer over and over again.

—MEGAN MCKENNA
in *Not Counting Women and Children*

In Chinese and Japanese monasteries, cooks are regarded as virtuosos whose preparation of food is a devotional practice.

Early in the trip I asked for vegetarian food. At every meal I have been offered a bowl of rice and cabbage cooked in a Northern Chinese style. Sometimes a dish of peanuts has livened the cuisine. I expect no change in the fare, and wait patiently for my food. The others begin to eat. They finish their meal. I am still waiting. I wonder if my dinner has been forgotten.

I am ready to fill my bowl with plain rice when the waiter walks into the dining room carrying an array of dishes which he arranges before me. He returns with more until there are almost a dozen dishes on the table. This is no meal. It's an offering.

Everyone becomes silent before such artistry. Wild black mushrooms shimmer in a glossy red sweet-and-sour sauce, leafy greens are bright and fresh and warmed with ginger. Spicy bean curd is flecked with fiery red peppers. Tiny slivers of carrots, fresh-sliced bamboo shoots, and deep-fried gluten puffs float in golden sesame sauce.

I stare at the food in awe, my mind blank. The only sound comes from the ceiling fan rhythmically stirring the humid air. Then the cook enters and approaches our table. He bows low before me. He is grateful to me, he explains, because since his years as a cook in a Buddhist monastery, he had little opportunity to cook vegetarian food for anyone who appreciates it.

The wild mushrooms, he tells me, were picked in a nearby forest. The greens are from gardens known for the quality of their vegetables. He bows slowly, and thanks me once again. I stumble over my own words of gratitude as he quietly disappears into the kitchen. I never see him again.

I didn't sleep that night. The cook's reverence and humility sliced through years of protective hardness and caught me without warning. His food was saturated with love, and its nurturance was almost too much to bear.

—ANNE SCOTT
in *Serving Fire*

Even the piles of food in the supermarket can function as temple bells, reminding us to appreciate the beauty of the creation.

Love life
everything—
pale lights
markets medley
of green lettuce,
red cherries,
golden grapes, and
purple eggplants—
all so extraordinary!
Incredible!
You get excited,
you talk to people
and people talk
to you,
you touch
and they touch you.
All this is magical,
like some
endless
celebration.

—EUGENE IONESCO
in *Learning by Heart*
by Corita Kent and Jan Steward

A simple act like drinking tea becomes a spiritual experience through the practice of being present.

Ryutan Shin stayed with Tenno (748–807) for three years, but having no instructions in Zen, as he expected, he asked, "It is some time since my arrival here, but I have yet had no words from you, master, in the way of spiritual teaching." Said the master, "Ever since your arrival here I have been teaching you in matters of spiritual enlightenment." Ryutan did not understand this and asked again, "When were such matters ever imparted to me?" The master's reply was: "When you bring me tea to drink, do I not take it? When you bring me food to eat, do I not accept it? When you bow to me, do I not acknowledge it by nodding? When was I ever at fault in instructing you in matters spiritual?" Dogo stood still for a while thinking about it. The master said, "If you want to see into the matter, see it at once; deliberation makes you miss the point for ever." This is said to have awakened the disciple to the truth of Zen.

—D. T. SUZUKI
in *Living by Zen*

Just a cup of tea. Just another opportunity for healing. Just the hand reaching out to receive the handle of the cup. Just noticing hot. Noticing texture and fragrance. Just a cup of tea. Just this moment in newness. Just the hand touching the cup. Just the arm retracting. The fragrance increasing as the cup nears the lips. So present. Noticing the bottom lip receiving heat from the cup, the top lip arched to receive the fluid within. Noticing the first taste of tea before the tea even touches the lips. The fragrance and heat rising into the mouth. The first noticing of flavor. The touch of warm tea on willing tongue. The tongue moving the tea about in the mouth. The intention to swallow. The warmth that extends down into the stomach. What a wonderful cup of tea. The tea of peace, of satisfaction. Drinking a cup of tea, I stop the war.

—STEPHEN LEVINE
in *Healing into Life and Death*

I

IMAGINATION

"Our spiritual famine has concluded, we are just beginning to restore the honor of the imagination," Episcopal priest Lauren Artress writes.

Artists, poets, and writers of all stripes reverence this faculty. As the expression of our creativity, it enables us to boldly explore the world.

"I am certain of nothing but the holiness of the heart's affections and the truth of imagination," English poet John Keats declares. It is his passport to both the inner and outer depths of things.

Another English poet, Percy Shelley, asserts: "The great instrument of moral good is imagination." We often forget that there are creative ways of bringing about change in our communities and society at large.

When Jesus suggests that we love our enemies, he is imaginatively expanding our concept of what it means to be a good person.

When Swiss psychologist C. G. Jung asks us to love those parts of ourselves that we find unappealing and dreadful, he is imaginatively challenging us to take a new path to personal renewal.

English children's book writer C. S. Lewis describes imagination as "the organ for meaning." It is the faculty that enables us to go beneath the surface to plumb the depths of our experience. Imagination also makes mystics of us all by encouraging us to put things together in new combinations.

"Imagination is the secret marrow of civilization," says Henry Ward Beecher, a nineteenth-century Protestant minister. "It is the very eye of faith." This power feeds both our appreciation of the present and our dreams for the future.

"There is no life of the spirit without the imagination," psychoanalyst Ann Ulanov writes. It opens up our eyes to new readings of the significance of our surroundings:

A tree is not only a beautiful part of nature but a spiritual teacher.

A clothespin is not only a practical object but a devotional resource when it sets the stage for meditation while we are hanging up the wash.

And a television drama is not just a source of entertainment but a gateway to spiritual transformation when we choose to make it so.

Imagination helps us become all we are meant to be as we take new routes into the world, explore creative ways of reframing our experiences, and use spiritual literacy to find meaning all around us.

And the best part is that with imagination there is always something new to be felt, seen, known, and appreciated. Writer and teacher Robert Sardello suggests that we really bring our souls alive "with the discipline of daily clothing the world with imagination." Try it and you'll be amazed at all the wild possibilities!

What would happen if we brought the same attention to our morning cup of coffee as the Japanese bring to the tea ceremony?

Coffee or tea or plain hot water are warming, soothing, stimulating. Preparing and serving a hot drink can be automatic or engrossing, sloppy or artistic, character-eroding or character-building.

More than once I've drawn attention to the Japanese tea ceremony. The ceremony is simply the preparation and serving and drinking of a bitter form of green tea. How mundane! Yet how exquisite! Exquisite because the movements and attitudes have been refined over generations and over years of practice by skilled participants so that every movement is choreographed for simplicity and grace.

How do you prepare and pour your coffee? How do you measure out sugar and cream? How do you stir? How do you raise the cup to your lips? Have you considered the behaviors and attitudes with which you participate in the simple ceremony of coffee drinking? From the moment of deciding to drink, through heating the water and taking the cup from the cupboard, until the cup is washed and put away, there is much to fill attention. When carried out properly, drinking a cup of coffee is no small thing.

—DAVID K. REYNOLDS
in *Pools of Lodging for the Moon*

Food, as one of the Creator's gifts, deserves to be treated with respect.

Food is already holy, not profane, and may never under any circumstances be desecrated, even as a possible demonstration of something that could be more sacred. We say grace before our meals—not to make our food holy, but to acknowledge gratefully that it is already holy. We don't gobble our food, play with it, or throw it around, because food is too sacred to be violated. A "food war" I witnessed in a college cafeteria was one of the most painful desecrations of sacred matter that I have ever suffered.

—WILLIAM MCNAMARA
in *Christian Mysticism*

The next time you have a tangerine to eat, please put it in the palm of your hand and look at it in a way that makes the tangerine real. You do not need a lot of time to do it, just two or three seconds. Looking at it, you can see a beautiful blossom with sunshine and rain, and you can see a tiny fruit forming. You can see the continuation of the sunshine and the rain, and the transformation of the baby fruit into the fully developed tangerine in your hand. You can see the color change from green to orange and you can see the tangerine sweetening. Looking at a tangerine in this way, you will see that everything in the cosmos is in it—sunshine, rain, clouds, trees, leaves, everything. Peeling the tangerine, smelling it, and tasting it, you can be very happy.

—THICH NHAT HANH
in *Mindfulness and Meaningful Work*
edited by Claude Whitmyer

CHORES

According to Jewish teaching, even such mundane chores as washing the dishes become acts of worship when they are done with consciousness and intention, and the Zen perspective does not seem so very different.

Now imagine that you are washing the dishes. You are concentrating on the act of washing, clearing the mind of all other thoughts. Any other thought that enters the mind is gently pushed aside, so that the task at hand totally fills the mind. You are totally aware of the act you are doing, and as far as you are concerned, nothing else exists in the universe.

Concentrate for a moment on a dish and realize that it is an expression of God's will and essence. Although it may be hidden, there is a spark of the Divine in the dish. There is also a spark of the Divine in the water with which you are washing the dish. When a person develops such an awareness, then even the most mundane act can become an intimate experience of the Divine.

—ARYEH KAPLAN
in *Jewish Meditation*

235

In the kitchen you can bring this presence to all your actions just by being more attentive.

As you wash the dishes, notice how your fingers curl around the edges of a plate or cup, feeling its shape and size. Become aware of the texture of smooth porcelain or the roughness of pottery. Feel the weight of each dish.

When you have thoroughly explored one dish, pick up another and explore it with this same sense of newness. Feel the sensations that come from the object in your hands; the perfect roundness of a bowl, the delicate weight of a wineglass, the delightful balance of a fork or spoon, each time realizing more fully the potential of your sense of touch.

As you try this out, you may become aware of your breathing. Notice too how you are standing. Perhaps you can feel how the weight of each object influences you.

What happens when you reach to the top shelf to put a bowl away? Your arms may need to find a different way of holding it for more balance. Become aware of your connection with the floor. Does it support you as you reach to put away the dishes?

Take time to feel what is most natural and easy.

The Zen master Suzuki Roshi said that there is no such thing as an enlightened person, there is just enlightened activity. By arriving at an attitude of quiet curiosity, even the most common task becomes an opportunity to explore our nature.

—BETTINA VITELL
in *A Taste of Heaven and Earth*

Chores give us practice in the disciplines of love and devotion. St. Thérèse of Lisieux, a nineteenth-century Carmelite Catholic nun, is convinced that God can best be served through little things or trifles. "To ecstasy, I prefer the monotony of daily toil," she writes. She advocates bringing care, compassion, and joy to the performance of small tasks. Two contemporary writers have similar views.

When we clean up after ourselves, whether it's a spilled jar, a broken chair, a disorganized study, or a death, we can see and reflect upon our own life and perhaps envision a new way that won't be so broken, so violent, so unconscious. By cleaning up our own homes we take responsibility for ourselves and for preserving what we love. But if our attitude is "my kingdom is not of this world," then there is a disturbing possibility that we'll finally do away with the world rather than clean it or ourselves. The feminine attitude of getting down on our hands and knees to scour—and at the most primitive level look at what needs cleaning—deserves our attention. For in this gesture of bended knees is some humility, some meditation, some time to recognize the first foundation of our homes.

—BRENDA PETERSON
in *Nature and Other Mothers*

The simplest, most direct method of creating sacredness into everyday surroundings is cleaning. I know this activity is usually relegated to the realm of drudgery, but it can become a practical means of infusing consciousness into your surroundings. Sacredness is experienced in the qualities of purity, orderliness, balance, and renewal. All of these are achieved through cleaning. In the process, neglected objects and corners of our living environments receive love and attention. The glow of consciousness passes into floors, furniture, dishes, and countertops, making them shine. Without spending a penny on redesign, the room is transformed.

—ANTHONY LAWLOR
in *The Temple in the House*

A young woman in Gail Godwin's novel Father Melancholy's Daughter *observes a holy day in Lent by cleaning her house.*

I decided to honor Maundy Thursday by cleaning the kitchen. This was the day for getting clean and starting over. In ancient times, penitents prostrated themselves before the congregation, and after prayers were read over them and hands laid on them, they were readmitted to communion. If you were high and mighty, it was your especial duty to humble yourself on this day, in keeping with the *mandatum* of Christ, "that you love one another even as I have loved you." Queen Elizabeth the First "kept her Maundy" in the great hall at Westminster by washing the feet of twenty poor women. In monasteries all over Christendom today, abbots and superiors knelt down on bare floors, washing and patting dry the feet of the lowliest kitchen monks. . . .

I attacked the spice shelf, unscrewing each bottle and sniffing; if there wasn't a definite smell of an herb or a spice, it went sailing into the trash bag. Better to have a clean space filled with nothing, than a cluttered space filled with things that were of no use to you anymore. My rubric for getting through this day.

I did a ruthless number on the refrigerator. Out went the rest of Miriam Stacy's tuna and noodle casserole, plastic container and all, . . . We had far too many plastic and metal-foil containers that jammed drawers when we tried to open them or clattered down on our heads from top cabinets, when we were looking for something else. . . .

The big black plastic garbage bag was filling fast. One must purify one's refrigerator with the same rigor as one purified one's heart.

—GAIL GODWIN
in *Father Melancholy's Daughter*

In the video series Discovering Everyday Spirituality with Thomas Moore, *best-selling author Robert Fulghum irons his shirt. He explains that this activity, which he does himself every day, is a spiritual practice. It provides connections to his past as he remembers the woman who taught him to iron; it allows him to pay attention to details, which are important in his life; and it is a quiet time for reflection.*

In the same series, poet and essayist Kathleen Norris is seen hanging her wash on the line. She explains how this chore gives her time for silence, meditation, and gratitude for the blessings of her senses.

I get started early, before six. It promises to be a good laundry day: a steady wind but not too strong. I come by my love of laundry honestly: my earliest memory is of my mother pulling clothes in from the sky on a line that ran out our apartment window in Washington, D.C. . . .

. . . I think of a friend who was dying, who had saved up all her laundry for my visit. "I can't trust my husband with it," she whispered conspiratorially. "Men don't understand that clothes must be hung on a line."

She was right. Hanging up wet clothes gives me time alone

under the sky to think, to grieve, and gathering the clean clothes in, smelling the sunlight on them, is victory.

—KATHLEEN NORRIS
in *Dakota*

HOBBIES

When I was a young boy, I collected foreign stamps. There were many things about this hobby that appealed to me. I enjoyed going to the store and purchasing stamps from different countries. Putting them in a book and meticulously arranging them on the page was part of a regular discipline that helped keep me centered.

The stamps were friends that had been sought out and honored. Each stamp was also a mystery because it had passed through several hands and traveled to different places before settling down with me. Just touching the stamps enabled me to move in my imagination beyond the boundaries of my small world.

I recalled my childhood hobby when I saw the film Searching for Bobby Fisher. *Seven-year-old Josh is a chess prodigy who learns new strategies from two very different teachers. One is an aggressive speed-chess player who makes the game into play. The other is a stern chess master who wants Josh to concentrate on cerebral competition. Both of them, as well as Josh's father, a sports writer, emphasize the importance of winning. His mother, on the other hand, wants her son to be true to the sensitive, feeling side of his personality. After losing a critical match, Josh fears that he does not have the killer instinct necessary to be a consistent winner. Eventually, however, he finds a way to be true to himself by balancing the need for mastery with his desire to play with compassion. Whatever our hobbies, they can become our spiritual teachers, once we learn to read their multiple meanings.*

Consider a jigsaw puzzle. Each piece has its place and no other piece can fit that place. Yet no one piece makes sense on its own. Each piece needs the whole for its integrity and coherence. And the whole needs each piece to fulfill its purpose and bring meaning and order to the puzzle. Once a piece is in its proper place, its separateness is surrendered. We know a piece is in its place when it blends with the whole and disappears.

What is true for a puzzle is true for Reality, with one exception: There is no hand putting us in our place. We must do that for ourselves. We must discover our place and take it. And when we do this, we discover the integrity and meaning of the whole; we discover the divine energy that flows through all things and links each to the other and all to God.

—RABBI RAMI M. SHAPIRO
in *Wisdom of the Jewish Sages*

There are many who garden in their spare time and find in this hobby a chance to be close to the earth, to work slowly and considerately, and to simply face the task before them. For those of us who come from families of gardeners, our gardens can also provide a feeling of connection with our ancestors, which is another sign of spirituality.

LISTEN

Standing in the garden,
left hand laden
with ripe strawberries. The sun

beams off the glassy
backs of flies. Three
birds in the birch tree.

They must have been there
all year.

My mother, my grandmother,
stood like this
in their gardens.

I am 43.
This year I have planted my feet
on this ground

and am practicing
growing up out of my legs
like a tree.

—LINDA LANCIONE MOYER
in *Christianity and Crisis*

Visits to museums can be like pilgrimages to holy places, as psychologist Shaun McNiff describes in the next reading.

My visits to the Peabody Museum changed the way I looked at the city. Old houses and streets lived many lives. They were simultaneously in the present and the past. Every day in grammar school I walked by the House of Seven Gables, and the Custom House, where Nathaniel Hawthorne worked, and looked out over Derby Wharf. The spirits of the previous generations were carefully collected in the Peabody Museum, which offered distinctly local and physical reflections of change, continuity, death, preservation. The museum felt like my private temple of the imagination, my treasury of images and soulful things. I traveled back to Federal Salem, rowed in wooden boats with Herman Melville and Queequeg, and threw harpoons from bowsprits. As I looked at the varied and grotesque metal heads and hooks of the harpoons, I imagined myself as a whale, stricken and dying. I bowed and drank tea with Chinese silk traders, canoed and swam with Polynesians, and swung the war clubs in the museum's glass cabinets imagining the killing of a human being.

—Shaun McNiff
in *Earth Angels*

We lived just a half-block from a museum when I was a girl, and I used to imagine myself into other times just as Shaun McNiff does in the passage above. However, I don't trace my interests in history and other cultures to those museum visits. I inherited the lifelong learner gene from my mother, Wildred Michael.

When she was a young wife in Indianapolis, my mother and about ten of her friends organized the Study Club. Every month they met at one of their homes where the hostess presented a program, usually focusing on something she had read, a place she had visited, or a current project. Everywhere else she lived, Mother was active in similar groups. Even her solitary time was spent studying, and she made our family trips into quests for new knowledge. I now see my mother's zeal for learning as one of her ways of being spiritual.

I remember one evening, when my father was saying good night to me, we had, as was our custom, what he called a "brief evening chat."

Putting on a serious face and feeling a bit nervous at the prospect of challenging what by then I knew to be a much-cherished activity, I managed to voice my query: "Why do Mom and you read out loud to each other?"...

I can still remember my father's words as he tried to tell me, with patient conviction, that novels contain "reservoirs of wisdom," out of which he and our mother were drinking. A visual image suddenly crossed my mind—books floating like flotsam and jetsam on Houghton's Pond, near Milton, Massachusetts, where we lived. I never told my father what had appeared to me, but he knew its essence by my glazed eyes. He made his pitch anyway: "Your mother and I feel rescued by these books. We read them gratefully. You'll also be grateful one day to the authors."

—ROBERT COLES
in *The Call of Stories*

In this book, we present "spiritual readings" of the world. We use the term very broadly to mean any take on our experience that looks for meaning and purpose. There is also a specific kind of spiritual reading called Lectio Divina. *Catholic priest Henri J. M. Nouwen explains that it is "reading with a desire to let God come closer to us. . . . The purpose of the spiritual reading is not to master knowledge or information, but to let God's Spirit master us. Strange as it may sound, spiritual reading means to let ourselves be read by God." Dorothy Day, cofounder of the Catholic Worker Movement, did this kind of reading.*

She considered books to be like so many cherished friends to whom she returned again and again to take up the conversation, as it were, wherever it left off at a prior reading. As Dorothy continued to mature, she entered each text with new perspective, so that it became a fresh conversation, with deeper insights gained. She found in reading a spiritual sustenance for everyday life. Nor was this nourishment limited to those works commonly associated with spiritual reading. Whether it be Scripture, a novel by Dostoevsky, or other fine writings, Dorothy was of the opinion that "The books will always be there. If we give up many other distractions, we can turn to them. We can browse among the millions of words written and often just what we need can nourish us, enlighten us, strengthen us—in fact, be our food just as Christ, the Word is also our food."

—Brigid O'Shea Merriman
in *Searching for Christ*

We can make any book into a holy text by entering into a dialogue with it and expressing ourselves freely in the process.

Ideally the pages of reading matter intended to be organic reading should have wide margins with ample room for writing. Ample margins allow space to pencil in your own thoughts, reflections and questions. Underscoring a thought and "fleshing out" an idea with your own thoughts is a way of entering into conversation with the writer. With a pencil as a prayer tool, you can write creatively your own commentary to the text. Now the book or magazine becomes an extension of you because you have personalized it. To then share it with another, especially if there is the freedom to pencil in comments, only increases its value.

—Edward Hays
in *Secular Sanctity*

Some individuals experience moments of enlightenment while meditating or communing with nature. St. Paul was knocked off his horse by a revelation while he was traveling. Many people report having epiphanies during worship. But my "Eurekas!" and "Ahas!" usually come when I am reading.

I have always underlined my books, but as a reviewer, I find the practice indispensable. I read very fast and make short scratches down the center of passages I want to return to. These underlines seem to be a source of amusement to people who borrow my books. Mary Ann advises them not to try to figure them out, but I am still questioned: "Why did you underline that?"

These scratches are my way of putting my mark upon a book. They are indications of my ongoing dialogue with an author who has engaged me. And they are my standing ovations for passages that have stirred my soul. A well-underlined book, I believe, is a book that has been taken to heart.

JOY

"Why aren't you dancing with joy at this very moment? is the only relevant spiritual question," Sufi seer Pir Vilayet Inayet Khan tells us. Your life is a glorious gift and you are loved by Lady Wisdom.

Israeli theologian Martin Buber also opens our eyes to this truth: "The beating heart of the universe is holy joy."

Look around and you'll see how the flowers, trees, squirrels, and stars all emanate delight in their being. The flowers give off a fragrance, the trees dance a samba for the breeze, the squirrels perform acrobatics, and the stars twinkle with glee.

Whenever you see an image of Buddha, Zen master Thich Nhat Hanh reminds us, he is always smiling. That smile reflects inner peace and joy.

When he is about to leave his disciples, Jesus tells them, "These things have I spoken to you, that my joy may be in you, and that your joy may be full." What a beautiful legacy—passing on abundant joy.

"Always remember," Rebbe Nachman of Breslov, the Hasidic teacher, says, "Joy is not incidental to your spiritual quest. It is vital." So cultivate it.

Why is it so hard for us to be joyful? Is it the pressures of life which give us no relief, or the suffering of the innocents, or the rampant injustice in the world? Is it perhaps the fact that we don't like ourselves very much and always feel guilty? Or is it the fear that seizes us when we think of tomorrow?

Julian of Norwich, a fourteenth-century English mystic,

speaks across the ages: "The fullness of joy is to behold God in everything." That is the secret in a nutshell. Behold the Divine Joy in the good and the bad, the just and the unjust, the past and the future, the magnificent moment and the tawdry one.

Listen now to Frederick Buechner, a contemporary Protestant writer: "The world is full of suffering indeed, and to turn our backs on it is to work a terrible unkindness maybe almost more on ourselves than on the world. But life indeed is also to be enjoyed. I suggest that may even be the whole point of it. I more than suspect that is why all the sons of God (and daughters) shouted for joy when He first brought it into being."

Give yourself permission to be dizzy with joy and thankful for all the blessings which abound in your days.

Give yourself permission to rejoice with others. As French Catholic novelist George Bernanos writes, "To find joy in another's joy, that is the secret of happiness."

Give yourself permission to feel good about helping others. As Mother Teresa of Calcutta, winner of the Nobel Peace Prize, knows, "She gives most who gives with joy."

Rejoice and be exceedingly glad.

JUSTICE

"Justice is like the Kingdom of God," writes English novelist George Eliot. "It is not without us as a fact; it is within us as a great yearning."

We yearn for fairness to preside in the relations among people. We yearn for a time when the inherent dignity of all individuals will be honored. We yearn for an era when the gross inequalities between the rich and the poor will be eradicated.

We seek liberty and justice for all. Aung San Suu Kyi, who was awarded the Nobel Peace Prize in 1991 for her work for democracy in Burma, calls freedom "a united determination to persevere in the struggle, to make sacrifices in the name of enduring truths." She believes, "to be free is to be able to do what you think is right." French philosopher Jean-Paul Sartre suggests, "Freedom is what you do with what's been done to you."

This gift from the Great Liberator is very precious. "It is dangerous to take human freedom for granted, to regard it as a prerogative rather than as an obligation, as an ultimate fact rather than as an ultimate goal. It is the beginning of wisdom to be amazed at the fact of our being free," Jewish theologian Abraham Joshua Heschel proclaims.

We could say the same things about justice. "Let justice roll down like waters, and righteousness like an ever-flowing stream," we read in Amos 5:24. What a high and holy vision!

"A person who lacks the verdancy of justice is dry," says German mystic Hildegard of Bingen, "totally without tender goodness, totally without illuminating virtue." The key word is "verdancy." The green growth of life is fellow-feeling.

The cynic with dry rot in his or her heart turns away from the injustice of the world. But "we were never promised a life free from fear and struggle. We were offered the hope that by committing ourselves to the struggle for a righteous society in solidarity with the wretched of the earth we would discover the secret of life." So writes Sheila Collins.

Justice comes alive within us or it doesn't come alive at all. Activist Catholic priest Daniel Berrigan says, "If faith does anything, as shown by the prophets and Jesus, it leads us into the injustice and suffering of the world." There is no escaping our obligations.

"Injustice anywhere is a threat to justice everywhere," civil rights leader Dr. Martin Luther King Jr. states. "We are caught in an inescapable network of mutuality tied to a single garment of destiny." American trial lawyer Clarence Darrow declares, "You can only be free if I am free."

Justice and freedom live through our words and deeds. Nancy Mairs, an American Catholic essayist, puts it all together for us: "That's what we're here for: to make the world new. We know what to do: seek justice, love mercy, walk humbly, treat every person as though she were yourself. These are not complicated instructions. It's much harder to decipher the instructions for putting together a tricycle than it is to understand these." Justice here. Justice now.

EXERCISE AND SPORTS

Physical activities often meet the criteria of spiritual practice. They engage body, mind, and spirit; they bring us to a broader understanding of community; and they put us in touch with some of the world's many mysteries. For example, there is something deeply spiritual about a daily run, about its solitude, its rhythms, its rituals.

RUN BEFORE DAWN

Most mornings I get away, slip out
the door before light, set forth on the dim, gray
road, letting my feet find a cadence
that softly carries me on. Nobody
is up—all alone my journey begins.

Some days it's escape: the city is burning
behind me, cars have stalled in their tracks,
and everybody is fleeing like me but some other direction.
My stride is for life, a far place.

Other days it is hunting: maybe some game will cross
my path and my stride will follow for hours, matching
all turns. My breathing has caught the right beat
for endurance; familiar trancelike scenes glide by.

And sometimes it's a dream of motion,
    streetlights coming near,
passing, shadows that lean before me,
    lengthened
then fading, and a sound from a tree: a soul, or an owl.

These journeys are quiet. They mark my days with adventure
too precious for anyone else to share, little gems
of darkness, the world going by, and my breath, and the road.
                        —WILLIAM STAFFORD
                        in *An Oregon Message*

In the next reading, Thomas Moore reflects upon the satisfactions he has experienced in combining two leisure-time activities: walking and conversing with another.

Walking inspires and promotes conversation that is grounded in the body, and so it gives the soul a place where it can thrive. I think I could write an interesting memoir of significant walks I have taken with others, in which intimacy was not only experienced but set fondly into the landscape of memory. When I was a child, I used to walk with my Uncle Tom on his farm, across fields and up and down hills. We talked of many things, some informative and some completely outrageous, and quite a few very tall stories emerged on those bucolic walks. Whatever the content of the talking, those conversations remain important memories for me of my attachment to my family, to a remarkable personality, and to nature.

—THOMAS MOORE
in *Soul Mates*

Best-selling author Robert Fulghum has an uncanny ability to find meaning in the commonplace. Here he makes a spiritual reading of his neighbor's nightly ritual.

Almost every evening I see him, walking both his old dog and a recently acquired puppy. It's a common scene—an ordinary event in most neighborhoods. You can almost set your clock by his reliable rhythm—coming by at ten and going back by at ten-thirty. Winter, summer, spring, and fall. Rain or snow, clouds or starshine, he walks the dogs. . . .

He said the dogs keep him doing something important for himself. The old dog finds his leash each evening and stands by the door, waiting. The old dog is driven by his lower intestine and bladder. The young dog frolics through the house, yapping and wriggling, driven by enthusiasm for any opportunity for action and adventure. But Sam is compelled by a need for what he tells his wife is "some fresh air." Whatever he calls it, she understands where he is going and why. While he is out of the house, she will do the dishes. For the same reasons, he goes out with the dogs. It is a sacred habit—a reflective time alone.

Sam says that on these walks he settles the affairs of the day and thinks about tomorrow. He calms down from the busyness of his life, notices the weather, the seasons, the trees, and the stars, and thinks about "all the big stuff." . . .

When my neighbor walks the dogs, he performs a ritual act of *sacer simplicitas*, to use the church Latin: "sacred simplicity." Walking the dog is in truth a ritual of renewal and revival on an intimate scale—a small rebirth of well-being on a daily basis.

—ROBERT FULGHUM
in *From Beginning to End*

Even the simple recreation of flying a kite can open a person up to a sense of the spiritual.

It may appear that the experience of true beauty is very difficult to achieve. This is definitely not true. In fact, the experience of beauty often arises naturally and unexpectedly. Several weeks ago, I went kiting with my children. It was a fine day. I have not flown a kite for a long time, and I am very glad that I did it again. For I discovered the beauty of kiting that day. To see the kite take off in the wind, to let it soar into the heights, to feel the tightness of the string in my hand and to run around laughing and screaming like a child—all these add up to an exhilarating experience. It was such a tremendous feeling of liberation. For a while, it looked as if the world was just one big kite, soaring into the blue sky. There was a lot of action in the sport, but I felt a genuine sense of stillness and harmony at the same time. I was one with the game. I was doing dynamic meditation.

—KENNETH S. LEONG
in *The Zen Teachings of Jesus*

The spiritual practice of play enables us to restore ourselves through activity that has no pragmatic value. We lose ourselves in the movement and find enchantment.

Lily would now take the skates out below that field of stars, the crunch of frozen snow, with the coyotes singing and howling, their cries echoing all around the narrow valley as if going in circles, start to finish and back to start again. She'd walk down to the pond and put the skates on, and with her hands behind her back and her chin tucked down, she would skate the way she and Joe had seen men and women do at a park in Seattle, so many years ago. It was a small pond, but she would skate as fast as she could anyway, using only her legs, slicing them back and forth like strong scissors, with the cold air racing past her face, and two moons to give her light: the real one cold as stone in the sky above her, and then the one frozen in the ice, reflected, the one that was just ahead of her and then beneath her, passing under her skates as she raced across it, an illusion, behind her, gone.

Lily would skate for hours, her long black hair flowing from beneath her cap. Her eyes watered with pleasure at the speed, and at the feel of it, and at the chance to be doing something that meant absolutely nothing at all, something other than gardening or cooking or cleaning—and she would skate until her legs were trembling, until she could no longer even stand.

She would lie down on the ice and rest, spread-eagled in the center of the pond. She would watch the moon, panting, her face bright as bone, and would imagine that it was watching her.

—RICK BASS
in *Platte River*

The first time I went snorkeling, I started a fish list. I decided to keep a record of every new fish I saw on vacation, and I loaded up my suitcase with books about tropical fish; it was important for me to know whether I was looking at a Blue Tang or a Bluehead Wrasse. When we got to the beach, I spent hours over the reef while Fred sat on the shore (efforts like mine were not his idea of a vacation). When I finally came back to land, I immediately checked all my books to find the names of creatures I could add to my list. Identifying everything made the experience more real, and in those days, it was my way of paying my respects to the fish.

After a few years, I quit taking my list on vacation, and I soon forgot the names of many of the fish. Visits to the reef began to be just that— visits. I became more interested in how my body related to the reef, how I could allow the waves to move me closer to it, and then away from it again. I paid attention to other things besides fish—how cloudy the water became on days when the waves were rougher, or how the color of the coral changed depending upon the color of the sky. I learned that I could relate to the fish, the reef, the ocean, and myself by just being there.

THE AVOWAL

As swimmers dare
to lie face to the sky
and water bears them,
as hawks rest upon air
and air sustains them,
so would I learn to attain
freefall, and float
into Creator Spirit's deep embrace,
knowing no effort earns
that all-surrounding grace.
—DENISE LEVERTOV
in *Oblique Poems*

In the next reading, novelist Lynne Sharon Schwartz describes learning to ride a bike as a deeply spiritual moment when we confront fear and discover the value of effortlessness, or what the Taoists call wu wei.

A few seven-year-olds are learning to ride bikes with the training wheels removed by eager parents who trot along behind, one hand steadying the back of the seat. At some arbitrary moment the parents let go. Immediately, the children feel the withdrawal of the hand anchoring them to the earth, rooting them, and they hastily concentrate all their efforts on keeping the wheels balanced. Their blood turns to fear; they can't relinquish their concentration and let the wheels roll, and yet it's the surfeit of concentration that undoes them. No longer spontaneous, like infants, they're sabotaged by effort, the mind turned in on itself. The bicycle starts rocking from side to side while the parents shout encouragement in English, Spanish, and Chinese: Just let go, relax and pedal. But the weight of concentration collapses in on the children; their panicky feet abandon the pedals and grope for firm ground. There they stand, shaky and forlorn, as the bicycle clatters to the pavement between their spread legs.

Yet how persistent they are, how bravely willing to climb back on, because for one immeasurably small instant between the removal of the steadying hand and the blood turning to fear, they felt the exhilaration of balance in motion, the blissful absence of effort, the joy of doing without doing.

—LYNNE SHARON SCHWARTZ
in *The Fatigue Artist*

My grandfather was a lawyer, a judge, and a farmer. He was frequently busy and conquesting, but I remember also that he sometimes entered into golden moments of *wu wei*. He and I used to go fishing at one of the little ponds on his farm. He would sit and hold his cane pole over the water, becoming as still as the stumps that jutted up from the water. I usually tired of fishing fairly soon and went on to other things, like dandelions. One day having given up on the fishing, I was playing in his old black truck when I noticed that his fishing bait was still on the seat. I remember being surprised that my grandfather had been out fishing an hour or more without bait.

I grabbed the bait basket and raced over to him. "Grandaddy, how can you fish without bait?"

He tilted back his hat and smiled as if he had been caught in some delicious secret. "Well, sometimes it's not the fish I'm after," he said, "it's the fishing."

—SUE MONK KIDD
in *When the Heart Waits*

Fly-fishing is the central theme of A River Runs Through It. *This film is based on Norman Maclean's autobiography in which he looks back on his experiences growing up with his younger brother Paul in Missoula, Montana. Their father teaches them the sport of fly-fishing, which has become his spiritual practice. In the film voice-over, Norman explains his father's worldview: "To him, all good things, trout as well as eternal salvation, come by grace, and grace comes by art, and art does not come easy." For Paul especially, mastery in fly-fishing is the solace he needs in an otherwise self-destructive life. Times spent at the river are mystical moments when the three men feel at one with each other and the universe. Peg Thompson describes something similar.*

When I go trout fishing, I carry everything I need for the day in my multipocketed vest and fanny pack. I begin at a place where a river crosses a road and hike upstream on an angler's path, fishing as I go. Soon I am alone, with only the stream and the rest of nature as my companions. Fishing, I become one with my surroundings. I move carefully and quietly. At times, I pause to feast on wild raspberries or blueberries, enjoy the mating ritual of dragonflies, or drink in the fragrance of spruce trees and moss. Often, I just relax on a smooth rock in the sun, awash with the sights, scents, and sounds of the place. I feel in complete harmony with myself and all creation.

—PEG THOMPSON
in *Finding Your Own Spiritual Path*

Patsy Neal, a basketball star, reflects upon the spiritual meaning she finds in this sport.

There are moments of glory that go beyond the human expectation, beyond the physical and emotional ability of the individual. Something unexplainable takes over and breathes life into the known life. One stands on the threshold of miracles that one cannot create voluntarily. . . . Call it a state of grace, or an act of faith . . . or an act of God. It is there, and the impossible becomes possible. . . . The athlete goes beyond herself; she transcends the natural. She touches a piece of heaven and becomes the recipient of power from an unknown source.

The power goes beyond that which can be defined as physical or mental. The performance almost becomes a holy place—where a spiritual awakening seems to take place. The individual becomes swept up in the action around her—she almost floats through the performance, drawing on forces she has never previously been aware of.

—PATSY NEAL
in *Sport and Identity*

"O sport, you are beauty!" wrote the founder of the modern Olympic Games, Baron Pierre de Coubertin. Even competitive sports can give athletes experiences of the spiritual practices of beauty, being present, and joy. For the XIV Olympic Winter Games in Sarajevo, Mary Ann

and I wrote a Viewer's Guide to ABC Sports' *television coverage of the events. In the guide, we quoted an article titled "Sport and Culture" by Rene Mahau: "In the action and rhythm which testify to mastery of space and time, sport becomes akin to the arts which create beauty. No athlete can accomplish a genuine feat without such perfect physical control, in time and space, that his movements and the rhythm of their timing are not to be differentiated from the finest ballet, the most splendid passages of prose verse, the most glorious lines in architecture." My contribution to the guide was a series of poems on winter sports. Here are two of them.*

SPEED SKATER

Energy is eternal delight,
wrote the poet William Blake.
Rounding the corner,
sending off a spray
of silver ice shavings
from his blades,
the speed skater understands.

He embodies life's
quickening force.
A human arrow,
he knows exactly
where he is going and
the fastest way to get there.

The single-mindedness
of the speed skater is
exceptional in a world of
so much squandered energy.

SLALOM SKIER

She is wrapped in a
cocoon of concentration.
It shows in her eyes, legs, arms.
Now is the only time.

This skier is totally focused.
Time slows as she marshals
all her energies for the run.
The mountain is serious.
It demands everything of her.

The flags whip by,
challenging her balance.
She twists and turns,
making all effort seem effortless.
Not until the end of the race is her
cocoon of concentration broken.
Joy, free as a butterfly,
bursts forth.

—FREDERIC BRUSSAT
in *The Beauty of Sports*

SABBATHS AND VACATIONS

Abraham Joshua Heschel, the great Jewish thinker, writes: "The Sabbath as a day of rest is not for the purpose of recovering one's lost strength and becoming fit for the forthcoming labor. The Sabbath is a day for the sake of life." In the next reading, Robert Fulghum recounts how he observes the Sabbath.

My wife and I try to live Sundays as if they were a different kind of day. I take this concept more from the Jewish tradition than from the Christian. We don't go anywhere; we don't have any obligations; we don't do any work. Instead, we listen to music, we read, we go for walks. We try to set ourselves aside from our busy lives on this day, allowing ourselves to simply enjoy being alive. We've noticed that having one sane day a week really makes a difference. We don't always manage to observe the Sabbath in this way, but when we do, it is indeed a special day.

—ROBERT FULGHUM
in *Handbook for the Soul*
edited by Richard Carlson
and Benjamin Shield

Best-selling author Sue Bender uses the term "little sabbaths" to describe pauses in the day.

"We all need a certain amount of fallow time," Yvonne reminds me.

"Watching the grass grow, sitting on the hillside, staring out the window daydreaming. When we don't have it, there is a deeper intelligence that won't come forth."

Mine is a racehorse rhythm, and once I get started in the morning it's difficult for me to stop. Now I can see that a pause—even a very *small pause*—is extremely useful.

These "little Sabbaths" replenish my body—and spirit.

—Sue Bender
in *Everyday Sacred*

Enjoying a pleasure usually associated with childhood is one way of taking a little sabbath.

As the stars again become visible tonight, I am reminded of a feast of leisure from my childhood days. I remember, on summer evenings, sitting outside on a quilt with Mama waiting for the stars to come out. Looking back at that moment with my adult eyes, I understand that God is Someone who has taken the time to sit on a quilt with me waiting for beauty. She is a Mother of Presence. I need only invite her into my moments of leisure. Her presence will empower my presence.

As I tried to bring a deeper quality of presence to all my works this day, I found God moving through the day with me, like a Mother, opening my eyes to beauty. Quietly, joyfully, gratefully, without complaining, I welcomed all the beauty that crossed my path.

—Macrina Wiederkehr
in *The Song of the Seed*

A carousel makes me feel four years old again, and I am convinced that the only way to be creative and constructive in our adult years—especially the later ones—is to get back in touch with the child we once were. . . .

It doesn't have to be a carousel for everyone. It might be fishing or a picnic or a game of miniature golf or going to a circus or anything else that takes us back in time and grants us a special, childlike freedom in which we accept all our thoughts and memories, sad and happy—and most of all, frees us from our grownup selves.

—EDA LeSHAN
in *It's Better to Be Over the Hill Than Under It*

Think of your next day off as a spiritual retreat offering refreshment for body, mind, and spirit. Poet Maya Angelou spells out just what that could mean.

Every person needs to take one day away. A day in which one consciously separates the past from the future. Jobs, lovers, family, employers, and friends can exist one day without any one of us, and if our egos permit us to confess, they could exist eternally in our absence.

Each person deserves a day away in which no problems are confronted, no solutions searched for. Each of us needs to withdraw from the cares which will not withdraw from us. We need hours of aimless wandering or spates of time sitting on park benches, observing the mysterious world of ants and the canopy of treetops.

If we step away for a time, we are not, as many may think and some will accuse, being irresponsible, but rather we are preparing ourselves to more ably perform our duties and discharge our obligations.

When I return home, I am always surprised to find some questions I sought to evade had been answered and some entanglements I had hoped to flee had become unraveled in my absence.

A day away acts as a spring tonic. It can dispel rancor, transform indecision, and renew the spirit.

—MAYA ANGELOU
in *Wouldn't Take Nothing for My Journey Now*

When a day away is not enough, we go on vacation. Thomas Moore in Care of the Soul *notes: "For the soul, it is important to be taken out of the rush of practical life for the contemplation of timeless and eternal realities." Sy Safransky, editor of* The Sun, *opens our eyes to a few of the spiritual benefits of getting away from the rush and hustle of our lives.*

We've come here to remind ourselves of what life seems intent on making us forget—those truths that run through the hands like sand. We've come to retrace the changing shoreline of our love, and rebuild what the busy days will wash away again. We've come, for a few days, to cut a deal with eternity: to talk without looking at the clock; to cheat boredom and jealousy and worry with the intensity of being together; to go beyond where the waves break in our hearts, to where it's calm instead of fearful, and bring that feeling back with us—if the sea, murmuring and mocking, will let us.

—Sy Safransky
in *Four in the Morning*

Many people use their leisure time to journey to faraway places. The soul and the spirit are challenged on such adventures.

That is why we need to travel. If we don't offer ourselves to the unknown, our senses dull. Our world becomes small and we lose our sense of wonder. Our eyes don't lift to the horizon; our ears don't hear the sounds around us. The edge is off our experience, and we pass our days in a routine that is both comfortable and limiting. We wake up one day and find that we have lost our dreams in order to protect our days.

Don't let yourself become one of these people. The fear of the unknown and the lure of the comfortable will conspire to keep you from taking the chances the traveler has to take. But if you take them, you will never regret your choice. To be sure, there will be moments of doubt when you stand alone on an empty road in an icy rain, or when you are ill with fever in a rented bed. But as the pains of the moment will come, so too will they fall away. In the end, you will be so much richer, so much stronger, so much clearer, so much happier, and so much better a person that all the risk and hardship will seem like nothing compared to the knowledge and wisdom you have gained.

—Kent Nerburn
in *Letters to My Son*

K

KINDNESS

"Whether one believes in religion or not—there isn't anyone who doesn't appreciate kindness," observes the Dalai Lama, leader of Tibetan Buddhists.

The spiritual practice of kindness consists of little acts—a word of thanks, a nod of approval, a tip at a restaurant, a smile to a weary worker, a greeting on the street, a hug for a friend. Remember William Wordsworth's poem: "The best portion of a good man's life/his little nameless, unremarkable acts/of kindness and love."

American novelist Henry James gets directly to the point: "Three things in human life are important. The first is to be kind. The second is to be kind. And the third is to be kind."

It isn't the bold initiatives or the grand strategies which make a difference. It is the trifles taken seriously which are at the heart of morality.

Rebbe Nachman of Breslov, a Hasidic master, says: "It's easy to criticize others and make them feel unwanted. Anyone can do it. What takes effort and skill is picking them up and making them feel good."

Kindness flows naturally out of empathy and hospitality. And a little appreciation can be powerful. Think about how many times someone's kind words have lifted your spirits and made you feel like a king or queen.

Etiquette is also part of the spiritual practice of kindness. In Earth etiquette, we don't walk on flowers or leave trash in parks. In house etiquette, we don't ignore or abuse our possessions. In animal etiquette, we don't ridicule our pets or frighten them.

"As we move around this world and as we act with kindness, perhaps, or with indifference or with hostility toward the people we meet, we are setting the great spider web atremble," Protestant writer Frederick Buechner muses. "The life I touch for good or ill will touch another life, and that in turn another, until who knows where the trembling stops or in what far place my touch will be felt." Our acts have reverberations which are felt way beyond our imagining.

Wendy Lustbader, a mental health counselor, writes: "The words 'genius' and 'generous' come from the Latin root 'genere' meaning 'to beget.' To have a genius for life is to possess the ability to generate warmth and well-being in others. Largesse literally enlarges our lives."

The spiritual life, Buddha says, is impossible without a generous heart. And in the Gospel of Luke, Jesus advises his followers to "forgive and you will be forgiven; give, and it will be given to you."

Kindness is sometimes viewed as one of those effete virtues lacking in charisma or clout. And yet it encompasses meaningful acts of love, words of encouragement, various kinds of etiquette, reverberations beyond our ken, generosity, and a salutary largesse. No wonder Rabbi Abraham Joshua Heschel near the end of his life concludes: "When I was young, I used to admire intelligent people; as I grow older, I admire kind people."

Although we are used to thinking of daydreaming as a waste of time, it can be an opening to meaningful moments of mystical awareness.

KINSHIP

I am aware
As I sit quietly here in my chair,
Sewing or reading or braiding my hair—
Human and simple my lot and my share—
　　I am aware of the systems that swing
　　Through the aisles of creation on heavenly wing,
　　I am aware of a marvelous thing,
Trail of the comets in furious flight
Thunders of beauty that shatter the night,
　　Terrible triumph of pageants that march
　　To the trumpets of time of Eternity's arch.
I am aware of the splendour that ties
　　All the things of the earth with the things of the skies,
　　Here in my body the heavenly heat,
　　Here in my flesh the melodious beat
　　Of the planets that circle Divinity's feet.
As I silently sit here in my chair,
　　I am aware
　　　—ANGELA MORGAN
　　　quoted in *The Dove in the Stone*
　　　by Alice O. Howell

Many of us are so driven and frantic that we live on little sleep and naps are the stuff of fantasy. But what does the lack of sleep do to us? Perhaps we do not fully understand a nap's significance.

Our word "sleep" comes from the German word "schlaff" which means "loose." To sleep, then, or to nap is to "hang loose," to be un-tight and to let go. Sleep at night or in short periods before bedtime is a beautiful expression of prayer since it is resting in God. It is letting go of our control of life. Sleep is a parable on prayer and it is also prayer. If we look only at the front side of sleep we might miss hidden implications. All things have a front and back door, and we should not be satisfied just to enter ideas from the front side only. The front door of sleep is bodily rest, but where does the back door lead?

The back door leads to the Prayer of Napping as an external sacrament of the inner ability to "let go" of managing every aspect of our lives. It is an expression that we are able to allow the Divine Mystery to take over in the midst of troubles and deadlines. It is an expression of faith that the Divine Presence is even concerned with our seemingly common work and difficulties. Sleep is a form of humility for it says, "God is saving the world." To let go for coffee breaks or naps and to do so without guilt allows God a chance to save the world!

—EDWARD HAYS
in *Pray All Ways*

Napped half the day;
no one
punished me!
—ISSA
in *The Essential Haiku*
edited by Robert Hass

It's not the doing, leisure teaches us, but the living that counts. And it's not the having but the appreciating that defines who we are.

If doing without makes you appreciate things more, I guessed that the people of Lake Wobegon should be the happiest people in the world. No purple mountain majesty there and no alabaster city, just waves of grain and the Co-op Elevator.

I liked what Pastor Tommerdahl said at Mrs. Lundberg's funeral. He spoke on the text "So teach us to number our days that we may apply our hearts unto wisdom," and to him, it meant that we should live each day as if it were our last. Mrs. Lundberg was the Asparagus Lady. She had a half-acre of it, my favorite vegetable, so delicious and it needed no planting, no weeding: it just jumped out of the ground by the thousands. Asparagus was the only extravagant thing about Mrs. Lundberg; otherwise she was like us.

If you lived today as if it were your last, you'd buy up a box of rockets and fire them all off, wouldn't you?

—GARRISON KEILLOR
in *Lake Wobegon Days*

Kentucky farmer and writer Wendell Berry surprises us with his spiritual reading of the juxtaposition of labor and leisure.

"Boys," Mat says, "it was a *hot* day. There wasn't a breeze anywhere in that bottom that would have moved a cobweb. It was punishing." He is telling Elton and Andy.

It was a long time ago. Mat was only a boy yet, though he was nearly grown. His Uncle Jack hired him to help chop out a field of tall corn in a creek bottom. It was hot and still, and the heat stood close around them as they worked. They felt they needed to tiptoe to get enough air.

Mat thought he could not stand it any longer, and then he stood it a little longer, and they reached the end of the row.

"Let's go sink ourselves in the creek," Jack said.

They did. They hung their sweated clothes on willows in the sun to dry, and sank themselves in the cool stream up to their noses. It was a good hole, deep and shady, with the sound of the riffles above and below, and a kingfisher flying in and seeing them and flying away. All that afternoon when they got too hot, they went there.

"Well sir," Mat says, "it made that hard day good. I thought of all the times I'd worked in that field, hurrying to get through, to get to a better place, and it had been there all the time. I can't say I've always lived by what I learned that day—I wish I had—but I've never forgot."

"What?" Andy says.

"That it was there all the time."

"What?"

"Redemption," Mat says, and laughs. "A little flowing stream."

—WENDELL BERRY
in *Remembering*

CELEBRATIONS

One of the central human needs is to be acknowledged and loved for who we are. That is why birthdays are high holy days.

Celebrating a birthday is exalting life and being glad for it. On a birthday we do not say: "Thanks for what you did, or said, or accomplished." No, we say: "Thank you for being born and being among us." . . . Celebrating a birthday reminds us of the goodness of life, and in this spirit we really need to celebrate people's birthdays every day, by showing gratitude, kindness, forgiveness, gentleness, and affection. These are ways of saying: "It's good that you are alive; it's good that you are walking with me on this earth. Let's be glad and rejoice. This is the day that God has made for us to be and to be together."

—HENRI J. M. NOUWEN
in *Here and Now*

We have a column in our newsletter called "Naming the Days." The title comes from the movie A Thousand Clowns, *based on the play by Herb Gardner. Murray Burns is a life-loving, wonder-filled New Yorker who is raising his twelve-year-old nephew. He specializes in celebrations, including seeing ships off, exploring the city's famous sights, and observing his own personal holidays—like the birthday of Irving R. Feldman, proprietor of the best kosher deli in his neighborhood.*

At one point, Murray recalls an epiphany. He was sitting on the express subway going to work, staring out the window watching the local stops whiz by. He was not feeling great or rotten; he was just not feeling. He realized he had to really concentrate to figure out what day of the week it was. And then he woke up: "You have got to own your own days and name them, each one of them, every one of them, or else the years go right by and none of them belong to you."

Our newsletter column names the days in upcoming months and suggests videos to watch, tapes to hear, or books to read to make each one special. We also name the days with our ritual tree, which stands at the entrance of our dining area. It is an eight-foot tree made of dry willow branches. We decorate it with pictures of people whose birthdays we want to remember—friends and family members as well as writers, actors, musicians, and others who have contributed to our enjoyment of

life. We also observe the holidays with our decorations. In November,
we hang our blessings on the tree for Thanksgiving, and in February we
put up little love notes for Valentine's Day.

Educator Gertrud Mueller Nelson believes that Christian families
should celebrate important days in the church year in the home. Here
are her ideas for Pentecost.

As one of the great feasts of the year, this birthday of the Church
cannot slip past. Inspired by the roar of the Spirit's wind and fire,
consider making a mobile. We hang ours in our "Holy Ghost
hole," the skylight, or from the chandelier over the dining table. A
red cardboard dove hovers on a thread with seven orange flames
around it, marked with the seven gifts of the Spirit. It sways and
dangles and moves in the drafts. Wear red clothes and eat red
food—strawberries, perhaps, that look like tongues of flame. At
each place at table make "name cards" with the gifts of the Spirit,
and family members may choose where they sit today, selecting
the gift they most love or most desire. At dinner, circle from one to
the next and hear a word about each of the Spirit's gifts and the
effect each brings. Then read "God's Grandeur" by Gerard Manley
Hopkins. It is also a pleasant thing to gather with friends on an
open field or in the park for an afternoon of kite-flying.

—GERTRUD MUELLER NELSON
in *To Dance with God*

Feast days and religious holidays are packed with spiritual meanings to
be recognized and observed. And we never know when a new under-
standing will come to us in the midst of the celebrations.

When I was twelve, I read in a magazine how I could spruce up my
Christmas presents with homemade wrapping. I used one of the arti-
cle's suggestions for my father's package. I made a chimney out of a
small box, then I cut up pink sponges and pasted them like bricks on its
side. The tag said, "To My Santa Daddy."

The evening after I quite proudly put this present under the tree, my
two older brothers, Colin and Philip, called me aside. "Mary Ann," they
said. "We saw your present for Dad, and we think you should change
the tag."

"Why?" I demanded a little defensively, thinking they were teasing
me, and I hate to be teased. But they were serious.

"No matter what you hear in school, no matter how old you get, or how smart," they advised, "never stop believing in Santa Claus."

I have remembered those words. I have remembered what those teenaged boys wanted their little sister to know. Stories are true. Don't be a cynic. Hold on to the magic. Years later, I came across this meditation on Santa Claus and realized that I still believe.

What has happened to me has been the very reverse of what appears to be the experience of most of my friends. Instead of dwindling to a point, Santa Claus has grown larger and larger in my life until he fills almost the whole of it. It happened in this way. As a child I was faced with a phenomenon requiring explanation. I hung up at the end of my bed an empty stocking, which in the morning became a full stocking. I had done nothing to produce the things that filled it. I had not worked for them, or made them or helped to make them. I had not even been good—far from it. And the explanation was that a certain being whom people called Santa Claus was benevolently disposed toward me. . . . What we believed was that a certain benevolent agency did give us those toys for nothing. And, as I say, I believe it still. I have merely extended the idea. Then I only wondered who put the toys in the stocking; now I wonder who put the stocking by the bed, and the bed in the room, and the room in the house, and the house on the planet, and the great planet in the void. Once I only thanked Santa Claus for a few dolls and crackers, now, I thank him for stars and street faces and wine and the great sea. Once I thought it delightful and astonishing to find a present so big that it only went halfway into the stocking. Now I am delighted and astonished every morning to find a present so big that it takes two stockings to hold it, and then leaves a great deal outside; it is the large and preposterous present of myself, as to the origin of which I can offer no suggestion except that Santa Claus gave it to me in a fit of peculiarly fantastic goodwill.

—G. K. Chesterton
in *The Tablet 2*

PRACTICING SPIRITUAL LITERACY: LEISURE

CONVERSATIONS/JOURNAL ENTRIES

- What childhood experiences with food have influenced your present eating attitudes and habits? What are your favorite foods? Are any foods taboo? How do you determine which foods best suit you?

- M. F. K. Fisher, the famous writer on food, notes: "Once in the life of every human, whether he be brute or trembling daffodil, comes a moment of complete gastronomic satisfaction. It is, I am sure, as much a matter of spirit as of body. Everything is right. Nothing jars. There is a kind of harmony with every sensation and emotion melted into one chord of well-being." Recall or imagine your perfect meal, and write about it in your journal.

- What chores give your daily life rhythm and purpose? What spiritual practices do you usually associate with these duties?

- What were your favorite hobbies as a child? How did they make you feel? What are your present hobbies? In what ways do they enrich your life and express your playfulness? What other spiritual meanings do you attach to these activities?

- What are some of the spiritual benefits for you of running, walking, swimming, or other aerobic exercise?

- "Thank God It's Friday" (TGIF) is a phrase which originated in the 1960s. What significance does it hold for you? What are your favorite activities on your days off?

- Vacations are soul-satisfying experiences. What needs do you want satisfied on a vacation? Describe or write about the best vacation you have ever had.

ACTIVITIES/PROJECTS

- Sit around the kitchen table and play the following game. Pick one or two foods and try to imagine how their personalities differ. What other relatives or neighbors on the food chain do they best get along with? If they could speak to you about your eating habits, what would they say?

- When you are cooking a meal, pause to consider the feelings and ideas that pass through you. What do you like best or least about this activity? How did you learn to cook? What parts of yourself do you feel are best expressed in cooking?

- Many restaurants accentuate the presentation of food on the plate. Set aside an evening to cook something special and then harmonize the colors, textures, and portions on the plate. Savor these with your senses. Involve children in making seasonal decorations for your table to complement the food presentation.

- Rent the Academy Award-winning film *Babette's Feast* and talk about its messages about food, cooking, art, grace, and God. How important is table fellowship in your spiritual tradition?

- Start a book or study club; see the back of this volume for the publication information on the many resources we have cited, any of which would be a good start for your group.

- Keep track of your daydreams in a notebook, as you would your night dreams. Try to discover what is blooming in these fertile fields of wonder.

SPIRITUAL EXERCISES/RITUALS

- Create a blessing service for your stove, refrigerator, toaster, bowls, pans, dishes, and cooking cutlery. Acknowledge their cocreator role in the preparation of meals in your home.

- Expand the repertoire of graces used at your meals. There are many good collections of prayers and graces from different spiritual traditions and from ancient and contemporary times. An especially fine one is *One Hundred Graces* selected by Marcia and Jack Kelly.

- Examine the ways you observe the Sabbath. Many religions encourage believers to stop their habitual activities on the Sabbath. Try giving up television, shopping, or talking for one day to see if these—or similar acts—increase the meaning of the Sabbath for you. What additional practices could you use to deepen and enrich your experience of this special time?

- Take a "little sabbath" for five minutes this afternoon, or better still, take a nap.

- Talk to someone who has gone on a spiritual retreat or check out David A. Cooper's *Silence, Simplicity and Solitude: A Guide for Spiritual Retreat.* Plan your own spiritual retreat.

- Protestant theologian Tom Driver has defined ritual as "a party at which emotions are welcome." With some loved ones create a celebration which expresses your joy and gratitude for the manifold blessings in your lives.

CREATIVITY

Creativity is God's gift to us. Using our creativity is our gift back to God.

—Julia Cameron

Why does anybody tell a story? It does indeed have something to do with faith, faith that the universe has meaning, that our little human lives are not irrelevant, that what we choose or say or do matters, matters cosmically.

—Madeleine L'Engle

The universe is made of stories—not atoms.

—Muriel Ruykeyser

There's a phrase in West Africa called "deep talk." When a person is informed about a situation, an older person will often use a parable, an axiom, and then add to the end of the axiom, "Take that as deep talk." Meaning that you will never find the answer. You can continue to go down deeper and deeper. Dreams may be deep talk.

—Maya Angelou

All art that really draws us to look at it deeply is spiritual.

—Wendy Beckett

An artist creates out of the materials of the moment, never again to be duplicated. This is true of the painter, the musician, the dancer, the actor, the teacher, the scientist, the businessman, the farmer—it is true of us all, whatever our work, that we are artists so long as we are alive to the concreteness of a moment and do not use it to some other purpose.

—M. C. RICHARDS

The outward work will never be puny if the inward work is great.

—MEISTER ECKHART

Good work that leaves the world softer and fuller and better than ever before is the stuff of which human satisfaction and spiritual value are made.

—JOAN CHITTISTER

"God is creating the entire universe, fully and totally in the present now," says Meister Eckhart, a thirteenth-century mystic. The world is a work-in-progress, and we are partners with God in its ongoing creation.

The creative path is not restricted to those society might call artists. "Every person," according to potter M. C. Richards, "is a special kind of artist and every activity is a special art." Her point is well illustrated in this chapter's collection of spiritually literate readings about creative activities.

We begin with the important step of sharing the stories of our lives. Our personal trials, triumphs, and transformations reflect our vision of the world and our place in it. In the words of novelist James Carroll, "We tell stories because we can't help it. We tell stories because we love to entertain and hope to edify. We tell stories because they fill the silence that death imposes. We tell stories because they save us."

Another way we gain insight into the shape and texture of our lives is by paying attention to our dreams. They give us messages about our fears, aspirations, and choices. "Dreaming," says archetypal psychologist James Hillman, "is a nightly dip, a skinny dip into the pool of images and feelings."

Films, television programs, and popular music also can be spiritual resources for us. These mediums contain priceless moments of beauty, enlightenment, moral encouragement, and personal meaning. All that is required to read them spiritually are the practices of hospitality and reverence, the ability to approach them as a religious person might enter a cathedral or temple—open to grace and mystery.

Every culture and wisdom tradition links the arts and spirituality. Music, dancing, singing, poetry, and painting are common avenues of adoration and praise. The arts convey our enthusiasm and house our yearning.

Creativity contributes to our sense of aliveness and our playfulness.

Crafts keep us focused on what is happening both around us and within us. One art teacher, Adriana Diaz, defines creations as "places where caring and daring come together." They open our eyes to nature and the body and give us fresh appreciation for both ritual and recreation.

In the preceding chapter, we saw that there are many opportunities for creativity in the everyday design and maintenance of our lives. In future chapters, we will see that creativity is essential in our relationships, whether we are practicing the art of love in an intimate relationship or trying to maintain a friendship across long distances. Creativity is equally important in the search to find innovative ways of dealing with the world's problems, and of serving others.

But perhaps the greatest challenge—or, at least it is perceived as such—is to bring creativity to our work. Shortly before her death in 1943, French mystic Simone Weil wrote, "Our age has its own particular mission or vocation, the creation of a civilization founded upon the spiritual nature of work." To make a spiritually literate reading of work, we need to locate all the letters of our alphabet in our workplaces. Then we can join the Balinese in saying, "We have no art. Everything we do is art."

ART AS PATHWAY

One afternoon, a musician was playing the violin and the Master was listening with great pleasure. A friend entered and said, "Stop this. They are announcing the afternoon prayer."

"No," said Rumi. "This also is the afternoon prayer. They both talk to God. He wants the one externally for His service and the other for His love and knowledge."

—STORY
quoted in *The Way of Passion*
by Andrew Harvey

Creativity is a pathway to the sacred. All the world's religions give credence to the idea that art pleases God and that creativity fuels our spiritual journey. In a radio interview, Desmond Tutu, Anglican archbishop of South Africa, suggests that our creativity should be used to enhance our world.

We were made to enjoy music, to enjoy beautiful sunsets, to enjoy looking at the billows of the sea and to be thrilled with a rose that is bedecked with dew. . . . Human beings are actually created for the transcendent, for the sublime, for the beautiful, for the truthful . . . and all of us are given the task of trying to make this world a little more hospitable to these beautiful things.

—DESMOND TUTU
quoted in *The NPR Interviews 1994*
edited by Robert Siegel

Appreciating the beauty around us is one way to recognize creativity. Clarissa Pinkola Estés gives other ways in the next reading.

Creativity is a shapechanger. One moment it takes this form, the next that. It is like a dazzling spirit who appears to us all, yet is hard to describe for no one agrees on what they saw in that brilliant flash. Are the wielding of pigments and canvas, or paint chips and wallpaper, evidence of its existence? How about pen and paper, flower borders on the garden path, building a university? Yes, yes. Ironing a collar well, cooking up a revolution? Yes. Touching with love the leaves of a plant, pulling down "the big deal," tying off the loom, finding one's voice, loving someone well? Yes. Catching the hot body of the newborn, raising a child to adulthood, helping raise a nation from its knees? Yes. Tending to a marriage like the orchard it is, digging for psychic gold, finding the shapely word, sewing a blue curtain? All are of the creative life.

—CLARISSA PINKOLA ESTÉS
in *Women Who Run with the Wolves*

Creativity puts us on a path of self-discovery that takes us deep inside ourselves. As we become more spiritually literate, we may discover that we are more interested in the process than in the end result.

There are many marvelous stories of potters in ancient China. In one of them a noble is riding through town and he passes a potter at work. He admires the pots the man is making; their grace and a kind of rude strength in them. He dismounts from his horse and speaks with the potter. "How are you able to form these vessels so that they possess such convincing beauty?" "Oh," answers the potter, "you are looking at the mere outward shape. What I am forming lies within. I am interested only in what remains after the pot has been broken."

—M. C. RICHARDS
in *Centering*

When the first whites started getting into Inuit country they found lots of tiny ivory carvings everywhere, even in dumps.

When these people were stuck in a storm, they carved these

things to pass the time. And then they threw them out because the activity was the thing.

—DOLORES LACHAPELLE
quoted in *Listening to the Land*
by Derrick Jensen

As we have seen, creativity contains elements of beauty, transformation, being present, and play. Three more stories illustrate how creative thinking expands our perceptions and our adaptability.

Buddha was once threatened with death by a bandit called Angulimal.

"Then be good enough to fulfill my dying wish," said Buddha. "Cut off the branch of that tree."

One slash of the sword, and it was done! "What now?" asked the bandit.

"Put it back again," said Buddha.

The bandit laughed. "You must be crazy to think that anyone can do that."

"On the contrary, it is you who are crazy to think that you are mighty because you can wound and destroy. That is the task of children. The mighty know how to create and heal."

—ANTHONY DE MELLO
in *The Heart of the Enlightened*

A friend's son was in the first grade of school, and his teacher asked the class, "What is the color of apples?" Most of the children answered red. A few said green. Kevin, my friend's son, raised his hand and said white. The teacher tried to explain that apples could be red, green, or sometimes golden, but never white. Kevin was quite insistent and finally said, "Look inside." Perception without mindfulness keeps us on the surface of things, and we often miss other levels of reality.

—JOSEPH GOLDSTEIN
in *Insight Meditation*

A large truck was moving through a railway underpass when it got wedged in between the road and the girders overhead. All the efforts of experts to extricate it proved useless, and traffic was stalled for miles on both sides of the underpass.

A little boy kept trying to get the attention of the foreman but was always pushed away. Finally in sheer exasperation, the foreman said, "I suppose you've come to tell us how to do this job!"

"Yes," said the child. "I suggest you let some air out of the tires."

—ANTHONY DE MELLO
in *The Heart of the Enlightened*

In the movie Dead Poets Society, *John Keating is an English professor who uses unorthodox teaching methods to emphasize the value of individuality. In one exercise, he has the boys in his class walk across the quadrangle, challenging each to find a gait that distinguishes him from the others. Another time, he orders his students, one by one, to stand on top of his desk for a different view of things. Seeing the world from a new perspective is what spiritual literacy is all about.*

Creativity is deeply humanizing. The next reading details how art creates a space where we can focus on our feelings.

You hear an old song and the face of a lost loved one suddenly appears, and in the space of the song the loved one grabs your loneliness by the collar and sends it out the door.

You stand before a painting and the peaceful landscape calls you in—or a scene of violent pain holds you in thrall—and for a minute that's longer than eternity you enter the serenity, or you rage and grieve along with the picture's tortured souls.

You read a piece of poetry and for the span of a minute—or an hour—you find a space to sit and listen to the sound of naked joy, or to stare into the face of unfathomable grief.

More than anything else, that's what good art does: not answer questions or set agendas, but create space—space to laugh, to mourn, and to wonder who and how and why we are.

—GRAZIANO MARCHESCHI
in *Wheat & Weeds and the Wolf of Gubbio*

STORIES AND DREAMS

We live in a story-shaped world. Usually the first stories we hear put us in touch with our loved ones, our family history, and the natural world.

When I was a child, full of anticipation, I would shake in my grandmother's arms as she held me in the warm Savannah nights and told me stories of the spirits that frequented her house. I could hear them knocking on the walls, and I saw their ephemeral traces for many years. She also told me stories about her childhood and youth, a time when life was lived at a walking pace. It was these nocturnal tellings, in fact, that set my imagination free. For through her, I began to see that the so-called inanimate world really had soul and that another way of seeing and understanding was possible, lessons that stand inside me to this day.

—JOAN HALIFAX
in *The Fruitful Darkness*

Considering what advice he would give the readers of his novels, sermons, and memoirs, Protestant minister Frederick Buechner writes, "Listen to your life. See it for the fathomless mystery that it is." Equally important for our spiritual journey is to be able to learn from the life stories of others.

Many years ago, Barbara Myerhoff was teaching a class at the University of Southern California in urban anthropology. As part of the course, the students were required to interview someone very different from themselves, someone with whom they would not normally converse. One young man in the class, who had lived an unusually protected and insulated middle-class life, was having such great difficulty in finding a subject that he considered dropping the course. However, the day the paper was due, he arrived in the class ecstatic.

"I was at my wit's end," he said, "when it occurred to me to interview our Guatemalan housekeeper. Naturally, I was very nervous because I had never really spoken to her, and it was rather late at night. But as I had to do the paper, I went to her room and knocked at her door. When I entered, I explained my need, asking if it would be a terrible nuisance for her to tell me something about her life. She looked at me strangely and my heart sank. After what seemed a very, very long time, she said quietly, 'Every night before I go to sleep, I rehearse the story of my life, just in case someone should ever ask me. *Gracias a Dios.*'"

—DEENA METZGER
in *Writing for Your Life*

Poets hail the commonplace and hallow the holy when it briefly and quietly brushes by us. As God's alert spies with reverent eyes, they are wonderful spiritual companions.

Loraine, who works in the fast-paced business of radio broadcasting, tells me she has memorized "The Lake Isle of Innisfree" by William Butler Yeats. She has spoken that poem aloud to herself so many times that the tranquil "Isle of Innisfree" has literally become an interior place for her, a place she knows like she knows her own home. She uses this poem to keep herself centered. She keeps a copy of it on her desk. She says it helps her to recall a sense of stillness. It becomes a source of inspiration and sustenance to her.

—JOHN FOX
in *Finding What You Didn't Lose*

Dreams also function as passports to inner worlds, and they constantly remind us of the mysterious, ambivalent, and shadow sides of ourselves.

It is said that a favorite student of Jung's went to visit him when he was in his eighties and living in a little tower on Lake Zurich. They went for a walk, and Jung began to tell him a dream. Jung would tell anybody his dreams: friends, students, the farmers who lived next door. He said that often their comments would give him some new insight that he couldn't reach himself; sometimes people would say things that felt so wrong that he got a hint of what might be right. This student, as he was walking, listened to the dream very carefully. In great awe—as the students, of course, would have been of Jung—he said, "Oh, Dr. Jung, it must be so marvelous, having worked on dreams for so long and being the age you are, to be able to understand your own dreams." And Jung said angrily, "No, no! Don't you understand that your dream always remains a mystery, particularly to yourself?"

—EDITH SULLWOLD
in *Sacred Stories*
edited by Charles Simpkinson
and Anne Simpkinson

I often dream I am a tightrope walker. I climb the rope ladder slowly, carefully, adjusting to its wrigglings. The wooden slats mutter to me all the way up. The rungs my right foot stands on say "If you are afraid of falling, you will fall," and the rungs my left foot presses say "If you believe you cannot fall, you will fall."

Eventually I arrive on the little platform at the top. I strip off my track suit and am revealed in all my sequinned glory. I look out and down at the upturned eyes, sparkling brighter than my costume. Then the spotlight pins me, and I hear its mocking tones.

It says "And probably in the end you will fall anyway."

And in my dream, I always listen politely and know it is true, and then I go out sparkling, flashing and dance on the void. That is the challenge, the moment of hope: to dance as near the edge of destruction as is possible, to be willing to fall and still not fall. And the audience cheers, because it is beautiful and because they know that this time I may indeed fall and because they know that that is precisely why it is beautiful, and I have made it beautiful.

—SARA MAITLAND
in *A Big-Enough God*

Once a young man believed that even though he struggled to claim the dark, hidden parts of himself, he couldn't accept the shadow side of himself. Then he had a telling dream.

Out in a very dark night, he had to walk slowly. Suddenly, feeling like a fool, he said to himself, "What are you doing out here without a flashlight?" Trying to find his way back home, he became aware of another presence—a dog, he thought.

Staying on the alert, he saw that the animal was not a dog but a wolf! At first he decided to kill the beast with his bare hands. Then,

L

LISTENING

We begin our lives listening to the many sounds surrounding us in the womb. When we are dying, the last faculty to shut down is usually hearing. In between, there is so much to see that we seldom take the time to cultivate the art of listening.

Listening uses other practices: attention, being present, openness. It is holy work, involving in the inventive phrase of W. A. Mathieu, a Sufi musician, "making an altar out of our ears."

Michael Lerner, editor of *Tikkun* magazine, notes that "Hear O Israel" is "the central mantra of the Jewish people." Christians are challenged to listen to the Word of God, and Buddhists to the dharma talks going on around them.

"God speaks to us every day only we don't know how to listen," the great Indian spiritual leader Mahatma Gandhi states. Perhaps St. Benedict, founder of a Catholic order, gives the best advice of all: "Listen, my children, with the ear of your heart."

"All things and all men, so to speak, call on us with small or loud voices," Protestant theologian Paul Tillich proposes. "They want us to listen. They want us to understand their intrinsic claims, their justice of being. But we can give it to them only through the love that listens."

All things in the universe want to be heard. The Divine Ear helps us lean toward them so we can hear more clearly.

We are also challenged to listen to the many voices inside us, particularly the voices of conscience and intuition. And we need to be willing to lend an ear to the stories of others. As Quaker writer Douglas Steere puts it, "Holy listening—to 'listen' another's soul into life, into a condition of disclosure and discovery, may be almost the greatest service that any human being ever performs for another." This kind of listening is life-giving.

"A wealth of [spiritual] teaching is available," rabbi and retreat leader David A. Cooper suggests. "Our work is not so much to find a teacher as to improvise our own receptivity and sharpen our ability to hear the teachings all around us."

There are the spiritual teachings of the old house that creaks in the wind, the cat who signals pleasure with a purr, and the waitress at the corner café whose cheerful chatter brightens the days of all who come in her orbit.

There are other important teachings to hear as well—those that come from obstacles, enemies, and the demons which haunt us. Are you listening?

Finally, as psychologist and scholar Jean Houston reminds us, we need to listen to the voices of people throughout the global village. She calls it the "habit of multicultural deep listening." And it is critical to the survival of the planet.

Listening is a spiritual craft because it plugs us into the world in so many ways. Keep listening.

LOVE

"In every moment of genuine love," Protestant theologian Paul Tillich observes, "we are dwelling in God and God in us." Recognizing and amplifying these moments is an important part of spiritual literacy.

Life sponsors so many courses on love. We start learning about it when we bond with our parents. Family relationships tutor us in intimacy and self-esteem. Friendship and first love open our eyes to the possibilities of new unions. Marriage and parenting give us a chance to get love right in another family setting. We also practice loving others through our work, volunteer services, and leisure activities.

No one can doubt that romantic love often provides the feeling fuel that makes things happen. Educator Gertrud Mueller Nelson writes: "It is heady stuff that launches ships and makes the world go round. It is a powerful taste of the divine as we experience it in one another."

Think about a moment when you have felt madly in love. Sufi mystics do it all the time. Recall how things revolved around your beloved and how everything else took on a special glow and warmth.

Matthew Fox, an advocate for creation spirituality, has a suggestion for us: "I propose we fall in love several times a day for the rest of our lives. You could fall in love with the galaxies—there are one trillion out there! . . . You could fall in love with fish and plants, animals, and birds, and with people, especially those who are different from us."

All of the world's religions point to the power of love and the obligation to love our neighbors. The radical Jesus Christ goes even further. He challenges us to love our enemies. Jewish mystic Rav Kook comments, "It is our right to hate an evil man for his actions, but because his deepest self is the image of God, it is our duty to honor him with love."

The ethic of altruistic love compels us to look after the oppressed and the outcast. Or as one worker among the vulnerable in Calcutta, Mother Teresa, describes it: "I am a little pencil in the hand of a writing God who is sending a love letter to the world."

The way we treat others supersedes all other spiritual matters. German mystic Meister Eckhart illustrates this point: "If a person were in rapture as great as St. Paul once experienced and learned that a neighbor were in need of a cup of soup, it would be best to withdraw from his rapture and give the person the soup she needs."

The best way to keep love blooming is to creatively reimagine it. Ceremonialist Scout Cloud Lee does just that: "Treat everyone you meet just like you would if you just had your breath taken away by the most beautiful person in the world. Treat each situation in the day as though you were head-over-heels in love."

Love does make the world go around. Elbert Hubbard, a famous American collector of sayings, knows why: "The love we give away is the only love we keep."

recognizing that was absurd, he realized that to survive, "I must make friends with this wolf!"

When he awoke, he understood that the wolf represented his savage soul, his secret shadow, and then the answer to his struggle was clear, *"The wolf is my own dark brother.* Instead of trying to overcome the terror of my hidden self, I must learn to own it, to make friends with it, so I can come to love the rest of myself."

—SHELDON KOPP

in *Blues Ain't Nothing but a Good Soul Feeling Bad*

There are so many creative ways that Spirit tries to speak to us. We have to keep listening.

Once I was complaining to a wise friend that I often awakened at about two o'clock in the morning and then could not get back to sleep. The friend asked me if I really wanted to know why I awoke. I did want to know, for the days after these sleepless nights were a grim ordeal. So he told me that God wanted to talk with me. With my watered-down liberal theological training, I thought he was making fun of me, and I said so. He replied sincerely: "God woke up Samuel in order to talk to him. Why do you think that the Holy One won't speak to you in your darkness? Do you think that God has changed?"

Since I had found that the Divine had directed me out of a dead-end street through my dreams, I thought that listening for God in a sleepless night might well be worth a try. The following night when I awoke, I got up and went to a place where I could be warm. With journal and pencil in hand, I spoke inwardly: "Well, God, here I am, what do you have on your mind?" To my utter amazement, something spoke back to me. I recorded both the questions and the answers. A real conversation followed, and these conversations have continued many nights during the past forty years.

—MORTON KELSEY

in *Set Your Hearts on the Greatest Gift*

MOVIES, THEATER, TELEVISION

If I were giving myself a title, it would not be Fred Brussat, Film Critic, it would be Fred Brussat, Film Recommender. I take this approach on the counsel of the writer of Hebrews in the Bible who suggests that it would be a very good thing to show hospitality to strangers just in case I might be entertaining angels unawares. Over the years, an amazing number of movie strangers have turned out to be angels bearing spiritual meanings.

"No form of art," Swedish director Ingmar Bergman says, "goes beyond ordinary consciousness as film does, straight to the emotions, deep into the twilight room of the soul." Films can be pathways to self-understanding, engagement with others, and connection with a community. Recognizing this, I have ritualized going to the movies.

I consider the time from when the lights go down in the theater and the opening titles finish rolling to be a sacred interlude. It links those of us ready to see the film with those who have made it and others who have already seen it. It is a time to call in wisdom.

While watching the film, I try to see how I might inhabit the drama unfolding on the screen. Some movies provide close encounters with situations that mirror our own experiences; they show us how people deal with success and failure, suffering and death. Other films provide a rendezvous with the shadow side of life or the demons which dog our days. Some movies encourage us to exercise our values and to take stock of our commitments, while still others open a window into the profound mysteries of good and evil, love and loss.

As I leave the theater, I say a word of thanks to those whose creativity and commitment have brought this vision to us. I plan time to contemplate the experience, to appreciate what I have witnessed, and to let the film steep in my heart.

In the next reading, best-selling writer Stephen King explains how films provide moral instruction.

Modern horror stories are not much different from the morality plays of the fifteenth, sixteenth, and seventeenth centuries, when we get right down to it. The horror story most generally not only stands foursquare for the Ten Commandments, it blows them up to tabloid size. We have the comforting knowledge when the lights go down in the theater or when we open the book that the evil-doers will almost certainly be punished, and measure will be returned for measure. . . .

. . . If the horror story is our rehearsal for death, then its strict moralities make it also a reaffirmation of life and good will and simple imagination—just one more pipeline to the infinite.

In his epic poem of a stewardess falling to her death from high above the fields of Kansas, James Dickey suggests a metaphor for the life of the rational being, who must grapple as best he/she can with the fact of his/her own mortality. We fall from womb to tomb, from one blackness and toward another, remembering little of the one and knowing nothing of the other . . . except through faith. That we retain our sanity in the face of these simple yet blinding mysteries is nearly divine. That we may turn the powerful intuition of our imaginations upon them and regard them in this glass of dreams—that we may, however timidly, place our hands within the hole which opens at the center of the column of truth—that is . . .

. . . well, it's magic, isn't it?

—STEPHEN KING
in *Danse Macabre*

The magic of movies can show up unexpectedly. When I was a young assistant minister in a suburban parish in the late 1960s, I decided to discuss short films with the women's group. I started with Polish director Roman Polanski's Three Men and a Wardrobe *since it was a parable about the treasures in one's life.*

The political makeup of the congregation was very conservative. After showing the film, I asked if anyone would like to share her response. One woman leapt to her feet, screamed "How could you bring a film by a Communist into the sacred halls of this church?" and stormed out, presumably on the way to see my superior. A tense silence passed over the seventy-five other women in the room.

My first impulse was to lash out at the woman, but I bit my tongue. My Adam's apple seemed to be caught in my clerical collar which by then felt like a noose around my neck. In the softest voice I could muster, I said, "Well, that's one reaction to the film. Are there any others?"

The women began to share their spiritual interpretations of the film. They offered perspectives that I had never even considered. The dialogue was rich, full, and exciting, and it went on for almost two hours. Afterwards, some of the women said they were usually too shy to join a discussion, but this time it seemed important that many opinions be expressed. I thanked the Holy Spirit for the woman who set things in motion with her vituperative response.

That film discussion showed me how art can be a catalyst to the honest expression of feelings and ideas. Sometimes, however, art does not touch the mind as much as it reaches the soul.

When I begin to lose heart, it does me good to recall a lesson in the dignity of art which I learned years ago at a theater in Assisi, in Italy. Helena and I had gone to see an evening of pantomime and no one else showed up. The two of us made up the entire audience. When the lights dimmed, we were joined by the usher and the ticket seller. Yet despite the fact that there were more people on stage than in the audience, the actors worked as hard as if they were basking in the glory of a full house on opening night. They put their hearts and souls into the performance and it was marvelous.

Our applause shook the empty hall. We clapped until our hands were sore.

—EDUARDO GALEANO
in *The Book of Embraces*

We all feed the lake. That is what is important. It is a corporate act. During my time in the theatre I knew what it was to be part of such an enlarging of the human potential, and though I was never more than a bit player or an understudy, I knew the truth of Stanislavsky's words: "There are no small roles. There are only small players." And I had the joy of being an instrument in the great orchestra of a play, learning from the play (how much Chekov taught me during the run of *The Cherry Orchard*), from the older actors and actresses. I was part of the Body. That's what it's all about.

—MADELEINE L'ENGLE
in *Walking on Water*

That is a good spiritual image, the ensemble as body. Theater, movies, and television emphasize by their very structure that every part is important and the story cannot be told well except through the entire community. This is perhaps no more apparent than in television dramas, which are known for their acting ensembles.

When we first began reviewing television movies in the early 1970s, in the days before VCRs were common, Fred used to go to network screening rooms. I always greeted him on his return with the question, "Did you cry?" Most times he reported that, to the amazement of the network publicity people, he had and profusely.

We learned from those experiences to respect a good television program's ability to touch our emotions, and we are still inveterate criers during TV dramas. Last episodes of favorite series are always occasions for weeping. But there have been many teary moments in regular episodes of our favorites over the years: St. Elsewhere, Hill Street Blues, China Beach, Beauty and the Beast, thirtysomething, Northern Exposure, Picket Fences, Homicide, Chicago Hope, *and* NYPD Blue.

One night on Chicago Hope *was almost too much for us to take. The hospital lawyer, Alan Birch, was shot by a member of a street gang. Jeffrey Geiger, just named the best cardiac surgeon in the country, could not save him. The loss of Alan became a spiritual emergency for this usually puffed-up doctor. He quit his job so that he could take care of his godchild, Alan's baby girl, declaring "I am not going to be the center of the rest of my life." You get to know these characters over weeks and weeks of watching them, and then they do something unexpected and yet perfectly in character. A moment of grace.*

One of the finest grace moments we can remember occurred on NYPD Blue. *Andy Sipowicz is a New York City detective who from surface appearances and first impressions you might call "rough-hewn." He's a volatile, gauche, recovering alcoholic not known for his sensitive behavior. During one episode he investigated the murder of the only child of two immigrants from Poland. The boy was found in an abandoned lot almost directly across the street from their apartment.*

The next day Andy returned to the scene to find the parents standing on the sidewalk. They pointed to a white bird at the top of a nearby building. The parents had decided that their son's spirit had returned in the form of the bird to assure them that his soul was all right. They asked if the detective could see the light coming from the bird. Andy looked up with the expression of a man who has seen too much death and is not easily surprised. But as he stood next to those grieving parents, he softened. "I think there is something there," he said quietly. And we saw it too.

ART

"Art," Paul Klee writes, "does not reproduce the visible, rather it makes visible." Whether we are creating it or observing it, art can move us beyond our ordinary ways of viewing the world.

One day, after a drawing exercise, one of my students said in amazement, "Every time I draw something I fall in love!" I wasn't surprised to hear this, because I know that when we wake up to the world around us in full form, with vivid colors, lines, and shapes, we become filled with awe and wonder. It is easy to fall in love with the things we've walked past so many times, because we realize that the world is offering itself to us like a lover longing for our embrace and recognition. Receiving the universe in all its diversity allows us a new self-appreciation, and coming to a level of self-acceptance and self-love prepares us to love the world in return. When this awareness lives at our core, celebration becomes a way of life.

—ADRIANA DIAZ
in *Freeing the Creative Spirit*

When we see pain on a tortured person's face, we might glimpse for a second the image of Jesus crucified, a reality that artists for centuries have shown in infinite variation and detail and one that enters the lives of all of us at one time or another. We might look at a woman in a jewelry shop with the eyes of D. H. Lawrence, who saw Aphrodite in the body of the woman washing her clothes in a river. We might see a Cezanne still life in a momentary glance at our own kitchen table. When a summer breeze blows through an open window as we sit reading in a rare half-hour of quiet, we might recall one of the hundreds of annunciations painters have given us, reminding us that it is the habit of angels to visit in moments of silent reading.

—THOMAS MOORE
in *Care of the Soul*

On a trip to New York my husband and I went to see the renovated warehouse that had become the downtown Guggenheim Museum.

The uncluttered long white exhibition space floated—a limitless expanse of calm and stillness. I was not prepared for the beauty of the white walls. And on the walls were white paintings. White walls, white paintings. Placed at intervals were four or five Brancusi sculptures. That was all. My heart was pounding. This was what a temple should feel like: a "temple of the soul." . . .

An "inner light" radiated from the paintings.

The space was silent—with that respectful, muffled silence of a cloister. The word *purity* came to mind.

And immense.

This was the "immensity within ourselves" I had read about and hadn't understood.

"It doesn't always have to be so hard," I heard myself say—the judge nowhere present at that moment. There are other ways of "seeing"—these paintings seemed to say. Other possibilities, infinite possibilities. Mysteries to be uncovered.

—SUE BENDER
in *Everyday Sacred*

Fred's and my friend Pat makes a pilgrimage to New York at least once a year to go to art exhibitions. One of my fondest memories is of the afternoon she took me to the Guggenheim Museum to see a Jean Dubuffet retrospective. I wondered if I would understand the work of this French artist (I had majored in political science in college and never took art classes), but Pat told me not to worry.

We started at the top of the Guggenheim's ramp, an exhibition hall that slopes downward in a spiral for several stories. We zigzagged up and down the ramp for hours as we compared different versions of the same subject, and also returned again and again to our favorites.

It was a revelation to me. For one thing, I had not expected the art to be so playful or to touch me so deeply. I was laughing and crying at the same time. I was particularly drawn to the primitive portraits: odd, bloated figures with expressions of glee. One face was made of butterflies. Was this an image of transformation? Never mind. I was having too much fun to ponder the meanings of the paintings. The clever titles—Traveler Without a Compass or Ecstasy in the Sky—would start me laughing. When I looked over at Pat, the more experienced art connoisseur, she too was grinning from ear to ear.

More than twenty years later, I can't remember my personal reactions to each painting, collage, or sculpture. It is a feeling that remains: unmuted joy.

I can measure my life by the moments when art transformed me—standing in front of Michelangelo's Duomo pieta, listening to Dylan Thomas read his poetry, hearing Bach's cello suites for the first time.

But not only there.

Sitting at a table in a smoky club listening to Muddy Waters and Little Walter talk back and forth to each other through their instruments; listening to a tiny Japanese girl play a violin sonata at a youth symphony concert; standing in a clapboard gift shop on the edge of Hudson Bay staring at a crudely carved Inuit image of a bear turning into a man.

It can happen anywhere, anytime. You do not have to be in some setting hallowed by greatness, or in the presence of an artist honored around the world. Art can work its magic any time you are in the presence of a work created by someone who has gone inside the act of creation to become what they are creating. When this takes place time stands still and if our hearts are open to the experience, our spirits soar and our imaginations fly unfettered.

You need these moments if you are ever to have a life that is more than the sum of the daily moments of humdrum affairs.

If you can create these moments—if you are a painter or a poet or a musician or an actor—you carry within you a prize of great worth. If you cannot create them, you must learn to love one of the arts in a way that allows the power of another's creation to come alive within you.

Once you love an art enough that you can be taken up in it, you are able to experience an echo of the great creative act that mysteriously has given life to us all.

It may be the closest any of us can get to God.

—KENT NERBURN
in *Letters to My Son*

CRAFTS

Pottery, woodworking, and sewing are popular crafts which are creative outlets and a means of personal transformation for many men and women. Some will tell you that the regular practice of a craft is an act of worship. Others are content to savor a realization similar to Carla Needleman's: "Craft is a way of working to be alive inside my skin."

Working with clay has brought me back to the primal link between my soul and the cycles of change and creativity in nature. Made of stone, water, and organic slime, clay is the elemental mixture found everywhere in the world, offspring of the earth itself. When I work with clay and ground myself in the elements of nature, I feel like I am coming home to the earth after a long time away, having been lost in a world of words and concepts. Working with clay wakes me up, calls me back to my senses, and gives my soul a tangible expression, a language with shape and size.

—MARJORY ZOET BANKSON
in *This Is My Body*

Donna Schaper, a United Church of Christ minister, discovers truths about herself while refinishing a chair, as does Episcopal priest Barbara Cawthorne Crafton while sewing.

The first thing people do when restoring old chairs is strip—strip right down to the bare wood. They do this to see what the original might have looked like and to determine if the thing is worth doing over. They strip away all the years of grime, the garish coats of paint piled one on top of the other. They get rid of all the junk that's been tacked on through the years and try to find the solid, simple thing that's underneath.

I'm like an old chair needing that stripping process. Every now and then I have to take a really hard look at the illusions I've built up in myself and my society, see what I've gotten myself into. Illusions? Yes, illusions; the excess baggage I carry around, the unnecessary, the socially expected, all that keeps me living off center too long. Stripping myself of all this is an intentional letting go of these illusions. It is a spiritual act of personal forgiveness. God lets us let go.

It's hard work to let God forgive me. I have to discover the original under all these coats I've added, strip away all the cynicism and anger I've built up, get rid of the junk I've taken on, defy my disappointments, and find what is real again.

—DONNA SCHAPER
in *Stripping Down*

I have taken over a basement room in which someone who lived here before left a Ping-Pong table. It is now my sewing room. The table is just the right height for me, and I can spread out the fabric on its expanse of dark green when I cut things out. It's cool there in the summer, and quiet. I listen to the radio and work away, and a flat piece of cloth takes on shape as I work, grows breast-shaped curves and hips, gathers itself into a waistband, to which I have added an inch because I am fatter than I wish I were.

This activity uses resources seldom called upon in the rest of my life. Beyond basic decisions about color, style, and fabric, there is little thought involved in sewing. Clothing construction follows the same rules whatever the garment. You sew a seam and finish the edges. Right sides go together unless it says otherwise. You press seams open, and darts toward the center or down. You do not argue with the seams about the degree of their openness, nor do you seek a dart consensus about which way *they* want to be pressed. There are virtually no moral ambiguities in sewing.

—BARBARA CAWTHORNE CRAFTON
in *The Sewing Room*

Book review editor and writer Phyllis Tickle tells the story of how her father crocheted a rosette coverlet as a prayerful reaction to World War II. A veteran of World War I, he began stitching in 1937 and continued until the war was over. At one point, he reflected on the coverlet's spiritual meaning: it is prayer, connections, and teacher.

He stood up and brushed the grains of rotted wood dirt off his pants legs. "I thought a lot about my mother while I was working the coverlet. Did you know that?"

This time I had no need to feign. I had indeed known that. I nodded.

"She used to say that she could tell what a piece of work had taught someone and who it was that had been willing to learn." The thin smile spread around the corners of his lips and rippled on toward its center above his chin. "I wondered what she would have said about the coverlet and me."

"Did it teach you anything?" Even though the innocence of the wildflowers and the silence of the apple trees had given me permission, his mood was still broken, yanked back from reverie to reportage.

"Yes, of course, it did." He was impatient of his answer if not of my question. "All of those things you would suppose from a long, complicated project like that . . . "

MEANING

"Human beings construct meaning as spiders make webs," observes writer Catherine Bateson. "This is how we survive, our primary evolutionary business."

We are both meaning seekers and meaning makers. We try to discover the purpose of our lives and to make sense of our experiences.

"What we are looking for on earth and in earth and in ourselves is the process that can unlock for us the mystery of meaningfulness in our daily lives," Jungian psychologist Alice O. Howell counsels. "We can only see half of anything. The other half is the meaning we give to what we see. . . . In every tree, apple, flower, there is an aha! waiting!" Significances beckon at every turn. To see them, we must be attentive, open, and hospitable.

"Meanings," according to philosopher Victor Frankl, "are inexhaustible. We need to develop our intuitive sense that allows us to smell out meanings hidden and dormant in life situations."

Part of every day's spiritual challenge is to decipher the lessons in an encounter on the street corner, an article read during lunch, a problem at work, a phone call from a relative, a television documentary, the criticism of a peer, or the silence just before the dawn. We constantly ask, What does this mean?

We also are challenged to interpret the messages in sacred texts. They put us in touch with the meanings discovered by our spiritual ancestors.

"In many traditional Jewish communities, when a child entered cheder, religious school, for the first time, that child was greeted by a curious sight: a chart of letters smeared with honey," Rabbi David Wolpe tells us. "The new student licked off the honey from the letters one by one, thus learning a critical lesson: learning is sweet, and the very letters of the word carry the sweetness."

A smorgasbord of spiritual learnings are available to us from the world's religions. We taste the sweetness. We also feast on meanings passed on from seeker to seeker during lectures at bookstores, workshops at conference centers, and gatherings of men's and women's circles.

Thich Nhat Hanh, a Buddhist poet, writer, and activist, states: "In each of us is a seed of understanding. That seed is God." Old Wise One enables us to comprehend the significance of our days.

"Spirituality lets meaning flow into daily life," Brother David Steindl-Rast adds. As a result, we are constantly weaving new constellations of meaning through our search for truth, our struggle for justice, and our acts of love.

In the end, as diarist Anais Nin reminds us, "There is not one big cosmic meaning for all. There is only the meaning we all give to our lives, an individual meaning." Find that meaning and share it with others.

Then his eyes drifted off of me again for just a moment and he said, "But mainly the coverlet showed me how it was—in what way it was, that is—that Mama was right. Stitches do take the time they are made in and spend it to change the people who are making them." His voice was hesitant and slightly higher than usual as if he were both tentative of his commentary and relieved to have found it. "Always remember that I told you that, Princess. Watch the people as much as their stitches." I always did.

—PHYLLIS TICKLE
in *My Father's Prayer*

Our friend Debra is living proof that stitches change the people who make them. Each year she makes one-foot-square quilts as gifts for her friends. This is an excerpt from the note that accompanied one of the quilts.

I spent the first three months of this year fighting with colors and patterns in an ill-fated attempt to take control over these quilts. In the end, I was forced to give up my original color scheme and to do this impossible pattern—composed of twelve three-inch squares with six of those squares having twenty-five pieces in them—that no one in her right mind would take on for seventeen quilts. But this pattern would not leave my mind, and I gave in and created what wished to be created. God often works that way in our lives, making suggestions with lesser or greater force. We have a choice about saying "yes," but life can be easier and clearer when we just give in and say "yes."

Notice that the pattern has no beginning and no end. More and more, that fits life as I understand it. I used to think that "next month will be less busy." Well, for many years now, "next month" hasn't ever arrived! My life, and the pace of it, might have brief rest stops (thank God!) but there is basically no beginning and no end . . . just breathers here and there.

The backing fabric is a wonderful piece of the quilt. (There is something wonderfully extravagant about strawberries in the middle of winter!) I found this fabric and really, really wanted to use it on the front of the quilt, where the off-white squares are now. I tried to do so even though I *knew* there wasn't enough contrast to use it there. Life needs contrasts, and I had to use the white fabric to set off the red and the green. Then I tried to use the strawberries for the border, but it pulled the eye away from the quilt and onto the border only, upsetting the balance of the whole piece. So, the strawberries landed on the back. God gave me this stunning fabric, and used it to teach me about extravagance, contrast, and balance. My life has been richly blessed with all of these this year.

—DEBRA FARRINGTON
in *Debra's 1995 Advent Quilt*

MUSIC

The Master once proposed a riddle: "What do the artist and the musician have in common with the mystic?"

Everyone gave up.

"The realization that the finest speech does not come from the tongue," said the Master.

—ANTHONY DE MELLO
in *One Minute Nonsense*

In medieval times, men and women talked about the music of the spheres. W. A. Mathieu, a composer, believes that we can hear music all around us if we learn to listen.

You can lie still in your room and hear room music. There exists, thus, spider music, moss music, cloud and thunderclap music, music of Gaia, and music of the spheres; any or all of these are sensible to saints and sinners. As ye are tuned, so ye shall hear.

Do not be surprised if, at the core of some such music, you find your own foggy fear, or your own loneliness. Or, at the flung edge of it, come up hopelessly lost. Gradually you learn how you yourself are a kindred one of those musics, one among many in a lavish opera. You are *made* of music—lonely music when you are lonely, vast music when you feel vast, even happy music sometimes. The whole stream of your life, already musical, is simply waiting for you to hear it.

—W. A. MATHIEU
in *The Musical Life*

Here is one artist's glimpse of what is involved in making music a spiritual endeavor.

Free now to be guided by their own inclination, my hands sunk deep into a progression of low, resonant chords in the bottom of the piano. Slowly, they built into an energetic crescendo that almost shook the piano and filled the hall. Gradually, this movement evolved into something else, and then into something else again. There was a truthfulness in my playing now that I hadn't felt comfortable to expose before. Why is this truthfulness so important, I wondered. Can't I just sit down and play? But there is more to it than that. I know that when I step onto this stage, just focusing on technique and what I have played before is not enough. It is being truthful to the moment that counts. That is all a performer can depend on. Even though it offers no guarantees, it is all that I have to give. Once that shift occurred, what had at first seemed like hours now felt like minutes, and all too soon it was over.

—MICHAEL JONES
in *Creating an Imaginative Life*

The spiritual practices of imagination, being present, and listening increase our appreciation of musical performances.

The record drops to the turntable and begins to turn. The tone arm lifts, moves sideways with disinterested mechanical grace, hovers for a moment over the edge of the record, then descends. The speakers crackle loudly and I realize the record is more badly scratched than I'd remembered. A single muted violin begins the quartet. The tone seems distorted. Maybe something's wrong with the needle. The second violin joins in, the viola and cello.

And once again the miracle happens. The flaws are forgotten, Ludwig van Beethoven is here in the room. He is addressing himself to me alone. I *know* him. Across 150 years, transmitted by lines and dots on paper, put into sound by four men playing wooden instruments in Boston, translated into electronic impulses and thence into the mechanical vibrations of a stylus on a master disk, mass-produced into records, translated back into electricity then sound, Beethoven's personal presence survives. Ten times removed in time and space and intermediaries, his *C-Sharp Minor Quartet*, Opus 131, still contains him, *is* him.

—GEORGE LEONARD
in *The Silent Pulse*

I went with my wife to see the opera *La Boheme*. I wasn't familiar with the plot, the acoustics in the hall weren't quite right, and I needed to read the supertitle translations but found them distracting. I was physically and mentally restless; soon my mind was wandering back to problem solving and reviewing tasks I was working on earlier in the day. It struck me that when I was working on *them*, I was thinking about going to the opera. So I tried using breath-awareness. It was difficult at first because it forced me to confront my restlessness. After a few minutes I figured out a way to glance occasionally at the supertitles, not to worry about every detail of the plot, and to enjoy the beauty of the voices even if I couldn't understand what they were singing. Pretty soon I was swept into the story. Breath-awareness prevented me from being lured back into pointless fantasizing about other times and places. As the poignant story reached its climax, I wept at least a pint of tears. I left the theater with a pleasurable sad-achy sensation in my heart that lingered for hours.

—TIMOTHY MILLER
in *How to Want What You Have*

In the movie The Dead, *Gretta and her husband are leaving a party in Dublin. She pauses on the stairs to listen to one of the guests sing* "The Lass of Aughrim." *The song unlocks a memory she has kept hidden away about a long-ago romance and its tragic end. A song can do that.*

Another sweet surprise of music is its healing balm. Oliver Sacks, a psychiatrist and writer, describes these effects of music on his mending leg.

Suddenly, wonderfully, I was moved by the music. The music seemed passionately, wonderfully, quiveringly alive—and conveyed to me a sweet feeling of life. I felt, with the first bars of the music, a hope and an intimation that life would return to my leg—that *it* would be stirred, and stir, with original movement, and recollect or recreate its forgotten motor melody. I felt—how inadequate words are for feelings of this sort!—I felt, in those first heavenly bars of music, as if the animating and creative principle of the whole world was revealed, that life itself was music, or consubstantial with music; that our living moving flesh, itself, was "solid" music—music made fleshy, substantial, corporeal. In some intense, passionate, almost mystical sense, I felt that music, indeed, might be the cure to my problems—or, at least, a key of an indispensable sort.

—OLIVER SACKS
in *A Leg to Stand On*

For many years popular music—especially rock and reggae—has been a necessary part of our lives. This music expresses our deep feelings and desires, and speaks to a whole spectrum of our ideas on love and freedom and justice. We have two favorite musical spiritual directors: Bruce Springsteen and Gladys Knight and the Pips.

Whenever we experience a setback, suffer a personal slight, or witness an injustice, we turn on "Badlands" by Bruce Springsteen. This rock song meets us in the pits of depression, when we are aware of "trouble in the heartland" and we feel "caught in a cross fire" as a result. From the song, we learn that "the broken hearts stand/as the price you gotta pay." Bruce tells us to "keep pushin' till it's understood,/and these badlands start treating us good." He urges us to be defiant: "It ain't no sin to be glad you're alive." He says we need to have faith: "I believe in the love that you gave me./I believe in the faith that can save me./I believe in the hope/and I pray that someday it may raise me/Above these badlands." Those ringing words root our resolve, and we vow not to give up or give in.

Whenever we are feeling exhausted and at the end of our personal resources, we turn on "I Can See Clearly Now," a ballad by Johnny Nash sung by Gladys Knight and the Pips: "I can see clearly now, the rain is gone." Oh, don't we wish. "I can see all obstacles in my way." That's for sure. "Gone are the dark clouds that had me blind." Okay, it's not as bad as it seems. "Here is my rainbow I've been praying for." All right! "It's gonna be a bright, bright sunshiny day." Oh yes! The buoyancy of the music invariably renews our souls and sends us back into the fray with energy and hope.

Someday I may get to personally thank Patti La Belle for sharing her magnificent voice and extraordinary heart in song. Until then, this will have to do.

Every week, for two winters and two summers, as I drove to and from the cancer clinic for treatments, I played her renditions of "Somewhere Over the Rainbow" and "There's a Winner in You" over and over. When I was frightened and thought I couldn't make one more trip, I played those songs to get me there. Afterward, when I was tired and afraid I couldn't make the drive home, I played them again. My spirits never failed to recover, and the miles just flew by. I found such courage and hope in her passionate music. In the midst of the darkest time of my life, that voice made me feel grateful to be alive. . . .

There's a song for everyone, one incalculable mix of melody and magic that so neatly wraps the heart that we are lifted out of the here and now. And something in us is healed. Search for your song.

—NANCY BURKE
in *Meditations for Health*

WORK

A man chopped underbrush at the edge of the forest, sold it, and lived on the modest profits. One day a hermit came out of the forest, and the man asked him advice for his life. The hermit advised him, "Go deeper into the forest!" The man went deeper into the forest and found wonderful trees, which he sold as timber. He became rich, but he suddenly recalled the advice of the hermit: "Go deeper into the forest!" And so he went deeper into the forest and found a silver mine. He worked it and became still more wealthy. One day he again recalled the hermit's words: "Go deeper into the forest!" And so he dared to press farther into the darkness of the mysterious forest. Soon he found wonderful precious stones. He took them in hand and rejoiced at their brilliance, but again the hermit's words occurred to him: "Go deeper into the forest!" Jewels in hand, he walked on and on. Suddenly, at dawn, he found himself again at the edge of the forest. So he took his axe and chopped the underbrush and sold it to his fellows.

—WILLIGIS JAGER
in *Search for the Meaning of Life*

303

Our assistant Carolyn Dutton really likes Jager's story. It is appropriate that we move from music to work with Carolyn because she straddles both worlds. A gifted fiddler, and the fastest typist we have ever known, Carolyn definitely understands about going "deeper into the forest."

When she first came to New York, Carolyn played for projects staged at La Mama, an experimental theater in downtown Manhattan. She moved on to off-Broadway productions and a few years ago was the fiddler for the Broadway production of Grapes of Wrath. *All the while she played in a succession of bluegrass, rock, and country bands. When she wasn't making music, she typed for us and managed our subscriptions.*

The traditional work ethic says that a career should be a steady progression upward to better and better positions until you reach the pinnacle of your profession. But few careers today are linear. One day Carolyn announced that she was going to be at La Mama every afternoon for a month playing violin for an actors' workshop. She was back at the edge of the forest where she had started.

"How do you feel about that?" I asked, thinking of many other workers who not only find themselves doing the same things again and again but also having to start completely over in new careers. It is not the money or the job that matters, she said. She goes where she is needed, where she can use her gifts.

TO BE OF USE

The people I love the best
jump into work head first
without dallying in the shallows
and swim off with sure strokes almost out of sight.
They seem to become natives of that element,
the black sleek heads of seals
bouncing like half-submerged balls.

I love people who harness themselves, an ox to a heavy cart,
who pull like water buffalo, with massive patience,
who strain in the mud and the muck to move things forward,
who do what has to be done, again and again.

I want to be with people who submerge
in the task, who go into the fields to harvest
and work in a row and pass the bags along,
who are not parlor generals and field deserters

but move in a common rhythm
when the food must come in or the fire be put out.

The work of the world is common as mud.
Botched, it smears the hands, crumbles to dust.
But the thing worth doing well done
has a shape that satisfies, clean and evident.
Greek amphoras for wine or oil,
Hopi vases that held corn, are put in museums
but you know they were made to be used.
The pitcher cries for water to carry
and a person for work that is real.

—MARGE PIERCY
in *Circles on the Water*

Then a ploughman said, Speak to us of Work.

And he answered, saying:

You work that you may keep pace with the earth and the soul of the earth.

For to be idle is to become a stranger unto the seasons, and to step out of life's procession, that marches in majesty and proud submission towards the infinite. . . .

Always you have been told that work is a curse and labour a misfortune.

But I say to you that when you work you fulfil a part of earth's furthest dream, assigned to you when that dream was born,

And in keeping yourself with labour you are in truth loving life.

And to love life through labour is to be intimate with life's inmost secret. . . .

And all work is empty save when there is love;

And when you work with love you bind yourself to yourself, and to one another, and to God.

And what is it to work with love?

It is to weave the cloth with threads drawn from your heart, even as if your beloved were to wear that cloth.

It is to build a house with affection, even as if your beloved were to dwell in that house.

It is to sow seeds with tenderness and reap the harvest with joy, even as if your beloved were to eat the fruit.

It is to change all things you fashion with a breath of your own spirit,
And to know that all the blessed dead are standing about you and watching. . . .
Work is love made visible.

—Kahlil Gibran
in *The Prophet*

Our work, what we do and how we do it, is a personal statement.

There is a recent book about the village of Akenfield in England, in which the author tells of the old farmers who could look at a field where ten people had ploughed and tell you the name of the man who had done each furrow. In it could be felt the character of that ploughman. In a similar way I have been told of Indian markets in South America where they sell rope and can tell you, just by looking at it, who made each particular piece. There is a great difference between such innate character and what is an attempt at a "personal" statement.

. . . Those farmers in Akenfield were asked why they took such care to make furrows so precise—the precision would not yield more beans—and they answered that it wasn't because they were paid more, it was because it was their work and they did it as best they could. It belonged to them, it was them. "It was his signature," writes Ronald Blyth about the farmer, "not only on the field but on life."

—Bernard Leach
in *The Potter's Challenge*

The reason I didn't see the mysticism in the Victory [delicatessen] is that in the ordinary sense there was nothing to see. The nothing was there, not in what Ernie was doing but in what he was not doing.

At first it would seem that Ernie was working while everyone else stood around. As you became familiar with the place, Ernie's work seemed to disappear. You would just stop noticing he was working. There he was, spinning in his grimy apron, no more mysterious than a toasted hard roll. He was certainly the center of everything that happened in the Victory but it was a strangely unnoticed center. It should have been obvious that he was actually preparing and serving food but it wasn't obvious.

I doubt whether Ernie knew the names of more than a few of us. But names didn't matter here. Identities had a lighter weight. To the degree that we knew each other at all, it was by our orders or our baseball teams, by the jokes we told or by the intimate details about our lives that we revealed with astonishing innocence. Even if Ernie didn't recognize you, it came to about the same thing. "What's yours, lady?" "What're you buying today, pal?"

—JAMES P. CARSE
in *Breakfast at the Victory*

I had come to Kotzebue on the adventure of helping to "build the first high school above the Arctic Circle," but the work itself was far from an adventure. It was hard, backbreaking labor. One day I was trying to dig a trench for a sewer line—no small task in a world of frozen tundra. An Eskimo man whose face and hands displayed the leathery toughness of many winters came by and watched me for a while. Finally he said simply and profoundly, "You are digging a ditch to the glory of God." He said it to encourage me, I know. And I have never forgotten his words. Beyond my Eskimo friend no human being ever knew or cared whether I dug that ditch well or poorly. In time it was to be covered up and forgotten. But because of my friend's words, I dug with all my might, for every shovelful of dirt was a prayer to God. Even though I did not know it at the time, I was attempting in my small and unsophisticated way to do what the great artisans of the Middle Ages did when they carved the back of a piece of art, knowing that God alone would see it.

—RICHARD J. FOSTER
in *Prayer*

A man lamented to his rabbi:

"I'm frustrated that my work leaves me no time for study or prayer."

The rabbi replied: "Perhaps your work is more pleasing to God than study or prayer."

—HASIDIC TALE
told in *Being God's Partner*
by Jeffrey K. Salkin

With creativity and imagination, it is possible to reframe any type of work and see it as a partnership with God in the ongoing creation of the world. In the next reading, Rabbi Jeffrey K. Salkin helps us see what this means.

A few years ago, a young taxi driver drove me to John F. Kennedy Airport on Long Island. After a few minutes of conversation, I discovered that Mike had belonged to my synagogue years before I came to the community.

"So, rabbi," he asked while we sat in heavy traffic, "what do you say to a Jew like me who hasn't been in a synagogue since his bar mitzvah ceremony?"

Thinking for a moment, I recalled that in Hasidic lore, the *baal aqalah* (the wagon driver) is an honored profession. So I said, "We could talk about your work."

"What does my work have to do with religion?"

"Well, we choose how we look at the world and at life. You're a taxi driver. But you are also a piece of the tissue that connects all humanity. You're taking me to the airport. I'll go to a different city and give a couple of lectures that might touch or help or change someone. I couldn't have gotten there without you. You help make that connection happen.

"I heard on your two-way radio that after you drop me off, you're going to pick up a woman from the hospital and take her home. That means that you'll be the first non-medical person she encounters after being in a hospital. You will be a small part of her healing process, an agent in her re-entry into the world of health.

"You may then pick up someone from the train station who has come home from seeing a dying parent. You may take someone to the house of the one that he or she will ask to join in marriage. You're a connector, a bridge builder. You're one of the unseen people who make the world work as well as it does. That is holy work. You may not think of it this way, but yours is a sacred mission."

—Jeffrey K. Salkin
in *Being God's Partner*

A spiritual reading of work assumes that every job has a meaning and a purpose in the grand scheme of things.

God puts you where God needs you. You are where you are *supposed* to be. The job you are doing may not be any easier on account of this, indeed it may be harder, even more urgent, but now you are centered, focused, clear. So this is where I am supposed to be. I always thought I was supposed to be somewhere else, doing something else, being someone else. But I realize now that I was mistaken. This does not mean that I can't or will not be doing something else. Just right now, I am where God wants me.

—Lawrence Kushner
in *The Book of Words*

This world was given to us to work on. Cultivating it we come to a deep understanding of the divine reality with which every part of creation is charged. Rilke says in one of his poems to God, "We grasp you only by acting." The German word for grasping means both holding something in your hands, seizing, and putting your hands into something, as you do when shaping clay. Only in this way do we grasp the divine reality.

—Brother David Steindl-Rast
in *The Music of Silence*

Typing, and in this computer age, mousing, are how I use my hands to grasp the divine reality. Since Fred still writes with a pen on yellow pads, it's good for our partnership that I really like to type. The skill came easily to me. By the time I took typing class in high school, my fingers were already used to moving in response to something that my eyes saw. I had been reading music and playing piano for years. So

NURTURING

"God," according to the thirteenth-century mystic Mechtild of Magdeburg, "is not only fatherly. God is also mother who lifts Her loved children from the ground to Her knee."

What a wonderful image conveying how we are cherished and nurtured by She Who Is! This care and concern for us is the cause of our deep trust and well-being.

African-American poet Maya Angelou writes in her memoirs: "God loves me. Each time I allow myself to say the words I am suffused with tears of gratitude and wonder. And I am reestablished as a giving, living, full human being with every right to everything right here on this earth."

Although it may take a long time to figure out just who we are and what we are called to do (and that may change many times), one thing is for sure—we must nourish self and help it grow.

"All you need is deep within you waiting to unfold and reveal itself," Eileen Caddy of the Findhorn community in Scotland observes. "All you have to do is to be still and to take time to seek for what is within, and you will surely find it."

Self-exploration under the auspices of the Divine Mother remains an adventure over the course of a lifetime. There is no end to the twists and turns of the journey. And the lure of personal growth pulls us along.

Writer Brenda Schaffer spells out the nature of this endeavor: "Growth means becoming more of who we already are, not what others want us to be. Growth means evolving and waking up, not remaining asleep in the illusion of the learned self."

If we are to bring out the very best that is inside us, we must take time to nurture ourselves. "When we truly care for ourselves, it becomes possible to care far more profoundly about other people. The more alert and sensitive we are to our own needs, the more loving and generous we can be toward others," American columnist Eda LeShan notes.

Taking care of ourselves may involve something as simple as a soothing bath or as complicated as a spiritual retreat taken far from home.

Ways to nurture others abound. What have you given birth to and nurtured this day? A fresh sense of family solidarity? A supportive letter to a friend? A project to improve the neighborhood where you live?

"We are here to witness creation and to abet it," nature writer Annie Dillard professes. "We are here to bring to consciousness the beauty and power that are all around us and to praise the people who are here with us."

And so the circle is complete. The Grandmother of the World nurtures us. We take care of the best that is in us. Then we tend to the needs of others.

As psychotherapist Molly Young Brown concludes: "Service comes naturally to us when we love and accept ourselves on a deep level. Our love bubbles up and overflows to those around us. We find our greatest satisfaction and fulfillment in making contributions to the world in ways that are uniquely our own."

while others in my class groaned and cursed the machines, I relaxed and got into a flow. I found that typing provided me with daily lessons in effortlessness. It still does that, and more.

A spirituality of work is based on a heightened sense of sacramentality, of the idea that everything that is, is holy and that our hands consecrate it to the service of God. When we grow radishes in a small container in a city apartment, we participate in creation. We sustain the globe. When we sweep the street in front of a house in the dirtiest city in the country, we bring new order to the universe. We tidy the Garden of Eden. We make God's world new again. When we repair what has been broken or paint what is old or give away what we have earned that is above and beyond our own sustenance, we stoop down and scoop up the earth and breathe into it new life again, as God did one morning in time only to watch it unfold and unfold and unfold through the ages. When we wrap garbage and recycle cans, when we clean a room and put coasters under glasses, when we care for everything we touch and touch it reverently, we become the creators of a new universe. . . . Work enables us to put our personal stamp of approval, our own watermark, the autograph of our souls on the development of the world. In fact, to do less is to do nothing at at all.

—JOAN CHITTISTER
in *There Is a Season*

Some of the most trying, and yet the most creative, periods in our lives are ones when we don't quite know where we are headed. The following vigil takes note of the significance of job transitions.

The world of my work is changing, and my professional identity, direction, and security are unsettled.

It is discouraging to think of all the time and effort I have invested. It seems like a sacrifice.
Perhaps I can begin to understand the original meaning of the word: "to make sacred."
Perhaps this is a sacred passage in which my insecurity is sacrificed for trust in whatever is to come.

*As one form dissolves, another takes its place. My work now is to
seek and to recognize a new form that will provide the opportunity for growth and reward.*

> —NOELA N. EVANS
> in *Meditations for the Passages
> and Celebrations of Life*

*The shadow side of expressing ourselves through our labors is worka-
holism, perfectionism, and excessive busyness. Various spiritual disciplines help us battle these excesses.*

Brother David Steindl-Rast reminds us that the Chinese word for
"busy" is composed of two characters: "heart" and "killing." When
we make ourselves so busy that we are always rushing around
trying to get this or that "done," or "over with," we kill something
vital in ourselves, and we smother the quiet wisdom of our heart.
When we invest our work with judgment and impatience, always
striving for speed and efficiency, we lose the capacity to appreciate
the million quiet moments that may bring us peace, beauty, or joy.
As we seek salvation through our frantic productivity and accom-
plishments, we squander the teachings that may be present in this
very moment, in the richness of this particular breath.

In the Book of Ecclesiastes, there is a proverb: "Better one hand
full of quiet than two hands full of striving after wind." Unprac-
ticed in the art of quiet, we hope to find our safety, our belonging,
and our healing by increasing our levels of accomplishment. But
our frantic busyness actually makes us deaf to what is healing and
sacred, both in ourselves and in one another.

> —WAYNE MULLER
> in *Legacy of the Heart*

*For many people the other shadow element that permeates work is an
obsession with money. We say we have to work because of it, but we do
not reflect on what it can and cannot do for us. Philosopher Jacob
Needleman believes we must creatively come to terms with money and
the role it plays in our lives.*

"What is most necessary for man," I said, "and what is given him in great abundance, are experiences, especially experiences of the forces within him. This is his most essential food, his most essential wealth. If man consciously receives all this abundance, the universe will pour into him what is called *life* in Judaism, *spirit* in Christianity, *light* in Islam, *power* in Taoism. . . ."

"And so," I concluded, "If I had to say what I think the role of money is in human life, I would take my stand on these teachings of the masters. I would say that one needs money to live and survive in the outer world, to fulfill one's obligations to the community and to nature, but that above and beyond this, the role of money is to serve as the instrument for getting understanding. We come to the bottom of civilization if, instead of understanding, we are going after 'information.' Information is the plastic version of understanding. Just as bank cards stand to gold, just as easy and deadly credit stands to honest need, obligation, and giving . . ."

—JACOB NEEDLEMAN
in *Money and the Meaning of Life*

Edward Hays, a Catholic priest, has some very specific guidelines for a spirituality of money.

(a) First, we should love our money and take pride in it. It is good to be proud of having earned it, for money is one sign of a job well done. Every paycheck is a pat on the back.

(b) Next, mindful that our money is a sacrament in which we can say, "This is me . . . this is my sweat and toil . . . ," we should use it to nourish our bodies, which it represents. So, part of our income goes for food, clothing, shelter and also for entertainment and fun. This expression of self-love is good and holy.

(c) The dollar bills in your billfold are not only a sign of you, but also of the community to which you belong. They are the frequent reminder that you belong to a certain nation whose money you use symbolically. So, with part of your money you pay taxes. You should rejoice that this communion of self helps to build highways, pay teachers' salaries and patch up the potholes in the street in front of your house. . . .

(d) Some of your money goes into our Social Security system and is given to the elderly and the needy. So, a part of you puts food on the plate of some aged man or woman or helps pay the rent of an elderly person. By means of this withholding payment you are able to put flesh on the words that Jesus speaks about seeing him in those who are in need. . . .

(f) Finally, in numerous ways we are inclined to use parts of our money on gifts to those we love, to friends and to those organizations and activities we feel are important to the world and to growth of the human spirit. Whenever we give a gift of money we could seal it with a kiss or a wink . . . saying, "This is my body . . . this is me . . . this is my love."

—EDWARD HAYS
in *Secular Sanctity*

In the next passage, Hays reminds us to be grateful for the allies we have in our work—especially those mechanical ones we often take for granted.

If your daily work involves the use of a telephone, computer, typewriter or any technological marvel, try seeing it in a new way. As your workday begins, trace on it the sign of the cross. If you can, accompany that ritual sign with a mini-prayer such as, "Friend and co-worker, together with God, let us redeem the world." Practice thanking your machine when you turn it off at the end of the day. You may even want to give it a name, as were horses and beasts of burden who helped to lift the load of labor in the old days.

The work of *making holy* does not exclude machines. In "fax," that work of praying with our machines may be one of our greatest challenges as we travel the twenty-first century.

—EDWARD HAYS
in *Feathers on the Wind*

Sometimes our machine partners surprise us with an epiphany. Often the spell-checker in my word processing program on the computer sends me messages. It stops on words that it does not recognize and offers a list of alternatives. Some stops are annoying. My program would prefer I not use the word "place," preferring I choose "plane" or "plate," neither of which will do in an entire chapter on place as home and spiritual ground. As I hit the "I" key for "Ignore," I question why this program really feels it has no place to call home.

The day the spell-checker tried to substitute "hopelessness" for "homelessness," I was challenged to do something to break that automatic association. Being married to a minister I had to laugh when the program stopped on "pastoring" and suggested that better terms might be "pasturing" (as in tending the flock?) or "pestering" (all that emphasis on moral laws?). I decided another time that my program was too inclined to maintain the status quo when it suggested that "alikeness" was a better word than "aliveness." The option of choosing "monitoring" for "mentoring" also was interesting. In what sense do we want our mentors to monitor our progress?

I'm not the only one who has reflections sparked by the spell-checker. Here's one from British novelist Sara Maitland from her book on feminist theology.

The spell-check programme on my word processor, which I have to say is both pagan and right-wing, does not care for the word 'sacred.' Every time I ran this text through the programme it wanted to change the word 'sacred' to the word 'scared.' I know that feeling, I have it; everyone in the Bible has it—they are always 'sore afraid' when they encounter the sacred: the Ark of the covenant, the burning bush, the angelic messenger, the authentic dream. In many societies the act of making something sacred also simultaneously makes it dangerous—you may not touch it, name it, look at it, represent it. There is a fear, and a respect. The proper word is awe. The sacred is awful: it is full of awe. Since the fear of the Lord is the beginning of wisdom there is nothing much wrong (indeed there is rather a lot right) with this feeling, with reminding ourselves of the grandeur, the otherness of God, along with the tenderness and generosity.

—SARA MAITLAND
in *A Big-Enough God*

In the next reading, a tradesman contemplates the history of his profession and its future, and in so doing sees his work as a source of meaning.

I am a building tradesman.
My hands are custodians of skills a thousand generations old, held in

trust for a thousand generations.
My predecessors created the Hanging Gardens of Nebuchadnezzar and
patiently put together the Parthenon.
My successors will construct platforms in space and way stations
on the stars.
I harness the rivers, bridge the inlets, disembowel the mountains,
and level the valleys to make the nation strong in war and
prosperous in peace.
The mightiest skyscraper begins with a stake I drive in the ground
and ends with the turn of the owner's key in a lock I
install.

—PETER TERZICK
in *Of Human Hands*
edited by Gregory F. Augustine Pierce

Whatever our work, the best that is in people is brought out in a creative and soulful environment.

No matter what we do, we can make it our ministry. No matter
what form our job or activity takes, the content is the same as
everyone else's: we are here to minister to human hearts. If we talk
to anyone, or see anyone, or even think of anyone, then we have the
opportunity to bring more love into the universe. From a waitress
to the head of a movie studio, from an elevator operator to the president of a nation, there is no one whose job is unimportant to God.

—MARIANNE WILLIAMSON
in *A Return to Love*

THREADS

Sometimes you just connect,
like that,
no big thing maybe
but something beyond the usual business stuff.
It comes and goes quickly
so you have to pay attention,

a change in the eyes
when you ask about the family,
a pain flickering behind the statistics
about a boy and a girl in school,
or about seeing them every other Sunday.
An older guy talks about his bride,
a little affectation after twenty-five years.
A hot-eyed achiever laughs before you want him to.
Someone tells about his wife's job
or why she quit working to stay home.
An old joker needs another laugh on the way
to retirement.
A woman says she spends a lot of her salary
on an au pair
and a good one is hard to find
but worth it because there's nothing more important
than the baby.
Listen.
In every office
you hear the threads
of love and joy and fear and guilt,
the cries for celebration and reassurance,
and somehow you know that connecting those threads
is what you are supposed to do
and business takes care of itself.

—JAMES A. AUTRY
in *Love & Profit*

Those who see their work as a ministry realize that how they treat others is of great importance. The spirituality of work is most evident in this interaction.

Cashiering in a supermarket may not seem like a very rewarding position to most. But to me it is.

You see, I feel that my job consists of a lot more than ringing up orders, taking people's money, and bagging their groceries. The most important part of my job is not the obvious. Rather it's the manner in which I present myself to others that will determine whether my customers will leave the store feeling better or worse because of their brief encounter with me. For by doing my job well I know I have a chance to do God's work too.

Because of this, I try to make each of my customers feel special. While I'm serving them, they become the most important people in my life.

—MAXINE F. DENNIS
in *Of Human Hands*
edited by Gregory F. Augustine Pierce

The readings in this chapter confirm that many men and women see their work as love made visible, as mystical, as meaningful, as a copartnership with God, as a ministry, and as service to others. There is only one step left to take, and that is the most creative of all.

Spirituality is like gravity. It must be taken into account because it is there. Ignore it and you are ignoring the most central fact of any human situation. The Hindus greet each other by bowing with folded hands against the breastbone. This miniceremony means: "I salute the divinity within you."

No workplace can be truly alive until we see the divinity within one another, until we experience behind the breastbone the breath of life, until we insist that our work will not be the humdrum product of a sleeping spirit but a glorious monument to who we really are.

—JOHN COWAN
in *The Common Table*

PRACTICING SPIRITUAL LITERACY: CREATIVITY

CONVERSATIONS/JOURNAL ENTRIES

- All of us can be mothers—bringing something precious, worthwhile, and wonderful into the world. What have you birthed recently with your creativity and imagination?
- Do a journal exercise on the following thought by English writer D. H. Lawrence: "The human soul needs actual beauty even more than bread."
- What is your favorite myth? How has it been relevant to your life?
- Recall an incident from this past week which would be worthy to add to the ongoing work of telling your life story. Or pick one experience from your youth that you want to pass on to a young person as a life lesson.
- Write a tribute to an individual who has affirmed your creativity and encouraged you to express yourself. Then be a cheerleader for someone else's creativity.
- Did you play an instrument, sing, dance, write, draw, act, or make movies as a child? Have you continued any of these activities as an adult? What impact have these creative pursuits had upon your character? What is the one thing in your life you have spent the most time practicing?
- Think about the role money plays in your life and the priority you have given to it. Write your thoughts on this subject in your journal.
- What persons, books, or films have given you a sense of the spiritual significance of your work?

ACTIVITIES/PROJECTS

- Read a story you cherished when you were young to some children. Talk with them about how the story still lives in you.
- Choose a novel that has changed your life. Send a copy to a friend with a note explaining your enthusiasm for it.
- Movies give us varied images of the creative process, the challenges faced by imaginative individuals, and the joys of self-expression. Rent one of these videos and discuss its portrait of an artist: *An Angel at My Table, Camille Claudel, Cinema Paradiso, Sylvia, Vincent and Theo.*
- Keep a journal in which you record your night dreams. On the left side of the page, write the narratives of what happens during your dreams. On

the right side, draw any images from the dreams that strike you as significant. Over time, watch for recurring themes and images. You may also want to talk about powerful dreams with someone who knows you intimately. Try to unravel their meanings together.

- Send a card to a friend who needs a little creative encouragement. Write an imaginative note on it and add a picture or a drawing.

- The next time you watch a serious television movie or a sensitive feature film, allow the characters in the story to dwell in you. See how their experiences compare with your own. Also square off with the character who is most unlike you, who is the "other." Embrace that character and see what you learn from him or her.

- Create a tape of music and songs that have served as your spiritual directors, that connect you with meaning and fill you with renewed energy and hope.

- Find one small way of making your work more playful. For example, post cartoons on your office door.

SPIRITUAL EXERCISES/RITUALS

- Make it a spiritual practice today to find and celebrate one beautiful moment or thing.

- Attend an art exhibition as a pilgrim visiting a holy place in search of spiritual sustenance.

- Paint or sew a banner for your place of worship, or better still, coordinate an art project with members of your community. You might use a passage from sacred literature as your inspiration, or create an original design.

- The next time you arrange flowers in a vase, write a letter to a friend, or conclude a business deal, view the activity as prayer and see what happens.

- Memorize a favorite poem and use a key line as a daily mantra or affirmation.

- Pause during your work day to consider how what you do is enriching the lives of others. Say a prayer of thanks for these chances to serve.

SERVICE

Small service is true service.

—William Wordsworth

If one is to do good, it must be done in minute particulars.

—William Blake

I don't know what your destiny will be, but one thing I do know: the only ones among you who will be really happy are those who have sought and found how to serve.

—Albert Schweitzer

Love and compassion are necessities, not luxuries. Without them, humanity cannot survive.

—The Dalai Lama

Helping out is not some special skill. It is not the domain of rare individuals. It is not confined to a single part or time of our lives. We simply heed the call of that natural caring impulse and follow where it leads.

—Ram Dass and Paul Gorman

The question of bread for myself is a material question, but the question of bread for my neighbor is a spiritual question.

—Nikolai Berdyaev

Service is the rent each of us pays for living—the very purpose of life.

—MARIAN WRIGHT EDELMAN

Noncooperation with evil is as much a duty as cooperation with good.

—MAHATMA GANDHI

Reconnecting politics to our best values is now the most important task of a political life.

—JIM WALLIS

We are bombarded by the daily news of needs—desperate stories about poor, sick, and hungry people around the world, accounts of victims of violence and despair, and reports on the widespread destruction of the environment. The calls for our caring are sometimes overwhelming, and we are tempted to look the other way. But spiritual literacy enables us to reenvision both service and politics. "Today's headlines," write cultural commentators Corinne McLaughlin and Gordon Davidson, "can be seen as a living alphabet through which humanity comes to know itself and God."

The world's religions all recognize the importance of an individual's service to others. In the words of sixteenth-century Catholic mystic Teresa of Avila, "God has no hands or feet or voice except ours and through these he works."

Mythologist Joseph Campbell tells a story on this point. A troubled woman came to the Indian sage Ramakrishna, saying, "O Master, I do not find that I love God." He asked, "Is there nothing, then, that you love?" She responded, "My little nephew." And he said to her, "There is your love and service to God, in your love and service to that child."

Service starts in the home where we learn to love and to respect each other, to honor differences, and to resolve conflicts. We begin by reading our immediate world for ethical challenges and opportunities. Spiritual service covers the daily decisions we make about our food, clothing, health, entertainment, and study. In our homes, we first practice listening, gratitude, and forgiveness. And peace, if it is to have any chance of surviving in global affairs, must first thrive in this intimate milieu. Put another way by Mahatma Gandhi, the political begins with the personal.

As we move from our homes to our neighborhoods, we notice signs of the needs and suffering of others. We try to find ways we can use our talents to make a difference. There is deep satisfaction to be gained in working together with others on service projects. It is one of the best ways to diminish the power of fear, helplessness, and hopelessness.

In the Buddhist tradition, the faithful are advised to examine the lives of the compassionate ones to see how they might respond to suffering. Christians do the same when they study the lives of the saints. The stories of these holy ones show us that service is not only a revered ideal, it is a practical reality. In our own communities, we can identify moral mentors who have similarly devoted themselves to acts of charity. They demonstrate the spiritual practices of hope, justice, kindness, and zeal.

Finally, we recognize that whatever we do affects the world. Catholic social activist Dorothy Day points out that good deeds are like a pebble cast into a pond: they create ripples that spread in all directions. Our acts of service in our homes and communities become part of an ever-widening circle of compassion that eventually encompasses the entire creation. In this interconnected world, we live locally knowing that our actions have an impact globally.

THE IMPULSE TO CARE

There is a marvelous story of a man who once stood before God, his heart breaking from the pain and injustice in the world. "Dear God," he cried out, "look at all the suffering, the anguish and distress in your world. Why don't you send help?"

God responded, "I did send help. I sent you."

—DAVID J. WOLPE
in *Teaching Your Children About God*

The call to service is a yearning from the heart to live and move beyond ourselves. Love, compassion, and gratitude lead many to a life of service.

We all have, without exception, a very deep longing to give—to give to the earth, to give to others, to give to the society, to work, to love, to care for this earth. That's true for every human being. And even the ones who don't find it, it's because it has been squashed or somehow suppressed in some brutal way in their life. But it's there to be discovered. We all long for that.

And there's a tremendous sorrow for a human being who doesn't find a way to give. One of the worst of human sufferings is not to find a way to love, or a place to work and give of your heart and your being.

—JACK KORNFIELD
in *Roots of Buddhist Psychology*

I am one of these people who have been loved every day of my life. I am a person who has been told by the words or actions of those people closest to me, "We just think you're great. You can just do anything. You can be anything." I remember thinking a long time ago that in this painful world, if you have been given the kind of things I've been given which is the gift of limitless expectations for your life, and security, and a nest to come from, one that was warm and safe, and you look around you and if you have any sensitivity at all, you know that's not the way most people got their start or live their lives. And for me I would think it would be the road to madness if you didn't try to give some of it away.

—KAY HARDIE
quoted in *Some Do Care*
by Anne Colby and William Damon

Service begins early and it begins at home. Spiritual teachers have emphasized this point for centuries. Traveling in India, Diana Eck, a professor of comparative religions, was exposed to the approach taken by Mahatma Gandhi: "His vision was to extend the ethics, the care, and the common sense of the household to the whole of humankind."

One special moment of beauty that stands out in my mind I experienced in a bus station. . . . I witnessed a little girl helping her brother get a drink at the water fountain. Attempting to lift him to the proper height turned out to be impossible. I was just at the point of giving them some assistance when quick as lightning she darted over to a shoeshine man, pointed to a footstool he wasn't using, dragged it to the water fountain, and very gently lifted up her thirsty brother. It all happened so fast and it was so simple, yet it turned out to be a moment of beauty that became a prayer for me. So much to be learned from such a little moment. Perhaps what touched me most was her readiness to seek out a way to take care of the need without waiting to be rescued. It was a moment of beauty: a small child with a single heart.

—MACRINA WIEDERKEHR
in *A Tree Full of Angels*

Each activity of daily life in which we stretch ourselves on behalf of others is a prayer of action—the times when we scrimp and save in order to get the children something special; the times when we share our car with others on rainy mornings, leaving early to get them to work on time; the times when we keep up correspondence with friends or answer one last telephone call when we are dead tired at night. These times and many more like them are lived prayer.

—RICHARD J. FOSTER
in *Prayer*

Ram Dass and Paul Gorman, who have written one of the best books on the nature of helping, also believe that the little things we do for others qualify as acts of service.

Caring for one another, we sometimes glimpse an essential quality of our being. We may be sitting alone, lost in self-doubt or self-pity, when the phone rings with a call from a friend who's *really* depressed. Instinctively, we come out of ourselves, just to be there with her and say a few reassuring words. When we're done, and a little comfort's been shared, we put down the phone and feel a little more at home with ourselves. We're reminded of who we really are and what we have to offer one another.

—RAM DASS and PAUL GORMAN
in *How Can I Help?*

Often the most fulfilling acts of service are the ones that grow naturally out of our God-given talents, interests, and skills.

We may need to think about service in a completely new way if we are to find an opportunity to do something we love. Our first thought may be to use our most expert skill, the thing we do best in our daily work, such as repairing cars, massaging aching bodies, practicing civil rights law, or negotiating international peace. But sometimes we need to look at our other talents and skills. We often think of these as hobbies—as [Jimmy and Rosalynn] Carter probably did, having put in a tongue-and-groove floor in their attic in Plains—but these activities may be just what we need to perform truly effective service. Maybe we can heal the world through arranging flowers, writing poetry, or baking bread in a shelter. Why not? The "serious" methods that have been tried—from the war on poverty to the war in the Gulf—haven't ended the pain; often they seem to have created more. We need to free our minds if we are to find new paths through the dark forest of suffering. We need experimentation and playfulness in the face of difficulty, no matter how paradoxical that may seem. As Tibetan Buddhist teacher Tarthang Tulku says, "We already know how to enjoy ourselves. When we are enjoying ourselves, we are productive and creative. It's just a matter of bringing that enjoyment into everything we do."

—RAM DASS and MIRABAI BUSH
in *Compassion in Action*

Activists Corinne McLaughlin and Gordon Davidson emphasize that our understanding of politics, like our view of service, needs to be broadened significantly.

"Politics is the way we live our lives," stated an early new paradigm group called the New World Alliance, which we helped cofound with forty other leaders in 1979. "It is not just running for office. It is the way we treat each other, as individuals, as groups, as government. It is the way we treat our environment. It is the way we treat ourselves. Politics has to do with where we shop, what we eat, how we maintain our health. It has to do with the kinds of schools we create, the energy we use, the neighborhood organizations we build, the work we do. Politics involves our way of seeing the world, of developing our consciousness, of awakening our whole selves. It has to do with our attitudes, our values, our innermost dimensions."

The old political paradigm assumed that events were caused solely by political leaders and public policies. The new emerging paradigm could be called "politics as if people mattered." It addresses causes inherent in our own human psyche, our thoughts and feelings, as well as in the karma of groups and nations.

—CORINNE MCLAUGHLIN and GORDON DAVIDSON
in *Spiritual Politics*

In the movie Amazing Grace and Chuck, *twelve-year-old Chuck is deeply concerned about nuclear weapons. He decides to give up his "best thing"—pitching on a Little League baseball team—as a protest. Soon other children and a famous basketball player named Amazing Grace decide to make similar moral stands. When Chuck wonders if their protest will have any effect, Amazing Grace describes the secret of achieving what in sports is known as a sweet moment in time when body and mind act as one. Likewise when doing good, the superstar recommends, "Just forget yourself and disappear in the act."*

The unself-consciousness of service is also a theme in the movie Beyond Rangoon. *Laura, an American tourist in Burma, is awakened one night by a demonstration in the streets outside her hotel. She joins the crowd who have gathered to greet Aung San Suu Kyi, the leader of the pro-democracy movement. Although this is a fictional story, the character is based on an authentic hero who was awarded the Nobel Peace Prize in 1991 in recognition of her nonviolent struggle against a totalitarian government.*

In Beyond Rangoon, *soldiers try to block Aung San Suu Kyi's path, but this fearless woman passes gently through them. Later, describing the scene to her Buddhist tour guide, Laura says, "All those people were watching and she was so brave." He explains, "Because she was not watching herself."*

Once upon a time there was a blacksmith who worked hard at his trade. The day came for him to die. The angel was sent to him, and much to the angel's surprise he refused to go. He pleaded with the angel to make his case before God, that he was the only blacksmith in the area and it was time for all his neighbors to begin their planting and sowing. He was needed. So the angel pleaded his case before God. He said that the man didn't want to appear ungrateful, and that he was glad to have a place in the kingdom, but could he put off going for a while? And he was left.

About a year or two later the angel came back again with the same message: the Lord was ready to share the fullness of the kingdom with him. Again the man had reservations and said: "A neighbor of mine is seriously ill, and it's time for the harvest. A number of us are trying to save his crops so that his family won't become destitute. Please come back later." And off the angel went again.

Well, it got to be a pattern. Every time the angel came, the blacksmith had one excuse or another. The blacksmith would just shake his head and tell the angel where he was needed and decline. Finally, the blacksmith grew very old, weary and tired. He decided it was time, and so he prayed: "God, if you'd like to send your angel again, I'd be glad to come home now." Immediately the angel appeared, as if from around the corner of the bed. The blacksmith said: "If you still want to take me home, I'm ready to live forever in the kingdom of heaven." And the angel laughed and looked at the blacksmith in delight and surprise and said: "Where do you think you've been all these years?" He was home.

—Megan McKenna
in *Parables*

SERVICE TO COMMUNITY

The Buddhist master Shantideva sets the mood for the next readings as we expand our service from the home to the community.

May I be the doctor and the medicine,
And may I be the nurse
For all sick beings in the world
Until everyone is healed.

May a rain of food and drink descend
To clear away the pain of thirst and hunger
And during the aeon of famine
May I myself change into food and drink.

May I be a protector for those without one,
A guide for all travellers on the way;
May I be a bridge, a boat and a ship
For all who wish to cross (the water).

May I always support the life
Of all the boundless creatures.

And until they pass away from pain
May I also be the source of life
For all the realms of varied beings
That reach unto the ends of space.

—Shantideva
in *A Guide to the Bodhisattva's Way of Life*

In this passage from a novel, a wife pays tribute to a nurse's care of her sick husband. Two more readings show that service can be as simple as being present and providing encouragement.

Nurses are good at this kind of thing, using one hand for things that normally require two. And if you get one like Wanda, you can see the caring along with the skill. She rubs Jay's back with strong, circular strokes, and I watch, spellbound. There is a mesmerizing quality to watching someone do almost anything with care: tailors in their dry-cleaner windows, hunched over sewing machines. Bakers making art out of frosting. Children with a new pack of crayons and fierce intent. We are meant to use what we have, whatever it is. We are meant to be less mindful of our insides, more outwardly directed. That's what I think, as I watch Wanda rub Jay down, as the minty smell of the lotion makes its way over to me. There is incredible value in being in service to others.

—ELIZABETH BERG
in *Range of Motion*

I have a friend, a chemotherapy nurse in a children's cancer ward, whose job it is to pry for any available vein in an often emaciated arm to give infusions of chemicals that sometimes last as long as twelve hours and which are often quite discomforting to the child. He is probably the greatest pain-giver the children meet in their stay in the hospital. Because he has worked so much with his own pain, his heart is very open. He works with his responsibilities in the hospital as a "laying on of hands with love and acceptance." There is little in him that causes him to withdraw, that reinforces the painfulness of the experience for the children. He is a warm, open space which encourages them to trust whatever they feel. And it is he whom the children most often ask for at the time they are dying. Although he is the main pain-giver, he is also the main love-giver.

—INDIVIDUAL
quoted in *How Can I Help?*
by Ram Dass and Paul Gorman

O

OPENNESS

Open yourself to the Tao,
then trust your natural responses;
and everything will fall into place.

So writes Lao-tzu in the *Tao Te Ching*. Openness means going
with the flow when the senses are on full alert, the mind is
receptive, the body is awaiting new input, and the soul is ready
to go sailing on a sea of possibilities.

In the film *Dances with Wolves*, the Native American chief
Kicking Bear says to United States Army Lieutenant Dunbar:
"I was just thinking that of all the trails in this life, there is one
that matters more than all the others. It is the trail of the true
human being. I think you are on this trail and it is good to
see."

The trail of the true human being is one of openness toward
others—even those who are strangers and alien to all we know
and believe. Lieutenant Dunbar, who takes the name Dances
with Wolves, opens himself up to the ways of the Lakota people and becomes very familiar with the path of animals. He
practices openness.

Empathy is a sign of openness. Consider the Lakota prayer:
"Great Spirit, help me never to judge another until I have
walked two weeks in his moccasins." Too much misunderstanding in the world is a result of our refusal to put ourselves
in the situation of others—especially outsiders and enemies.

"Jesus said one word, and a dead man sat up," writes the
Sufi poet Rumi, "but creation usually unfolds, like calm

breakers." Openness means that we don't want to miss one moment of what's going on, whether it is mind-bending miracles or the slow epiphanies of the natural world.

"All real living is meeting," notes Jewish scholar Martin Buber. Joan Puls, a Catholic sister, calls openness "the attitude and condition that is at the heart of all spirituality."

This is the heart of our humanity—being here, open and giving to others. There is so much that is lost and never retrieved when we close off to others.

We need each other. "The begging bowl of the Buddha," Catholic monk Thomas Merton explains, "represents not just a right to beg, but openness to the gifts of all human beings as an expression of this interdependence of all beings . . . Thus when a monk begs from the layman it is not as a selfish person getting something from someone else. He is simply opening himself to his interdependence."

Be open like the monk with a begging bowl. Be open like a flower to the sun. Be open like an artist awaiting her muse.

Trust your natural responses to the world as Lao-tzu advises. Walk the trail of the true human being. Let the miracles and the calm breakers transform you. Make the most of the deep in you meeting the deep in another. And recognize that like a monk with a begging bowl, your openness to the gifts of the universe is what holds you in its warm embrace.

When I was very ill, I had to receive weekly intravenous treatments. This went on for almost two years. Somewhere in the middle I lost my courage. It is hard to say which collapsed first, my soul or my veins, but collapse they both did. One day the search for a healthy vein became too painful. I pushed the needle away and cried. A nurse brought to my side a young girl, of about ten, who had battled cancer all her life. This child smiled at me and said, "You should have got one of these." Lifting her T-shirt, she showed me the hole that had been cut into her abdomen so that she could receive her treatments through a permanent plastic port. Then she put her hand, so small and soft, on mine and said, "You can take it." And I did.

—NANCY BURKE
in *Meditations for Health*

Sometimes those we help turn out to be healers for us, showing us important spiritual lessons that we can apply to our own situations.

I recall a minister who had been experiencing long bouts of depression because of the seeming lack of success in his parish. One day he went to visit a woman who was very ill. As he started to leave the room, the woman spoke to him: "You have been such an important person in my life. I want you to know that I have great love for you." These kind words sailed straight into the minister's heart. He told me that he just couldn't believe it but by the time he reached his office he could sense that something different was stirring within him. During the next several weeks the depression lifted and he felt a tremendous rejuvenation in his life.

—JOYCE RUPP
in *Little Pieces of Light*

The practice of loving kindness must find its root deep within us. The story is told that Mohandas Gandhi once settled in a village and at once began serving the needs of the villagers who lived there. A friend inquired if Gandhi's objectives in serving the poor were purely humanitarian. Gandhi replied, "Not at all. I am here to serve no one else but myself, to find my own self-realization through the service of these village folk."

As Gandhi wisely points out, even as we serve others we are working on ourselves; every act, every word, every gesture of genuine compassion naturally nourishes our own hearts as well. It is not a question of who is healed first. When we attend to ourselves with compassion and mercy, more healing is made available for others. And when we serve others with an open and generous heart, great healing comes to us.

—WAYNE MULLER
in *Legacy of the Heart*

Increasingly, the homeless population is made up of children. Every day at the shelter, I interact with these homeless children. I share their joys and their sorrows. I am a part of their lives. As I see them struggle, my children come to mind. Some balance is struck between these children and my children. When I see a homeless child crying because her mother is too busy looking for work to pay her any attention, I remind myself to spend time with Chelsea. When a volunteer calls to say he cannot come today to take a homeless boy to a ball game, I promise myself that I will take Jeremy to one soon. When a homeless girl plays in the yard with broken toys, I rush home that day to play with Kristen.

It is a strange gift. The plight of homeless children makes me more sensitive to my own family. Were it not that God knew exactly where I was needed, I doubt I would be much of a father.

—MICHEAL ELLIOTT
in *Partners in Grace*

Talk to anyone who is a volunteer and you will learn about the personal satisfactions that accrue from his or her service.

The joy that compassion brings is one of the best-kept secrets of humanity. It is a secret known to only a very few people, a secret that has to be rediscovered over and over again.

I have had a few glimpses of it. When I came to Daybreak, a community with people who have mental disabilities, I was asked to spend a few hours with Adam, one of the handicapped members of the community. Each morning I had to get him out of bed, give him a bath, shave him, brush his teeth, comb his hair, dress him, walk him to the kitchen, give him his breakfast, and bring him to the place where he spends his day. During the first few weeks, I was mostly afraid, always worrying that I would do something wrong or that he would have an epileptic seizure. But gradually I relaxed and started to enjoy our daily routine. As the weeks passed by, I discovered how I had come to look forward to my two hours with Adam. Whenever I thought of him during the day, I experienced gratitude for having him as my friend. Even though he couldn't speak or even give a sign of recognition, there was real love between us. My time with Adam had become the most precious time of the day. When a visiting friend asked me one day: "Couldn't you spend your time better than working with this handicapped man? Was it for this type of work that you got all your education?" I realized that I couldn't explain to him the joy that Adam brought me. He had to discover that for himself.

—HENRI J. M. NOUWEN
in Here and Now

Caregivers also may come upon spiritual truths through their activities.

Early one morning in June, months after his Earth Day experience, Jonathan was preparing to give a massage at an AIDS clinic to a Baptist man who had tested HIV positive. (Jonathan did volunteer service for the agency after completing a twenty-hour training course in giving massages.)

"This man I'll call Robert was very religious," Jonathan related. "He turned a lot of his life over to God. I liked him, respected him, and had given him weekly massages over the last year. Generally he was quite restrained and nonverbal, and he didn't talk much about his personal life. He was always poised and calm, but when he talked about his relationship to God, he became excited, eloquent, like a poet. His language was beautiful, very coherent, and fluent...."

When Robert turned over, Jonathan moved to the end of the table and crouched to get a better angle to massage Robert's leathery feet. Jonathan kneaded the inside sole of one foot with his thumbs, beginning at the heel, up to the big toe and down again. He massaged from the inside of the foot across the center to the outside. Just as he began to repeat the process, he suddenly found himself emotionally swept up in a second illumination.

"I was still crouched down when suddenly it hit me that this man, Robert, was a child of God. I knew it sounded weird. Normally I would never say anything like that about somebody. Sometimes I felt very reverential about doing massages on people and thought different things, but at that moment all my thoughts left. I was overwhelmed, and felt that I was touching the body of a holy person. I was overcome by the holiness of his body, of the body itself, of his being, the holiness of my connection to him. I truly believed that he was a child of God. I was close to crying."

—RICHARD SOLLY
in *Call to Purpose*

There is a Talmudic saying, "Goodwill is the mightiest practical force in the universe." Opportunities to express that energy are everywhere.

Everything in our lives has brought us to exactly where we are. When we don't already know what is calling us to act, all we need to do is look and listen right where we are—it will probably be near. Maybe not geographically near, because our neighborhoods are not only physical, but it will be near.

When asked where she thought people should start looking, peace activist Fran Peavey said, "There are opportunities for service all the time. One time, driving a cab, I picked up a woman in her nightgown. She had been walking in her sleep and she was lost. I helped her find her way home. . . . Wherever you are, whatever you're doing, you can serve there. It doesn't have to be a big idea. It can be right where you are."

—RAM DASS and MIRABAI BUSH
in *Compassion in Action*

In the movie Nobody's Fool, *Sully is an aging handyman who has been a loser most of his life, except in his service to others. In one scene, he notices that a neighbor lady has become confused and is wandering*

down the street in her nightgown. In a blink Sully comes to her aid, escorting her home as if she were his date to the prom.

This scene reminds us of a story told by Dr. Gerald Epstein, who practices mind/body medicine in the Western spiritual tradition. Jerry encourages his students—mostly doctors, social workers, therapists, and body workers—to consider themselves educators and sharers of knowledge, not "helpers." He is suspicious of any role which places a professional in a position of authority over a client, for this takes away the individual's freedom. The healer's role is to share wisdom and to be present with support. Here's the story Jerry tells to illustrate this point.

A model of the spiritual physician can be found in an old Arabian story about a sheikh who dies and leaves his three sons seventeen camels. He has stipulated that the oldest son should get half the camels, the second son a third, the youngest son one ninth. The three sons are in a quandary, as they cannot possibly fulfill their father's wish with seventeen camels. They finally go to a sage in their community for help. He listens to their story, ponders it for a moment, then tells them that he will lend them his camel to help them solve their dilemma. He asks that they return the camel if and when they have no further need for it. They go home with the camel, and now they have eighteen. The eldest son takes his half, or nine camels; the second son takes his third, or six camels; and the youngest takes his one ninth, or two. Nine plus six plus two equals seventeen. They then return the eighteenth camel to the sage.

The story beautifully illustrates the healer's role. The sons were in some distress, experiencing problems for which they could find no ready solution The sage did not investigate their past or make any interpretation. He did not presume to become an authority and dictate to them an answer that he regarded as the only true one. He made no judgments about them, nor offered any unnecessary prognosis. He simply *lent a hand*.

—GERALD EPSTEIN
in *Healing into Immortality*

[The Desert Dweller] has lived in the desert so long that all of its moods have long since become a part of the daily rhythm of his life. But it is not that fact that is of crucial importance. For many years, it has been his custom to leave a lighted lantern by the roadside at night to cheer the weary traveler. Beside the lantern, there is a note which gives detailed directions as to where his cottage may be found so that if there is distress or need, the stranger may find help. It is a very simple gesture full of beauty and wholeness. To him, it is not important how many people pass in the night and go on their way. The important thing is that the lantern burns every night and every night the note is there, "just in case."

Years ago, walking along a road outside Rangoon, I noted at intervals along the way a roadside stone with a crock of water and, occasionally, some fruit. Water and fruit were put there by Buddhist priests to comfort and bless any passerby—one's spiritual salutation to another. The fact that I was a traveler from another part of the world, speaking a strange language and practicing a different faith, made no difference. What mattered was the fact that I was walking along the road—what my mission was, who I was—all irrelevant.

—HOWARD THURMAN
in *Meditations of the Heart*

Naturalist Wendell Berry writes: "The real work of planet-saving will be small, humble and humbling and (insofar as it involves love) pleasing and rewarding." The next reading illustrates one woman's determination to do her little bit of planet-saving.

I can't remember when I first met Maggie. She blended in with the sand and surf. You could see her walking along the shore in her white tennis shoes, floppy straw hat, and oversized print dress. She always carried a crumpled brown paper bag that matched the texture and color of her skin. I remember her most vividly at daybreak or in the evening when I went out jogging, but I later discovered that her walks were regulated by the tides, not by the sun or the clock. She came out at low tide when the beach was wide and smooth.

Maggie always walked with her head down. She would stop every now and then and pick something up, examine it, and either discard it or put it in the brown sack. I assumed she was collecting shells. We had a nodding and then a grunting acquaintance for many months before I ventured to ask her what kind of shells she was after.

"Not shells at all," she retorted in an accent more appropriate to Maine than Florida. No wasted words here. Phrases, not sentences, communicated her purpose and her desire for privacy. "Glass." She threw away a green pebble that had once been a Ballantine beer bottle. "Sharp glass. Cuts the feet. Surfers land on it. It sure ruins their summer."

—BOB LIBBY
in *Grace Happens*

... each of us can do something. Walking three miles to work won't heal the whole ozone layer, but it is something one person can do. And although we each can't do everything, together we can make a difference. Each of these bignesses is made up of many small parts. Individual people, sometimes working in groups. Individual moments. It is like the AIDS quilt, stitched together by the NAMES Project. Each patch is small, personal, and handmade. Each one reflects the person who made it and his or her friend, lover, or child who died of AIDS. Each patch is different: sweet, sophisticated, loving, stylish, outrageous. Together they make an immense blanket of love, care, sadness, and beauty. Like the Vietnam Veterans Memorial in Washington, D.C., which lists the names of all the Americans who died in that confusing war, it is difficult to see the quilt without feeling simultaneously the poignancy of each individual patch and the power of the entire statement.

—RAM DASS and MIRABAI BUSH
in *Compassion in Action*

SERVICE TO THE POOR

One of the most persistent and pernicious misunderstandings of the spiritual life is that it is only directed inward, that contemplation and action are somehow incompatible. Four stories from different traditions challenge this assumption.

St. John of the Cross, alone in his room in profound prayer, experienced a rapturous vision of Mary. At the same moment he heard a beggar rattling at his door for alms. He wrenched himself away and saw to the beggar's needs. When he returned, the vision returned again, saying that at the very moment he had heard the door rattle on its hinges, his soul had hung in perilous balance. Had he not gone to the beggar's aid, she could never have appeared to him again.

—DAVID WHYTE
in *The Heart Aroused*

The Hasidic masters tell the story of the rabbi who disappeared every Shabat Eve, "to commune with God in the forest," his congregation thought. So one Sabbath night they deputed one of their cantors to follow the rabbi and observe the holy encounter. Deeper and deeper into the woods the rabbi went until he came to the small cottage of an old Gentile woman, sick to death and crippled into a painful posture. Once there, the rabbi cooked for her and carried her firewood and swept her floor. Then when the chores were finished, he returned immediately to his little house next to the synagogue.

Back in the village, the people demanded of the one they'd sent to follow him, "Did our rabbi go up to heaven as we thought?"

"Oh, no," the cantor answered after a thoughtful pause, "our rabbi went much, much higher than that."

—JOAN CHITTISTER
in *There Is a Season*

One day Rumi asked one of his young, snotty disciples to give him an enormous amount of rich and delicious food. This young disciple was rather alarmed because he thought Rumi was living an ascetic lifestyle. Rumi used to pray all night and eat hardly anything. The disciple thought, "Aha, now I've really got the master—what he really wants is to go off somewhere secretly and eat all this food!" So he decided to follow Rumi. He followed him through the streets of Konya, out into the fields, out into yet further fields. Then he saw Rumi go into a ruined tomb. "I'm finally going to unmask his pretensions," the young disciple thought. But what he found was a totally exhausted bitch with six puppies, and Rumi was feeding the dog with his own hands so that she could survive to feed her children. Rumi knew that the disciple was following him, of course, and turned to him smiling and said, "See?" The disciple, extremely moved, said, "But how on earth did you know that she was here? How did you know that she was hungry? This is miles away from where you are!" Rumi laughed and laughed, "When you have become awake your ears are so acute that they can hear the cries of a sparrow ten thousand miles away."

—ANDREW HARVEY
in *The Way of Passion*

A man is vouchsafed a vision of the afterlife. He is first shown a great hall with a long banquet table filled with ambrosial delights. Each diner is equipped with a three-foot-long spoon, but no matter how much they contort their arms, thrusting their elbows into their neighbors' faces, their utensils are too long to maneuver even a single morsel into their gaping mouths. They sit together, opposite and side by side, in mutual misery.

"This," says the man's otherworldly guide, "is Hell."

The visitor is then taken to another place and sees an identical banquet table set with the same sumptuous viands and the same impossible silverware. Only here the denizens are well fed, utterly joyous, glowing with health and well-being.

"This," pronounces the host, "is Heaven."

The man is baffled. "What's the difference?"

"In Heaven," says the guide, pointing delightedly as a person lifts his long-handled spoon across the table to the parted lips of a neighbor, "they feed each other."

—CARYLE HIRSHBERG and MARC IAN BARASCH
in *Remarkable Recovery*

Although many of us sincerely want to help others, we may be tempted to put off service projects until that mythical moment when we feel less pressured or harassed.

A young man eagerly described what he dreamed of doing for the poor.

Said the Master, "When do you propose to make your dream come true?"

"As soon as the opportunity arrives."

"Opportunity never arrives," said the Master. "It's here."

—ANTHONY DE MELLO

in *More One Minute Nonsense*

Even when we think we are ready to jump to someone's aid, our efforts may be sidetracked by the shadow elements of service, such as bureaucracies and unrealistic expectations.

Good causes are dangerous. They attract the right people for the right reasons; thus the traps are more subtle. Being devoted to truth is one thing; being devoted to an organization devoted to truth is something else. Ram Dass tells one of my favorite stories, about God and Satan walking down the street. The Lord bends down, picks something up, and gazes at it glowing radiantly in his hand. Curious, Satan asks what it is. "This," answers the Lord, "is truth." "Let me have that," says Satan, "I'll organize it for you."

—SY SAFRANSKY

in *Four in the Morning*

Years ago I was practicing meditation in India. Anybody who spends any time at all in India must come to terms with the countless number of people begging. It is just part of reality there, and one is in relationship to it one way or another. I was in the bazaar one day buying some fruit. There were a lot of beggars around, and one little boy was holding out his hand. He looked hungry, so I took one of the oranges I had bought and gave it to him. It felt good to respond to him. But he just took the orange and walked away. Not a smile, not a nod, not a thank-you, nothing. Only when he did that, only in the absence of a response, did I see clearly that some part of my mind, some part of my generosity, some part of my motive had wanted an acknowledgment. I had not been expecting effusive thanks for the orange, but I had wanted something. And this child just took the orange and walked away.

—JOSEPH GOLDSTEIN

in *Transforming the Mind, Healing the World*

345

Denial, abstraction, pity, professional warmth, compulsive hyper-activity: these are a few of the ways in which the mind reacts to suffering and attempts to restrict or direct the natural compassion of the heart. This tension between head and heart leaves us tentative and confused. As we reach out, then pull back, love and fear are pitted against one another. As hard as this is for *us*, what must it be like for those who need our help?

—RAM DASS and PAUL GORMAN
in *How Can I Help?*

Whenever the old battle between the head and the heart starts up, it is inspiring to consider the zeal of Mother Teresa, Dr. Martin Luther King Jr., Mahatma Gandhi, and others. But even for extraordinary people like these, service can be hazardous duty.

Burnout is a surrender, Dr. Martin Luther King once said at a conference in 1964. A lot of us were sitting at a table talking about the subject because we had witnessed it in others and in ourselves. He explained his somewhat startling choice of words this way: "We have just so much strength in us. If we give and give and give, we have less and less and less—and after a while, at a certain point, we're so weak and worn, we hoist up the flag of surrender. We surrender to the worst side of ourselves, and then we display that to others. We surrender to self-pity and to spite and to morose self-preoccupation. If you want to call it depression or burnout, well, all right. If you want to call it the triumph of sin—when our goodness has been knocked out from under us, well, all right. Whatever we say or think, this is arduous duty, doing this kind of work; to live out one's idealism brings with it hazards."

—ROBERT COLES
in *The Call of Service*

In his memoir, Dr. David Hilfiker writes about his years working with poor people in inner-city Washington, D.C. It is truly arduous duty requiring that he deal with problems stemming from insufficient funding, ineffective programs, public indifference, and the alarming attitudes adopted by some of the people he serves.

When I first entered this universe of visible suffering, I assumed that provoking political change was just a matter of getting the ordinary, everyday people around me to understand what was happening; then—as had been true for "Crazy Jack" and others in Minnesota— there would be an outpouring of money and concern for the welfare of the poor. But as I saw homeless men with feet black, oozing, and gangrenous from frostbite discharged from emergency rooms; as hospital social workers threatened to discharge elderly demented men back to the streets; as alcoholics seeking help at the city detoxification center were turned away "because they weren't drunk enough"; as child protection workers dragged their feet or refused outright to investigate abusive situations we reported—I began to realize that the poverty I was seeing was much deeper than I could have imagined. Apparently the homelessness, the lack of medical attention, the malnutrition, the staggering infant mortality rate had been in some way *accepted*. They had become "tolerable evils." It would not be enough to inform people of what was happening. In some sense they already knew, and were numbed to it. . . .

Despite my eagerness, however, there was no way to prepare myself to face the unraveling of the social fabric, the larger loss of community that was the truth of inner-city Washington. I was initially shocked and angry at a system that had abandoned those least able to help themselves. There was no housing; medical care was inaccessible; public education was a disaster; jobs with living wages were unavailable. Most of my new patients had the same kinds of medical illnesses I had tended in Minnesota, but they also suffered from a kind of neglect I had not imagined possible.

That shock, though, I could at least see coming. What caught me completely off guard was my patients' internalization of their abandonment. Children who had not been adequately loved now saw themselves as unlovable; young people who had been inadequately trusted could now trust no one; adults who had been pushed down too many times now saw failure as inevitable; addicts for whom no treatment was offered had now—for practical purposes—given up on the possibility of a meaningful life. I was not prepared for the hostility, the seeming ingratitude, the noncompliance, the irrationality that is so much a part of the inner-city reality.

—DAVID HILFIKER
in *Not All of Us Are Saints*

347

P

PEACE

"To a large extent, the future lies before us like a vast wilderness of unexplored reality," Christian philanthropist Sir John Templeton writes. "The God who created and sustained the evolving universe through eons of progress and development has not placed our generation at the tag end of the creation process. God has placed us at the beginning. We are here for the future."

And as pioneers of tomorrow, we have to practice peace right now. French philosopher Simone Weil reminds us that "violence obliterates anybody who feels its touch." Most of the tragedies of the twentieth century bear out her point.

In marked contrast to our history, the wisdom traditions challenge us to be gentle, compassionate people, to practice peace.

We begin in our homes with how we treat those who are nearest and dearest to us. "Violence," Jesuit peace activist John Dear tells us, "occurs when we forget and deny our basic identity as God's children, when we treat one another as if we were worthless instead of priceless."

The practice of peace involves introspection. "If you love peace," says Mahatma Gandhi, the world's foremost advocate for nonviolence, "then hate injustice, hate tyranny, hate greed—but hate these things inside yourself, not in another."

The practice of peace continues in the neighborhood and at work where our sense of community has grown tattered and frail. Nobel Peace Prize winner Mother Teresa brings to mind what is at stake here: "If we have no peace, it is because we have forgotten that we belong to each other."

Peace also involves the practice of lovingkindness and compassion in the midst of the daily grind where tempers flare and tensions reign. Here is a place to join with Zen teacher Robert Aitken, who pledges: "I take up the way of not killing. I vow to cultivate my love and to apply it in my daily life at home and in the large community. I vow to moderate my lifestyle for the protection of all things."

The little steps we take in the name of peace and nonviolence enable us to feel a connection with others all over the world who are taking their own small steps for peace. "As peacemakers," Catholic writer Henri J. M. Nouwen suggests, "we must resist resolutely all the powers of war and destruction and proclaim that peace is the divine gift offered to all who affirm life."

We are here for the future to do what we can by practicing peace and nonviolence. Why now? Because like the Indian mystic poet Kabir, we can say, "Something inside of me has reached to the place where the world is breathing." To feel the breathing of the world is to join with songwriter John Lennon in his plea, "All we are saying is give peace a chance."

We are here for the future. Writer Coleman McCarthy voices our understanding: "The earth is too small a star and we too brief a visitor upon it, for anything to matter more than the struggle for peace."

PLAY

Giver of Life created the world in play and the world remains an unfinished masterpiece. That is why there is truth in American philosopher Ralph Waldo Emerson's aphorism: "It is a happy talent to know how to play."

Inside us is a child who remembers the energy and delight of play. That child helps us feel the pleasures of being.

Imaginative play is the source of creativity. Whenever we express our deepest self, we become cocreators in the ongoing refinement of the universe. This is true whether we are writing a poem, restoring an antique table, singing in a church choir, or fixing a new dish for dinner.

"Imaginative play," psychologist Frances E. Vaughan believes, "is a key that opens the doors of intuition." We follow an intuitive hunch and it leads us to a surprising love relationship, a new line of work, or a leisure-time project that renews our soul.

And finally, imaginative play gives us another way of approaching the texts of our lives and all we encounter in our daily experience. Sophia delights in our spontaneity.

Play is a pathway to laughter. All the spiritual traditions have holy fools, clowns, or tricksters who try to tease people into a fuller appreciation of the paradox and mystery of life. The stories of Zen masters, Hasidic sages, Christian saints, and Muslim mystics keep us on our toes.

For example, there is the Apache myth of the Creator giving human beings the ability to talk, to run, and to look. But He was not satisfied until He also gave them the ability to laugh. Only then did the Creator say, "Now you are fit to live."

A sense of humor gives us a lightness of being, to use the felicitous phrase of novelist Milan Kundera. Jews have such high regard for this human faculty that they celebrate Purim annually. This holy day emphasizes eating, drinking, and joking around.

Doris Donnelly, a teacher of spiritual theology, describes a curious custom in the Greek Orthodox tradition. Believers gather on Easter Monday to trade jokes. "Since the most extravagant 'joke' of all took place on Easter Sunday—the victory, against all odds, of Jesus over death—the community of the faithful enters into the spirit of the season by sharing stories with unexpected endings, surprise flourishes, and a sense of humor."

Jan Steward, who writes about rituals, is not surprised that churches have potluck suppers. "Celebration," she suggests, "is a kind of food we all need in our lives, and each individual brings a special recipe or offering so that together we will make a great feast." As Martin Luther, leader of the Protestant Reformation, says in his *Table Talks*, "Our loving God wills that we eat, drink and be merry."

Playing around is a good and holy thing. Don't ever let anyone tell you otherwise. It enables us to express ourselves creatively, to use our intuition and imagination, to savor pleasure and the lightness of being, and to make our humble contribution to the unfinished masterpiece of the world.

We heard a story about Dorothy Day. We're not sure of all the details, but it goes something like this: A reporter came to interview Dorothy at her office. He could see her talking to a man who was either drunk or mentally ill. Time passed and the reporter grew impatient. Dorothy finally turned and said, "Are you waiting to speak to one of us?" Obviously, Dorothy did not think that she was more important than the person she was with. This is an example of service through respect. Here is another.

One day a woman came in and donated a diamond ring to the Worker. We all wondered what Dorothy would do with it. She could have one of us take it down to a diamond exchange and sell it. It would certainly fetch a month's worth of beans. That afternoon, Dorothy gave the diamond ring to an old woman who lived alone and often came to us for meals. "That ring would have paid her rent for the better part of a year," someone protested. Dorothy replied that the woman had her dignity; she could sell it if she liked and spend the money for rent, a trip to the Bahamas, or keep the ring to admire. "Do you suppose God created diamonds only for the rich?"

—Tom Cornell
quoted in *Dorothy Day*
by Robert Ellsberg

Of all the spiritual practices we bring to acts of service, perhaps the most important is hope.

I remember talking with a friend who has worked for many years at the Catholic Worker, a ministry to the poor in New York City. Daily she tries to respond to waves of human misery that are as ceaseless as surf in that community. Out of my deep not-knowing I asked her how she could keep doing a work that never showed any results, a work in which the problems keep getting worse instead of better. I will never forget her enigmatic answer: "The thing you don't understand, Parker, is that just because something is impossible doesn't mean you shouldn't do it!"

—Parker J. Palmer
in *The Active Life*

There is a Zen saying, "No seed ever sees the flower." Anyone involved in compassionate service eventually learns this truth.

Effort is its own reward.

We are here to do,
And through doing to learn;
and through learning to know;
and through knowing to experience wonder;
and through wonder to attain wisdom;
and through wisdom to find simplicity;
and through simplicity to give attention;
and through attention
to see what needs to be done. . . .
　　　　　—BEN HEI HEI
　　　　　　in *Wisdom of the Jewish Sages*
　　　　　　by Rabbi Rami M. Shapiro

SERVICE TO THE WORLD

The mind and heart reel upon folding up the paper. Just another day of broken hearts and lives around the world. Sitting back in my blue armchair my eyes close. A dream floats across. I hold the smooth round globe in my arms like a baby. My eyes wander over the surface as if I am entering into it. Lightly my fingers explore the oceans, the beaches, the rivers, and climb the mountains. This is my home planet, now held as a lovely child in my arms. The inner eye sees some of the faces, some of the struggles, some of the delight, the dreams of each place on that globe. As my fingertips touch a place on the globe the troubles of each location flash into view. I wish I could give some relief for the wrinkles of pain in each land, each river, each ocean.

I hold the globe close to my breast and sob. My fingers curl around thousands of miles, thousands of weapons, thousands of birds and fish, thousands of people longing, as I do, for peace. There is no way to invent a way out of the suffering of the present. It simply has to be lived and loved now in the real. My ears strain to listen deeply to the messages that I may carry the wisdom of the earth to keep going. Faithfully I rock the globe patting it softly, snuggling it into my bosom, singing a lullaby my grandmother taught me, "Byo oh bye yoh bye yoh, bye yoh bye yoh bye."

—FRAN PEAVEY
in *By Life's Grace*

A spiritually literate understanding of service begins with our involvements at home and in our communities, and then it expands to embrace world issues. Judaism uses the concept of the repair of the world to explain how the local and the global are connected.

Energy in the form of light is trapped in gross matter. Sparks of holiness are imprisoned in the stuff of creation. They yearn to be set free, reunited with their Source through human action. When we return something to its proper place, where it belongs, where it was meant to be; when we use something in a sacred way or for a holy purpose; when we treat another human being as a human being, the captive sparks are released and the cosmos is healed. This liberation of light is called the Repair of Creation.

The process occurs also within each individual. According to one legend, once there was a primordial person as big as the whole universe whose soul contained all souls. . . .

This person is identical with the universe and, for this reason, each human being is at the same time both riddled with divine sparks and in desperate need of repair. Each person is the whole world. And every human action therefore plays a role in the final restitution. Whatever we do is related to this ultimate task: To return all things to their original place in God. Everything a person does affects the process.

—LAWRENCE KUSHNER
in *The Book of Words*

I am reminded of the story of the teacher who tears to shreds a map of the world and, thinking it an impossible task, gives it to a recalcitrant student to put together. Within ten minutes the boy is back, the task completed. Astounded, the teacher asks him how he did it. The boy replies: "When I turned the pieces over, I found a torn-up man. I put him together, and when I looked at the other side the world was whole again."

—SOOZI HOLBECHE
quoted in *The Way Ahead*
edited by Eddie and Debbie Shapiro

Sheila Cassidy, who was jailed as a prisoner of conscience in Chile, believes that all pain and suffering in the universe has a purpose in what she calls "the Divine Economy."

I believe,
no pain is lost.
No tear unmarked,
no cry of anguish
dies unheard,
lost in the hail of gunfire
or blanked out by the padded cell.
I believe that pain
and prayer
are somehow saved,
processed,
stored,
used in the Divine Economy.
The blood
shed in Salvador
will irrigate the heart
of some financier
a million miles away.
The terror,
pain,
despair,
swamped
by lava, flood or earthquake
will be caught up
like mist and fall again,
a gentle rain
on arid hearts
or souls despairing

in the back streets
of Brooklyn.
—SHEILA CASSIDY
in *Sharing the Darkness*

How do we take the first steps toward healing the world's pain and suffering? Chickasaw essayist Linda Hogan describes one path.

In 1986, I heard Betty Williams, a 1977 Nobel Peace Prize laureate from Northern Ireland, lecture in South Dakota. One afternoon Williams had witnessed the bombing death of Irish children. A little girl died in Williams's arms. The girl's legs had been severed in the explosion and had been thrown across the street from where the woman held the bleeding child. Williams went home in shock and despair. Later that night, when the shock wore off, the full impact of what she'd seen jolted her. She stepped outside her door, screaming out in the middle of the night. She knocked on doors that might easily have opened with weapons pointed at her face, and she cried out, "What kind of people have we become that we would allow children to be killed on our streets?" Within four hours the city was awake and there were sixteen thousand names on petitions for peace.

—LINDA HOGAN
in *Dwellings*

In 1978, NBC aired a television miniseries called Holocaust. It was the first of many powerful TV movies to dramatize the horrors of the Nazi campaign to exterminate the Jews during World War II. The public's response to depictions of this tragedy invariably ends with the vow "Never Again!"

Fred and I wrote a Viewer's Guide to Holocaust and were therefore invited to many of the press functions organized to assess audience reactions. A speaker on each occasion was Rabbi Marc Tannenbaum from the American Jewish Committee. He sat on the podium and listened to historians talk about the film's accuracy and to Holocaust survivors share their varied opinions of it. Then Rabbi Tannenbaum stood up and talked about the boat people of Cambodia. The campaign of terror by the Khmer Rouge against the Cambodian people was in full swing at that time, and thousands of people were fleeing the genocide in dangerously unseaworthy vessels.

I remember thinking, "Here he goes again" when, for the third time, I heard Tannenbaum begin the boat people speech. Other people at the press conference clearly did not appreciate what they considered to be a change of subject. A few TV critics became restless, wanting to focus on information about the Holocaust they could use in their reviews. Not a few of the survivors became visibly upset with his speech, some murmuring that the horror of the Holocaust was unique.

But Tannenbaum kept talking about the suffering of the boat people. Never again? Now is again! He said so over and over. Today, when I hear news reports from Rwanda, Bosnia, Tibet, Burma—oh, the list does go on—I still hear his insistent, prophetic voice.

Rabbi Marc Tannenbaum did not turn away from the world's pain, nor does Buddhist educator Sharon Salzberg in the next reading.

I handed my passport to a uniformed Soviet official. He looked at my picture, and he looked at me, and he looked at my picture, and he looked at me. The look he gave me was, I think, the most hateful stare I have ever received from anybody in my life. It was an icy rage. It was the first time in my life that I had experienced that kind of energy so directly and personally. I just stood there, shocked. Finally, after quite a long period of time, the official handed me back my passport and told me to go.

I went to the transit lounge of the airport, where my traveling companions were waiting for me. I was very upset. I felt as though the man's energy had poisoned my being. I had absorbed his hatred, and I was reacting strongly to it. Then, in one moment, everything shifted. I thought, "If being exposed to his energy could make me feel so terrible after ten minutes, what would it be like to live inside that energetic vibration all the time?" I realized that this man might wake up, spend much of the day, and go to sleep in a state quite similar to the one I had just experienced from him. A tremendous feeling of compassion came into me for him. He was no longer a threatening enemy, but rather someone in what seemed to be intense suffering.

—SHARON SALZBERG
in *Lovingkindness*

For some individuals, the call of conscience takes precedence over the rational calculus of society that measures everything in terms of results.

I have another friend who has devoted most of his adult life to resisting the madness of war through actions of justice and peace. He has done everything from painfully unearthing the seeds of violence in his personal life to living in poverty so as to stay below the taxation level. He owns nothing in his own name because, if he did, the government could collect it as back-taxes. The money he "should" have given the government over the years, and more, he has donated to peace and justice projects.

Does he have any results to show for his efforts? Has he been effective? Hardly—at least, not by the normal calculus. His years of commitment to peacemaking have been years of steady increase in wars and rumors of wars. So how does he stay healthy and sane? How does he maintain a commitment to this sort of active life? His answer completes the koan offered by my friend at the Catholic Worker: "I have never asked myself if I was being effective, but only if I was being faithful." He judges his action, not by the results it gets, but by its fidelity to his own calling and identity.

—Parker J. Palmer
in *The Active Life*

This is not an invitation to add us to mailing lists, but I will admit that I read requests for support. While Fred sorts through film screening invitations and press releases, I open the rest of the mail. After the bills are filed and the personal notes are read, I turn my attention to the letters from nonprofit organizations.

I am especially interested in the ones who keep me informed about their projects; I even read newsletters. I had never heard of the guinea worm but once I did, I was glad the Carter Center had been working to eradicate it. I sign cards for Amnesty International to forward to political prisoners so they know people care about them. I send housewarming notes to people moving into a Habitat for Humanity home. And I give money to further all kinds of causes.

I feel that these letters in a small way keep me connected to the needs of the world. Even those citing grim statistics about animal species nearing extinction, children starving in our cities, and threats to environmental laws do not depress me. For the letters are really about hope and faith and people trying to make a difference. I know there are no quick fixes to the thorny long-term problems we face, but it does my heart good to know that there are people around the world who do not react like the woman in the next story.

There was a woman who wanted peace in the world and peace in her heart and all sorts of good things, but she was very frustrated. The world seemed to be falling apart. She would read the papers and get depressed. One day she decided to go shopping, and she went into a mall and picked a store at random. She walked in and was surprised to see Jesus behind the counter. She knew it was Jesus, because he looked just like the pictures she'd seen on holy cards and devotional pictures. She looked again and again at him, and finally she got up her nerve and asked, "Excuse me, are you Jesus?" "I am." "Do you work here?" "No," Jesus said, "I own the store." "Oh, what do you sell in here?" "Oh, just about anything!" "Anything?" "Yeah, anything you want. What do you want?" She said, "I don't know." "Well," Jesus said, "feel free, walk up and down the aisles, make a list, see what it is you want, and then come back and we'll see what we can do for you."

She did just that, walked up and down the aisles. There was peace on earth, no more war, no hunger or poverty, peace in families, no more drugs, harmony, clean air, careful use of resources. She wrote furiously. By the time she got back to the counter, she had a long list. Jesus took the list, skimmed through it, looked up at her and smiled. "No problem." And then he bent down behind the counter and picked out all sorts of things, stood up, and laid out the packets. She asked, "What are these?" Jesus replied, "Seed packets. This is a catalog store." She said, "You mean I don't get the finished product?" "No, this is a place of dreams. You come and see what it looks like, and I give you the seeds. You plant the seeds. You go home and nurture them and help them to grow and someone else reaps the benefits." "Oh," she said. And she left the store without buying anything.

—MEGAN MCKENNA
in *Parables*

Michael and Justine Toms and the staff of New Dimensions Radio in Ukiah, California, have started a chorus for peace called the Earth Circle. They have invited their listeners and supporters to sit in a worldwide

circle on the first day of every month at 8 A.M. San Francisco time, "to pray and/or meditate, at the same instant, from wherever you are, for five minutes—to resonate with us and others as we focus on taking responsibility for who we are as a species on the planet, and on whatever situation most needs healing on the planet." To bring the strength of diversity to the circle, the New Dimensions people encourage participation by individuals from the widest possible religious, cultural, and ethnic backgrounds.

The Earth Circle demonstrates the spiritual practices of compassion, connections, hope, justice, peace, and unity. So does the action described in the next reading.

Stopping at high noon for a moment of reflection is a spontaneous gesture of human consciousness. I remember when Tetsugen Glassman Sensei was being ordained the Abbot of Riverside Zendo in New York. It was a grand affair. Zen teachers from all over the country were gathered together to celebrate the event, with candles and incense and white chrysanthemums and black and gold brocade garments. In the middle of this solemn celebration, the beeper on somebody's wristwatch suddenly went off. Everybody was surreptitiously looking around to find the poor guy to whom this had happened, because generally you are not even supposed to wear a wristwatch in the Zendo. To everybody's surprise, the new Abbot himself interrupted the ceremony and said, "This was my wristwatch, and it was not a mistake. I have made a vow that regardless of what I am doing, I will interrupt it at noon and will think thoughts of peace." And then he invited everyone there to think thoughts of peace for a world that needs it.

—BROTHER DAVID STEINDL-RAST
in *The Music of Silence*

John Wesley, who in the eighteenth century founded the Protestant Methodism movement, devoted his life to helping others. Here he lays out as spiritually literate an understanding of service as anyone writing today.

Do all the good you can
by all the means you can,
in all the ways you can,

in all the places you can,
at all the times you can,
to all the people you can,
as long as ever you can.
—JOHN WESLEY
quoted in *Spiritual Illuminations*
edited by Peg Streep

PRACTICING SPIRITUAL LITERACY: SERVICE

CONVERSATIONS/JOURNAL ENTRIES

- Talk about the people and experiences that have most influenced you to be a caring person. If a specific incident triggered your caring impulse, write about it in your journal.
- Think back over your life and choose two caregivers you admire. If you have not previously done so, write them letters expressing your appreciation for their caring, or write tributes in your journal.
- Describe a fulfilling act of service you have performed. What benefits did you derive from the experience?
- Give three reasons why you give money or time to an organization or group involved in service.
- Name some of the obstacles and rationalizations that have kept you from becoming more involved in service to others.
- What is the most creative service project you have seen, read about, or experienced?
- Replay in your mind a recent occasion when someone helped you out just when you needed it. How did it feel? Write a paragraph or two about what you learned from this experience of service.
- What have you found to be the best way to help poor, disadvantaged, or needy people? Do you follow your heart or your head when someone you meet on the street asks you for money?
- What degree of responsibility do you feel for the increasing gap between the rich and the poor in the world, and for other problems such as violence in society and racial prejudice?

ACTIVITIES/PROJECTS

- Compile a list of volunteer opportunities with service organizations, being sure to indicate which groups have things for children to do. Distribute your list where you worship, work, or study. The Chamber of Commerce, United Way, or a community association of charitable organizations can provide information on local groups. In addition, *The Encyclopedia of Associations*, published by Gale Research, Inc., and available in the reference sections of most libraries, includes descriptions of nearly 23,000 national and international organizations; a name and keyword index enables you to find a group working in almost any area.

- Find a service project that you and your friends and/or members of your family can do together. Commit time to it for at least one month.

- As a household project, recognize someone in your community who has provided "Outstanding Service." Make a certificate or send a note with some flowers or food treats.

- At work, keep a notepad near you and write down different ways you could help out or be of service to fellow workers.

- Involve yourself in the peaceful resolution of a dispute at home, at work, or in your community.

- Go to the library and read articles or books until you are up to speed about a particular world problem that stirs your passion. Make a list of things you can do about it.

- We all need the stirring example of service-oriented people to inspire us. Rent one or more of the following video portraits of moral mentors: *Cry Freedom,* the story of South African freedom fighter Stephen Biko and newspaper editor Donald Woods; *Gandhi,* the Academy Award–winning film about the Indian peace activist; *King,* a rounded look at the Christian nonviolent advocate for the rights of African-Americans; *Mother Teresa,* a documentary about the Catholic nun's work; *Romero,* a film about the Catholic archbishop who fought for justice in El Salvador; and *Sakharov,* a drama about the Russian physicist who spent his last years crusading for human rights.

SPIRITUAL EXERCISES/RITUALS

- Find stories about service in the sacred literature of your spiritual tradition. One example is the parable of the Good Samaritan in the Christian New Testament.

- Create a living prayer by providing a service to someone in your neighborhood this week.

- Sacrifice is an important spiritual practice in many traditions. Give up one thing, besides money and time, for a cause you believe in.

- During your next service project, monitor your inner work and see how the curriculum of service is deepening you.

BODY

The first step on a spiritual path today is a return to a sense of one's own body.

—MARTHA HEYNEMAN

Our body is precious. It is a vehicle for awakening. Treat it with care.

—BUDDHA

If we bless our bodies, they will bless us.

—GLORIA STEINEM

Eroticism, being in relation, calls the inner life into play. No longer numb we feel the magnetic pull of our bodies toward something stronger, more vital than simply ourselves. Arousal becomes a dance with longing. We form a secret partnership with possibility.

—TERRY TEMPEST WILLIAMS

Our health is a voyage and every illness is an adventure story.

—MARGIAD EVANS

Diseases can be our spiritual flat tires—disruptions in our lives that seem to be disastrous at the time but end by redirecting our lives in a meaningful way.

—BERNIE SIEGEL

Diminishment and death are not the last word—the way to new life is physical.

—SALLIE MCFAGUE

The world's religions encourage us to view the body as a reliable companion, as a capable mediator of our experience of the world, as a vehicle for transformation, and as a temple of God. Jews regard the body and soul as being inextricably linked, and Christians emphasize the incarnation of the sacred in human flesh. Hindus celebrate the body as a vessel for salvation, while both Buddhists and Taoists practice healing arts which attend to the breath and energy lines in the body. Native Americans and some primal religions consider the body's movement in dance to be a form of prayer.

Despite this acknowledgment by the world's religions of the body's sacred role, there is a contemporary malady that Protestant theologian Sallie McFague describes this way: "The most prevalent spiritual disease of our time is not wanting to be here, not wanting to be in a physical body." The writers represented in this chapter, we could say, are working on a cure.

The global spirituality movement has given rise to several hopeful developments. The body arts of massage, yoga, tai chi, and others increasingly are seen as ways to practice both attention and listening to the body. We show reverence for our bodies when we exercise regularly, eat healthy foods, enjoy sensuous experiences, and simply relax.

Growing naturally out of this revisioning of the body is a reunion of sexuality and spirituality. If relationship is the nexus of our encounters with the Divine One, sexual expression of love is devotion. We have begun to understand what the mystical poets have known all along—that our most intimate acts of loving another person also signify our feeling of oneness with the sacred.

Illness in our body is another point of connection. In the words of cancer survivor Marc Ian Barasch, "Disease and healing are not just physiological processes. They are spiritual detonations." Every illness can be a journey of self-discovery through which we learn about our

limitations, our vulnerabilities, and our strengths. The spiritual practices of prayer, imagination, forgiveness, and faith are essential tools in
the body/mind/spirit healing kit.

Illness can even lead to transformation. "Our culture," best-selling
author Deepak Chopra observes, "provides us with so little opportunity
to confront the basic meaning of life that sickness and death have filled
the void by becoming conversion experiences." The ample "literature of
personal disaster," as writer Nancy Mairs calls it, demonstrates how
people have been set on a new course while dealing with devastating
illnesses.

Death, then, becomes the ultimate spiritual teacher, not merely at the
end of life but throughout it. An old Buddhist monk is asked if he fears
death. "How could I?" he replies gently. "I have been preparing for it for
sixty years."

Finally, there is a new respect for the sacred dimensions of near-death
experiences, the process of dying, grieving rituals, and life-after-death
revelations. This awareness brings many spiritually literate people to
agreement with Protestant minister Samuel H. Miller: "We believe that
death does not have the last word. Life has depths in it which death does
not touch; it has heights which death cannot reach; it has powers which
death cannot quell."

LISTENING TO THE BODY

The Church says: *The body is a sin.*
Science says: *The body is a machine.*
Advertising says: *The body is a business.*
The body says: *I am a fiesta.*
> —EDUARDO GALEANO
> in *Walking Words*

Spiritual literacy enables us to reject negative images of the body and join the fiesta. Consider the fluid and free expression of the body in dance, for example. One of my fondest family memories is of the time Mary Ann and I watched my younger sister, Laurie, dance at a disco in New York City. She could improvise with the different currents of sound, undulating and swaying in a state of total abandon. Her movements looked as if they came as naturally to her as breathing.

Laurie and her partner were so spontaneous and dramatic that the rest of the dancers stopped to watch them. I realized that she had found a total and honest bodily expression of her soul—a way of honoring life in all of its dimensions.

When Caleigh was two, she developed a marvelous, though probably not uncommon, routine. It was profoundly ritualized. After her bath she would make a beeline for the living room. There, under its cathedral ceiling and amid toys not yet picked up, she would lope in circles. Susan and I saw her as a filly in a field of prairie grass. She would toss her strawberry blond hair, sometimes lifting one foot in the most fascinating and peculiar way, and keep on circling—inevitably counterclockwise. The beauty of her step was so compelling that I would sit entranced, sometimes for a quarter of a hour, while she played out her celebration. As far as we knew, she had never seen a filly in a field or a unicorn in a Disney movie. We had not taught her the dance, and we marveled at its constancy and kinesthetic energy.

—RONALD L. GRIMES
in *Marrying & Burying*

Psychoanalyst and cantadora *Clarissa Pinkola Estés and workshop leader Mark Gerzon have discovered that our bodies can be read on many levels..*

The body uses its skin and deeper fascia and flesh to record all that goes on around it. Like the Rosetta stone, for those who know how to read it, the body is a living record of life given, life taken, life hoped for, life healed. It is valued for its articulate ability to register immediate reaction, to feel profoundly, to sense ahead.

The body is a multilingual being. It speaks through its color and its temperature, the flush of recognition, the glow of love, the ash of pain, the heart of arousal, the coldness of nonconviction. It speaks through its constant tiny dance, sometimes swaying, sometimes a-jitter, sometimes trembling. It speaks through the leaping of the heart, the falling of the spirit, the pit at the center, and rising hope.

The body remembers, the bones remember, the joints remember, even the little finger remembers. Memory is lodged in pictures and feelings in the cells themselves. Like a sponge filled with water, anywhere the flesh is pressed, wrung, even touched lightly, a memory may flow out in a stream.

To confine the beauty and value of the body to anything less than this magnificence is to force the body to live without its rightful spirit, its rightful form, its right to exultation. To be thought ugly or unacceptable because one's beauty is outside the current fashion is deeply wounding to the natural joy that belongs to the wild nature.

—CLARISSA PINKOLA ESTÉS
in *Women Who Run with the Wolves*

By taking a biography of our body, we can learn to know it better than we did when we were younger. So take a moment and interview your own body. . . . If you are visually rather than verbally oriented, draw a portrait of your body. Encounter not only the front, which you see in a mirror, but your sides and back. Probe its depths; discover its strengths; acknowledge its weaknesses; locate its wounds. Converse with the parts of your body of which you are proud, and those of which you are ashamed. Do not only speak the lines of an interviewer asking questions. Also play the part of your body giving its replies. Do not do this silently, but out loud. Be honest with your body, and ask it to be honest with you. It will help you decide what kind of nourishment, energy, and purpose you are seeking in the second half of your life.

Our bodies can be our wisest teachers, our most enlightened gurus. Perhaps it is a headache or backache, slumping shoulders or chest pain, failing eyes or constipated bowels. Almost always, hidden in our wound, is something that will enrich and deepen our lives. Your body ultimately knows itself far better than any other person can. In its cells have been stored every experience that has ever happened to you since before you were born. It knows more about you than your own mother, more about you even than your mind. Our bodies will teach us more than we can imagine, if only we will listen.

—MARK GERZON
in *Listening to Midlife*

We can get in touch with the stories and messages in our bodies through massage, exercise, and other forms of bodywork, and also through simple observations of how we look and feel.

From time to time a friend comes to my house to give me a massage. But I decided that "massage" is a very inappropriate word for it. I decided this should be called "listening to the flesh." She touches my body, and in each place she touches, the body has stored pain and joy, memories, knowledge of many kinds. And I begin to listen—to my arm, my shoulder, my belly, the soles of my feet, my tongue, my uterus. I begin to walk in the landscape of my body, the landscape of my flesh. And I begin to write the autobiography of my flesh.

371

Perhaps my toe wants to tell me a story about my childhood, of the slimy places it touched, the sharp-edged stones, of the times when it still reached my mouth, toe or thumb being equally good. Perhaps my womb wants to cry the story of the child I lost, of what wanted to be formed and what slipped out into darkness before it could be held securely by the arms near the heart.

Maybe my throat wants to tell me of all the songs held back. Held back in fear, or in doubt, or in anger, all the songs that the heart already knows but that I have not voiced. Perhaps I need to walk in that place, down my throat to the vocal cords.

—BURGHILD NINA HOLZER
in *A Walk Between Heaven and Earth*

The history of a life is here, written into cells and carved into skin. My body has memories of its own carried in the tension of my shoulders, in a characteristic way of holding my head, in a crease of concentration between my eyes. My body, absorbing pain and pleasure with equal ferocity, has kept a careful record of the passing time.

I try to see myself as others see me, to note the crinkles in the corners of my eyes, to acknowledge that the fullness around my hips obliterates every trace of my once-adolescent lankiness. My age is visible in the way I rise from sitting on the floor, the way I collapse into bed at night, in my losing battle with sagging stomach muscles.

Yet though I am determined to face the ravages of time, when I look into the mirror, I feel touched in the most profound way by the sight of this old flesh-and-blood friend.

Women have been taught to concentrate on how their bodies look, not how they feel, to see themselves as objects of someone else's attention, rather than the subjects of their own. And yet the truth is that I know my body from within, as no one else will ever know it. It is adaptable, expressive, and responsive, as if by magic. It has introduced me to every pleasure, shared in every wondrous discovery. It fits me. And despite all its shortcomings, it has been a comfort to me more times than not.

—LINDA WELTNER
in *No Place Like Home*

In the early 1970s, Mary Ann and I used to conduct youth ministry workshops around the country. One evening we were having dinner with a young minister when he said, "Pastor Brussat, I really love what we did in the workshop, but there is something about your presentation that bothers me." He paused.

I gave him my permission to speak freely, and he continued. "You should do something about your face." Trying not to register too great a reaction on that face, I replied, "What do you mean?"

"Well," said the minister. "You have a look of quiet, stern arrogance. It might put people off." I nodded, not knowing what else to do.

"I've figured out what it is that creates this impression," he went on. "It's your hair style." I wore my hair then, as I do now, combed straight back from my high forehead. "It's the way you flaunt your receding hairline."

I looked more carefully at my earnest adviser. He had taken most of the little hair he had from the top of his head and brushed it down over his brow in the style of a choirboy. Body language speaks volumes— both his and mine.

Life for me is like an ocean, with waves sometimes high, sometimes low, sometimes smooth, sometimes rough; so sometimes I'm high, sometimes I'm smooth, sometimes I'm low and sometimes I'm troubled. To carry the ocean analogy a little further, the current is life and the waves are essential for the movement of the ocean and for all the life that it holds inside. Waves are a natural response to all of the forces in the universe.

I am the same way, my faces are natural consequences of my being a human being, living and growing, and I need to know that storms as well as the beautiful sunshine are part of life. So I take pride in my stormy face, my sunshiney face, and I accept them as natural for that context. I don't have to put on a happy face when I feel stormy. I can put on a face that belongs with that. And I don't have to put on a face of doubt when I feel sunshiney inside.

—VIRGINIA SATIR
in *Your Many Faces*

A deckhand on a ship we used to sail was a rather severe young man with a squint. Whenever we asked him, "How are you today?" he would invariably respond, "Partly cloudy, chance of rain." Then he would smile, and we knew that he had made a place in his life for both sunshine and shadow.

Our body's language can be eloquent. Our gestures, postures, and facial expressions convey and influence the many emotions that pass through us. So do the ways we arrange our bodies, clothe them, and care for them. A friend who is a television executive has a weekly manicure no matter how busy she is. She feels better when her nails look nice, and she says with a wink, "It's wonderful to know that for one-half hour every week, someone will hold my hand."

In the movie Stacking, unhappily married Kathleen yearns for a new life beyond the Montana town where she has always lived. One day a photographer bound for California stops by the cafeteria where she works and asks her to come with him to that flowered paradise. Although she turns him down, Kathleen paints her fingernails the color of hibiscus to symbolize her desire for a change. Later, in a moment of despair and resignation to her fate, she angrily cleans off the polish.

Many spiritual traditions emphasize the sacred dimensions of body care through bathing. In India, Orthodox Hindus start the day bathing in a river. Some Zen students believe that a half-hour bath equals a half-day of meditation. There is even a Japanese saying that a bath is a gift from the gods. Here is a reading on bathing from the Jewish tradition.

Once, when Hillel had concluded a class with his disciples, he left the House of Study with them.

The disciples asked him, "Master, where are you going?"

He replied: "To fulfill a religious obligation."

"What is this religious obligation?" the disciples wanted to know.

He replied: "I am going to the bathhouse in order to have a bath."

The disciples were astonished, and they asked, "Is that really a religious obligation?"

He answered: "Yes! If somebody who is appointed to scrape and clean the statues of the king that stand in the theaters and circuses is paid for the work and even associates with the nobility, how much more should I, who am created in the image and likeness of God . . . take care of my body?"

—Rabbi Hillel
quoted in *Jewish Wisdom*
by Rabbi Joseph Telushkin

The spiritual practice of wonder is evoked when we think of how amazing our bodies are. Deepak Chopra points out that "The skin replaces itself once a month, the stomach lining every five days, the liver every six weeks, and the skeleton every three months." Novelist John Updike contemplates a scab and discovers a sacred message: "A scab is a beautiful thing—a coin the body has minted, with an invisible motto: In God we trust." Japanese poet Buson considers a very common posture and fashions a haiku of gratitude.

> My arm for a pillow,
> I really like myself
> under the hazy moon.
> —BUSON
> in *The Essential Haiku*
> edited by Robert Hass

And no one can ignore the body's natural rhythms and requirements.

> His Holiness the Abbot
> is shitting
> in the withered fields.
> —BUSON
> in *The Essential Haiku*
> edited by Robert Hass

I struggle with a negative view of my body. As a boy I was skin and bones, and was often the subject of ridicule. By middle age, I was normal weight but still carried with me a negative body image. One day while showing friends around the resort in Antigua where we vacation, I slipped on the algae and fell down, slamming my head against the rocks. There was a good one-inch-wide gash in my scalp.

The nurse at the hotel took care of the wound, declaring that it was not very deep and did not require stitches. But the next morning, I noticed some blood on my pillow and pointed it out to the maid. "No problem," she said. "I'll clean it. I heard you cut your head."

A few days later, I met the maid in the hallway. I was about to say something about my cut being healed when she beat me to the point. "Preacherman," she said with a big smile, "you have good flesh."

Good flesh! Those were the sweetest words I had ever heard about my body. I told Mary Ann I wanted to emblazon them across a T-shirt. It was such a simple miracle really, a cut healing quickly, but it helped me to cherish and appreciate my body as I never had before.

THE NETWORK OF THE IMAGINARY MOTHER
(excerpt)

Blessed be my brain
    that I may conceive of my own power.
Blessed be my breast
    that I may give sustenance to those I love.
Blessed be my womb
    that I may create what I choose to create.
Blessed be my knees
    that I may bend so as not to break.
Blessed be my feet
    that I may walk in the path of my highest will.

—ROBIN MORGAN
in *Upstairs in the Garden*

Some of the wisdom traditions teach that one's body is a reflection of the entire universe. "I am a little world," Renaissance poet John Donne proclaims. The next readings about toes and fingers show how even the small countries of the body world alert us to the value of such spiritual practices as attention, peace, and meaning.

Some years ago, I used to run for my health. I did it religiously but badly. I was as strong as a horse, but according to one observer, I ran "funny." My weight dropped lower than it should have been. When I first began, I had trouble with my right knee, and then the trouble left the knee and moved to the calf, then to the ankle, and then back to the knee and so on.

    My wife offered to pull my toes, a strange, primordial custom probably preserved by her family since the Stone Age, in which the toes are pulled, one at a time, until they click. Her family finds satisfaction in this ritual. In my family, we kept our hands off one another; all body parts were private parts. Now, as I lay on the davenport twisted in pain, I allowed my wife to pull my right little toe, not because I thought it would help but because she would find it satisfying. The toe clicked. My right ankle, calf, and knee loosened into complete relaxation. The pain was gone.

The next day I ran and suffered a little. As I stepped gingerly out of the shower, I reached down and tugged on my little toe. It worked again. And again. And again.

—John Cowan
in *The Common Table*

There are so many things that can provide us with peace. Next time you take a shower or a bath, I suggest you hold your big toes in mindfulness. We pay attention to everything except our toes. When we hold our toes in mindfulness and smile at them, we will find that our bodies have been very kind to us. We know that any cell in our toes can turn cancerous, but our toes have been behaving very well, avoiding that kind of problem. Yet, we have not been nice to them at all. These kinds of practices can bring us happiness.

—Thich Nhat Hanh
in *For the Love of God*
edited by Benjamin Shield
and Richard Carlson

Each finger of the human hand has a psychological and symbolic character, surprisingly constant across different cultures. The little finger is a child, the weak member who must be protected. The second finger waits, it wears the ring, and it follows the high-standing middle finger that so frequently stands for the penis. The index finger is the one that makes point, turns the pages, is the one that Christ raises in teaching. The thumb, in the French Salic Law, was said to be worth half a hand. It is the symbol of human strength and ability. And among all cultures, the palm is a common ground that when exposed means peace and when concealed in a fist means war.

—William Bryant Logan
in *Dirt*

According to the craftsmen of the Middle Ages, that's why we have spiral patterns on our fingertips. They thought the whorls there are the marks left by the soul entering or leaving the body. In this imaginative way of thinking, we infuse the people and things we touch in the world with soul by the care and attention of our touch. Our soul emerges from this mysterious place inside us and out through our fingertips, ensouling the wood we carve, the gardens we cultivate, the children and animals and lovers we touch. To me, this is a poetic way of imagining how we bring soul back into our personal lives—by paying attention to the very way we touch, as with the way we prepare food or the care we give our work or the manner in which we touch the earth.

> —PHIL COUSINEAU
> in *Handbook for the Soul*
> edited by Richard Carlson
> and Benjamin Shield

Spiritual readings of the body, like William Logan's and Phil Cousineau's, often emphasize the symbolic. Almost every body part, in one culture or another, has been regarded as signifying something more than what it is on the surface.

That evening, my husband invented a parable. A young painter comes to Michelangelo and says, "I've seen your religious paintings. Teach me to depict the human soul."

"Fine," says Michelangelo. "Learn to paint a human knuckle. Observe the knuckle closely. See all its bones and webs of skin, and the exact way it puckers. Study its minute shifts of color. You may paint a soul only by painting a knuckle."

> —BONNIE FRIEDMAN
> in *Writing Past Dark*

Mother let me play with one of her hands. She laid it flat on a living-room end table beside her chair. I picked up a transverse pinch of skin over the knuckle of her index finger and let it drop. The pinch didn't snap back; it lay dead across her knuckle in a yellowish ridge. I poked it; it slid over intact. I left it there as an experiment and shifted to another finger. Mother was reading *Time* magazine.

Carefully, lifting it by the tip, I raised her middle finger an inch and released it. It snapped back to the tabletop. Her insides, at least, were alive. I tried all the fingers. They all worked. Some I could lift higher than others.

"That's getting boring."

"Sorry, Mama."

I refashioned the ridge on her index-finger knuckle; I made the ridge as long as I could, using both my hands. Moving quickly, I made parallel ridges on her other fingers—a real mountain chain, the Alleghenies; Indians crept along just below the ridgetops, eyeing the frozen lakes below them through the trees.

—ANNIE DILLARD
in *The Annie Dillard Reader*

Annie Dillard as a child intuits that there is more to a body than flesh and bone. Body is a unity of the physical, emotional, mental, and spiritual. But we don't always live by that understanding. The next story, from the Native American tradition, offers a simple explanation for those times we do not feel all together.

One tale is about how the person's shadow lives a life of its own. Each night, when one lies down to sleep, the shadow departs, going out to explore the world it is not free to explore during the day. The shadow may become quite intrigued by the large and strange world, and be reluctant to return home at daybreak. So it is necessary for the person, early in the morning, to hum the shadow home. Each person has a song that only its shadow will recognize, and the shadow must obey the hum. If one is too busy, or too thoughtless, to hum the shadow home, the whole day will be difficult. Until the shadow comes home, the person is not whole, is not all together. It is like the person who got up on the wrong side of the bed—part of him is still missing. Humming the shadow home is necessary for harmony, for inner unity.

—MARY JOSÉ HOBDAY
in *Western Spirituality*
edited by Matthew Fox

QUESTING

"If we are spiritual beings on a human path rather than human beings who may be on a spiritual path," Jungian analyst Jean Shinoda Bolen suggests, "then life is not only a journey but a pilgrimage or quest as well." It is a quest for meaning, fulfillment, and wholeness.

This image of journey, quest, or pilgrimage is a theme in all the wisdom traditions. When a monk asks, "What is the Tao?" Master Unmon replies, "Walk on." It's important to keep moving. Or as Confucius says, "It does not matter how slowly you go, so long as you do not stop."

In the Bible, journey plays a central role in the Old and New Testaments. The Jews wandered in the wilderness on the way to the Promised Land. Jesus of Nazareth took the long, hard road to Jerusalem. And Saul was converted—transformed—to Paul on the road.

Throughout history, people looking for spiritual renewal have undertaken pilgrimages to sacred sites. Once in a lifetime, Muslims are under the obligation to journey to Mecca. They set out with high hopes for the quickening of their faith.

For many of us the inward quest is equally important. Trappist monk Thomas Merton writes: "Our real journey in life is interior; it is a matter of growth, deepening, and of an ever greater surrender to the creative action of love and grace in our hearts."

The point of questing is to polish our souls, to come to terms with the shadow, to explore what naturalist Loren Eiseley calls "the ghost continent" within.

This ongoing endeavor takes discipline, courage, and perseverance. As the Indian philosopher and poet Sri Aurobindo reminds us, "The spiritual journey is one of continuously falling on your face, getting up, brushing yourself off, looking sheepishly at God and taking another step."

Psychologist Jacquelyn Small notes, "At certain points along the journey, people begin to crave a larger context. . . . They long to be in the supportive and joyful company of others who are seekers like themselves." Companions who can share our experience and insights are essential on the inward quest.

The word question is derived from the Latin *quaerere* (to seek) which has the same root as the word quest. This makes sense. Questions are powerful allies on a spiritual journey. They stretch our mind, body, and soul.

"A very powerful question may not have an answer at the moment it is asked," social activist Fran Peavey observes. "It will sit rattling in the mind for days or weeks as the person works on an answer. If the seed is planted, the answer will grow. Questions are alive."

And we are more alive when actively involved with questing and questions. Keep moving. Keep crossing inner and outer borders. Keep asking.

SEXUALITY

The body teaches us that sexuality is not to be separated from other physical expressions of our being. Everything is part of our unique fleshly signature.

We sing ourselves every instant, with our bitten lips, our constrained voices, our message machines, our walk, our run, our way of stepping onto a bus, our compulsion to apologize, our lust to accuse, our styles of hugging and kissing.

Once in my life I kissed a woman on the mouth romantically. The surprising thing about it was that she kissed in the exact same way she held a pencil and walked down the street in sandals and shook salt into a bowl of soup. Her gestures had a coherence that was utterly natural. I had expected a secret to be revealed when I kissed her, but discovered that she expressed her secret constantly, as we all do, night and day.

—BONNIE FRIEDMAN
in *Writing Past Dark*

In the next reading, Nancy Mairs, a Catholic, laments the body-denying tradition in some branches of Christianity, which is most evident in the denigration of sexual pleasure. She offers a body-affirming approach. Then, one of her Christian predecessors endorses sexuality as sacred.

You would think, wouldn't you, that a faith founded on the premise of incarnation—of the Word-that-speaks-all-into-being made flesh to dwell among us—would hold in certain respect, perhaps in outright reverence, the body, the very form in which the divine had elected to be housed. . . .

. . . The world may well end if you cut down its trees and pave it over, it may well end if you permit its people to go unfed and unclothed and uneducated while you prosper. But the world will not end if you touch your genitals. The world will not end even if you touch someone else's genitals. I can think of sound reasons for choosing not to do so, but fear and disgust should not be among them. Your body is not a pesthouse, it is simply a body: who you are: part of God's creation, a small part, true, but as real and lovely as the rest. If you love every part, evil will not enter the world through you.

—NANCY MAIRS
in *Ordinary Time*

Professor Heiko Oberman of the University of Tubingen in West Germany speaks of how Luther, a former Augustinian friar who married, found the art of lovemaking not only delightful but sacred. In a letter to a friend, Luther is quoted as saying, "As you penetrate your wife, I'll penetrate mine, and we'll be united in Christ." Luther goes on to state that the best place to be at Christ's Second Coming is to be united in the act of making love.

—EDWARD HAYS
in *Secular Sanctity*

Essayist Sallie Tisdale calls lovemaking "a symphony of experiences, infinitely complicated with meaning." Sexual love is one arena where the practice of being present gives way to devotion and mystery.

Through sex we enter the timeless, boundary-less moment. We partake of the one experience above all others in life which allows us the bliss of true union. Here ego and all its concerns are erased, and the self is dissolved in utter surrender. To know, feel, and discover this in the presence of another human being, as we are invited to do in making love, is to be brought face-to-face with one of the greatest mysteries of human existence—that we are spirit, embodied, and that as human beings, we are partaking in this miracle.

To experience your sexual relationship in this way is to elevate it to the sacred encounter it is. In so doing, you will experience your body as a vessel of the divine, your orgasm as a gift of the spirit, and your beloved as he or she with whom you are gifted to share a taste of eternal bliss.

—DAPHNE ROSE KINGMA
in *Heart & Soul*

The height of sexual love, coming upon us of itself, is one of the most total experiences of relationship to the other of which we are capable, but prejudice and insensitivity have prevented us from seeing that in any other circumstances such delight would be called mystical ecstasy. For what lovers feel for each other in this moment is no other than adoration in its full religious sense, and its climax is almost literally the pouring of their lives into each other. Such adoration, which is due only to God, would indeed be idolatrous were it not that in that moment love takes away illusion and shows the beloved for what he or she in truth is—not the socially pretended person but the naturally divine.

Mystical vision, as has always been recognized, does not remain at the peak of ecstasy. As in love, its ecstasy leads into clarity and peace. The aftermath of love is an anticlimax only when the climax has been taken and not received. But when the whole experience was received the aftermath finds one in a marvelously changed and yet unchanged world, and here we are speaking of spirituality and sexuality in the same breath. For the mind and senses do not now have to open themselves; they find themselves naturally opened, and it appears that the divine world is no other than the everyday world.

—ALAN WATTS
in *Nature, Man, and Woman*

"Erotic is what those deep relations are and can be that engage the whole body—our heart, our mind, our spirit, our flesh. It is that moment of being exquisitely present," Terry Tempest Williams writes. And eroticism is expressed in a variety of ways.

Walking is safe sex for me. You see, you take your deep, sighing breaths and your hair tosses in the wind and you lift your chin a little to gulp in more fresh air, and you close your eyes a little against the warmth of the emerging sun, and your feet and your legs pump in unison and your thighs rub against each other in a rhythm, and you perspire a lot, and your T-shirt and shorts fill with moisture until you could wring them out by the time you've done a mile or so, and you're panting during the second mile, and your joints are growing looser and warmer, and your mind is floating and swaying with the tops of the trees, and everything is, for a few blessed moments, right. Walking as orgasm.

—BettyClare Moffatt
in *Soulwork*

ILLNESS

A spiritually literate perspective can find in illness a teacher and an opportunity for profound change. Kat Duff writes about these aspects of illness in a remarkable memoir about her battle with chronic fatigue syndrome. She observes: "Illness offers an extraordinary and at times frightening vantage point from which to view the terrain of one's life." She notes that a Navajo word for disease translates as "fragmentation and reassemblage." Our experiences with pain and disease remind us that our bodily journey through life is a pilgrimage toward wholeness.

Once upon a time, a fabulously wealthy king had a son whom he adored. The boy was bright and handsome—perfect in every way—except one: He had a severely hunched back. This saddened the king no end. So he proclaimed that a huge reward would go to the person who figured out how to heal the boy's back. Months and months passed without a solution. Wise men and women with good ideas traveled to the palace from all over the region. But no one knew what to do.

Then one day, a famous guru happened into the kingdom and heard about the problem. "I don't want your reward," said the tiny woman (who was herself all scrunched over with age and wrinkled up like a prune). "But," she added, "I do have your answer." This was her advice: In the center of your courtyard, you must construct a sculpture—an exact replica of your dear son, with one exception: Its back must be straight and lovely in appearance. That's all. Trust God for the healing.

With that, the Master disappeared and the king's artisans set to work. In no time, a beautiful marble sculpture sat in the center of the courtyard. Every day as the little boy played, he studied the figure admiringly. He started to feel, "Why that's me! That looks exactly like me." Every day, the prince gazed lovingly at the sculpture until he identified with it.

Bit by bit, the boy's back straightened. One day, a year or so later, as the king watched his son frolicking in the gardens, he suddenly noticed the prince's back was totally healed. The young boy's identification with the marble sculpture had been so complete that he believed it represented him—straight back and all. Body obeyed belief.

> —MARSHA SINETAR
> in *To Build the Life You Want, Create the Work You Love*

Our beliefs about illness may affect the healing process, and many people attribute their remissions and recoveries to the spiritual practices of prayer, forgiveness, zeal, joy, and hope. When we or our loved ones do not get well, illness may then point us toward the spiritual practice of mystery, and we admit there are questions about pain and disease for which the only answer is "I don't know."

Sick people often identify causes for their ailments that their family and friends find unbelievable, such as the wind, nuclear radiation, or a bad marriage. My parents have learned to nod along when I offer my latest theory about the underlying cause of my immune deficiency, whether it is parasites from India, the mercury fillings in my teeth, or family karma, but the fact is that they are all true in the strange coordinates of this illness. Cures are equally unbelievable. Who would imagine that someone could recover from a terminal case of cancer by receiving massive doses of radiation, or drugs first developed for chemical warfare, much less by watching funny movies? I have begun to suspect that in the otherworld reality of illness, anything and everything can kill and heal, whether it is digitalis in heart medicine, a lover's touch, or God's grace. There is no apparent rhyme or reason to the geography of illness, only the ultimate authority and agency of physical pain.

> —KAT DUFF
> in *The Alchemy of Illness*

Growing up a doctor's daughter, I learned early in life from my father not to panic at the first sign of illness. Dr. Lewis Thomas, in his best-selling book Lives of a Cell, *succinctly captures my family's attitude: "The great secret, known to internists and learned early in marriage by internists'*

wives, but still hidden from the general public, is that most things get better by themselves. Most things, in fact, are better by morning."

In the next reading, Lewis Thomas suggests that casting disease as the enemy—something we must arm ourselves against—may be fashionable, but it is not wise.

Watching television, you'd think we lived at bay, in total jeopardy, surrounded on all sides by human-seeking germs, shielded against infection and death only by a chemical technology that enables us to keep killing them off. We are instructed to spray disinfectants everywhere, into the air of our bedrooms and kitchens and with special energy into bathrooms, since it is our very own germs that seem the worse kind. . . .

These are paranoid delusions on a societal scale, explainable in part by our need for enemies, and in part by our memory of what things used to be like. Until a few decades ago, bacteria were a genuine household threat, . . . Most of these have now left most of us, thanks to antibiotics, plumbing, civilization, and money, but we remember. . . .

The microorganisms that seem to have it in for us in the worst way—the ones that really appear to wish us ill—turn out on close examination to be rather more like bystanders, strays, strangers in from the cold. They will invade and replicate if given the chance, and some of them will get into our deepest tissues and set forth in the blood, but it is our response to their presence that makes the disease. Our arsenals for fighting off bacteria are so powerful, and involve so many different defense mechanisms, that we are in more danger from them than from the invaders. We live in the midst of explosive devices; we are mined.

—LEWIS THOMAS
in *The Lives of a Cell*

My father, Carroll Brussat, beat cancer twice in his later years. How did he do this? Part of it was his belief in the power of positive thinking, and another part was his voracious will to live. But I am convinced that his healing process was set in motion by his repeated telling of the story of his battle with the disease. Father seemed to derive fresh energy from these accounts of the doctor who helped him and the physicians who failed him. He took great pride in learning all he could about cancer and

then taking charge of his own healing regimen. When the disease faded, he wrote several articles about what had happened to him in order that others might benefit from his experience.

Anatole Broyard, a New York Times *book reviewer, used the same strategy in his losing battle with cancer.*

Just as a novelist turns his anxiety into a story in order to be able to control it to a degree, so a sick person can make a story, a narrative, out of his illness as a way of trying to detoxify it. In the beginning I invented mininarratives. Metaphor was one of my symptoms. I saw my illness as a visit to a disturbed country, rather like contemporary China. I imagined it as a love affair with a demented woman who demanded things I had never done before. I thought of it as a lecture I was about to give to an immense audience on a subject that had not been specified. Having cancer was like moving from a cozy old Dickensian house crammed with antiques, deep sofas, snug corners, and fireplaces to a brand-new one that was all windows, skylights, and tubular furniture.

—ANATOLE BROYARD
in *Intoxicated by My Illness*

Fred and I have found it useful over the years to identify the emotional correlates to our physical symptoms, having discovered that dealing with an emotional issue can directly influence our physical recovery and vice versa. One year, for example, I sprained both my ankles. My mind/body teacher, Dr. Gerald Epstein, has observed in his clinical practice that for right-handed people, injuries on the left side of the body correlate to emotional issues with the past and injuries on the right side of the body correlate to issues about the future.

The year I sprained my ankles, Fred and I were in transition and were making important decisions about our publications. I was finding it hard to give up what we had been doing for years, although our interests, energy, and the marketplace were all signaling that it was time to make a change. On my way home one day, I slipped off a curb and sprained my left ankle. Clearly, I was having trouble stepping out of the past.

Even when we had decided to move in new directions, I was hesitant since I could not be sure that we would find an audience for our new plans and that they would support us financially. I wanted some guar-

antee of a successful outcome. Around that time, I fell at an uneven patch of the sidewalk and sprained my right ankle. It was just as diffi-cult to step into the future as out of the past. My ankles were telling me to stay in the present—to do what I could do day by day. Obsessing about past regrets and future outcomes was literally tripping me up.

Marion Woodman, a Jungian therapist, writes that illness is a com-mentary on the modern lifestyle: "The harder we look at our aches and ailments, the more we will be startled by the painful truths they are trying to convey about our dangerously disembodied way of life."

Our national debate on health care is symbolic of deeper questions than insurance coverage, cost containment, and doctor's fees. It's about whether we see health related only to our physical body, or to our whole being—body, mind, and spirit. Can we take individual responsibility for our health, preventing "dis-ease" through con-scious living, rather than seeing our bodies as machines we can abuse and then have repaired at the medical "body shop" with everyone paying the bills.

The health care debate on a deeper level is really about what creates a healthy life. And it leads us to ask if we can be truly healthy and free of disease if we are living lives of greed, anger, fear, and selfishness. It also raises the issue of whether we can be healthy individuals in a morally degenerating, crime-ridden soci-ety. Can we recognize that individual health is connected to the health of all?

—CORINNE MCLAUGHLIN and GORDON DAVIDSON
in *Spiritual Politics*

Whereas it is valuable to explore the complex factors that influence health, the blame game has no place in a spiritual understanding of dis-ease or healing.

Some people once brought a blind man to Jesus and asked him, "Rabbi, who sinned, this man or his parents, that he was born blind?" They all wanted to know why this terrible curse had fallen on this man. And Jesus answered, "It was not that this man sinned, or his parents, but that the works of God might be made manifest in him." He told them not to look for why the suffering came but to listen for what the suffering could teach them. Jesus taught that our pain is not punishment, it is no one's fault. When we seek to blame, we distract ourselves from an exquisite opportunity to pay attention, to see even in this pain a place of grace, a moment of spiritual promise and healing.

—WAYNE MULLER
in *Legacy of the Heart*

Don't turn your head. Keep looking
at the bandaged place. That's where
the light enters you.
        And don't believe for a moment
that you're healing yourself.

—JELALUDDIN RUMI
in *The Essential Rumi*
translated by Coleman Barks
with John Moyne, A. J. Arberry,
and Reynold Nicholson

Illness and pain are powerful teachers. Nothing gets our attention quite like them.

For most of us, it became clear that horror can last only a little while, and then it becomes commonplace. When one cannot be sure that there are many days left, each single day becomes as important as a year, and one does not waste an hour in wishing that that hour were longer, but simply fills it, like a smaller cup, as high as it will go without spilling over. Each moment, to the very ill, seems somehow slowed down, and more dense with importance, in the same way that a poem is more compressed than a page of prose, each word carrying more weight than a sentence.

—NATALIE KUSZ
in *Road Song*

I woke before dawn with this thought. Joy, happiness, are what we take and do not question. They are beyond question, maybe. A matter of being. But pain forces us to think, and to make connections, to sort out what is what, to discover what has been happening to cause it. And, curiously enough, pain draws us to other human beings in a significant way, whereas joy or happiness to some extent, isolates.

—MAY SARTON
in *Recovering, A Journal*

In the next reading, a physician finds in the biblical admonition to "love thy neighbor" the basis for a spiritual approach to pain and illness.

In mind medicine, we can become spiritual friends to ourselves by assuming a new attitude toward our afflictions. We undergo a change of heart. Instead of being adversarial toward our illness, we seek to create cooperation between the illness and ourselves. We treat it as an authentic and genuine part of our being, not as an alien to be shunned and despised. Rather, it is a messenger that reflects our own inner imbalances and needs to be integrated back into our lives. The integration takes place through love. We treat the illness with love or a loving attitude. We bear in mind the ancient biblical injunction: "Love your neighbor as yourself." The illness is our closest neighbor, closer than any family members or friends. When we are in pain, we are closer to that pain than to anything or anyone else. So—love it! Again, biblical wisdom says, "Do not do unto others as you would not have them do unto you." Do not hate your ailment. It will hate you back. Replace hate with love.

—GERALD EPSTEIN
in *Healing into Immortality*

Whereas the biblical traditions put the emphasis on love, Eastern traditions put the emphasis on balance. The writer of the next passage is a leading teacher of Japanese shiatsu or acupressure massage therapy.

In the Orient, the human body is viewed as a finely balanced unity of interdependent parts. More important, the whole is greater than the sum of its parts.

REVERENCE

"The challenge of the saints of the twenty-first century," Catholic priest Edward Hays declares, "is to begin to comprehend the sacred in the ten thousand things of our world; to reverence what we have come to view as ordinary and devoid of spirit."

Look around. There is so much that is deserving of our respect and honor. The sacred is in, with, and under the ten thousand things of the world. And we are spiritual sleuths trying to find the fingerprints of the Subtle One.

In *The Book of Rites*, Confucius says, "Always and in everything let there be reverence." He realizes that this is a building block of a better world.

Ecologist and philosopher Thomas Berry explains the significance of this all-encompassing attitude: "Every being has its own interior; its self, its mystery, its numinous aspect. To deprive any being of this sacred quality is to disrupt the larger order of the universe. Reverence will be total or it will not be at all."

German dramatist Johann Wolfgang von Goethe feels that "the soul of the Christian religion is reverence." That assessment is shared by Oliver Wendell Holmes Sr., an American author, who writes, "I have in my heart a small shy plant called reverence; I cultivate that on Sunday morning."

The Jains in India consider reverence for life and nonviolence to be the lodestar of their religion. One of their prayers goes: "May I always have a friendly feeling toward all living beings in the world and may the stream of compassion always flow from my heart toward distressed and afflicted living beings."

German Protestant theologian Jurgen Moltmann points out that reverence in our times means "defending God's creation against human aggression, exploitation, and destruction."

Physician and theologian Albert Schweitzer makes reverence for life the foundation of his ethics. He counsels: "Profound love demands a deep conception and out of this develops reverence for the mystery of life. It brings us close to all beings." Schweitzer's reverence for life enables us to honor the Friend of the World by cherishing all parts of the creation. And that includes everything from the Grand Canyon to the ant that makes its way across our path.

Ecophilosopher Henryk Skolimowski goes even further: "Reverential thinking creates a field of good energy; ultimately it is a healing thinking. Reverential thinking is not a luxury, but it is a condition of our sanity and grace."

This ecological way of looking at the Earth and the community of life hopefully can resurrect the spirit of St. Francis, the thirteenth-century Italian monk who rejoiced in the natural world and his role in it as a loving member of the family of all living and nonliving things.

Our parting words come from physician Larry Dossey: "There is only one valid way, thus, to partake of the universe—whether the partaking is of food and water, the love of another, or indeed, a pill. That way is characterized by reverence—a reverence born of a felt sense of participation in the universe, of a kinship with all others and with matter."

You are a living entity that is composed of mind, body, and spirit. An Oriental diagnostician views all three realms as one. There is no separation, only unity.

In Oriental diagnosis, we see the body as an orchestra whose music is the soul. Remove any instrument, or change the way it is played, and you alter the music entirely. To bring out the full breadth of the spirit, you must finely tune each organ as if it were an instrument. It must function optimally, as if it were being played by a virtuoso. Yet you must never forget that each organ must blend harmoniously with the rest of the body—all the other pieces of the orchestra—to bring forth the most complete and beautiful being, which is you.

—WATARU OHASHI
in *Reading the Body*

Gretel Ehrlich, an essayist who lives in the American West, was hit by lightning on her ranch. To recover physically from this jolt to her being, she had to slow down and explore a balanced path.

Takashi, the farmer-monk from southern Japan who visited me at the beach house, said, "You have always been so strong. Now it is time to learn about being weak. This is necessary for you."

How could I grow strong by becoming weak, I asked. I was being purposefully naive. What he was asking for was balance. Health cannot be accomplished any other way. I pondered the dampening of this forceful energy, which had always welled up inside me. How does one do such a thing and not ask for death in the process? But that was the point: I didn't have to *do* anything. There was still a lot I had to learn about getting well.

—GRETEL EHRLICH
in *A Match to the Heart*

A study published in The New England Journal of Medicine *in January 1993 revealed that one in three American patients routinely uses alternative therapies. Applying the spiritual practices of attention, connection, listening, and teachers, we discover healers in all kinds of settings.*

A physician told me of a patient of hers who could no longer work because of fatigue and chronic back pain. One day this patient decided to watch her cat and do whatever the cat did. When he stretched, she stretched; when he rested, she rested; when he ate, she ate; and so it went. The cat showed her how to get in touch with her own instinctual rhythms. It was a profound lesson after which she was able to listen to her own body. She developed a growing sensitivity to the language of her body and learned how to help it heal.

—ANNE SCOTT
in *Serving Fire*

A woman told me she had taken home a church bulletin. In it was the quote: "The light shall never be overcome by the darkness." She felt drawn to that quote and placed it on her refrigerator door. The next day she went to the doctor for a physical and discovered that she had a tumor in her breast. She told me that the quote she had saved was her greatest strength in the days to come. Even as she went for surgery she felt the light within her overcoming the darkness. . . . When she learned the wonderful news that her tumor was benign she felt deep gratitude for the inner strength she had received from finding that simple quote.

—JOYCE RUPP
in *May I Have This Dance?*

For centuries, shamans have used compassion in their healing.

Flora Jones, a Wintu shaman from Northern California, heals through the experience of "feeling with" the patient: "I feel for the sores, the aches, and the pains. When I put my hand over the body I can feel every little muscle and every little vein. I can feel the soreness. It hurts me. If they have heart trouble, my heart just beats. Any place they are hurting, I hurt. I become a part of their body."
—PETER KNUDTSEN
in "Flora: Shaman of the Wintu," *Natural History*

The same process lives on through modern-day doctors and health care providers who treat patients with dignity.

If I as a doctor spend an hour of my clinic time talking to a woman who has only a few weeks to live, I am making a clear statement of her worth. I am giving her time that could have been spent with people who will get better, who will be able to contribute once again to the common good. I am affirming the worth of one individual person in a world in which the individual is at risk of being submerged or valued only for his strength, intellect or beauty. It is a prophetic statement about the unique value of the human person, irrespective of age, social class, or productivity. It is an affirmation that people matter just *because they are people*, because God made them and loves them, just as they are, not because they are good or witty or physically beautiful.

—SHEILA CASSIDY
in *Sharing the Darkness*

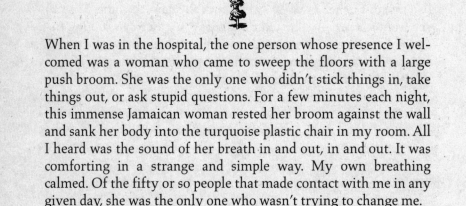

When I was in the hospital, the one person whose presence I welcomed was a woman who came to sweep the floors with a large push broom. She was the only one who didn't stick things in, take things out, or ask stupid questions. For a few minutes each night, this immense Jamaican woman rested her broom against the wall and sank her body into the turquoise plastic chair in my room. All I heard was the sound of her breath in and out, in and out. It was comforting in a strange and simple way. My own breathing calmed. Of the fifty or so people that made contact with me in any given day, she was the only one who wasn't trying to change me.

One night she reached out and put her hand on the top of my shoulder. I'm not usually comfortable with casual touch, but her hand felt so natural being there. It happened to be one of the few places in my body that didn't hurt. I could have sworn she was saying two words with each breath, one on the inhale, one on the exhale: "As . . . Is . . . As . . . Is . . ."

On her next visit, she looked at me. No evaluation, no trying to figure me out. She just looked and saw me. Then she said simply, "You're more than the sickness in that body." I was pretty doped up, so I wasn't sure I understood her; but my mind was just too thick to ask questions.

I kept mumbling those words to myself throughout the following day, "I'm more than the sickness in this body. I'm more than the suffering in this body." I remember her voice clearly. It was rich, deep, full, like maple syrup in the spring. . . .

I reached out for her hand. It was cool and dry. I knew she wouldn't let go. She continued, "You're not the fear in that body. You're more than that fear. Float on it. Float above it. You're more than that pain." I began to breathe a little deeper, as I did when I wanted to float in a lake. I remembered floating in Lake George when I was five, floating in the Atlantic Ocean at Coney Island when I was seven, floating in the Indian Ocean off the coast of Africa when I was twenty-eight. Without any instruction from me, this Jamaican guide had led me to a source of comfort that was wider and deeper than pain or fear.

It's been fifteen years since I've seen the woman with the broom. I've never been able to find her. No one could remember her name; but she touched my soul with her compassionate presence and her fingerprints are there still.

—DAWNA MARKOVA
in *No Enemies Within*

"Each person," says Albert Schweitzer, "carries his own doctor within." The path to wellness often leads to the spiritual practice of yearning.

The sick person's best medicine is desire—the desire to live, to be with other people, to do things, to get back to his life. When I was in the hospital, I was always gazing out of the window at the real world, which had never looked more desirable. I'd like to suggest, to invent or imagine or recall, ways of keeping one's desire alive as a way of keeping oneself alive.

—ANATOLE BROYARD
in *Intoxicated by My Illness*

In the movie Awakenings, *Leonard suffers from a sleeping sickness that has kept him immobilized for thirty years. When he is at last able to move and speak again, he announces without bitterness: "I've been away for quite some time . . . I'm back." As we watch him rejoice in his daily activities over the next weeks, it is impossible not to feel along with him the preciousness of the physical sensations we too often take for granted, and, like him, to be grateful.*

My illness gave the idea of the sacral in my life a depth it lacked in the classroom. One might agree with Durkheim that "the contrast between sacred and profane is the widest and deepest the human mind can make." Yet for myself I find all sorts of things now—even "profane" things—to be sacred. Our few acres of grass and trees at White Hedges, whether morning, dusk or full moon—I get a shiver of delight from gazing at them. I expand it to the larger plot of land I call my country, with its own brand of sacredness. I look at the old sundial on the lawn, and know it is always later than I think, and the dial becomes an image of the sacredness of time itself, of which so little remains. The sacral is the ritualizing of all the things—small and large—that are invested with life's essential meaning. . . . If I had to sum up in a phrase the difference my illness made in me, it would be that I have become the familiar of the sacral, and that every day of my life has learned to carry its own transcendence.

—MAX LERNER
in *Wrestling with the Angel*

DEATH

In the film Little Big Man, *Old Lodge Skins is an elderly Native American who decides it is time for him to die. He climbs to the top of a mountain, says a prayer, declares "This is a good day to die," and lies down on the earth. As he waits, he feels a drop of rain on his face. And then another. The old man opens his eyes and gets up. "I was afraid of that," he says as he prepares to head back down the mountain. "Sometimes the magic works. Sometimes it doesn't."*

Most of us are not as comfortable with death as Old Lodge Skins. We have difficulty with all three stages of this part of the spiritual journey: preparing for the time of death, dying, and dealing with what happens afterward. Therefore, keeping death before us is an essential task of everyday spirituality.

Each time we look into the bathroom mirror, we should remember that it is a magic mirror which can help us on the Way. Looking in the bathroom mirror is a good time to talk to ourselves. We are alone, and so there is no fear of being accused of vanity in taking extra time to look at ourselves. Looking at our image, we can speak words of encouragement or correction: "You drank too much last night, George . . . look at your eyes!" We can also examine the face in front of us with the eye of an inspector, noticing each new sign of aging. The bathroom with its private, magic mirror is a wonderful place for a mini-wake, a place to mourn our own deaths. If we can, as we pass through life, properly mourn our little deaths as each one comes—each new gray hair, new wrinkle or blemish— then we will die happy deaths. Proper mourning allows us to accept and embrace the aging process as natural. Those who pretend that they are not aging—dying slowly—who use creams, ointments and dyes to pretend it is otherwise, only find themselves in an impossible race with Old Boney Death.

—EDWARD HAYS
in *Secular Sanctity*

GESTALT AT SIXTY
(excerpt)

I am not ready to die,
But I am learning to trust death
As I have trusted life.
I am moving
Toward a new freedom
Born of detachment,
And a sweeter grace—
Learning to let go.

I am not ready to die.
But as I approach sixty
I turn my face toward the sea.
I shall go where tides replace time,
Where my world will open to a far horizon
Over the floating, never-still flux and change.
I shall go with the changes,
I shall look far out over golden grasses
And blue waters.

There are no farewells.

Praise God for His mercies,
For His austere demands,
For His light
And for His darkness.
            —MAY SARTON
                in *Selected Poems of May Sarton*
                edited by Serena Sue Hilsinger
                and Lois Brynes

Robert Fulghum offers another tactic for keeping death in focus.

A caption for this photograph: *A man sitting on a folding chair in a cemetery, as a light rain fell and the sun shone at the same time, on the first day of summer in 1994.*

If you were there, standing close by, you would notice that the sod beneath his chair was laid down in small square sections, suggesting it had been removed and then carefully replaced.

The man owns the property upon which he sits. He has paid for the site, paid to have the ground dug up, to have a cement vault installed, and to have the ground restored.

He is sitting on his own grave. Not because his death is imminent—he's in pretty good shape, actually. And not because he was in a morbid state of mind—he was in a fine mood when the picture was taken. In fact, while sitting there on his own grave, he has had one of the most affirmative afternoons of his life.

Sitting for an afternoon on his own grave, he has had one of those potent experiences when the large pattern of one's life is unexpectedly reviewed: the past, birth, childhood, adolescence, marriage, career, the present, and the future. He has confronted finitude—the limits of life. The fact of his own death lies before him and beneath him—raising the questions of the when and the where and the how of it. What shall he do with his life between now and then?

            —ROBERT FULGHUM
                in *From Beginning to End*

One of the great paradoxes of life is that it often takes a brush with death, or a diagnosis of a terminal disease, to wake us up to the preciousness of the present moment.

In many cases, people who've become aware of their mortality find that they've gained the freedom to live. They are seized with an appreciation for the present: every day is my best day; this is my life; I'm not going to have this moment again. They spend more time with the things and people they love and less time on people and pastimes that don't offer love or joy. This seems like such a simple thought—shouldn't we all spend our lives that way? But we tend not to make those kinds of choices until somebody says, "You have twelve months to live."

—BERNIE SIEGEL
in *Handbook for the Soul*
edited by Richard Carlson
and Benjamin Shield

An acute sense of mortality, combined with the poignancy of time passing, breeds a love for all things. When my grandmother was dying of cancer, she wanted to live to see the roses in her garden in June. When they came, it was as if she was seeing the fullness and glory of the world for the first time: Christ's blood flowing through the rose. She was a devout Christian living this experience as the Resurrection.

—ANDREW HARVEY
in *Dialogues with a Modern Mystic*

In The Tibetan Book of Living and Dying, *Buddhist teacher Sogyal Rinpoche suggests: "There is no greater gift of charity you can give than helping a person to die well." This gift often involves nurturing, reverence, and making room for mystery by letting go.*

I was on my way to a wedding a couple of years ago when I saw a crowd bustling about a person lying on the ground. I stopped my car and got out to see what was going on. There was a woman lying on the ground, her fists clenched as if she were holding on for dear life. It turned out that she was one of the four women who had been stabbed by an Arab in the Kiryat Hayovel neighborhood of Jerusalem. The medic was at her side, trying to resuscitate her. It was the first time in my life that I actually saw someone struggling, literally holding on to life, and gradually slipping away into death. I forgot about the wedding and sat down beside her, holding her, being with her. There was nothing I could do for her but that. The medic was doing his best. But I felt as if I had been "summoned" to stay with her. As I held her, I became very aware of this woman, of a life slowly but surely leaving this world. The gleam in her eyes gradually dimmed and the clenched fists eventually relaxed. I felt that I had "accompanied" her and that somehow this perfect stranger, whose name I did not even know, whom I had never met before—this perfect stranger was no longer a stranger.

At that moment, I felt closer to her than to anyone I had ever known.

—JEFF FRIEDMAN
quoted in *Wrestling with the Angel*
edited by Jack Riemer

When I was in seminary, I did a summer internship at a suburban parish. One day I heard the loud crashing sound of an automobile accident on the highway in front of the building. I ran to the scene and found a badly injured man bleeding profusely from the head. He was in a dazed condition, and kept trying to get up. Instead of offering prayers, I knelt and embraced him, encouraging him in his confusion to be still and wait for help.

Later, I was criticized by my superior, who stated that my job was not to touch dying or injured people but to simply minister with prayers and words of consolation. He said that if I were ever in a situation like this one again, the best course was to keep my hands off the person. I could be sued by the victim for further injuring him or holding him against his will.

Despite this minister's advice, I continued to use touch as a form of prayer in my ministry. Two weeks later at a hospital where a woman had died, I gathered her four family members into something akin to a football team huddle. They later told me that this spontaneous gesture was a healing moment in their grieving process, and had spoken to them more deeply than any words I could have offered. The huddle enabled them to literally embody their support and love for each other.

I asked the doctor to leave me alone with my father, or as alone as he and I could be in the middle of the emergency room bustle. As I sat there and watched him struggle to go on living, I tried to focus on what the tumor had done with him already. This wasn't difficult, given that he looked on that stretcher as though by then he'd been through a hundred rounds with Joe Louis. I thought about the misery that was sure to come, provided he could even be kept alive on a respirator. I saw it all, all, and yet I had to sit there for a very long time before I leaned as close to him as I could get and, with my lips to his sunken, ruined face, found it in me finally to whisper, "Dad, I'm going to have to let you go." He'd been unconscious for several hours and couldn't hear me, but, shocked, amazed, and weeping, I repeated it to him again and then again, until I believed it myself.

After that, all I could do was to follow his stretcher up to the room where they put him and sit by the bedside. Dying is work and he was a worker. Dying is horrible and my father was dying. I held his hand, which at least still felt like his hand; I stroked his forehead, which at least still looked like his forehead; and I said to him all sorts of things that he could no longer register. Luckily, there wasn't anything I told him that morning that he didn't already know.

—PHILIP ROTH
in *Patrimony*

Being present to a loved one who is dying is one of the most difficult experiences most of us ever have. The next reading brings into this moment the spiritual practice of connections and the understanding that we are never alone.

A patient of mine was dying from lung cancer. The day before his death, I sat at his bedside with his wife and children. He knew he had little time left and he chose his words carefully, speaking in a hoarse whisper. Although not a religious person, he revealed to us that recently he had begun to pray frequently.

"What do you pray for?" I asked.

"I don't pray for anything," he responded. "How would I know what to ask for?" This was surprising. Surely this dying man could think of *some* request.

"If prayer is not for asking, what is it *for*?" I pushed him.

"It isn't 'for' anything," he said thoughtfully. "It mainly reminds me I am not alone."

Jiddu Krishnamurti, one of the most revered spiritual teachers of this century, once asked a small group of listeners what they would say to a close friend who is about to die. Their answers dealt with assurances, words about beginnings and endings, and various gestures of compassion. Krishnamurti stopped them short. There is only one thing you can say to give the deepest comfort, he said. Tell him that in his death a part of you dies and goes with him. Wherever he goes, you go also. He will not be alone.

—LARRY DOSSEY
in *Healing Words*

On an episode of the television series Picket Fences, *young Kimberly Brock, who wants to be a doctor, is squeamish about having to do a dissection in class. She goes to see Carter, a pathologist and the town's coroner. Kimberly has never been in a morgue before and declares the place rather creepy. Carter responds with a spiritual reading of the morgue. He recalls something his anatomy professor told him about the cadavers. He was to think of them as patients who "have granted us a great privilege to enter a cathedral where no one has set foot before."*

Then, with what could be called a bow of gratitude, Carter reads Kimberly a Latin saying he keeps near the autopsy room: "This is the place where death nurtures life." In the next passage from a novel, the living repay the service.

"Dr. Hagopian, in what capacity did you work with the defendant?"

"He was my assistant in the morgue at the University Hospital in Madison, Wisconsin."

"Will you tell the jury exactly when he worked for you?"

"It was the summer of '86."

"Before his graduation."

"Yes, he was a junior."

"And what was the nature of his work?"

"He helped me with the autopsies."

"Did his behavior strike you in any way as unlike the behavior of those who have worked with you in this capacity before?"

"There were a few things," answered Dr. Hagopian. "He read aloud to the corpses. A bedtime story, he called it."

"Do you recall what he read to them?"

"I do, because I found it fascinating. I'd never heard anything like it. He read to them from the *Tibetan Book of the Dead*. Sometimes he came early to work so he'd have time to give them a whole chapter."

"Was there anything else you recall as inappropriate about his behavior at that time?"

"Well, he sang during the autopsies. He has a great voice."

The courtroom was very still. Turned to stone, all of them, thought Sam, except Mrs. Woolman, who was nodding at him, and Ellen, who was rocking in her seat.

"What did he sing?"

"Different things. 'You Are My Sunshine,' 'Hark the Herald.' We sang 'Hark the Herald' a lot."

—NANCY WILLARD
in *Sister Water*

All the world's religions have rituals to help us say good-bye to the deceased, but many mourning rituals we design ourselves.

I remember so well the day I went to the home of a family whose teenage daughter had been killed in a car accident. It was a moment full of deep sorrow and I knew that it would be no easy visit. Helen took me to her daughter's bedroom. There, on the bed, she had placed all of the major mementos of her daughter's few and swift school years. I remember especially the school jacket with a bright, shiny medal she had won the day before she died. Helen pointed out the mementos and spoke both proudly and poignantly of her daughter's short but full life. We stood there bonded in silent sadness, tears in our eyes and hearts. Then we joined the other members of the family and friends who had gathered. Each one who entered the home was greeted in this same manner.

Now, many years later, as I reflect on that visit, I realize what a beneficial ritual that was. It never occurred to me at the time that Helen was praying a goodbye; but looking back on it, I see how she was doing exactly that. Each time she escorted another visitor to the room and stopped to ponder, she was living out the pain of her daughter's death. The mementos of her daughter were the images that Helen needed to link her with the child she had birthed, nurtured and deeply loved, the child she had swiftly lost in a blur of tragic time.

—JOYCE RUPP
in *Praying Our Goodbyes*

One of the most poignant of our community customs is the *Celebration of Memories* ceremony. The night before a sister is buried the community gathers at her coffin to remember together the moments of her life that taught us all something about life. The simple ritual turns death into life at the very moment we feel its loss most. It is a model, this finding life in loss, for dealing with death of all kinds.

—JOAN CHITTISTER
in *In a High Spiritual Season*

A Native American perspective sets death in the context of the life of the tribe and the powerful presence of the ancestors. The Swamish chief Seattle explains this view in a speech delivered to the governor of the Washington Territory in 1854.

To us our ancestors are sacred and their resting place is hallowed ground. You wander far from the graves of your ancestors and seemingly without regret . . . Your dead cease to love you, and the land of their nativity, as soon as they pass the portals of the tomb and wander way beyond the stars. They are soon forgotten and never return. Our dead can never forget the beautiful world that gave them being . . .

Every part of this soil is sacred in the estimation of my people. The very dust upon which you now stand responds more lovingly to their footsteps than to yours, because it is rich with the blood of our ancestors, and our bare feet are conscious of the sympathetic touch.

And when your children's children think themselves alone in the field, the store, the shop, upon the highway, or in the silence of the pathless woods, they will not be alone. At night when the streets of your cities and villages are silent and you think them deserted, they will throng with the returning hosts that once filled and still love this beautiful land. The white man will never be alone.

Let him be just and deal kindly with my people, for the dead are not powerless. Dead, did I say? There is no death, only a change of worlds.

—CHIEF SEATTLE
quoted in *Western Spirituality*
edited by Matthew Fox

Primal religions also celebrate the presence of ancestors.

Those who are dead are never gone:
They are there in the thickening shadow.
The dead are not under the earth:
they are in the tree that rustles,
they are in the wood that groans,
they are in the water that sleeps,
they are in the hut, they are in the crowd,
the dead are not dead.
Those who are dead are never gone,
they are in the breast of the woman,
they are in the child who is wailing
and in the firebrand that flames.
The dead are not under the earth:
they are in the fire that is dying,
they are in the grasses that weep,
they are in the whimpering rocks
they are in the forest, they are in the house,
the dead are not dead.

—BIRAGO DIOP
quoted in *The Fruitful Darkness*
by Joan Halifax

Gabriel Horn is a contemporary Native American writer who here describes the eternal return of the Spirit.

When we are born, it's like taking a cup of spirit out of the gene pool of life that the Mystery provides. We must pour that cup back when we die, like a drop of rain that falls back into the ocean where it originated, except that the drop of spirit we take into this world

S

SHADOW

The shadow, according to American poet Robert Bly, is "the long bag that we drag behind us" containing all the dark parts of ourselves that we would like to keep secret.

The shadow may include our anger, selfishness, jealousy, pride, insecurity, wildness, or destructiveness.

Although these qualities are an integral part of us, we want to hide them or deny them. Eventually, they get out of the bag when we project them onto others—husband, wife, child, friend, neighbor, coworker, or another race and culture.

The spiritual practice of shadow involves being able to recognize these elements—and deal with them—when they make an appearance in our lives. According to Jungian analyst Robert A. Johnson, "To honor and accept one's own shadow is a profound spiritual discipline."

But it is much easier to demonize enemies and blame things on something outside ourselves. Nations do this as well as individuals. "If only it were all so simple. If only there were evil people somewhere insidiously committing evil deeds, and it were necessary only to separate them from the rest of us and destroy them," Russian writer Alexander Solzhenitsyn laments. "But the line dividing good and evil cuts through the heart of every human being. And who is willing to destroy a piece of his own heart?"

Now is the time to accept the evil that lives in us. "The only devils in the world," said Indian spiritual leader Mahatma Gandhi, "are those running around in our hearts."

There is a vicious thug, a serial killer, a terrorist inside us. To deny this truth is to live in an air-conditioned fantasy world.

And don't be fooled. "Evil is unspectacular and always human," poet W. H. Auden asserts. "He shares our bed and eats at our table." We inflict pain on others in small daily doses—little acts of selfishness, indifference, and neglect. The shadow lives in our snubs, grudges, criticisms, and self-pity.

"The full and joyful acceptance of the worst in oneself," writer Henry Miller suggests, "may be the only sure way of transforming it." Give up trying to deny your evil or to escape from your imperfections and limitations. Listen to what your demons have to say to you.

Richard Rohr, a Catholic priest who directs a center for both contemplation and action, says, "God calls us to take the path of the inner truth—and that means taking responsibility for 'everything' that's in you: for what pleases you and for what you're ashamed of. . . . In the spiritual life, nothing goes away. There is no heavenly garbage dump. Everything belongs."

Remember, too, that the Eternal Light is often discovered during a dark night of the soul. Others have experienced dark times before you. Check out the Psalms in the Bible.

Accept and own your shadow. Name your demons and learn from them. Realize you are not alone. And as St. Francis of Assisi advises, "Love the leper inside."

SILENCE

"Silence is something like an endangered species," remarks psychotherapist Gunilla Norris. "The experience of silence is now so rare that we must guard it and treasure it."

The clamor of the world assaults us from all directions. As part of our spiritual practice we must make a place for silence.

"Be still and know that I am God," we read in the Bible. It's a good directive. We can take a cue from Quakers, who design their worship services around silence. Native Americans also treat stillness with respect. They aren't afraid of waiting for long periods of time for messages from the Great Spirit.

Rabbi David A. Wolpe tells us: "Judaism perceives a certain stillness, an almost indescribable placidity and perfection that we can sometimes glimpse behind the turmoil of the world. It is not something we can see or hear, but it can be felt. There is a corner of Eden still tantalizingly in view."

What a stirring image—a corner of Eden in our lives where we can commune with the Most High and feel at one with the world. In that silence we nurture our bodies and souls. And as writer Sue Patton Thoele puts it, "Only in the oasis of silence can we drink deeply from our inner cup of wisdom."

That sacred place where words and activity come to a halt is a necessary part of a full life. Writer Max Picard notes: "Silence stands outside the world of profit and utility. It cannot be exploited for profit; you cannot get anything out of it. It is 'unproductive,' therefore it is regarded as useless. Yet there is more help and healing in silence than in all useful things."

Trappist monk Thomas Merton realizes, "It is in deep solitude and silence that I find the gentleness with which I can truly love my brother and sister." Silence, you see, is a seedbed where our connections to others take root and grow. Think of the monks and nuns and other religious whose silent prayers and meditations hold up the world.

"God is the friend of silence," states Mother Teresa of Calcutta, a servant of the poor. "See how nature—trees, flowers, grass—grow in silence? The more we receive in silent prayer, the more we can give in our active life." Silence animates compassion and sets in motion the service of others.

No wonder the American social critic Norman O. Brown calls silence "the Mother Tongue." And let's not overlook Austrian poet Rainer Maria Rilke's advice: "Our task is to listen to the news that is always arriving out of silence." Listen and attend.

Heed the counsel as well of playwright Samuel Beckett, who demonstrates in such plays as *Waiting for Godot* the value of listening to the silences in conversations. And don't forget religious writer Eugene Kennedy's thought: "There are times when silence is the most sacred of responses."

Silence is a special place you must go to regularly. Silence is a grace that nurtures, heals, reveals, and renews. "No spiritual exercise," counsels St. Seraphim of Sarov, "is as good as that of silence." Be still and know. Be still. Be.

should increase in size. It can do this if we become closer to the spiritual things of life rather than the material. That way we put back more than we came in with. This assures each generation of enough spirit-power to be born spiritually strong, with innate understandings and knowledge.

The key idea . . . is to fill our cups with goodness. That way, when we die, all that goodness pours back into the Mystery and into those we love. A slow death by cancer is not a choice of death anyone would make, but for Simone's mother, it allowed the spirit of her life to fill up with even more goodness.

—GABRIEL HORN
in *Native Heart*

In Buddhism, Taoism, and Confucianism, death is a pathway to rebirth. Mourning rituals are as much about freedom and joy as they are about ending.

Many years ago, when visiting Japan, I saw a group of monks carry a cage of white birds to the top of a hill. It was an unusual sight, so I followed them. . . . It was a long and hard climb. I began to tell myself I was nuts and should turn back. My chest heaved. My calves screamed. It was foggy, damp, cold.

And then we arrived. Encircling the cage, the monks chanted in low and resonant tones, their palms pressed together, their shaven heads bowed, their orange robes dancing as the mist rolled around their ankles. One of them leaned over and opened the cage door. A score of white doves erupted into the sky—rising, circling, flapping their way to freedom.

I was clicking the shutter wildly when one of the monks tapped me on the shoulder. In very halting English, he asked me about my camera. I put it in his hands. As he was looking at the lens, I asked him why they had released the birds. He smiled softly, responding, "One of our brothers has passed. These birds will be companions for the liberation of his soul."

—DAWNA MARKOVA
in *No Enemies Within*

*The resurrection of the dead is a central belief in the Christian tradi-
tion. Catholic priest John R. Aurelio expands the idea of resurrection to
include moments when a deceased loved one is felt to be present sacra-
mentally: "We can do what Jesus did. Because of our love we can give
others gifts that they will remember us by. Those are the sacraments
that exist between us. Those also become doorways for afterdeath experiences with those we love."*

Emil had what the French would call *joie de vivre,* a zest for life. He
would aptly be described by countless people as the most unforget-
table character they ever met. For a man who held no public office,
no rank in civic organizations, and a modest status job as a real-
estate broker, his circle of friends literally extended to hundreds of
people. . . .

He was a presence wherever he went, but never an ostentatious
one. He was hardly ever the center of attention; nor did he crave it.
He simply had a remarkable way of making everyone in the room
with him feel special, even the proverbial wallflower with whom he
always spent extra time. He was so full of life it was contagious,
even bothersome at times. At a family cottage on the lake, he would
never let the sun go down without an audience. No matter what
people were doing at the time—usually sitting down for dinner or
playing cards—he would roust everyone, forcibly if necessary, and
herd us outside to watch the sun sink majestically into the lake. In
spite of our protests, we would all take a moment to stare at it in
silent and rapt attention. When it was over Emil would give us permission to go back and continue whatever we were doing. . . .

When he died of a heart attack just before Christmas he left a
gaping hole in many lives. We all knew that someone very special
was irretrievably lost to us. Or was he? Early the following summer a group of us were gathered at the family cottage once again.
We were all busily involved in whatever we were doing when
someone looked out the window and said, "Look everybody. It's an
Emil sunset." Without even being summoned we all dropped what
we were doing and went outside to watch the blazing sun go down.
No one spoke. At that moment, we all knew that Emil was actually
there with us. He was present to us because he had left us the sunset as his sacrament and we all knew it and felt it.

—JOHN R. AURELIO
in *Returnings*

PRACTICING SPIRITUAL LITERACY: BODY

CONVERSATIONS/JOURNAL ENTRIES

- If you interviewed your body, what would it say about its strengths, weaknesses, and wounds?

- When was the last time your body spoke to you about some problem and you refused to listen? Was the result an illness? Recall an instance when your body vividly revealed a piece of wisdom to you.

- Do you see eroticism as a positive spiritual force in your life? If not, what are some of the obstacles and blocks which prevent you from embracing it?

- Austrian scientist and philosopher Rudolf Steiner maintains that the illnesses of adulthood are catalysts to personal growth. Do you agree or disagree? What insights into yourself and your style of living have you gained from a sickbed?

- What would you do if you were told that you only had a year to live? a month? a week? If someone could forecast the future, would you want that person to tell you when and how you are going to die? Why or why not?

- Write a journal exercise on your personal interpretation of the following phrase from James Joyce's *Ulysses:* "Mr. Duffy lived just a short distance away from his body."

- What is your greatest fear about death? What is your vision of a finely finished death? How do you imagine your death?

ACTIVITIES/PROJECTS

- Monitor your body closely for a week and see what it reveals about its stress, relaxation, and care.

- Go back through your photo albums and study the history of your body. Pick out pictures of yourself as a young child, at age ten, in your teens, and in succeeding decades. During which period did you feel best about your body? Were you ever unhappy or ashamed of your body? In the photographs, what does your body language reveal about you? How have your attitudes toward your body changed over the years?

- Write a contract with your body in which you list the steps you will take to improve your health and to ward off disease. Be specific. Your doctor may be able to give you recommendations based on the results of a physical examination. Health magazines often carry articles on this subject. In addition, Dr. Andrew Weil in his book *Spontaneous Healing* suggests "An Eight-week Program for Optimal Healing Power," which you could adapt to your own body's needs.

- Interview an alternative health practitioner—such as a massage therapist, acupuncturist, or herbalist—about his or her work.

- Rent the video *Regarding Henry*. In this story, Henry is an aggressive and amoral lawyer whose comfortable life is upended when he is shot in the head by a thief. As he recovers from the wound and the memory loss resulting from it, Henry surprises everyone by transforming his attitudes toward his work and his family. His journey becomes a spiritual as well as a physical one as he seeks new sources of meaning and purpose.

- Three films on video spotlight the path of learning that can accompany the processes of dying, death, and grieving. In *The Doctor*, a surgeon who is diagnosed with throat cancer is tutored in the meaning of life and death by a woman dying of a brain tumor. *My Life* documents the spiritual journey of a young man dying of cancer. *Truly Madly Deeply* focuses on a woman who is in mourning for her dead lover. Through a surprising development, she is compelled to come to terms with their relationship and the underworld of grief.

SPIRITUAL EXERCISES/RITUALS

- Take a shower or a bath, thinking of your body as a temple of God. The next time you engage in your exercise program, consider your movements as devotional acts or prayers.

- Write blessings for the different parts of your body.

- Read the poetry of Rumi, Kabir, Mirabai, or "The Song of Songs" in the Bible to see how sexuality and spirituality are intertwined.

- Talk to religious leaders in your community—for example, the chaplain at the hospital—about the services they provide to ill and dying people and their families.

- Meditate on this thought by German theologian Elizabeth Moltmann-Wendell: "Eternal Life begins here in us with our bodies."

- Create a brief memorial service for a loved one on the anniversary of his or her death. Try to reconnect with this person whose spirit is still bearing fruit in your life.

RELATIONSHIPS

Spiritual maturity is an acceptance of life in relationship.

—JACK KORNFIELD

For many of us today . . . intimate relationship has become the new wilderness that brings us face to face with our gods and demons. . . . When we approach it in this way, intimacy becomes a path—an unfolding process of personal and spiritual development.

—JOHN WELWOOD

This is intimacy: its touch is ever new, revealing the precious moments we have to live and to connect with things. No love is ever lost in this universe.

—GUNILLA NORRIS

Relationships are the Holy Spirit's laboratories in which He brings together people who have the maximal opportunity for mutual growth.

—MARIANNE WILLIAMSON

Relationships are meant to be signs of God's love for humanity as a whole and each person in particular.

—HENRI J. M. NOUWEN

It is very significant indeed that physics now sees the whole universe as a web of dynamic interrelationships. When we come to the human person, our lives are also a network of interrelationships.

—BEDE GRIFFITHS

Most individuals have found God most clearly in and through others. The love of others is the love of God experienced in this life.

—WENDY WRIGHT

Relationships with other people form the spiritual web of our lives, with crucial strands being marriages, partnerships, family, and friends. According to many religious traditions, our deepest values are expressed through these essential bonds.

In religions which recognize a divine spark within every human being, all personal interactions can be seen as encounters with the holy. In Christianity, the concept of the Trinity—often phrased as Father, Son, and Holy Spirit—envisions the sacred as being relational. In the moral code of Confucianism, the health of the society derives from the maintenance of proper relationships with family, friends, and community.

For those who regard spirituality primarily as a journey toward wholeness, relationships are a training ground. "Being human is an accomplishment like playing an instrument," essayist Michael Ignatieff observes. "It takes practice." Relationships provide us with opportunities to practice enthusiasm, gratitude, hospitality, love, play, and questing. At the same time, they may expose our shadow sides, drawing out our anger, envy, hatred, pain, greed, and shame. These bonds also constantly school us in the spiritual practice of mystery. Sometimes there is just no rational explanation for why and when we feel linked to another.

Mystery is at the heart of intimate relationships. As a character in one of Joyce Carol Oates's novels puts it: "Marriage was the deepest, most mysterious, most profound exploration open to humankind; she had always believed that, and she believed it now. . . . The plunging into one another's soul, this pressure of bodies together, so brutally intimate, was the closest one could come to a sacred adventure." Partners are drawn together by desires and dreams, and then they improvise a relationship to navigate the sometimes treacherous waters of communication, career, finances, aging, and much more. The intricate and daily working out of two become one is a deeply spiritual endeavor.

Family relationships provide other examples of connection. According to psychologist Paul Pearsall, "The family is a soul center and apex of spiritual energy. It is a place where we learn what everything means and how to make everything meaningful." There, we are tutored in politics, economics, and moral thinking, and we discover the significance of yours, mine, and ours. Parents, brothers, and sisters are companions on our spiritual journeys, giving us crucial points of reference. And as with marriage, there is a primal mystery at the heart of family life extending back in time to our ancestral roots.

"From rocking horse to the rocking chair, friendship keeps teaching us about being human," writes cultural observer Letty Cottin Pogrebin. Making and keeping friends is a spiritual challenge requiring the diligent practice of kindness, listening, and nurturing. But the benefits are inestimable: the intimate sharing of ideas and ideals, unwavering support that is both honest and hopeful, mutual admiration and faithfulness. From childhood buddies to adult mentors and spiritual friends, these special individuals draw out the best that is in us. They are witnesses to our self-discoveries and spiritual unfolding.

The readings in this chapter reveal that relationships are some of the best practice drills available to help us polish our spiritual literacy skills. Marriages, partnerships, family, and friends are animated by powerful energies, and they are drenched with wonder.

RELATIONSHIPS AS A PATH

In the first chapter of this book, we talk about four spiritual literacy filters which enhance our perceptions of the meaning of our experiences. This is a good time to recall the filters because they are useful in helping us see how relationships are a spiritual path.

Sacramentalism recognizes that relationships are reminders and reflections of Spirit's relationship with us. Panentheism emphasizes the relational nature of the cosmos. Divinization assumes that we see the divine in each other. The nontheistic approach of interbeing is based on the fundamental assertion that everything is connected to everything else; the universe is woven together by relationships.

Bede Griffiths is known for his sensitivity to the truths of all religions. He tells the following story to make the point that the supreme reality—Brahman in Hinduism—is present in our interactions.

One day [a disciple] was going along the road when an elephant broke loose and was charging towards him. He just stood there, looking at the elephant, saying to himself, "All this is Brahman. Nothing can happen to me." The elephant took him up in his trunk and threw him off by the side of the road, where he was picked up unconscious. They brought him back to the guru and the man complained to him, "You said all is Brahman. I thought the elephant was Brahman—how can this hurt me?" The guru replied, "Yes, but the mahout who was riding the elephant was shouting to you to get out of the way, and he also was Brahman."

—BEDE GRIFFITHS
in *River of Compassion*

Relationships provide many images of the spiritual practices of unity and connections, which can be recognized both in the movement toward sacred wholeness and in the many subtle ways we influence each other.

Some seem to be born with a nearly completed puzzle.
And so it goes.
Souls going this way and that
Trying to assemble the myriad parts.

But know this. No one has within themselves
All the pieces to their puzzle.
Like before the days when they used to seal
jigsaw puzzles in cellophane. Insuring that
all the pieces were there.

Everyone carries with them at least one and probably
Many pieces to someone else's puzzle.
Sometimes they know it.
Sometimes they don't.

And when you present your piece
Which is worthless to you,
To another, whether you know it or not,
Whether they know it or not,
You are a messenger from the Most High.
—LAWRENCE KUSHNER
in *Honey from the Rock*

I was on a train on a rainy day. The train was slowing down to pull into a station. For some reason I became intent on watching the raindrops on the window. Two separate drops, pushed by the wind, merged into one for a moment and then divided again—each carrying with it a part of the other. Simply by that momentary touching, neither was what it had been before. And as each one went on to touch other raindrops, it shared not only itself, but what it had gleaned from the other. I saw this metaphor many years ago and it is one of my most vivid memories. I realized then that we never touch people so lightly that we do not leave a trace. Our state of being matters to those around us, so we need to become conscious of what we unintentionally share so we can learn to share with intention.

—PEGGY TABOR MILLIN
in *Mary's Way*

Take a lump of clay,
Wet it, pat it,
Make a statue of you
And a statue of me
Then shatter them, clatter them,
Add some water,
And break them and mold them
Into a statue of you
And a statue of me.
Then in mine, there are bits of you
And in you there are bits of me.
Nothing ever shall keep us apart.

—KUAN TAO-SHENG
quoted in *Of Love and Lust*
by Theodor Reik

A good relationship has a pattern like a dance and is built on some of the same rules. The partners do not need to hold on tightly, because they move confidently in the same pattern, intricate but gay and swift and free, like a country dance of Mozart's. To touch heavily would be to arrest the pattern and freeze the movement, to check the endlessly changing beauty of its unfolding. There is no place here for the possessive clutch, the clinging arm, the heavy hand, only the barest touch in passing. Now arm in arm, now face to face, now back to back—it does not matter which. Because they know they are partners moving to the same rhythm, creating a pattern together, and being invisibly nourished by it.

—ANNE MORROW LINDBERGH
in *Gift from the Sea*

The spiritual practice of hospitality encourages us to have all kinds of relationships, no matter what happens.

When I was in Jerusalem for three months I had an Israeli landlady in her fifties. Her TV set was broken and she called a repairman. It took him four visits to fix the screen. "But you knew even before he came the first time what was wrong. He could have brought the correct tube and fixed it immediately." She looked at me in astonishment. "Yes, but then we couldn't have had a relationship, sat and drunk tea and discussed the progress of the repairs." Of course, the goal is not to fix a machine but to have relationships.

—NATALIE GOLDBERG
in *Writing Down the Bones*

I was sitting on a beach one summer day, watching two children, a boy and a girl, playing in the sand. They were hard at work building an elaborate sand castle by the water's edge, with gates and towers and moats and internal passages. Just when they had nearly finished their project, a big wave came along and knocked it down, reducing it to a heap of wet sand. I expected the children to burst into tears, devastated by what had happened to all their hard work. But they surprised me. Instead, they ran up the shore away from the water, laughing and holding hands, and sat down to build another castle. I realized that they had taught me an important lesson. All the things in our lives, all the complicated structures we spend so much time and energy creating, are built on sand. Only our relationships to other people endure. Sooner or later, the wave will come along and knock down what we have worked so hard to build up. When that happens, only the person who has somebody's hand to hold will be able to laugh.

—HAROLD KUSHNER
in *When All You've Ever Wanted Isn't Enough*

In order to savor the delights of relationships, we must learn to live in the present moment. A great teacher of this spiritual practice is Greek novelist Nikos Kazantzakis's famous character Zorba.

I've stopped thinking all the time of what happened yesterday. And stopped asking myself what's going to happen tomorrow. What's happening today, this minute, that's what I care about. I say: What are you doing at this moment, Zorba? . . . I'm kissing a woman. Well, kiss her well, Zorba! And forget all the rest while you're doing it; there's nothing else on earth, only you and her!

—ZORBA
in *Zorba the Greek*
by Nikos Kazantzakis

Another way to taste the enchantments of relationships is through the spiritual practice of gratitude.

In ancient Japan it is said that after a night of making love, the man had to write a poem so that when his lover awakened she might find the poem next to her sleeping mat. This ancient Japanese custom was intended to link together sensuality and love. The poem and the consideration behind its creation was a reassurance that the sexual exchange was a fruit of love and not just a "taking." . . .

The thanksgiving gift of the poem was but one way to assure the woman that she was truly loved. Not only women, but men as well, need to be frequently reassured that they are loved. Expressions like that of the lover's poem, expressions that are both thanksgiving and affection, are essential to any human love affair. They are equally essential in our love affair with God.

—EDWARD HAYS
in *Secular Sanctity*

The next two stories highlight a shadow side of relationships. It is something that may be inevitable—criticism—but there are different ways to respond.

While traveling separately through the countryside late one afternoon, a Hindu, a Rabbi, and a Critic were caught in the same area by a terrific thunderstorm. They sought shelter at a nearby farmhouse.

"That storm will be raging for hours," the farmer told them.

"You'd better stay here for the night. The problem is, there's only room enough for two of you. One of you'll have to sleep in the barn."

"I'll be the one," said the Hindu. "A little hardship is nothing to me." He went out to the barn.

A few minutes later there was a knock on the door. It was the Hindu. "I'm sorry," he told the others, "but there is a cow in the barn. According to my religion, cows are sacred, and one must not intrude into their space."

"Don't worry," said the Rabbi. "Make yourself comfortable here. I'll go sleep in the barn." He went out to the barn.

A few minutes later, there was a knock at the door. It was the Rabbi. "I hate to be a bother," he said, "but there is a pig in the barn. In my religion, pigs are considered unclean. I wouldn't feel comfortable sharing my sleeping quarters with a pig."

"Oh, all right," said the Critic. "*I'll* go sleep in the barn." He went out to the barn.

A few minutes later, there was a knock at the door. It was the cow and the pig.

—BENJAMIN HOFF
in *The Te of Piglet*

There was once a rabbi who was revered by the people as a man of God. Not a day went by when a crowd of people wasn't standing at his door seeking advice or healing or the holy man's blessing. And each time the rabbi spoke, the people would hang on his lips, drinking in his every word.

There was, however, in the audience a disagreeable fellow who never missed a chance to contradict the master. He would observe the rabbi's weaknesses and make fun of his defects to the dismay of the disciples, who began to look on him as the devil incarnate.

Well, one day the "devil" took ill and died. Everyone heaved a sigh of relief. Outwardly they looked appropriately solemn but in their hearts they were glad for no longer would the master's inspiring talks be interrupted or his behavior criticized by this disrespectful heretic.

So the people were surprised to see the master plunged in genuine grief at the funeral. When asked by a disciple later if he was mourning over the eternal fate of the dead man, he said, "No, no. Why should I mourn over our friend who is now in heaven? It was for myself I was grieving. That man was the only friend I had. Here I am surrounded by people who revere me. He was the only one who challenged me. I fear that with him gone, I shall stop growing." And as he said these words, the master burst into tears.

—ANTHONY DE MELLO
in *The Heart of the Enlightened*

Many spiritual teachings emphasize that relationships are multifaceted, bringing both blessings and responsibilities.

[Here is] a story of a Hasidic rabbi, renowned for his piety. He was unexpectedly confronted one day by one of his devoted youthful disciples. In a burst of feeling, the young disciple exclaimed, "My master, I love you!" The ancient teacher looked up from his books and asked his fervent disciple, "Do you know what hurts me, my son?"

The young man was puzzled. Composing himself, he stuttered, "I don't understand your question, Rabbi. I am trying to tell you how much you mean to me, and you confuse me with irrelevant questions."

"My question is neither confusing nor irrelevant," rejoined the rabbi, "For if you do not know what hurts me, how can you truly love me?"

—MADELEINE L'ENGLE
in *Walking on Water*

A spiritually literate perspective on relationships understands that what we do to others, we do also to ourselves and to all those related to us in the great chain of being.

A man rowed a small boat upstream, heading toward home, when he felt another small boat, heading downstream, collide with his boat. Since he had the right of way, he felt angry. Turning, he yelled at the other boatman, "Watch where you're going! Be more careful!"

The other man apologized, and passed by without further incident. But an hour later, as the man continued upstream, he felt another boat collide with his. Furious, he turned to yell at the reckless person. His anger vanished when he saw that the boat was empty—it must have come loose from its moorings. Calmly, he pushed it aside and continued on his journey.

He never lost his temper again, because from then on, he treated everyone like an empty boat.

—DAN MILLMAN
in *No Ordinary Moments*

MARRIAGES AND PARTNERSHIPS

Sacred literature abounds with stories of how individuals have sensed the sacred through their experiences of intimacy. James Kavanaugh starts off this section with his take on one couple's relationship.

I see the birth of God in the old Italian couple who run a grocery store in my neighborhood. They do not often speak of God or Jesus or salvation, but I know they feel the divine presence. This couple love each other and greet me with a kind word and a smile. They smile when I buy a half-pound of hamburger for some homemade chili. The store is their home, their life, their community. They know almost everyone by name, or at least, by face. They charge more than a supermarket, but they give more. And when I leave the store, I somehow feel more human, more in touch with the realities of life, more a man, closer to God. They work every day from nine till nine. They eat lunch and dinner together while they work. And when I say, "You work too hard," they answer, "This is where we are the happiest." And I believe them. They do not work at all; they spend the day serving their friends. Then they go home, have a glass of wine, and watch TV and say their simple prayers to a friendly God or light a candle to their madonna. Sometimes they play cards or reminisce. Then they go to bed. At times I sing a little when I leave their store, not because I have been "saved," but because in the beauty of this vision of man, I sense in my life the Living God.

—JAMES KAVANAUGH
in *God Lives . . . From Religious Fear
to Spiritual Freedom*

God calls man and woman into a different relationship. It is a relationship that looks like two hands that fold in an act of prayer. The fingertips touch, but the hands can create a space, like a little tent. Such a space is the space created by love, not by fear. Marriage is creating a new, open space where God's love can be revealed to the "stranger": the child, the friend, the visitor.

This marriage becomes a witness to God's desire to be among us as a faithful friend.

—HENRI J. M. NOUWEN
in *Here and Now*

French writer Colette once said, "What a wonderful life I've had. I only wish I had realized it sooner." We often undervalue our intimate relationships in the same way.

Husband: "I'm going to work hard, and someday we are going to be rich."

Wife: "We are already rich, dear, for we have each other. Someday maybe we'll have money."

—ANTHONY DE MELLO
in *The Song of the Bird*

In her memoir about her long marriage, children's book author Madeleine L'Engle revels in the fulfillment of shared experiences of beauty, and then Deena Metzger writes about the value of shared imagination.

We have both, throughout the forty years of our marriage, continued to respond with excitement to the same beauty—for instance, to certain pieces of music. I remember driving up to Crosswicks one early spring day when we heard, over the car radio, the beautiful flute solo from Gluck's *Orfeo,* and our response of delight was such that it has always been special music for us. On a cold and dank day we walked along a beach in southern Portugal, arm in arm, gazing with awe at the great eyes painted on the prows of the fishermen's boats. One night we stood by the railing of a freighter and were dazzled by the glory of the Southern Cross against the blackness of an unpolluted sky. If this kind of simultaneous recognition of wonder diminishes, it is a sign of trouble. Thank God it has been a constant for us.

—MADELEINE L'ENGLE
in *Two-Part Invention*

I was having lunch at an inn in northern England. There was a middle-aged, respectable English couple sitting at a table next to me. One could see they had been married for a long time. In my imagination, he was a colonel in the British army, someone who, having achieved something modest and satisfying in his life, was coming to the end of the public drama. I don't know what possessed him, but as he was drinking his tea and I was drinking mine, he leaned over to me and said, sotto voce, "My wife has always wanted to live in a tree."

That image has lived with me for twenty-five years. It was not her longing that moved me, it was how thoroughly she and he were embodying that image, were living it in the imagination, if not in reality. In my mind, and perhaps in theirs, she was already living in a tree, and though I saw her quite plainly sipping tea in this very, very civilized inn, I also saw her, and continue to see her, living forever in the treehouse of her imagination.

—DEENA METZGER
in *Writing for Your Life*

In a partnership, it usually doesn't take us long to learn that no one is perfect. It is accepting each other's imperfections that's hard work.

One afternoon, according to an old Sufi tale, Nasruddin and his friend were sitting in a cafe, drinking tea, and talking about life and love.

"How come you never got married, Nasruddin?" asked his friend at one point.

"Well," said Nasruddin, "to tell you the truth, I spent my youth looking for the perfect woman. In Cairo, I met a beautiful and intelligent woman, with eyes like dark olives, but she was unkind. Then in Baghdad, I met a woman who was a wonderful and generous soul, but we had no interests in common. One woman after another would seem just right, but there would always be something missing. Then one day, I met her. She was beautiful, intelligent, generous and kind. We had everything in common. In fact, she was perfect."

"Well," said Nasruddin's friend, "what happened? Why didn't you marry her?"

Nasruddin sipped his tea reflectively. "Well," he replied, "it's a sad thing. Seems she was looking for the perfect man."

—SUFI TALE
in *Chop Wood, Carry Water*
by Rick Fields, with Peggy Taylor,
Rex Weyler, and Rick Ingrasci

Someone once said marriage is patch, patch, patch, and its mystery and surprise derive from just that.

You know what getting married is? It's agreeing to taking this person who right now is at the top of his form, full of hopes and ideas, feeling good, looking good, wildly interested in you because you're the same way, and sticking by him while he slowly disintegrates. And he does the same for you. You're his responsibility now and he's yours. If no one else will take care of him, you will. If everyone else rejects you, he won't. What do you think love is? Going to bed all the time? Poo! Don't be weak. Have some spine! He's yours and you're his. He doesn't beat you or abuse you, and you've made about the same bargain. Now that you know what it's like to be married, now that all the gold leaf has sort of worn off, you can make something of it, you can really learn to love each other.

—JANE SMILEY
in *At Paradise Gate*

When the children were little and broke one of their toys, Howard would promise to fix it, to make it as good as new. But, oh, dear reader, I'd married him—and toys are one thing, marriage another. Dr. Lewin spoke more conservatively to us of forgiveness, of renewal. At first, Howard had resisted counseling as much as he'd resisted putting the house up for sale. He'd sit in Dr. Lewin's office, brood-

TEACHERS

"Imagine that every person in the world is enlightened but you," Buddha says. "They are all your teachers, each doing just the right things to help you learn patience, perfect wisdom, perfect compassion."

But are we ready to see the people ahead of us in a long line at the bank as teachers of patience? And can those who criticize us open our eyes to wisdom? Do we really need strangers to teach us compassion?

"Everything that happens to you is your teacher," counselor Polly Berrien Berends observes. "The secret is to learn to sit at the feet of your life and be taught." That means being constantly alert and throwing out pride.

Jesus, a great teacher, uses stories, parables, and difficult questions to bring people into a close encounter with the Wisdom of the World. Indirection is his forte.

The Chinese philosopher Lao-tzu, another master teacher, shows great respect for mystery. In the *Hua Hu Ching*, he writes: "The highest truth cannot be put into words./Therefore the greatest teacher has nothing to say./He simply gives himself in service, and never worries."

The best spiritual guides are individuals who teach by their entire being. That's why in a famous Hasidic story, a disciple goes to see his rebbe, not to hear what he has to say but to carefully watch how he ties his shoelaces.

David A. Cooper, a rabbi and retreat leader, suggests: "In the end, everyone is our teacher, on one level or another. The child is our teacher, our friends, our family, the stranger on the street. Every experience is a challenge; a teaching is always hidden in it. Every thought that bubbles up in our minds can teach us things about ourselves—if we are able to listen."

The curriculum for our spiritual education is wide-ranging and practical. A new course is starting every minute. Marilyn Barrett, a therapist, describes her garden as "an informal classroom, a kind of laboratory where I learn vital things overlooked in my formal education."

In living room salons, study circles, reading clubs, and film discussion groups, informal education is booming today. Few of these gatherings have a designated teacher. As Jungian writer Alice O. Howell notes, "Forming a circle is a symbolic way of asserting that the true teacher is always invisible in our midst." Collaborative soul making, where everyone is a teacher, is one of the spiritual adventures of our times.

And it's important to recognize that this kind of education—soul making—continues throughout the life cycle. "Every period has something new to teach us," Benedictine sister Joan Chittister observes. "The harvest of youth is achievement; the harvest of middle age is perspective; the harvest of age is wisdom."

Teachers are all around you. Watch for them, remembering the wise counsel of the second-century Jewish sage Ben Azzai: "Treat no one lightly and think nothing is useless, for everyone has a moment and everything has its place."

TRANSFORMATION

"There's a part of every living thing that wants to become itself," writer Ellen Bass observes, "the tadpole into the frog, the chrysalis into the butterfly, a damaged human being into a whole one. That is spirituality." It is also a capsule description of the holy grail of transformation.

The quest for wholeness is a global phenomenon. Individuals in all parts of the world are involved in inner work, trying to get in touch with soul, imagination, and creativity. Some are searching for a connection with the Sacred Source through contemplation, rituals, and retreats. Others are drawn to explore the spiritual dimensions of relationship.

Sam Keen, a freelance philosopher, looks at how this impulse toward renewal is reflected in the world's religions: "The great metaphors from all spiritual traditions—grace, liberation, being born again, awakening from illusion—testify that it is possible to transcend the conditioning of my past and do a new thing."

What we have been does not determine who we are. "One discovers that destiny can be directed," French-American diarist Anais Nin writes, "that one does not have to remain in bondage to the first wax imprint made on childhood sensibilities. Once the deforming mirror has been smashed, there is a possibility of wholeness."

Essayist Normandi Ellis talks about a friend who calls himself a "human becoming in the spirit of growth, change, and development that is part and parcel of this life." We want to bring to the fore parts of ourself that have been overlooked. Indeed, whenever we are involved in the process of personal reformation or renewal, we must face the shadow. As Andrew Harvey, a modern-day mystic, points out, "The very things we wish to avoid, neglect, and flee from turn out to be the 'prima materia' from which all real growth comes."

Be on the lookout for resources that will unlock your inner potential. Be on the lookout for imaginative experiences that will stop you in your tracks and turn you around.

One of the great examples of personal transformation is St. Paul. In Romans 12:2, he suggests, "Be transformed by the renewing of your minds."

The African-American novelist Alice Walker challenges Christians with the following thought: "The transformation required of us is not simply to be 'like' Christ, but to be a Christ." And that means, in the words of Protestant minister Samuel Miller, we need "to match our inward transformation with the magnitude of the world's need."

In the rigorous and true aphorism of our era, the personal must become the political. The wholeness we seek is not a private retreat but a project to ensoul the world. Or, as best-selling author Rabbi Harold Kushner concludes, "The ultimate goal is to transform the world into the kind of world God had in mind when he created it."

ing and silent, like a prisoner in the docket, as I leveled charges against him. But then he began to defend himself and bring those old countercharges, until we were interrupting each other and shouting, while Dr. Lewin beamed at us across the steeple of her hands. "Listen to yourselves," she said. "Still so much passion!"

Had it endured, despite everything, or had it merely been revived? I'm not sure. But at his little cousin's concert that afternoon, as she sawed her way through Mendelssohn's *D minor Trio*, we held hands like the sweethearts we'd once been. . . .

That night, when the party was over, Howard went to our bedroom and lay in wait for me, wearing only his suit of tarnished flesh. I walked toward the bed through the pewter light, dressed in all the awful beauty of my years. We looked at one another.

—Hilma Wolitzer
in *Silver*

Visiting someone in a hospital recently, I watched an elderly couple. The man was in a wheelchair, his wife sitting next to him in the visitors' room. For the half hour that I watched they never exchanged a word, just held hands and looked at each other, and once or twice the man patted his wife's face. The feeling of love was so thick in that room that I felt I was sharing in their communion and was shaken all day by their pain, their love, something sad and also joyful: the fullness of a human relationship.

—Eda LeShan
in *It's Better to Be Over the Hill Than Under It*

Once when I was going through a difficult time, my husband touched his finger to the tears winding down my face, then touched his wet finger to his own cheek. His gesture spoke volumes to me. It said: "Your tears run down *my* face, too. Your suffering aches inside *my* heart as well. I share your wounded place."

—Sue Monk Kidd
in *Communion, Community, Commonweal*

Perhaps all couples would do well to recognize the difficulties of relationships right from the start. In the next reading, the spiritual practice of shadow is ritualized.

I recently heard about a couple who had the good sense to call upon the shadow in a wedding ceremony. The night before their marriage, they held a ritual where they made their "shadow vows." The groom said, "I will give you an identity and make the world see you as an extension of myself." The bride replied, "I will be compliant and sweet, but underneath I will have the real control. If anything goes wrong, I will take your money and your house." They then drank champagne and laughed heartily at their foibles, knowing that in the course of the marriage, these shadow figures would inevitably come out. They were ahead of the game because they had recognized the shadow and unmasked it.

—ROBERT A. JOHNSON
in *Owning Your Own Shadow*

The longer people stay together, the more they realize the importance of compromise.

I believe a good relationship is a lot like two rocks with rough edges that are in a bag together. Over time as they come into repeated contact, bumping into one another, chips are knocked off each of them, rough edges are smoothed out. Eventually you get two pretty smooth stones with polished surfaces, but it does take a while.

—INDIVIDUAL
quoted in *Going the Distance*
by Lonnie Barbach and David L. Geisinger

However, not all marriages are meant to last.

A wonderful moment occurs in the film *The First Monday in October*, that eloquently makes this point. One of the Supreme Court judges returns home to find his wife packing to leave him. She complains that although he is not a bad man, he simply doesn't see her, doesn't feel her emotional needs. He is just blind to her and the emotional nuances of their relationship. He pleads for another chance. She finally pauses and asks him to close his eyes. She tells him that she will not divorce him if he can describe the wallpaper in their bedroom that they have occupied for twenty-five years. He can't, and she leaves.

—GLEN A. MAZIS
in *The Trickster, Magician & Grieving Man*

Rituals help us come to terms with the end of a relationship.

Several years ago psychologist Onno Van der Hart was working with a woman who was having a great deal of trouble letting go of her broken marriage. One day, in therapy, Van der Hart handed her a brick as a symbol of her old relationship, and then instructed her to carry it around in her purse for the next week. As the week went on, and her purse grew heavier and heavier, the woman began to get a clear understanding of how burdensome the weight of her old attachment had become. The brick was a symbol that focused her attention on the intrinsic meaning of the relationship. The idea that holding onto this attachment wasn't in her best interest was hardly a new message. But this time, by symbolizing the oppression with a tangible symbol, that message was delivered in a language she could understand on a deeper level. Finally ready to let go of this old burden, she marked the change in a personal ceremony by crushing the brick of her old relationship with a hammer and scattering the pieces. The relationship was now truly ended, and she was able to move into a new stage of growth.

—KATHLEEN WALL and GARY FERGUSON
in *Lights of Passage*

Tom and Jean decided to separate after being together for three years. Couples counseling had helped them recognize that they still loved each other, but that they had grown in different ways. Their old relationship no longer suited either of them, and to keep it up only led to fights and pain. They wanted to remain friends but did not know how to let go of their past way of relating. They decided to do a ritual. . . .

. . . They dug a hole and placed some artifacts of their relationship in it—a few gifts, a letter, a shared pillowcase. During the week, Tom had written a poem, and Jean had made a picture, symbolizing the significance of what they previously had together. They shared these creations with each other and discovered they had each included what they had hoped the relationship would become.

Together they put the drawing and poem into the hole and set them on fire. They acknowledged these symbols of their past and of their hopes and let their desires and their old form of relating pass away as the papers burned . . .

. . . When the fire was out, they covered it with dirt and planted flowers over the remains of their old relationship. As they watered the flowers, they said a prayer that what had died could find life in a new and better form. They then held each other and wept together, glad that they did not have to go through this ending alone.

—RENEE BECK and SYDNEY BARBARA METRICK
in *The Art of Ritual*

In Anne Tyler's novel Breathing Lessons, *a long-married couple realize that improvisation is and always has been expressive of their love for each other.*

"And then our first anniversary," Maggie said. "What a fiasco! Mother's etiquette book said it was either the paper anniversary or the clock anniversary, whichever I preferred. So I got this bright idea to construct your gift from a kit I saw advertised in a magazine: a working clock made out of paper."

"I don't remember that."

"That's because I never gave it to you," Maggie said.

"What happened to it?"

"Well, I must have put it together wrong," Maggie said. "I mean I followed all the directions, but it never really acted like it was supposed to. It dragged, it stopped and started, one edge curled over, there was a ripple under the twelve where I'd used too much glue. It was . . . makeshift, amateur. I was so ashamed of it, I threw it in the trash."

"Why, sweetheart," he said.

"I was afraid it was a symbol or something. I mean a symbol of our marriage. We were makeshift ourselves, is what I was afraid of."

He said, "Shoot, we were just learning back then. We didn't know what to do with each other."

"We know now," she whispered. Then she pressed her mouth into one of her favorite places, that nice warm nook where his jaw met his neck.

—ANNE TYLER
in *Breathing Lessons*

The spiritual practices of enthusiasm and play can give rise to meaningful marriage rituals.

Kay Holler relates a daily ritual that her husband, Steve, initiated in their home, a ritual which seems small but is large with significance. "Every evening since we've been married, Steve comes home from work and shouts from the front door, 'The luckiest man in the world is home!' I've been hearing this for two and a half years now," writes Kay, "and it still makes me feel good."

—KAY HOLLER
quoted in *Why Not Celebrate?*
by Sara Wenger Shenk

In addition to including nicknames for each other—Bear and Tiger Woman—Rick and Carol's play often incorporated their two cats. Both of their animals were very affectionate and would invariably jump into their laps or sleep with them in their bed if given the chance. When Rick and Carol cuddled together on the floor in front of the fireplace, their two cats would pile on top of them and purr contentedly in a manner that reminded Carol of the way that kittens will snuggle together for warmth. Thus was born their term for snuggling together—"A Cat Pile." When either of them wanted some affection, they would say, "Let's make a cat pile."

—WILLIAM BETCHER
in *Intimate Play*

A young professional couple developed a morning ritual of rising about an hour and a half before work and going jogging together. It's often just about dawn when they head out during winter, their breath clouding the air and their golden retriever in tow. Afterward they shower and sit down in the kitchen for a light breakfast. There they can look out at the bird feeder and share their dreams from the night before. They don't try to interpret them, but they talk about what the dreams make them think of. Sometimes they find meanings in their dreams, but at others they are content just to share them. It's an intimate time that helps them begin their day feeling taken care of.

—WILLIAM BETCHER
in *Intimate Play*

As a couple we have a practice of counting moments of happiness. We got the idea from a quotation in May Sarton's Endgame *which we used in our first book,* 100 Ways to Keep Your Soul Alive. *Sarton suggests that it is wrong to expect that there will be a time of happiness in our lives. Rather, there are moments of happiness, and "almost every day [contains] at least one moment of happiness."*

We have decided that marriage is like that. On our twenty-fifth wedding anniversary, we each wrote a list of moments of happiness we had shared. It took us most of the morning to write them and then read them back and forth to each other. We laughed to discover how many moments appeared on both lists. We have never separated our weekdays from the weekends, so we were not surprised that our memories came from both our work and our play. Counting our blessings that anniversary, we could see a long and steady stream of moments when being together has nourished our souls and given us a taste of the presence of God.

FAMILY

Whether in our birth family or one of our own creation, we find a connection there that makes even ordinary occurrences meaningful. Therapist Robert A. Johnson tries to define this ineffable experience.

Many years ago a wise friend gave me a name for human love. She called it "stirring-the-oatmeal" love. She was right: Within this phrase, if we will humble ourselves enough to look, is the very essence of what human love is, and it shows us the principal differences between human love and romance.

Stirring the oatmeal is a humble act—not exciting or thrilling. But it symbolizes a relatedness that brings love down to earth. It represents a willingness to share ordinary human life, to find meaning in the simple, unromantic tasks: earning a living, living within a budget, putting out the garbage, feeding the baby in the middle of the night. To "stir the oatmeal" means to find the relatedness, the value, even the beauty, in simple and ordinary things, not to eternally demand a cosmic drama, an entertainment, or an extraordinary intensity in everything. Like the rice hulling of the Zen monks, the spinning wheel of Gandhi, the tent making of Saint Paul, it represents the discovery of the sacred in the midst of the humble and ordinary.

—Robert A. Johnson
in *We*

In the 1995 movie Moonlight and Valentino, *Rebecca's husband has just been killed in an accident. Her family and friends gather to help her through the various stages of grief. At one point, her best friend suggests they go to the home of a long-married couple, supposedly to water the plants. They end up sitting on the porch. "Do you feel it?" asks the friend wistfully. She calls it the "Tomkins' porch feeling," that certain quality of contentment, the legacy of a deep and long love in the family context. The "Tomkins' porch feeling" reminds us of the "vibration" described by the grandson in the next reading.*

In my grandmother's house there was a vibration, recurrent and mysterious, like the diminishing echo of a cello chord. This sound was unmistakable to a boy of five, though it was so faint I could not be sure whether it was a real sensation or a memory.

What was its source? . . .

My first working hypothesis about the source of the mysterious vibration was this: All these ancient and decaying things, having been handled and knocked around by my relatives since the dawn of Time, absorbed the life force of these people who had used and abused them. And once in a while the collection's energy, having risen to a critical level, would discharge itself into the atmosphere like a sigh of relief, wind through a ghostly wind chime, making a vibration nearly audible. . . .

But not for another twenty years would I understand that the vibration in my grandparents' house was love. That is a conceptual understanding that had to be guided by an intuition, which then was nourished by a lot of reading and reflection. My grandparents were in love. They loved each other. They loved their children and grand-children, and were loved in return, though probably not quite as much. Their children loved one another, the way sisters and broth-ers do. My grandfather and grandmother loved God, each in his or her own special and sometimes peculiar ways; and . . . their love for God was reciprocated, in some graceful proportion.

It was not my grandparents' love for each other, or for their children, or for me, that made the air hum in the twilight. No particular expres-sion or impression of love caused that vibration, but love itself, ever so briefly made perceptible. Love sounded a chord now and again, this chord of intense pleasure tinged with melancholy, to remind me that all of the component notes had been ringing there for generations. In visual terms, it was like noticing all at once that the rainbow of colors flowing from a prism is derived from a ray of pure sunlight.

—Daniel Mark Epstein
in *Love's Compass*

Once upon a time there was a woman who longed to find out what heaven is like. She prayed constantly, "O God, grant me in this life a vision of paradise." She prayed in this way for years until one night she had a dream. In her dream an angel came and led her to heaven. They walked down a street in paradise until they came to an ordinary looking house. The angel, pointing toward the house said, "Go and look inside."

So the woman walked in the house and found a person prepar-ing supper, another reading the newspaper, and children playing with their toys. Naturally, she was disappointed and returned to the angel on the street. "Is this all there is to heaven?"

The angel replied, "Those people you saw in that house are not in paradise, paradise is in them!"

—Edward Hays
in *Feathers on the Wind*

U

UNITY

In Psalm 133 we read, "How very good and pleasant it is when kindred live together in unity!"

Indeed it is. Our spirits soar when we work with others on a common cause. We thrill to the unison of a choral performance when all the voices blend into one grand sound.

The yearning for human unity is a universal one. "I cannot affirm God if I don't affirm man," American editor Norman Cousins declares. "If I deny the oneness of man, I deny the oneness of God. Therefore I affirm both. Without a belief in human unity, I am hungry and incomplete."

Today, however, the prospects for that belief seem very slim. The walls which divide people have gotten taller and thicker. The barriers between men and women, old and young, gays and straights, First World and Third World, haves and have-nots, continue to proliferate.

Yet even in the face of these negative developments, the dream of unity persists. Many are in agreement with Russian novelist Leo Tolstoy, who announces, "I now understand that my welfare is only possible if I acknowledge my unity with all the people of the world without exception."

Mahatma Gandhi of India explores the ramifications of this attitude: "I believe in the essential unity of all people and for that matter, of all that lives. Therefore, I believe that if one person gains spiritually, the whole world gains, and if one person falls, the whole world falls to that extent."

The kinship of all peoples in our age of global spirituality recognizes that we have a common stake in the survival of the planet. There must be an end to ethnic warfare and ancient enmities.

Let peacemakers and mediators arise in the four corners of the earth and practice their trade. They identify with the words of Baha'u'llah, the founder of Baha'ism: "O contending peoples and kindreds of the earth! Set your faces toward unity, and let the radiance of its light shine upon you. Gather ye together, and for the sake of God resolve to root out whatever is the source of contention among you."

Let the religions of the world share their resources and work together to bring mutuality, compassion, and justice to all parts of the planet. "The religious community has the saving vision," Protestant minister William Sloane Coffin suggests. "It is the ancient prophetic vision of human unity, now become an urgent pragmatic necessity."

The Weaver of Oneness wants us to be united with each other—neighbors with neighbors, communities with communities, religions with religions, nations with nations.

Let unity be expressed in your solidarity with others and in your good deeds. "Kings and cabbages go back to compost, but good deeds stay green forever," writer Rick de Marinis notes. "Under the skin we are all related, and the common ground of blood, bone and meat makes us charter members of the same humble club, say what you will about superficial differences."

In our families, we learn to have faith and to live spiritually—nurturing, trusting, and honoring each other's secrets.

"Said your prayers?"

"Yes Pa, long since. And I said em *my* way."

"Lying here on your back, in the hot pitch dark?"

"Yes, Father dear."

"Liss, I've told you. Serious prayers are—"

"'—Said on your knees, on the hard oak floor, with a good bright light so you don't fall asleep.'"

Whit said "My sentiments, more or less exactly."

"Rest easy, Pa. You're safe another day. I've seen to that."

He was in the doorway with both hands overhead, hooked in the framing. Liss was the one who always knew him. He could wipe his face as blank as chalk, she'd always see the one scared cell. He said "How so? You hired me an escort?"

"God and I have a deal."

"Can you tell me?" Whit said. He recalled his own childhood so clearly that it always surprised him to find Liss thinking of him as she did. At her age, he could hardly see the adults, much less pray for them.

Liss thought it out carefully. "Prayers are the biggest secret I've got. So please don't ask. Just trust me again."

He said "You're all I trust on Earth." It had slipped past his guard; but when he said it again in his mind, it felt near enough to the truth to stand.

Liss laughed again. But this time her voice dipped so low that Whit barely heard her above the tub water. "Don't load me too heavy," she said. "I may break."

He said "You won't."

She said "Good *night*" and a wide yawn caught her.

—REYNOLDS PRICE
in *The Foreseeable Future*

Family relationships give us many opportunities to reap the riches of the spiritual practices of enthusiasm and wonder—especially as demonstrated by children and grandchildren.

When my daughter was small she got the dubious part of the Bethlehem star in a Christmas play. After her first rehearsal she burst through the door with her costume, a five-pointed star lined in shiny gold tinsel designed to drape over her like a sandwich board. "What exactly will you be doing in the play?" I asked her.

"I just stand there and shine," she told me. I've never forgotten that response.

—SUE MONK KIDD
in *When the Heart Waits*

Whoever will not welcome the realm of God as a little child welcomes it will not enter into it. My father was once walking on the beach with his three-year-old grandson when the little boy stopped, picked up a tiny fragment of a seashell, and began to examine it. My father bent down and, looking at the tiny fragment, he asked the boy, "How could you see such a little shell?" "Because," said the boy, "I have little eyes."

—THOMAS W. MANN
in *To Taste and See*

Our families often reveal the ties of mutual love and support which are mirrors of the Provider's love for us.

A boy and his father were walking along a road when they came across a large stone. The boy said to his father, "Do you think if I use all my strength, I can move this rock?" His father answered, "If you use all your strength, I am sure you can do it." The boy began to push the rock. Exerting himself as much as he could, he pushed and pushed. The rock did not move. Discouraged, he said to his father, "You were wrong. I can't do it." His father placed his arm around the boy's shoulder and said, "No, son. You didn't use *all* your strength—you didn't ask me to help."

—DAVID J. WOLPE
in *Teaching Your Children About God*

*My father once taught me about using all my strength when he encour-
aged me to take his help. The summer after my second year of college, I
convinced my roommate Mark to accompany me on a trip from Milwaukee to New York City. We would find jobs and then in the evenings
I would write about the experience. It sounded good to me. My father
thought it was a terrible idea. However, when he realized I was determined
to go, he gave me enough money to return home if things went poorly.*

*Poorly is not quite the word I would use now to describe the disastrous
events of the next few days. Arriving in Manhattan during a rain storm,
Mark and I immediately tried various employment agencies, but the offices
were crammed with job seekers and we were out-of-towners with little
work experience. We found a cheap hotel and slept anxiously. By the third
day, we started to run out of money so we slept on the subway.*

*I decided to visit the headquarters of my church denomination. An
executive listened to my story and said, "Son, if and when you ever
become a minister, I hope you'll get some common sense. No one with
an ounce of sanity would come to New York City without a job, a relative, or a friend. I suggest you put your pride in your back pocket and
head back to Milwaukee. There is nothing I can do for you." I took my
father's money and bought a bus ticket.*

*When I got home, dazed, bedraggled, hungry, and humiliated, my
father never said "I told you so." He must have realized that I had
learned a life lesson about being on my own in a big city, but he let me
keep it to myself. He had made the only point I needed to know when he
gave me a safety net for my first journey into the urban wilderness.*

*Polly Berrien Berends, who runs workshops on children's spiritual-
ity, says that parenthood is the world's most intensive course in love.
Poet Gary Snyder adds that having a child in the house is like living
with a Zen master; it requires attention, patience, and selflessness. Practicing peace, love, and forgiveness in the family is a holy mission.*

Many people, as they become spiritual, seek what is called "selfless
service" in order to deepen their practice. But if you want selfless
service, all you need do is have children. When Mother Teresa is
speaking to the wealthy matrons who have gathered to support
her work, she tells them that before they think of feeding the
starving, and clothing and housing the poor, they should first look
to their own family. She asks if their families are in harmony.
"Before you go out into the world to serve others, how is *your*
home?" And several of the matrons look helplessly at each other,
perhaps having discovered that being married with children can be

more painfully confusing than even helping the dying abandoned on the streets of Calcutta. That it is easier to "march for peace" than maintain a peaceful family.

—STEPHEN and ONDREA LEVINE
in *Embracing the Beloved*

A woman came to see me who was suffering greatly because of her daughter. She told me her daughter was real bad trouble. "She's run away to live with my other daughter down in Tennessee, and now she's forged a check with her sister's name on it, and she's gotten pregnant and she's only sixteen. I've been a seamstress all my life, supporting the kids and myself since my husband ran out when the youngest was still in the womb. Now she's run away, and you can't imagine what it's like. . . ."

I'm shortening the story. It actually took about fifteen minutes to run it all down. I just listened as openly as I could. I could feel her pain and discouragement and felt my heart hurt at the hard life she had had. At the same moment I felt very quiet inside, figuring maybe all I had to offer was to be with her. A little bit I felt she was wearing the albatross of this story, like the Ancient Mariner, and I was just another in a long line of people who had heard it. So when she finished I said, "Right."

She sensed I wasn't getting caught, and her immediate reaction was, "No, you don't understand." And she recited the whole thing one more time, fifteen more minutes. And when she'd finished the second time, I said again, "Right."

This time she stopped for a moment. She'd heard me. She paused, and then said with a kind of wry smile, "You know, I was kind of a hellion when I was a kid, too." She just let it go.

—INDIVIDUAL
quoted in *How Can I Help?*
by Ram Dass and Paul Gorman

At the heart of parenting is denying self. A friend of mine once said that she saw parenting as a journey in dying to self, a way in which she could enter Christ's journey. She is a mother of four, a gifted choreographer, dancer, and educator, and I respect her spirituality embedded in the daily. Her words and example come back to me now in tangible reality. I think of them often: dying to self. Family is where I learn the core of Jesus' words: "Take up your cross and follow me." "Find yourself by losing yourself," "Love God, love your neighbor . . . summing up the law."

But so often it is easier to love your neighbor than it is to love your own family. We at least don't have to live with our neighbor, rub shoulders and feet day after day. Yet what closer neighbor can there be than those we live with: roommate, sister, brother, spouse, child, partner, parent. As family, we are beloved neighbors, learning love in the midst of covenant—dying to self.

—CELESTE SNOWBER SCHROEDER
in *In the Womb of God*

The need to know and to be known—part of the spiritual practices of questing and transformation—are familiar desires for most parents.

A parent's view of what's wrong or right with his kid is probably less accurate than even the next-door neighbor's, who sees the child's life perfectly through a gap in the curtain. I, of course, would like to tell him how to live life and do better in a hundred engaging ways, just as I tell myself: that nothing ever neatly "fits," that mistakes must be made, bad things forgotten. But in our short exposures I seem only able to talk glancingly, skittishly before shying away, cautious not to be wrong, not to quiz or fight him, not to be his therapist but his Dad. So that in all likelihood I will never provide a good cure for his disease, will never even imagine correctly what his disease is, but will only suffer it with him for a time and then depart.

The worst of being a parent is my fate, then: being an adult. Not owning the right language; not dreading the same dreads and contingencies and missed chances; the fate of knowing much yet having to stand like a lamppost with its lamp lit, hoping my child will see the glow and venture closer for the illumination and warmth it mutely offers.

—RICHARD FORD
in *Independence Day*

In the Swedish film My Life as a Dog, *Ingemar is a twelve-year-old boy who is sent to live with relatives in the country because his mother is dying. As a stay against his loneliness and the bewilderment he feels inside, he replays in his mind one magic time of true communion with her: At a lake, Ingemar entertained his mother with a back flip, and she responded with a sunny golden laugh. Family memories are soul food, reminders of sacred and enduring connections.*

As I stepped out into the sunlight I smelled cigar smoke. I stopped and looked to see where it was coming from, but saw no one. I was about to shrug, dismiss it and walk down the stone stairs, but I found myself whispering, "Wait, stop now." Though it was me who whispered, the words gave me the eerie sense that it was someone else whispering.

I stood at the top of the stairs. Suddenly, I realized the smoke smelled exactly like the El Producto cigars my father smoked at home when I was a child. Then it was a constant source of conflict because it sickened me. How many times I whined and nagged my father to put out his cigar while we drove to church. But outside the library I found the smell strangely aromatic and refreshing. Though no one was in sight, the smell in the open air was pervasive, as if someone were smoking right alongside me. I felt a presence that I identified as my father.

I was immediately overwhelmed with gratitude and love for him, feeling a closeness to him that I had never experienced. For me, the effect of the experience was so deep and lasting that I regard the moment as sacred, a gift, a revelation based on an awareness that I had never before experienced.

—RICHARD SOLLY
in *Call to Purpose*

Grief—like memory—is another spiritual vessel of great meaning. And it is usually first experienced in the family.

I once saw in a cemetery in India an old woman just sobbing away at the grave of her son who had been tortured by Tamil terrorists. She spread herself over the whole grave and sobbed. She held the grave with two hands and sobbed and sobbed. And I thought to myself and said to my companion, "I don't want to love if that is what love is," and he said, "Are you crazy? What she feels is so immeasurably beautiful because she grieves that much, she loves that much, and love lives on in her." Love's glory was in her weeping, love's glory was in her sobbing, love's glory was in the abandonment of her grief. That is love's glory, and love's glory has blood all over it.

—ANDREW HARVEY
in *The Way of Passion*

In the "Ritual" episode of the video series Discovering Everyday Spirituality with Thomas Moore, *Donna Schaper, a writer and United Church of Christ minister, talks about the rituals that enrich her family life during a typical day. In the morning, this family of five check in with each other and share their schedules. Both parents work, and the three children are involved in music, sports, and other activities. They all feel more connected when they know what the others are doing.*

At bedtime, Donna asks her son to tell her one good thing and one bad thing that has happened during the day. Through this ritual of attention, she shows him that she is interested in the details of his life and, while she cannot always fix everything or explain everything, he can count on her presence. Acknowledging the variety of her children's experiences in this way, Donna adds, is a "form of thanksgiving."

In his book about rituals built around the hours of the monastic day, Benedictine monk David Steindl-Rast suggests some other family observances for evening times.

If you have children, you can bring the spirit of Compline into your home by spending some special time with them at the day's end. Soothe them with sweet stories, sing together, bless them, pray with them. Lead them from a fear of the night, which is so natural to small children, into a trust in the night as a time to merge with the loving mystery in which we are all immersed.

This gentle, deliberate ending of the day completes the circle of the hours.

—BROTHER DAVID STEINDL-RAST
in *The Music of Silence*

Vigils venerate key moments in the parent-child relationship.

I celebrate and welcome the new life that has come into mine!

One of the lessons you will need to learn is about sharing—and I need to learn this lesson, too.
There are those around us who are entitled to be involved as you grow and change, and I need to feel secure enough to share you with them.
My role in your world is distinct and irreplaceable, and remembering that can make my sharing easier.

I love you. I believe in you. I wish only the best for you.

My child, you leave my home but not my heart.

I will miss those parts of your life that have overlapped mine— your activities, your friends, the lights left on, the music from your room.
I have wished so often for moments of peace and quiet.
Now I wish for graceful adjustment to the stillness you leave behind.

Your years in my care have blessed me as I have watched the unfolding of your life. It is with pride and tenderness that I now release that life to follow its own promise. I love you. I believe in you. I wish only the best for you.

—Noela N. Evans
in *Meditations for the Passages
and Celebrations of Life*

Rituals also help maintain family ties across distances.

My son David sends a card almost every week to his grandmother, aged eighty-nine. I don't know how this ritual got started, but I do know he spends a lot of time looking for just the right card, one he thinks will please her. This *practice* has been going on for more than three years, and he says it's a challenge to keep finding "special" new cards.

453

This year on her birthday David went east to visit his grandmother. "I never understood how much getting a card means to Grandma," he told us when he returned. "She looks forward to checking the mail. I could really see how happy she was when she got a few birthday cards."

—Sue Bender
in *Everyday Sacred*

The spiritual practice of deep listening is essential to the growth and vibrancy of family life.

WHEN SOMEONE DEEPLY LISTENS TO YOU

When someone deeply listens to you
it is like holding out a dented cup
you've had since childhood
and watching it fill up with
cold, fresh water.
When it balances on top of the brim,
you are understood.
When it overflows and touches your skin,
you are loved.

When someone deeply listens to you,
the room where you stay
starts a new life
and the place where you wrote
your first poem
begins to glow in your mind's eye.
It is as if gold has been discovered!

When someone deeply listens to you,
your bare feet are on the earth
and a beloved land that seemed distant
is now at home within you.

—John Fox
in *Finding What You Didn't Lose*

Finally, one of the best gifts parents can pass on to their children is the spiritual practice of gratitude.

FATHER'S VOICE

"No need to get home early;
the car can see in the dark."
        He wanted me to be rich
        the only way we could,
        easy with what we had.

And always that was his gift,
given for me ever since,
        easy gift, a wind
        that keeps on blowing for flowers
        or birds wherever I look.

World, I am your slow guest,
one of the common things
        that move in the sun and have
        close, reliable friends
        in the earth, in the air, in the rock.
            —WILLIAM STAFFORD
                in *Stories That Could Be True*

FRIENDSHIP

I can remember the scene as vividly as if it were yesterday. My best friend Skipper and I were seven-year-old boys living in Wauwatosa, Wisconsin. One day, after playing in the verdant valley behind his house, we sat down in our favorite place between two tall trees. We looked into each other's eyes and promised that when we grew up we would be cowboys out West. And no matter what happened we would be friends forever.

The valley seemed to conspire with this shining moment in our lives. The sun was bright, the sky was blue, and the two trees served as silent witnesses to our vow. But circumstances beyond our control pulled us apart. My family moved to another part of the city. Years passed, and I never saw Skipper again. But I have not forgotten the ardor of that perfect instant of mutuality with him. Although we never rode the range together, our friendship lives on in my mind.

In Soul Mates, *Thomas Moore writes: "Each friend is indeed a world—*
a special sphere of certain emotions, experiences, memories, and qualities
of personality. . . . We are all made up of many worlds and each friend-
ship brings one or more of those worlds to life." My early friendship with
Skipper took me to a world of possibilities. It showed me the value of shar-
ing my dreams with another, a gift I have carried into many of my adult
relationships.

Every friendship has its own peculiar characteristics, and we can
access them through the spiritual practices of imagination and being
present.

Imagine yourself and your most intimate friend in a deep conversation, feeling one another's feelings while talking soul talk.
Effortlessly your speech turns into music: two braided instruments,
a clarinet and a cello, or a French horn and trombone, or two alto
flutes, or a soprano saxophone and an electric bass. What would
that sound be?

—W. A. MATHIEU
in *The Musical Life*

Another place where I find soul, one of the strongest places, is in
the presence of other people whom I meet at soul level. It happens
whenever a dialogue takes place in which both people are truly
present, tuning in to really hearing each other and reflecting back.
A sense of discovery occurs, as when musicians get together and
improvise a musical dialogue, a dialogue that depends on letting go
of ego and defenses. To voice something you're feeling and put
observations into words with another person who is totally present is a creative act embodying soul and love.

—JEAN SHINODA BOLEN
in *Handbook for the Soul*
edited by Richard Carlson and Benjamin Shield

Paul D sits down in the rocking chair and examines the quilt
patched in carnival colors. His hands are limp between his knees.
There are too many things to feel about this woman. His head
hurts. Suddenly he remembers Sixo trying to describe what he felt

about the Thirty-Mile Woman. "She is a friend of mine. She gather me, man. The pieces I am, she gather them and give them back to me in all the right order. It's good, you know, when you got a woman who is a friend of your mind."

—TONI MORRISON
in *Beloved*

People sometimes talk about becoming friends instantly, but usually this relationship takes time. The Chinese have the right attitude expressed in a proverb: The fifth cup of tea between friends is the best.

It is possible to take our closest relationships and our best friends for granted. The heart cannot live without intimacy. We all need special people in our lives to whom we can show our souls. But relationships need to be nurtured, nourished, and celebrated. Friendships won't last without food. How do you feed your friendships?

—MACRINA WIEDERKEHR
in *A Tree Full of Angels*

My oldest friend knows how to feed her friendships. I met Joy when I was a teenager and she was right out of college. Over the years, Joy and I kept in touch sporadically. When we both settled in New York, we made more direct efforts. The relationship was never the same from year to year, and there was one period when we didn't talk at all.

Now our friendship is nourished on mutual understanding, respect for each other's interests, and appreciation for the care we have felt for more than thirty-five years. But I will be the first to say that we have a friendship today because Joy puts real effort and devotion into it. She's the one who remembers holidays, who phones in regularly to see how I am doing, who writes a condolence letter when I have experienced a loss, or sends an encouraging card when I am under stress. When I beg off a date because I have too much work to do, she'll say, "You have to eat. I'll come down; we'll just get a bite."

Joy is the kind of friend who is sensitive enough to know what you need and then provide it. She brings the spiritual practices of attention, listening, and play to friendship. In the next readings, friends meet each other with silence, compassion, and hospitality.

I also remember the time that a friend came to me and told me that his wife had left him that day. He sat in front of me, tears streaming from his eyes. I didn't know what to say. There simply was nothing to say. My friend didn't need words. What he needed was simply to be with a friend. I held his hands in mine, and we sat there . . . silently. For a moment, I wanted to ask him how and why it all had happened, but I knew that this was not the time for questions. It was the time just to be together as friends who have nothing to say, but are not afraid to remain silent together.

Today, when I think of that day, I feel a deep gratitude that my friend had entrusted his grief to me.

—Henri J. M. Nouwen
in *Here and Now*

I was a neurotic for years. I was anxious and depressed and selfish. Everyone kept telling me to change.

I resented them, and I agreed with them, and I wanted to change, but simply couldn't, no matter how hard I tried.

What hurt the most was that, like the others, my best friend kept insisting that I change. So I felt powerless and trapped.

Then, one day, he said to me, "Don't change. I love you just as you are."

—Anthony de Mello
in *The Song of the Bird*

According to therapist Paula Hardin, "relationships provide the fastest and clearest way to see shadow parts of ourselves." To have a friend bring our flaws and failings into focus can be liberating.

During a lecture trip to Texas, I had bought a large cowboy hat for Raymond, one of the handicapped members of the house in which I lived. I looked forward to coming home and giving him my gift.

But when Raymond, whose needs for attention and affirmation were as boundless as my own, saw my gift he started yelling at me: "I don't need your silly gift. I have enough gifts. I have no place for them in my room. My walls are already full. You better keep your gift. I don't need it." His words opened a deep wound in me. He made me realize that I *wanted* to be his friend, but instead of spending time with him and offering him my attention, I had given him an expensive gift. Raymond's angry response to the Texan hat confronted me with my inability to enter into a personal relationship with him and develop a real friendship. The hat, instead of being seen as an expression of friendship, was seen as a substitute for it.

—Henri J. M. Nouwen
in *Here and Now*

Not even mutual admiration is, by itself, enough to keep a friendship alive that long. For one thing, we discover somewhere along the line that even people we admire have feet of clay. The best of us is flawed. Our flaws show through eventually; we disappoint our friends, and sometimes their disappointment hurts enough to wound our friendship. Or even worse, we may discover that the traits we so much admired were put-ons, cosmetics hiding a shabby interior. And we cannot count on any friendship to survive the feeling of being conned.

Besides, even friends who admire each other a lot drift apart when one of them moves to another part of the country. If I move away, don't see my friend again for five years, and do not stay in close touch, our friendship is likely to die of malnutrition, with dignity maybe, and peacefully, but with the same result as any dying. I may still admire him, but I would admire him as a person who *used to be* my friend.

I feel a good deal of melancholy when I think of it, but it is true that we cannot count on mutual admiration to make friendships last forever, any more than we can expect friendships to last because friends like each other or are useful to each other. If friendships like these do happen to last a lifetime, it is probably because they are more than friendships of affection, or usefulness, or admiration. Most likely, they are held together because the friends are committed to each other.

—Lewis B. Smedes
in *Caring & Commitment*

VISION

"I will pour out my spirit on all flesh; your sons and your daughters shall prophesy, your old men shall dream dreams and your young men shall see visions." So go the familiar words from Joel 2:28 in the Bible.

The Sacred Parent speaks in our dreams and in our visions. Sons and daughters, old and young, all have roles to play.

"Vision," according to English writer Jonathan Swift, "is the art of seeing things invisible." This gift belongs to those who can see the good hidden away in the kernels of setbacks, suffering, and pain. It resides in those who never give up hope when less stalwart souls are ready to pack up their bags and go home. It stirs in the love of those who refuse to capitulate to cynicism on either a private or a public level.

Native Americans are particularly attuned to the spiritual practice of vision. Their vision quests are journeys undertaken by youth as a rite of passage or by tribal leaders for renewal. The individual ventures into the wilderness alone, returning only when he or she has had a vision—a personal insight into a spiritual path or a revelation about the destiny of the tribe.

At one point or another in our lives, we must all undergo something similar to a vision quest. "We do not receive wisdom," French writer Marcel Proust suggests. "We must discover it for ourselves after a journey through the wilderness, which no one else can make for us."

Vision has to do with morality. American philosopher Ralph Waldo Emerson writes: "The high, contemplative, all-consuming vision, the sense of right and wrong, is alike in all. Its attributes are self-existence, eternity, intuition, and command. It is the mind of the mind."

Meditation teacher Jon Kabat-Zinn is more specific: "Our vision has to do with our values, and with our personal blueprint for what is most important in life."

Vision is also about taking a stand. Protestant minister Peter Marshall, who was once chaplain to the United States Congress, proposes, "Give us clear vision that we may know where to stand and what to stand for, because unless we stand for something, we shall fall for anything."

And vision is about matters of depth, breadth, and height. Writer Stephen S. Wise explains, "Vision looks inward and becomes duty. Vision looks outward and becomes aspiration. Vision looks upward and becomes faith."

So nourish the visionary gleam that lies within you. Cultivate the art of seeing invisible things. Find your own wisdom. Hone your sense of right and wrong. Take a stand when you must.

Russian novelist Boris Pasternak understands what vision means: "It is not the earthquake that controls the advent of a different life but storms of generosity and visions of incandescent souls."

When a relationship becomes stale or difficult, the ritual of empathy or of walking a mile in another's shoes helps clarify what may be going on.

An old friend seems to be deliberately avoiding me. He has moved, not sent me his new address, and not responded to my letter, which the postal service must have forwarded to him. I am angry and sad. Then it occurs to me that he feels he needs things from friends that he doesn't think I can provide. Maybe he's right. I'm married, he's single; I have children, he doesn't; I have a career, he's in school; and so on. With a little effort, I recall the times I have neglected old friends for similar reasons. I am still disappointed but not so mad, not so sad.

—TIMOTHY MILLER
in *How to Want What You Have*

Sending and receiving correspondence illuminates the riches of a relationship.

Letters are the stories of our souls. Unlike a telephone call, a letter can be picked up again and again. It can be deeply pondered. It can be eaten. Always serve letters with a cup of tea and a footstool. Celebrate "the reading" slowly. It is irreverent to read a letter fast.

I treasure my letters like early morning sunrises. I see the rays between the lines. I hear the dreams and yearnings, the gratitude and the delight. I hear the questions and the musings, all coming from the heart of this newly published author. A letter bears its own copyright. Standing before my mailbox holding an original very limited edition in my hands is like standing before a feast.

—MACRINA WIEDERKEHR
in *A Tree Full of Angels*

In the film 84 Charing Cross Road, *based on a true story, a couple become good friends just through writing letters. Helene, a writer who lives in New York, orders out-of-print books from a London bookstore. Frank, one of the employees there, takes a personal interest in her*

witty orders, and they begin to exchange letters. During the twenty years they correspond, they never meet face-to-face. Yet their relationship has all the marks of a great friendship—a deep sharing at the soul level and an opening up of new worlds of experience and meaning.

I am reminded of this film when I send E-mail notes to friends I have met on a computer network. Fred and I have our doubts sometimes about technology's impact on relationships. For instance, we both question the value of telephone voice mail, especially when we catch ourselves and others using it to avoid being reached. It is possible to dodge people for days by leaving messages on machines.

The computer, however, has been a wonderful container of friendship for me. My spiritual friend and I regularly talk about our journeys via E-mail messages. Through private and public meetings on the Internet, I can talk with friends about a variety of topics, from feminism to favorite TV shows. I recognize that these are very specific friendships, but they are friendships nonetheless, and they help me stay involved with a wider circle than my immediate one. They add a breadth of experience to my life that I might otherwise not know.

Catholic priest Edward Hays offers a few final thoughts on correspondence as a spiritual experience.

You and I are meant to be "letters" to the world. People who "read" us receive a message from the Divine Mystery. Now, *there's* a delightful vocation—to be a sort of "valentine" from God to a love-hungry world! But if we are to be living, divine letters, "words made flesh," we, of all people, should keep alive and treat with respect the beautiful custom of letter writing. As we take time to do this, let us remember that such activity is always prayer. Let us remember that it is also prayer to receive and read a letter. Perhaps we could pause at the conclusion of having penned a note to a friend and trace the sign of the cross upon the letter to remind ourselves of this fact. Or, we could breathe part of our spirit into the envelope. More than just a puff of breath, we could send along with our message a part of our soul. Since love is invisible, some ritual or sign helps us to remember what it is we are really sending when we send a letter to someone we love.

—EDWARD HAYS
in *Secular Sanctity*

The kind of energy and love exchanged in letters is also available through prayer. Many people derive both solace and strength from knowing that their friends are praying for them.

Every day I take my friends to my prayer. They are remembered in my heart. During this time of remembering I am reminded of the sacred connections that can happen during prayer. I bring a friend from Little Rock into the sacred space within. Then I gather up someone from New York City and walk into my heart with her. Finally all of these wonderful people, many of them strangers to each other, are there in the sacred space of my heart. It feels like a great homecoming. I truly believe that these saints of God receive energy from each other simply by being gathered together in my heart. They may be strangers to one another but the Christ-connection that they share makes them kinfolks.

—MACRINA WIEDERKEHR
in *Seasons of Your Heart*

Every night I carry a band of friends, family members, and a few strangers into my prayers. A few are unemployed, some are struggling with illness or despair, and others are facing transitions in their lives. I have a special list—"Fred's List," my friends call it—of people I pray will find someone to love who will love them. Most of these individuals know that they are part of my evening ritual, and in the case of my list for love relationships, they even make a point of telling me when they can be removed. Until then, they can count on me night after night.

Rewarding relationships spring up in all kinds of places. The people in the next readings recall times when teachers were friends to them.

"When I went back to teach—you know how it is. There's the opening-night party in the Gates Room. Mr. Shipman came over to me and welcomed me back, just as nice. And I thought: 'Doesn't this man know how much I hated him? Doesn't he remember that he *failed* me? Coming up to me like an old friend.'

"Then he said he was going to give me one piece of advice—that you know you've been at St. Paul's too long when the stuff that sixteen-year-olds say starts to make sense. And he laughed. I'd never seen the man laugh."

Anthony put his head back. He liked a story, always had. "What you're talking about is grace," he said.

"Is it?"

I like the simplicity of the word. Old ladies in church use it. Old drunks who don't drink anymore use it. Grace, Tillich says, is accepting that you are accepted. Children say grace at table. Bosomy blond Baptists and tweedy Episcopalians use it. Teenagers are the only ones who shun the word, as if it might snatch from them the magic of their power.

—Lorene Cary
in *Black Ice*

Thank God for that rain out the window and for Mr. Clemente, who allowed us in ninth grade to listen to it for no reason, in the middle of the day. That one moment carried me a long way into my life.

I didn't know it then. At the time, I think, it made me a little nervous—it was too naked, too uncontrolled, too honest. I thought it odd. In those days I was watching my step, making sure I knew the rules, keeping things in control. I wore the same long, pleated skirt every day, blue cardigan sweater, oxford shoes, and carried a brown leather school bag, even while the other girls were wearing makeup, nylons, heels. I never felt that I fit in. . . . For fear that people would think I was weird—I saw no one around me I could identify with—I tried not to be noticed. I became a nerd. And here was Mr. Clemente who asked me to listen to the rain, to connect a sense organ with something natural, neutral, good. He asked me to become alive. I was scared, and I loved it.

—Natalie Goldberg
in *Long Quiet Highway*

Sometimes we need to expand our understanding of friendship to catch all the nuances of its spiritual power. We may even discover through it the sacred significance of our lives.

Sometimes I think we get caught in a trap when we think about friendship. The idea becomes stereotyped: a friend is someone we know a long time and see often. Not necessarily so. . . .

A friend can be someone you have known all your life or someone you met a week ago—or someone you never met except
through a book or a beautiful movie or a play or a piece of music or
a painting. Or someone who has served as a role model and made
you proud to be a fellow human being. My friends include Monet
and Mozart, Arthur Miller and Arthur Laurents, Federico Fellini
and Thomas Wolfe, Louisa May Alcott and Eleanor Roosevelt, and
a hundred other human beings who have lifted my spirits and
made me more than I was before they touched my life. They
remind me that friendship is the source of love and growth, whatever form it may take.

—EDA LESHAN
in *It's Better to Be Over the Hill Than Under It*

One day the teacher, Frederick Wilkerson, asked me to read to him.
I was twenty-four, very erudite, very worldly. He asked that I read
from *Lessons in Truth*, a section which ended with these words:
"God loves me." I read the piece and closed the book, and the
teacher said, "Read it again." I pointedly opened the book, and I
sarcastically read, "God loves me." He said, "Again." After about
the seventh repetition I began to sense that there might be truth in
the statement, that there was a possibility that God really did love
me. Me, Maya Angelou. I suddenly began to cry at the grandness
of it all. I knew that if God loved me, then I could do wonderful
things, I could try great things, learn anything, achieve anything.
For what could stand against me with God, since one person, any
person with God, constitutes the majority?

—MAYA ANGELOU
in *Wouldn't Take Nothing for My Journey Now*

*We met Ieva in 1969, when she was working in the Philadelphia office
responsible for Lutheran youth ministry programs. She was the secretary who mimeographed the first issues of our publication. She was
there when we got our first subscribers and our first grant. When we
could finally afford to have the magazine printed, Ieva was the one who
took it to the press. Her enthusiasm nourished our first attempts to
relate spirituality and culture.*

Today Ieva is a single mother of three and a minister in the Lutheran Church of Sweden. She serves the Latvian congregation of Stockholm, counsels Christians in Latvia, and over the years has done pioneer work in women's theological education. Her spiritual journey has been long and dramatic, and we have marveled at her unflagging energy and her passionate commitment to ministry. The few times in recent years when we have been able to meet in Stockholm or New York have been mutually empowering.

Ieva is our soul friend and our spiritual ally—someone who has been there for us through good and bad times. We speak a language of the heart, even when weeks pass and we are not in contact. Instantly, when we hear her voice, the connection that we know is always there sparks to life with a bounty of new blessings.

With Ieva we laugh easily and often. We laugh over good times, and we laugh—like the clown sculptures we have given each other—in spite of sadness and disappointments. Laughter—to use a phrase by Protestant theologian Harvey Cox—is our way of crossing ourselves. It is a mark of our faith, and it enables us to face uncertainty. What is never uncertain is her faithfulness to us as a friend.

It is expressed so simply. "I used something from you in a sermon last week," she will mention. "I've been thinking of you," she will inevitably say. She believes in us and what we are doing. We believe in her and what she is doing. Ieva's presence in our life is a grace, a sacramental sign that God loves us.

PRACTICING SPIRITUAL LITERACY: RELATIONSHIPS

CONVERSATIONS/JOURNAL ENTRIES

- What spiritual practices have you found helpful in raising the level of intimacy in your relationships?
- "Love is an act of imagination," therapist Ethel Spector Person writes. "For some of us it will be the greatest creative triumph of our lives." In your journal, list some of the ways you have found to keep love alive in your primary relationship.
- Write about situations when your partner has been a spiritual teacher for you? What have you learned?
- Recall a moment of meaning from your early family life and share it with a member of your family today.
- Do a journal exercise around the following Arabian proverb: "A friend is one to whom one may pour out all the contents of one's heart, chaff and grain together, knowing that the gentlest of hands will take and sift it, keep what is worth keeping, and with a breath of kindness blow the rest away." Include a tribute to such a friend in your life.
- Why do you think friendship is such a common theme in movies and television shows?
- What are the chief benefits of having friends who have known you for a long time? What are some of the major barriers you face in sustaining a long-term friendship? During what stages of your life has friendship meant the most to you?

ACTIVITIES/PROJECTS

- Make a list of seven keys to sustaining an enduring and fulfilling marriage or partnership. Compare your list with your partner's, and choose one activity to do together this week.
- Make a collage or a clay sculpture that captures in an image or a figure your understanding of what marriage is like. If you have a family with children, do the same activity about your family.
- Identify one ancestor in your family tree and do something to honor his or her spirit.
- Set aside a family evening for a reading of poems or short stories that are especially meaningful and pleasurable to you.

- Send a note of appreciation to a friend who shares your enthusiasms and always is supportive.
- "Love doesn't make the world go round," Franklin P. Jones has observed. "Love is what makes the ride worthwhile." Rent one of our favorite ten films on video about love: *The Accidental Tourist, Always, Breathing Lessons, Defending Your Life, Everybody's All American, Moonstruck, Murphy's Romance, On Valentine's Day, 1918,* and *Summer Solstice.*
- Families of all types deal with spiritual challenges. Here are ten of our favorite films on this theme: *Avalon, The Dollmaker, The Man in the Moon, Men Don't Leave, On Golden Pond, Parenthood, Places in the Heart, See You in the Morning, Terms of Endearment,* and *What's Eating Gilbert Grape.*
- "Every friendship plays a different tune on your soul," novelist and essayist Wilfrid Sheed has noted. Here are ten of our favorite videos on this subject: *Age Old Friends, Beaches, The Big Chill, The Boy Who Could Fly, City Slickers, Clara's Heart, 84 Charing Cross Road, Fried Green Tomatoes, Stand by Me,* and *Thelma and Louise.*

SPIRITUAL EXERCISES/RITUALS

- For a specific time every day during the next week, sit with your partner in silence. See if this turns into a period for meditation or prayer.
- Using the spiritual practice of wonder, refashion one daily activity that you do as partners so that it deepens your soul.
- Every family has daily rituals which have spiritual significance, although some of them are taken for granted. Share stories about a ritual you observed in your birth family, and a ritual in your household today. Talk about areas where you might incorporate spiritual practices, such as blessing prayers, into such family activities as watching television, going to the grocery store, or washing the car.
- The Japanese hold moon-viewing parties. Have a family celebration the next time there is a full moon.
- When your family comes home from a vacation, do a ceremony to emphasize that you are returning to start over again.
- Create a ritual to celebrate your friendship with another person who has shared your spiritual journey.

COMMUNITY

The moving finger of God in human history points ever in the same direction. There must be community.

—HOWARD THURMAN

Community means different things to different people. To some it is a safe haven where survival is assured through mutual cooperation. To others, it is a place of emotional support, with deep sharing and bonding with close friends. Some see community as an intense crucible for personal growth. For others, it is primarily a place to pioneer their dreams.

—CORRINE McLAUGHLIN AND GORDON DAVIDSON

In a real sense all life is interrelated. All [people] are caught in an inescapable network of mutuality, tied in a single garment of destiny.

—DR. MARTIN LUTHER KING JR.

Community. Somewhere, there are people to whom we can speak with passion without having the words catch in our throats. Somewhere a circle of hands will open to receive us, eyes will light up as we enter, voices will celebrate with us whenever we come into our own power. Community means strength that joins our strength to do the work that needs to be done. Arms to hold us when we falter. A circle of healing. A circle of friends. Someplace where we can be free.

—STARHAWK

The new survival unit is no longer the individual nation; it's the entire human race and its environment. This newfound oneness is only a rediscovery of an ancient religious truth. Unity is not something we are called to create; it's something we are called to recognize,

—WILLIAM SLOANE COFFIN

Our lives extend beyond our skins, in radical interdependence with the rest of the world.

—JOANNA MACY

Throughout our lives, we are nourished and sustained by communities. They fulfill our yearning for support, solidarity, and meaning. With spiritual literacy we recognize them as divine milieus where we can grow and flourish for all our days.

Our experience of community begins with our childhood friends who give us the affirmation we seek outside the family and who show us some first things about love and kindness. At schools and universities, we expand our horizons in communities of learning and pick up points about justice, vision, and imagination. Later, in our careers, we often must practice listening, nurturing, and peace as we work with others. Back home in our neighborhoods, we develop our capacities for connections, hospitality, and zeal.

Some of us may turn to support groups to help us deal with a problem, or we may band together with others fighting for a common cause. These special communities give us a trusting environment where we can express our feelings, share our stories, and try to make a difference.

In both our private and public lives, we experience faith, grace, and joy as we contemplate mystery in religious or spiritual congregations. Discussion clubs, salons, and electronic communities are also available to us for the exchange of ideas and the sharing of information. Memberships in men's and women's groups meet our needs for fellowship too, and become a place to practice questing and transformation. And there are all those ad hoc communities which arise spontaneously out of crises—wars, natural disasters, accidents, and personal traumas—and call up our capacity for compassion, forgiveness, and prayer.

We belong to still more communities. There is our generational cohort, our age mates, with whom we move through history. Many of us maintain ethnic or nationalistic ties which are often expressed in communal activities. And now more than ever, we are part of a global community which, according to anthropologist Margaret Mead, "is united by shared knowledge and danger." Then, too, there is the community of our ancestors, called the communion of saints in some traditions, who are available to support and direct us from the invisible world.

Spiritual readings of these experiences yield many meanings. But the most important is the most obvious: we are embedded in communities, circles within circles of communities, both small and large, focused and abstract. Holding up the ideal of unity, we strive to break down the walls which separate us from others—not only other nations and peoples, but other species and the natural world.

"'Everything belongs' has become my motto and mantra," says Catholic priest and retreat leader Richard Rohr. By keeping an open mind and spirit, we reach out to the stranger and to all those who are different from us.

In one of his ecological treatises, scientist Gregory Bateson asks, "What pattern connects the crab to the lobster and the orchid to the primrose and all four of them to me? And me to you?" The mystics say love is the pattern that stitches the universe together. As the readings in this chapter attest, the Guardian of the Galaxies has created us for life together in love, for community.

PORTRAITS OF COMMUNITY

The creation of a community reflects a natural and very powerful urge to connect, do good, and change the world. And we are strong when we stand and work together.

THE LOW ROAD
(excerpt)

Two people can keep each other
sane, can give support, conviction,
love, massage, hope, sex.
Three people are a delegation,
a committee, a wedge. With four
you can play bridge and start
an organization. With six
you can rent a whole house,
eat pie for dinner with no
seconds, and hold a fund raising party.
A dozen make a demonstration.
A hundred fill a hall.
A thousand have solidarity and your own newsletter;
ten thousand, power and your own paper;
a hundred thousand, your own media;
ten million, your own country.

It goes on one at a time,
it starts when you care
to act, it starts when you do
it again after they said no,

it starts when you say We
and know who you mean, and each
day you mean one more.
—MARGE PIERCY
in *The Moon Is Always Female*

I once heard a story from an old African-American man in the mid-south. He came out of an alley as I was sitting amidst the graffiti of the inner-city "park." Some people would call him crazy, for he spoke to anyone and no one. He shuffled along with one finger held out as though to test the wind's direction. *Cuentistas* recognize such persons as having been touched by the gods. In our tradition, we'd call such a man *El Bulto,* The Bundle, for souls such as he carry a certain kind of ware and show it to any who will look, anyone who has the eyes to see it and the sense to shelter it.

This particular kindly *El Bulto* gave me this story. It is about a certain kind of ancestral transmission. He called the story "One Stick—Two Stick." "This is the way of the old African kings," he whispered.

In the story, an old man is dying, and calls his people to his side. He gives a short, sturdy stick to each of his many offspring, wives, and relatives. "Break the stick," he instructs them. With some effort, they all snap their sticks in half.

"This is how it is when a soul is alone without anyone. They can be easily broken."

The old man next gives each of his kin another stick, and says, "This is how I would like you to live after I pass. Put your sticks together in bundles of twos and threes. Now, break these bundles in half."

No one can break the sticks when there are two or more in a bundle. The old man smiles. "We are strong when we stand with another soul. When we are with another, we cannot be broken."
—CLARISSA PINKOLA ESTÉS
in *Women Who Run with the Wolves*

Once several members of a Hasidic congregation had become helplessly lost in a dense forest. They were delighted when unexpectedly they came upon their rabbi who was also wandering through the woods. They implored, "Master, we are lost! Please show us the way out of the forest."

The rabbi replied, "I do not know the way out either, but I do know which paths lead nowhere. I will show you the ways that won't work, and then perhaps together we can discover the ones that do."

—SHELDON KOPP
in *Blues Ain't Nothing but a Good Soul Feeling Bad*

Communities link us with others through time. We discover these connections through religious rituals, special observances, and the occasional surprise.

We are communities in time and in a place, I know, but we are communities in faith as well—and sometimes time can stop shadowing us. Our lives are touched by those who lived centuries ago, and we hope that our lives will mean something to people who won't be alive until centuries from now. It's a great "chain of being," someone once told me, and I think our job is to do the best we can to hold up our small segment of the chain. That's one kind of localism, I guess, and one kind of politics—doing your utmost to keep that chain connected, unbroken.

—DOROTHY DAY
quoted in *Dorothy Day*
by Robert Coles

In the oldtime religion of my youth, we believed that through the ritual of what we called "the Lord's Supper," we communed with the saints, with all those who had gone before.

I was struck with this old image at a retirement dinner as the retiree invoked the names of company people long dead and spoke of them as if they were just on some kind of sabbatical. He talked of what they had taught the people who had taught him, and how he had tried to teach others who were now teaching the beginners.

As he spoke, we realized that a true community has no limit in time. He made us feel the extension of our community of work, into a time long before us and into a time yet to come. As if the work exists in and of itself, and we come and go from it in a kind of continuum of endeavor, in a kind of communion.

—JAMES A. AUTRY
in *Love & Profit*

REFLECTION

The Christian doctrine
of the communion of saints
is simple, really.
All it says is
that once you buy the farm
you still live on the farm.
All it says is
that those who have gone before us
are still with us.
All it says is
that past generations
still count
and must be taken into account.
In other words,
we're all in this together.
All of us.

—MITCH FINLEY
in *Whispers of Love*

Once I began going to church, the age-old religious rituals marking the turning of the year deepened and gave a fuller meaning to the cycle of the seasons and my own relation to them. The year was not only divided now into winter, spring, summer, and fall but was marked by the expectation of Advent, leading up to the fulfillment of Christmas, followed by Lent, the solemn prelude to the coming of the dark anguish of Good Friday that is transformed in the glory of Easter. Birth and death and resurrection, beginnings and endings and renewals, were observed and celebrated in ceremonies whose experience made me feel I belonged—not just to a neighborhood and a place, but to a larger order of things, a universal sequence of life and death and rebirth. . . .

Going to church, even belonging to it, did not solve life's problems—if anything, they seemed to escalate again around that time—but it gave me a sense of living in a large context, of being part of something greater than what I could see through the tunnel vision of my personal concerns. I now looked forward to Sunday because it *meant* going to church; what once was strange now felt not only natural but essential.

—DAN WAKEFIELD
in *Returning*

I recall a recent phone conversation with my mother. . . . The church she attends had purchased new hymnals. The old ones had been stacked by the exit, and the minister announced that any member of the congregation who wished to have one could just pick one up on the way out.

As she left the church, my mother stopped to pick up a hymnal for her older sister who because of illness was no longer able to attend services. The first one that she picked up had been damaged, so she put it back, rummaged around quickly in the pile of books, then drew one out whose cover looked fairly decent. "I wasn't paying much attention to what I was doing," she told me. "I was just letting my fingers find the book they wanted."

Later on the way home, my mother took time to examine more closely the book she had picked up for her older sister. To her astonishment and delight, when she opened it she saw on the title page an official statement saying that this hymnal had been purchased for the church by her older sister as a memorial to her husband. Out of the hundreds of old hymnals that her church was giving away, my mother had randomly chosen the one book that would mean the most to her sister—the very one my aunt had donated to the church many years previously!

—DAVID SPANGLER
in *Everyday Miracles*

Experiences in community can be healing, bringing us to a new life. In this passage from a novel, a guilt-ridden man attends a funeral service.

The organ music dwindled away. Dr. Prescott rose and announced a prayer, and still no one arrived to fill that empty pew.

The prayer was for the living. "We know Thy daughter Lucy is safely by Thy side," Dr. Prescott intoned, "but we ask Thee to console those left behind. Comfort them, we pray, and ease their pain. Let Thy mercy pour like a healing balm upon their hearts."

Like a healing balm. Ian pictured something white and semi-liquid—the bottle of lotion his mother kept by the kitchen sink, say—pleasantly scented with almonds. Could the balm soothe not just grief but guilt? Not just guilt but racking anguish over something impulsively done that could not be undone?

Ordinarily indifferent to prayers (or to anything else even vaguely religious), Ian listened to this one yearningly. He leaned forward in his seat as if he could ride the words all the way to heaven. He kept his eyes tightly shut. He thought, *Please, Please. Please.*

In the pews around him he heard a rustling and a creaking, and he opened his eyes and found the congregation rising. Struggling to his feet, he peered at the hymnbook Cicely held in front of him. "... with me," he joined in belatedly, "fast falls the eventide ... " His voice was a creak. He fell silent and listened to the others—to Cicely's clear soprano, Mrs. Jordan's plain, true alto, Dr. Prescott's rich bass. "The darkness deepens," they sang, "Lord, with me abide!" The voices ceased to be separate. They plaited themselves into a multistranded chord, and now it seemed the congregation was a single person—someone of great kindness and compassion, someone gentle and wise and forgiving. "In life, in death, O Lord," they finished, "abide with me." And then came the long, sighed "Amen." They sat down. Ian sat too. His knees were trembling. He felt that everything had been drained away from him, all the grief and self-blame. He was limp and pure and pliant as an infant. He was, in fact, born again.

—ANNE TYLER
in *Saint Maybe*

Some community experiences enable participants to focus on the deeper meanings of the spiritual practice of play.

One of the first things I noticed on my longer retreats, ... was how like an exercise class the liturgy seemed. It was sometimes difficult to rise early for morning office; at other times during the day it seemed tedious to be going back to church, but knowing that the others would be there made all the difference. Once there, the benefits were tangible, and I usually wondered how I could have wished to be anywhere else. When I compared all this to an aerobics class, a monk said, "That's exactly right."

... It is serious play indeed. It means that somewhere, as I write this, as you read it, people are singing Psalms and praying for us all. Knowing that most of us won't notice or care, they are making us a gift of their very lives. Here we approach the ultimate play in a monastery, the monk's sense that his being there at all is a sign of God's play with him.

—KATHLEEN NORRIS
in *Dakota*

The world was not arranged for our personal convenience, and we have to learn to adjust to the presence of other communities. The author of the next passage traveled a great distance to India for a silent retreat.

Just below my cottage was a big, open field, and a few weeks after I arrived a group called the Delhi Girls came to it. The Delhi Girls were a kind of paramilitary Girl Scout troop. Not only did they set up camp, but they also set up loudspeakers. From six o'clock in the morning until ten o'clock at night, they played loud Hindi film music.

I watched my mind go through a tremendous range of emotions, from real anger, even rage, to a feeling of self-importance: "How can they do this to me? I came here to get enlightened!" It took quite a while for my mind to work through all of that, to let go of the feeling of self-importance and self-righteousness, and just to let things be. But when my mind finally settled down, it did let go in that way. Then the din of film music in the middle of a meditation retreat was no longer a problem.

—JOSEPH GOLDSTEIN
in *Transforming the Mind, Healing the World*

Signs of human community—its meaning and its beauty—can be found all around us, if we only look.

Convention centers are the basilicas of secular religion. . . .

We associate with other people like us to affirm ourselves. We come for people reasons, not professional reasons. Loneliness is one great burden of being a solitary human being. To spend time in the company of others who have our concerns, values, interests, beliefs, or occupation is to get confirmation of who we are—to feel connected to a larger image of ourselves.

It's true that many gatherings seem concerned only with business—with products, sales, and economic gain. What's wrong with that? What we do for a living defines much of who we are, and being with other people who make and sell potato peelers or whatever is no less important to those who come together than any other event that draws people together. The judgment of the value of the convention is made by those who are involved, not outsiders who see only the surface.

—ROBERT FULGHUM
in *From Beginning to End*

One night, I did leave the house and walked for hours, wishing to disencumber myself. But my bones failed me and the lights of an all-night diner were irresistible. I entered the steamy, greasy warmth, felt the meat smell cling to my clothing. I sat down at the counter and picked up a matchbox. On it was printed ACE 24-HOUR CAFE—WHERE NICE PEOPLE MEET. And tears came to my eyes for the hopefulness, the sweetness, the enduring promise of plain human love. And I understood the incarnation for, I believe, the first time: Christ took on flesh for love, because the flesh is lovable.

The waitress looked at me, an old man with a night's growth of gray-green beard. My eyes, I knew, were feverish, the mad eyes she must have got used to on the late-night shift. She said, "How about another cup of coffee, dear?" I smiled and thanked her.

—MARY GORDON
in *The Company of Women*

I took part in a retreat once in which the leader gathered the group into a circle and handed out three balls of colored yarn. She asked us to toss the balls back and forth to one another across the circle, each holding onto a piece of it. The result was a beautiful, multi-colored web stretched across the center of the circle. "Each of you take turns and wiggle your thread," the leader instructed. What we found was that every movement vibrated the entire web. And it dawned on me—this immeasurable truth we were portraying. We are each a thread woven into the vast web of the universe, linked and connected so that our lives are irrevocably bound up with one another. I looked at those faces around the circle in a new way. The old adage, "I am my brother's keeper"—or in this case, my sister's keeper—melted into something new: I am my sister. And suddenly I wanted to gather them to me and do what I could to heal them and bless them and affirm to them how beautiful they were.

—SUE MONK KIDD
in *Communion, Community, Commonweal*
edited by John S. Mogabgab

When Brooke and I were in Spain, we found ourselves in the Donana National Park, one of the last remaining wetlands in Europe. We were there during spring migration, so we were able to witness waves of birds from both the European and African continents.

The wetlands happen to be on the edge of a beautiful town called El Rocio. We went on a Sunday morning to see the flamingos and the spoonbills. On the edge of the marsh is a beautiful white-washed adobe *santuario*. An old woman handed each person a large candle. She said, "Light this candle with your desire in mind, let your desire pierce your heart, and take it home with you."

The people lighted their candles with their desires in mind, then moved into an alcove to put their candle onto a huge iron rack. In this white-tiled room with a statue of the Mother of Dew, each person stood next to their candle and tended to their desire, watching while the wax melted. When the wax had melted sufficiently to make a ball of it, each person took the wax home as a talisman.

The room was searing—there had to be hundreds, even thousands of candles, all burning at the same time, with people attending to their individual desires. It was wonderful. Brooke said to me, "My desire is melting into everyone else's." And that was

WONDER

"The sense of wonder, that is our sixth sense and it is a natural religious sense," English writer D. H. Lawrence declares.

The Great Artist calls us to luxuriate in this sense-luscious world. And there is so much to see, touch, smell, taste, and hear!

"Each grain of dust contains something marvelous," notes Joan Miró, the Spanish painter, "but in order to understand it, we have to recover the religious and magical sense of things that belong to primitive people."

Indigenous tribes all over the world see the sacred in all things and rejoice in the discovery of new marvels. Curiosity is their vitamin. In other cultures, it may be up to children to keep wonder alive. They tutor adults in the art of surveying life with fresh eyes.

Jelaluddin Rumi, the Sufi poet and seer, advises: "Observe the wonders as they occur around you./Don't claim them. Feel the artistry/moving through, and be silent."

There are so many wonders in a world of this and that. Quicken our pulses, Universal Miracle Worker, so we don't miss anything.

British essayist G. K. Chesterton writes, "At the back of our brains, so to speak, there [is] a forgotten blaze or burst of astonishment at our own existence. The object of the artistic and spiritual life [is] to dig for this submerged sunrise of wonder."

Let the artist within you come alive to the report of your senses. You are heir to the wonderful estate of earth and its dowry of delights.

"Wonder," English historian Thomas Carlyle states, "is the basis of worship." We are stopped in our tracks by the majesty of creation and the gift of our lives. We need to practice "awe-aerobics," as American comedian Lily Tomlin recommends in one of her skits.

The practice of wonder is also a part of prayer as Jewish theologian Abraham Joshua Heschel reveals: "To pray is to take notice of the wonder, to regain a sense of the mystery that animates all beings, the divine margin in all our attainments."

The wonder that engenders worship and pulsates in prayer also leads us back to the everyday. "A mature sense of wonder," American philosopher Sam Keen clarifies, "does not need the constant titillation of the sensational to keep it alive. It is most often called forth by a confrontation with the mysterious depth of meaning at the heart of the familiar and the quotidian."

The world is moving toward us with a flood of epiphanies. Join the parade of wonders. We hallow and hail the Higher Power's presence in the kingdom of surprises which is our daily round and rhythm.

And we agree with the sentiments of Mary Oliver in her poem "When Death Comes":

> When it's over, I want to say: all my life
> I was a bride married to amazement.
> I was the bridegroom, taking the world into my arms.

precisely the point. When you're in that collective space in a ritu-
alistic way, there is no way your desire won't merge with everyone else's desire. They are the desires of our highest selves.

—TERRY TEMPEST WILLIAMS
quoted in *Listening to the Land*
by Derrick Jensen

*One of the side effects of an emergency—a spiritual one or any other
kind—is that it creates communities, as Jungian analyst Jean Shinoda
Bolen discovers in the next reading.*

I was probably driving at least 60 MPH, when I fell asleep at the
wheel. I woke up with my car moving through tall weeds that were
hitting my windshield; it felt like I was in a dream. I was disoriented about whether I was dreaming and where I was, and it took
me a moment to know that I was awake and in my car and that I
had better put my foot on the brake. Within minutes after the car
stopped, two very concerned men ran down the embankment to
see if I was all right. They were Good Samaritans who had come to
help, and witness to what had happened. When I fell asleep at the
wheel, I was in the outside lane. The men said that they were right
behind me and saw my car headed straight for a telephone pole,
and that I had missed it by only three or four feet. . . .

When I realized how close a call it had been, it felt as if I had had
guardian angels looking after me, and as if these men who on a
long empty stretch of highway had immediately stopped to help
were human guardian angels as well.

—JEAN SHINODA BOLEN
in *Crossing to Avalon*

*Grief creates another type of community. We are one with the dead and
with each other.*

It was her fourth birthday party. She and her friends had just bought
ice cream from the traveling ice cream man, but as she walked out from
behind the white ice cream truck, she walked right under the rear
wheels of an oncoming fully-loaded coal truck. If someone hadn't

yelled, he wouldn't have known to stop. There was nothing that could be done because there was very little left of her at all. The children, the little girl's mother, some other adults, and the truck driver—a large overweight middle-aged man in a coal-stained sweaty T-shirt—stood mutely in a circle. There were one or two attempts at pious utterings: "God takes the little ones first because he loves them most;" "She's better off now that she is with God." The silence was piercing.

The little girl's mother, a small woman, began to weep and scream and beat on her head and face with her fists. As she stood there and beat on herself, everyone else stood in frozen paralysis. We stood there for a long time.

Then without uttering a word the truck driver opened his arms, turned his hands outward, and looked at the woman. She walked slowly toward him into his embrace. He wept. She wept. The freeze was broken. The silence, the paralysis, was broken. We all wept. We wept. We held hands. We hugged.

The little girl was dead. We were dead, and with the simple motion of lifting up his hands and arms, the truck driver had offered us a ritual that gave us life and transformed us.

—MICHAEL DWINELL
in *Fire Bearer*

A few doors away, my attention is arrested by one of the most unusual memorials that I have seen in the South Bronx. In bright white paint against a soft beige background is a painting of a large and friendly-looking dog, his tail erect, his ears alert for danger. Above, in yellow letters, I read "MOONDOG," which appears to be the nickname of the person who has died. "Gone is the face. . . . Silent is the voice. . . . In our hearts we'll remember," reads the epitaph.

As I am standing on the sidewalk copying these words, a plump Hispanic woman rises from the stoop nearby and comes up to my side.

"Is this where he died?" I ask.

"Yes," she answers. "He was shot right there, inside the door."

"Why was he killed?"

"He was protecting a woman who was pregnant."

"Did the woman live?"

"The woman lived. She's fine."

"Did the baby live?"

"The baby's doing fine."

"How old was the man who died?"

"He was almost 21."

I ask her how he got his nickname.

"He loved dogs. He used to bring them home." Her voice is jovial and pleasant.

"Did you know him well?"

"He was my son," she says.

—JONATHAN KOZOL
in *Amazing Grace*

BUILDING COMMUNITY

How do we build community? In the following reading, Chilean poet Pablo Neruda recalls an incident in his childhood that influenced his approach to poetry and his appreciation of human unity.

One time, investigating in the backyard of our house in Temuco the tiny objects and miniscule beings of my world, I came upon a hole in one of the boards of the fence. I looked through the hole and saw a landscape like that behind our house, uncared for, and wild. I moved back a few steps, because I sensed vaguely that something was about to happen. All of a sudden a hand appeared—a tiny hand of a boy about my own age. By the time I came close again, the hand was gone, and in its place there was a marvellous white sheep.

The sheep's wool was faded. Its wheels had escaped. All of this only made it more authentic. I had never seen such a wonderful sheep. I looked back through the hole but the boy had disappeared. I went into the house and brought out a treasure of my own: a pine cone, opened, full of odor and resin, which I adored. I set it down in the same spot and went off with the sheep.

I never saw either the hand or the boy again. . . .

I have been a lucky man. To feel the intimacy of brothers is a marvellous thing in life. To feel the love of people whom we love is a fire that feeds our life. But to feel the affection that comes from those whom we do not know, from those unknown to us, who are watching over our sleep and solitude, over our dangers and our weaknesses—that is something still greater and more beautiful because it widens out the boundaries of our being, and unites all living things.

That exchange brought home to me for the first time a precious idea: that all humanity is somehow together. That experience came to me again much later; this time it stood out strikingly against a background of trouble and persecution.

It won't surprise you then that I have attempted to give something resiny, earthlike, and fragrant in exchange for human brotherhood. Just as I once left the pine cone by the fence, I have since left my words on the door of so many people who were unknown to me, people in prison, or hunted, or alone.

That is the great lesson I learned in my childhood, in the backyard of a lonely house. Maybe it was nothing but a game two boys played who didn't know each other and wanted to pass to the other some good things of life. Yet maybe this small and mysterious exchange of gifts remained inside me also, deep and indestructible, giving my poetry light.

—PABLO NERUDA
quoted in *Twenty Poems*
translated by James Wright and Robert Bly

The sharing of gifts takes many forms in a community.

I was walking one Sunday afternoon several years ago with an older friend. We went by the ruining log house that had belonged to his grandparents and great-grandparents. The house stirred my friend's memory, and he told how the oldtime people used to visit each other in the evenings, especially in the long evenings of winter. There used to be a sort of institution in our part of the country known as "sitting till bedtime." After supper, when they weren't too tired, neighbors would walk across the field to visit each other. They popped corn, my friend said, and ate apples and talked. They told each other stories. They told each other stories, as I knew myself, that they all had heard before. Sometimes they told stories about each other, about themselves, living again in their own memories and thus keeping their memories alive. Among the hearers of these stories were always the children. When bedtime came, the visitors lit their lanterns and went home. My friend talked about this, and thought about it, and then he said, "They had everything but money."

They were poor, as country people have often been, but they had each other, they had their local economy in which they helped each other, they had each other's comfort when they needed it, and they had their stories, their history together in that place.

—WENDELL BERRY
in *What Are People For?*

There was once an old Jewish man. All he ever did in his spare time was go to the edge of the village and plant fig trees. People would ask him, "Why are you planting fig trees? You are going to die before you can eat any of the fruit that they produce." But he said, "I have spent so many happy hours sitting under fig trees and eating their fruit. Those trees were planted by others. Why shouldn't I make sure that others will know the enjoyment that I have had?"

—MEGAN MCKENNA
in *Parables*

The spiritual practice of love builds community, as do kindness and gratitude, and prayer.

Try saying this silently to everyone and everything you see for thirty days and see what happens to your own soul: "I wish you happiness now and whatever will bring happiness to you in the future." If we said it to the sky, we would have to stop polluting; if we said it when we see the ponds and lakes and streams, we would have to stop using them as garbage dumps and sewers; if we said it to small children we would have to stop abusing them, even in the name of training; if we said it to people, we would have to stop stoking the fires of enmity around us. Beauty and human warmth would take root in us like a clear, hot June day. We would change.

—JOAN CHITTISTER
in *In a High Spiritual Season*

Thank someone for something. Go out of your way today to acknowledge the generosity of a person you know. It doesn't matter if you have known this man or woman your entire life, or have just met him or her and don't know if you will ever see the person again. Thanking him for a service rendered, or a favor given, or for help of some kind will enlarge your personal community to include yet another person.

Do you patronize a business establishment that always provides you with excellent service? Thank the proprietor, or tell an employee how much you appreciate the way you are treated every time you walk in, and ask him to pass the message on to the owner of the business. Or write a quick note to this effect and give it to the person you are talking to.

Thanking someone for a service rendered builds community, as well as friendship. It makes even the most insignificant encounters, like a stranger holding the door for you at the deli, all the more meaningful. It's a way for two people who will probably never know each other's names to connect, even for a moment.

—ALAN EPSTEIN
in *How to Have More Love in Your Life*

Most of us begin by praying for those people closest to us—our families and other loved ones, our spiritual friends, and those dependent on us. Whenever I invite intercessions from retreat groups, I am reminded of this: people quite naturally name those closest to them. There is nothing wrong with this; in fact, it is very right. But it is easy to get stuck within this intimate circle. With maturity, our horizons should broaden from the narrow circle of those known to us to include all those in need or suffering, whole nations as well as individuals. When I quiet my words and let myself simply be open, I find myself praying for the people who are dying *right now*, the babies who are being born *right now*, the frail old woman lying sleepless in a nursing home *right now*, the prisoners who are being tortured *right now*.

—MARGARET GUENTHER
in *Toward Holy Ground*

Community is created and renewed when individuals act in love and serve each other. A story called "The Messiah Is One of You" illustrates this truth.

Once upon a time there was an abbot of a monastery who was very good friends with the rabbi of a local synagogue. It was Europe, and times were hard. . . .

The abbot found his community dwindling and the faith life of his monks shallow and lifeless. Life in the monastery was dying. He went to his friend and wept. His friend, the rabbi, comforted him and told him: "There is something you need to know, my brother. We have long known in the Jewish community that the Messiah is one of you."

"What," exclaimed the abbot, "the Messiah is one of us? How can that be?"

But the rabbi insisted that it was so, and the abbot went back to his monastery wondering and praying, comforted and excited.

Once back in the monastery, walking down the halls and in the courtyard, he would pass by a monk and wonder if he was the one. Sitting in chapel, praying, he would hear a voice and look intently at a face and wonder if he was the one, and he began to treat all of his brothers with respect, with kindness and awe, with reverence. Soon it became quite noticeable.

One of the other brothers came to him and asked him what had happened to him. After some coaxing, he told him what the rabbi had said. Soon the other monk was looking at his brothers differently and wondering. The word spread through the monastery quickly: the Messiah is one of us. Soon the whole monastery was full of life, worship, kindness, and grace. The prayer life was rich and passionate, devoted, and the psalms and liturgy and services were alive and vibrant. Soon the surrounding villagers were coming to the services and listening and watching intently, and there were many who wished to join the community.

After their novitiate, when they took their vows, they were told the mystery, the truth that their life was based upon, the source of their strength and life together: The Messiah is one of us. The monastery grew and expanded into house after house, and all of the monks grew in wisdom, age, and grace before the others and the eyes of God. And they say still, if you stumble across this place, where there is life and hope and kindness and graciousness, that the secret is the same: The Messiah is one of us.

—MEGAN MCKENNA
in *Mary*

CHALLENGES TO COMMUNITY

In our communities, we are often challenged to live with those who are different from us, even those with whom we profoundly disagree. In these situations, it is useful to remember the spiritual practice of shadow, in which we recognize and deal with undesirable aspects of ourselves, including our fear, our intolerance, our bigotry, and our shame.

Recently I witnessed a moment of deep soulfulness between two strangers. I was at a bus stop, sitting next to a woman reading a newspaper, but I was totally engrossed in the performance of a fourteen-year-old on a skateboard. He had his baseball cap turned around with the bill in back, and he was skating beautifully and very fast. He buzzed by us once, then twice. When he came by a third time, he accidentally knocked the woman's newspaper out of her hands. She said, "Oh, why don't you grow up!"

I watched him glide down to the corner of the block, where he stood talking with his buddy. The two of them kept looking back over their shoulders at the woman. She hesitated for a moment, then rolled up her paper, tucked it under her arm, and walked into the street, motioning to him. "Won't you come here?" she called. "I want to talk to you."

Very reluctantly, he skated over to her, turned his cap around with the bill in front, and said, "Yeah?"

She said, "What I meant to say was that I was afraid that I might get hurt. I apologize for what I did say."

His face lit up, and he said, "How cool!"

> —ANGELES ARRIEN
> in *Nourishing the Soul*
> edited by Anne Simpkinson,
> Charles Simpkinson, and Rose Solari

There was a time when my aggravation with the system focused on Caspar Weinberger, secretary of defense. I'm sure he was no worse than many others, but there was something about his cold arrogance and apparent lack of wisdom that infuriated me. So I got a picture of Caspar and placed it on my *puja* (prayer) table with all my spiritual heroes. Then, each morning when I lit my incense and honored the beings represented on the puja table, I'd feel waves of love and appreciation toward my guru, Buddha, Christ, Anandamayi Ma, Ramana Maharshi, and Hanuman. I'd wish them each good morning with such tenderness. Then I'd come to Caspar's picture, and I'd feel my heart constrict, and I'd hear the coldness in my voice as I said, "Good morning, Caspar." Each morning I'd see what a long way I still had to go.

But wasn't Caspar just another face of God? Couldn't I oppose his actions and still keep my heart open to him? Wouldn't it be harder for him to become free from the role he was obviously trapped in if I, with my mind, just kept reinforcing the traps by identifying him with his acts? . . .

The Indian poet Kabir said . . . "Do what you do to another person, but never put them out of your heart." It's a tall order. But what else is there to do?

—RAM DASS
in *Compassion in Action*
by Ram Dass and Mirabai Bush

There is a danger, in issue-oriented groups not based on community, that the enemy is seen as being the one outside of the group. The world gets divided between "the good" and "the bad." We are among the good; the others are the bad. In issue-oriented groups, the enemy is always outside. We must struggle against all those who are outside of our group, all those who are of the other party.

True community is different because of the realization that the evil is inside—not just inside the community, but inside me. I cannot think of taking the speck of dust out of my neighbor's eye unless I'm working on the log in my own. Evil is here in me. Warfare is inside my own community, and I am called to be an agent of peace there. But warfare is also in me and I am called to seek wholeness inside of myself. Healing begins here, in myself. Wholeness and unity begin inside of myself. If I am growing toward wholeness, then I'll be an agent of wholeness. If our community is an agent of wholeness, then it will be a source of life for the world around it.

—JEAN VANIER
in *From Brokenness to Community*

On the subway car there was an old black woman, a bag lady, stooped, asleep or unconscious, her smell overwhelming—so overwhelming that her end of the car was empty, because others who got on gave her a very wide berth. A white man in his mid or late twenties stepped on board and immediately began to fan the air with grand gestures. He said "Oh, God!" loudly and to no one in particular but with great self-importance, his eyes scanning the passengers for someone with whom to complete the drama of his observations. He chose a young black boy of about twelve or thirteen years of age, sweet-faced, gentle-eyed, a knapsack of books on his back, a school kid in a baseball jacket with an adolescent daydream written across his face. The white man looked over at him and scolded in a very loud voice: "You see that? That's why you'd better learn how to work!" Heads turned. The kid looked stricken, then giggled tensely, looked back at the subway car full of those robotic eyes. A wall fell across the introspection of only a moment before, and he smiled a smile of pure incipient rage.

—PATRICIA J. WILLIAMS
in *The Rooster's Egg*

A woman complained to a visiting friend that her neighbor was a poor housekeeper. "You should see how dirty her children are—and her house. It is almost a disgrace to be living in the same neighborhood as her. Take a look at those clothes she has hung out on the line. See the black streaks on the sheets and towels!"

The friend walked up to the window and said, "I think the clothes are quite clean, my dear. The streaks are on your window."

—ANTHONY DE MELLO
in *The Heart of the Enlightened*

In many urban areas, large populations of homeless people live as constant reminders that there is a shadow side to the good life, a consequence of our internal poverty.

The tormented, lost wanderers of our city are all about us; they huddle, sleep, awaken, stagger about, hold out their beggar hands. We wear their presence like a great societal shroud—our own. In them that other city, a city of shame, stirs to life. Day and night. . . .

495

THE MYSTERY

The letter "X" is often used to symbolize the unknown. In this Alphabet of Spiritual Literacy, it signifies the Great Unknown at the center of the universe—the Mystery.

"The first mystery is simply that there is a mystery. A mystery that can never be explained or understood. Only encountered from time to time. Nothing is obvious. Everything conceals something else. . . . Spiritual awareness is born of encounters with the mystery," Rabbi Lawrence Kushner tells us.

The world is drenched in mystery and no matter what we do, we can never cut through it all and grab hold of the answer, the one explanation. "X" factors abound, upsetting our rational conclusions.

German Catholic theologian Karl Rahner admits, "I must confess to you in all honesty, that for me, God is and has always been absolute mystery." That's the right spirit. Put away all the paraphernalia designed to unmask the Creator of the Universe. Let God be God.

"There are many theological questions which can be asked—even interesting ones, for which the truest answer this side of the grave is, 'I don't know,'" Episcopal Bishop James A. Pike states. Who can understand the nature of evil or the reasons for the great suffering in the world? Who can pin down why human beings are so prone to self-destruction? Reason comes up short trying to answer these piercing questions. "The eye goes blind," the poet Rumi warns, "when it only wants to see *why*."

Jewish theologian Martin Buber asserts, "Real faith means holding ourselves open to the unconditional mystery which we encounter in every sphere of our life which cannot be compressed in any formula."

French writer Francis Rene de Chauterbriand has it right: "There is nothing beautiful or sweet or great in life that is not mysterious." The erotic touch that stirs our desire, the majesty of a rainbow from horizon to horizon, the feelings of power in a sacred place, the voice of a deceased ancestor in our ears, the unconditional love of a pet dog.

Accept the mystery of being loved by the Divine Magnet. "Once that happens, nothing is accidental, casual or futile anymore," notes Catholic priest and writer Henri J. M. Nouwen.

"You are hugged by the arms of the mystery of God," declares Hildegard of Bingen, a thirteenth-century mystic. "There is a mystic in every one of us yearning to play again in the universe," Matthew Fox, a modern-day mystic, affirms. Set the mystic free. And heed the words of Rumi, the Sufi seer:

> If you want what visible reality
> can give, you're an employee.
>
> If you want the unseen world,
> you're not living your truth.
>
> Both wishes are foolish,
> but you'll be forgiven for forgetting
> that what you really want is
> love's confusing joy.

The homeless live out, in dreadful, literal detail, the poverty we would rather conceal—from God, from ourselves. They are icons of the "other side" of ourselves; they are icons of modern life turned inside out. That shroud again, its seams and rents shamefully exposed.

Their language—their curses and ravings, their unaccountable silence—is a code. It is a totting up of the cost: the lives we lead, the lives we long to lead. Lives of appetite, envy, racism—that "good life" so commended to all, so lethal and leveling; the cost of weapons and waste and war, the fuel of the great voracious urban engine.

The homeless are the shadow at the heart of things, the shadow we flee. It is named death.

—DANIEL BERRIGAN and MARGARET PARKER
in *Stations*

There is a story about St. Francis and the Wolf of Gubbio. The version we like best is told by Catholic theologian John Shea in his book Starlight, *and he credits it to the storyteller Bob Wilhelm, plus or minus a few details. Here is a paraphrase of the story:*

The people of the little Italian city of Gubbio are understandably very proud of their beautiful home. Then one night a shadow comes out of the nearby woods and prowls the streets. In the morning the people of Gubbio find a mangled and gnawed dead body. This happens again and again. Finally an old woman says that she has seen a wolf on the streets at night. The terrified people decide to ask a holy man who has a reputation for being able to talk to animals for his help. They send a delegation to get St. Francis.

They have very specific ideas on what St. Francis should tell the wolf. First, he should preach to him and remind him to obey the commandment against killing and to follow Christ's commandment about loving God and neighbors. And then, just in case, since a wolf is, after all, a wolf, he should tell the wolf to move to someone else's city.

Francis goes into the forest to meet the strange shadow, addressing it as "Brother Wolf." Then he returns to the town square. "My good people of Gubbio, the answer is very simple. You must feed your wolf." The people are furious, especially with the suggestion that this uninvited beast in their midst is somehow to be regarded as "their wolf." But they do feed it, and the killing stops.

For more than a year now, we have had an encampment of homeless people on our block. There is scaffolding on the building at the corner, and it provides protection from the elements. Every night around six o'clock, a group of about twenty people construct sleeping quarters out of cardboard boxes. Twelve hours later the maintenance men from the building remove the empty boxes, clean up any trash, and wash down the sidewalks. Considering the reputation of homeless shelters in the city, I have figured that this arrangement may be the best one available to many of these people.

But Fred and I seem to be in the minority in our building. At one of our co-op meetings, the "problem of the homeless" came up, and I listened to the complaints and fears of my neighbors about the "wolf" in our midst. The homeless are dirty. They get drunk and throw up on the street. They are bums. They could be deranged. One did ask for money. They should follow the American commandment and get a job.

I mention that I have seen the outreach counselors from the homeless coalition talking with these people about other options, yet the same individuals choose to return to our block night after night. Perhaps we should realize that they are our neighbors now. They impress me as a pretty quiet group. Lots of times they are reading when I walk by, and most of the time they are sleeping. "I saw one of them get mad and yell at this man on the street," someone reports. The consensus: the homeless are dangerous.

Now someone says he will speak to the building manager. If they would quit cleaning up after the homeless, they would go away. How about if a group from the community went to talk to them? (I'm thinking now, "And say what? Go away?") We could call the police and report that the homeless are threatening us, and the police would make them move. "Where?" I ask, "There isn't any low income housing available, and the shelters are overcrowded and turning people away." The reply comes from several voices: "To someone else's street."

My neighbors never consider sending for a holy man to help in this situation. But I am reminded of how similar we are to the people of Gubbio when, a few days later, I hear what one of my neighbors has said about me: "We need to talk to Mary Ann again about the homeless. I think she's feeding them."

I'm not, I confess. I do send money to support the work of the homeless advocacy groups who have some concrete ideas about what can be done. But, in all honesty, I do not know what is the best way to offer hospitality to these strangers in our midst.

In the next reading, Thomas Moore considers how some of the problems in our communities are related to the loss of soul.

. . . Only in a thoroughly unrelated world can we poison nature without conscience, neglect our children and the poor, and righteously slay thousands of enemy soldiers because we don't have the patience or imagination for negotiation.

As a tonic for our troubled world, friendship and behaving with consideration and care may seem light and even frivolous, but that could be because we have lost a sensitivity to the values of soul. Our soullessness appears in our tough pragmatism and in our bottom-line thinking. Even our social sciences seem more secure studying hard issues such as chemicals, traumas, and direct family influences as sources of our problems, instead of the philosophical issues that lie deep in society. In compensation, some turn to otherworldly spirituality, seeking to transcend the limits of human knowledge and effort through preternatural means. In neither case is soul nurtured. We need a return to the simple virtues of friendship and manners if we are to restore life to humane dimensions and values.

—Thomas Moore
in *Soul Mates*

Community can also be enriched and deepened by meaningful rituals.

Circle to Reclaim Sacredness and Safety

A woman was raped on a Sunday morning while running on a walking path in a small town. The circle was called on the following Sunday morning by a local peace group. About seventy-five women and men gathered on the same path and walked in silence along it, following two women playing a heartbeat rhythm on their drums, all mindful of the atrocity perpetrated here and all the many others who are raped and abused.

When the group arrived at the site they formed a circle and after the circle was cast various people read poems and statements and led a few songs. A small rock carved as a goddess was passed to each person in the circle and they were asked to speak their feelings, prayers, and commitments and to place these into the goddess-rock as they held it in turn. A woman and man then buried the goddess along the pathway, reclaiming the area as sacred ground and asking for protection for all those who pass there. Everyone left the circle committed to finding ways to end violence against women.

—SEDONIA CAHILL and JOSHUA HALPERN
in *The Ceremonial Circle*

The spiritual practices of forgiveness, justice, openness, and compassion extend community into powerful territory.

Lloyd LeBlanc has told me that he would have been content with imprisonment for Patrick Sonnier. He went to the execution, he says, not for revenge, but hoping for an apology. Patrick Sonnier had not disappointed him. Before sitting in the electric chair he had said, "Mr. LeBlanc, I want to ask your forgiveness for what me and Eddie done," and Lloyd LeBlanc had nodded his head, signaling a forgiveness he had already given. He says that when he arrived with sheriff's deputies there in the cane field to identify his son, he had knelt by his boy—"laying down there with his two little eyes sticking out like bullets"—and prayed the Our Father. And when he came to the words: "Forgive us our trespasses as we forgive those who trespass against us," he had not halted or equivocated, and he said, "Whoever did this, I forgive them." But he acknowledges that it's a struggle to overcome the feelings of bitterness and revenge that well up, especially as he remembers David's birthday year by year and loses him all over again: David at twenty, David at twenty-five, David getting married, David standing at the back door with his little ones clustered around his knees, grownup David, a man like himself, whom he will never know. Forgiveness is never going to be easy. Each day it must be prayed for and struggled for and won.

—HELEN PREJEAN
in *Dead Man Walking*

Compassion means
that if I see my friend and my enemy
in equal need,
I shall help them both equally.
Justice demands
that we seek
and find the stranger,
the broken, the prisoner
and comfort them
and offer them our help.

    —MECHTILD OF MAGDEBURG
     Meditations with Mechtild of Magdeburg
     by Sue Woodruff

An old Rabbi once asked his pupils how they could tell when the night had ended and the day had begun.

"Could it be," asked one of the students, "when you can see an animal in the distance and tell whether it's a sheep or a dog?"

"No," answered the Rabbi.

Another asked, "Is it when you can look at a tree in the distance and tell whether it's a fig tree or a peach tree?"

"No," answered the Rabbi.

"Then what is it?" the pupils demanded.

"It is when you can look on the face of any man or woman and see that it is your sister or brother. Because if you cannot see this, it is still night."

    —HASIDIC TALE
     quoted in *Peacemaking Day by Day*

PLEASE CALL ME BY MY TRUE NAMES

Don't say that I will depart tomorrow—
even today I am still arriving.

Look deeply: every second I am arriving
to be a bud on a Spring branch,

to be a tiny bird, with still-fragile wings,
learning to sing in my new nest,
to be a caterpillar in the heart of a flower,
to be a jewel hiding itself in a stone.

I still arrive, in order to laugh and to cry,
to fear and to hope.
The rhythm of my heart is the birth and death
of all that is alive.

I am the mayfly metamorphosing
on the surface of the river.
And I am the bird
that swoops down to swallow the mayfly.

I am a frog swimming happily
in the clear water of a pond.
And I am the grass-snake
that silently feeds itself on the frog.

I am the child in Uganda, all skin and bones,
my legs as thin as bamboo sticks.
And I am the arms merchant,
selling deadly weapons to Uganda.

I am the twelve-year-old girl,
refugee on a small boat,
who throws herself into the ocean
after being raped by a sea pirate.
And I am the pirate,
my heart not yet capable
of seeing and loving.

I am a member of the politburo,
with plenty of power in my hands.
And I am the man who has to pay
his "debt of blood" to my people
dying slowly in a forced-labor camp.

My joy is like Spring, so warm
it makes flowers bloom all over the Earth.
My pain is like a river of tears,
so vast it fills the four oceans.

Please call me by my true names,
so I can hear all my cries and laughter at once,
so I can see that my joy and my pain are one.

Please call me by my true names,
so I can wake up
and the door of my heart
could be left open,
the door of compassion.

—THICH NHAT HANH
in *Call Me by My True Names*

MYSTICAL EXPERIENCES

"We are here," Thich Nhat Hanh says, "to awaken from the illusion of our separateness." Our deepest sense of community comes in mystical moments when we feel at one with all the creation. The setting may be quite ordinary; the experience, extraordinary.

I was five and lying in high grass. A bee hummed close to my eye and frightened me. Then the bee started to suck honey and at that very moment I became sun, bee, flower and grass. "Me" had evaporated with my fear.

Then, when I was eleven, on a country road, I saw a snow flurry approach from afar. The first few snowflakes fell around my feet from the dark wintry sky. I saw how some of the flakes melted immediately on impact, others stayed. Again, Me disappeared, melted with snowflakes, became one with road and sky and snowstorm. It has happened often, always when least expected.

A few hours before leaving on this journey, driving somewhere in New Jersey, I lost my way back to the parkway. At last at a traffic light stood a pedestrian, a very fat man in a battered homburg hat. A greasy cigar stump stuck out straight from what looked more like a snout than a face.

"How do I get to Route 4?" I called out.

"Route 4," he repeated, chewing on his cigar. "Nothing to it!" His little eyes twinkled with kindness. "Take a left at the second light, can't miss it!" He had put his fat hand on my sleeve and given a friendly squeeze.

I looked at him and saw. I tried to thank him, but no sound came. I made a kind of bow. The jelly had become Man.

What is spiritual experience? A snowflake melting, a bee sucking honey, a fat man at a traffic light. Trivia.

—FREDERICK FRANCK
in *Fingers Pointing Toward the Sacred*

*I was just a five-year-old boy when I had my first spiritual experience.
I lay down in the grass on a neighbor's lawn and looked across the
street. There under a clear blue sky, my best friend's mother was hanging out the wash in the wind. A deep feeling came over me that I was
one with her, the grass, the sky, the wind, and the wash.*

I remember this illumination happening to me one noontime as I
stood in the kitchen and watched my children eat peanut butter and
jelly sandwiches. We were having a most unremarkable time on a
nondescript day, in the midst of the most quotidian of routines. I
hadn't censed the table, sprinkled the place mats with holy water, or
uttered a sanctifying prayer over the Wonder bread. I wasn't feeling particularly "spiritual." But, heeding I don't know what
prompting, I stopped abruptly in mid-bustle, or mid-woolgathering,
and looked around me as if I were opening my eyes for the first
time that day.

The entire room became luminous and so alive with movement
that everything seemed suspended—yet pulsating—for an
instant, like light waves. Intense joy swelled inside me, and my
immediate response was gratitude—gratitude for everything,
every tiny thing in that space. The shelter of the room became a
warm embrace; water flowing from the tap seemed a tremendous
miracle; and my children became, for a moment, not my progeny
or my charges or my tasks, but eternal beings of infinite singular-
ity and complexity whom I would one day, in an age to come,
apprehend in their splendid fullness.

—HOLLY BRIDGES ELLIOTT
in *Beholding God in Many Faces*

I was sitting alone on the downtown IRT on my way to pick up the
children at their after-school music classes. The train had just pulled
out of the Twenty-third Street station and was accelerating to its

505

YEARNING

There is within all of us a great yearning for transcendental meaning or a connection with the Heart of the Universe. As Nicaraguan poet and priest Ernesto Cardenal puts it, "We have always wanted something beyond what we wanted."

Desire is a great force field of energy that takes us beyond ourselves. It keeps us in touch with our senses and creates an appreciation for the multidimensional pleasures of life.

It animates our erotic feelings and sends us whirling into the wonderful dance of sexuality. It funds our capacity to know and be known. And it fuels our fascination with beauty and mystery.

"The great pathfinders," according to philosopher Sam Keen, "testify that the motive for the spiritual life is awakening desire rather than grim duty."

This desire is boundless; it is hard to pin down with definitions. Third-century Christian philosopher St. Augustine expresses it well when he declares, "O Lord, You have created us for Yourself, and our hearts are restless until they rest in Thee."

Part of the restlessness stems from our feelings of incompleteness. There is something missing which only the power and presence of the Supreme One can fill. In Psalm 42:1, we read, "As a deer yearns for running streams, so I yearn for you, my God."

There is something awesome about entering the territory of the Endless Fountain where things are not neatly mapped out or clearly designated. Fortunately, many pioneers of desire have gone before us and left behind spiritual resources that can help us find our way.

It is our boundless desire that enables us to cross borders to new places. It is our boundless desire that keeps us moving even through dark nights of the soul. And it is our boundless desire that brings us home with the intention of sharing our good news with others.

"You have nothing infinite except your soul's love and desire," says fourteenth-century Catholic mystic Catherine of Siena. It is this deep yearning that spurs our search for the Compassionate One.

Etty Hillesum, a victim of the Nazi concentration camps, offers another view: "Our desire must be like a slow and steady ship sailing across endless oceans, never in search of safe anchorage." Our hearts are restless but there is no final resting point.

Instead there are spiritual practices which express our yearning for the Shining One. They help us luxuriate in the mysteries of world, self, and the Sacred.

Love your spiritual yearning and strengthen it. Your heart's desire is a passport to a pluriverse of meanings.

YOU

The seed of the Blessed One is planted in us but we have trouble accepting this reality. "Our deepest fear is not that we are inadequate," writes best-selling spirituality author Marianne Williamson. "Our deepest fear is that we are powerful beyond measure. It is our light, not our darkness, that most frightens us. We ask ourselves, who am I to be brilliant, gorgeous, talented, and fabulous? Actually who are you not to be? You are a child of God."

Nicaraguan Catholic priest Ernesto Cardenal adds: "God has been thinking of me since before I was born, for all eternity. God loves us more than we love ourselves."

Why is it so hard to accept the good news? Perhaps because we are our own worst enemies. Perhaps because others make us feel like damaged goods. Perhaps because we think it's too much of a burden to bear.

"Do you know what you are?" Spanish cellist Pablo Casals asks. "You are a marvel. You are unique. In all the world there is no other . . . exactly like you." Sing your unique song with gusto. And remember the advice of the Bal Shem Tov, a Jewish mystic, "Compare not yourself with anybody else lest you spoil God's curriculum."

We are each a unique blend of good and evil. The choice is ours in every moment which parts of ourselves to put out into the world. Thorin, speaking to Bilbo in J. R. R. Tolkien's *The Hobbit*, says, "There is more in you of good than you know . . . some courage and some wisdom blended in measure."

Tap into that courage and unspool that wisdom. "We have a thrifty God," observes art historian Sister Wendy Beckett, "who lets nothing that is good within us ever go to waste."

The German mystic Meister Eckhart repeats the point: "Become aware of what is in you. Announce it, pronounce it, produce it and give birth to it."

You do not need to try to become special. The Godseed inside makes you already special. "The Greek Orthodox have a spiritual injunction that implores a person to 'become what you are,'" explains writer Holly Bridges Elliott. "This means by virtue of your creation in the image of God and by your baptism, remember your true humanity, remember that your authentic self is inhabited by God and is a holy creation."

You have an assignment and a purpose in life. This is your mission, should you choose to accept it.

"God's dream is to be not alone but to have humanity as a partner in the drama of continuous creation," Rabbi Abraham Joshua Heschel writes. Life is a great adventure, we are partners with the Godhead, and though our role may be small, the honor is still ours.

"The world needs all of our power and love and energy, and each of us has something to give," essayist Merle Shain reflects. "The trick is to find it and use it, to find it and give it away, so there will always be more. We can be lights for each other, and through each other's illumination we will see the way. Each of us is a seed, a silent promise, and it is always spring."

cruising speed. All around me people sat bundled up in mufflers, damp woolen coats, and slush-stained boots, reading newspapers or staring off blankly as the train jerked along the track. The air was cold and close, with the smell of stale tobacco clinging to winter coats. An elderly pair exchanged words in a Slavic tongue; a mother read an advertising sign to her three bedraggled, open-mouthed children.

Then suddenly the dull light in the car began to shine with exceptional lucidity until everything around me was glowing with an indescribable aura, and I saw in the row of motley passengers opposite the miraculous connection of all living beings. Not felt; saw. What began as a desultory thought grew to a vision, large and unifying, in which all the people in the car hurtling downtown together, including myself, like all the people on the planet hurtling together around the sun—our entire living cohort—formed one united family, indissolubly connected by the rare and mysterious accident of life. No matter what our countless superficial differences, we were equal, we were one, by virtue of simply being alive at this moment out of all the possible moments stretching endlessly back and ahead. The vision filled me with overwhelming love for the entire human race and a feeling that no matter how incomplete or damaged our lives, we were surpassingly lucky to be alive. Then the train pulled into the station and I got off.

—ALIX KATES SHULMAN
in *Drinking the Rain*

★★★
☰
★ ★★

The day I first saw inner earth from a bus window, I was one of many travelers poised between homes. We sat arm to arm, skin to skin. For a little while we were all anyone else had, homeless. At every abrupt turn the bus made, we were thrown helter skelter into one another, while outside of our windows the vast outer world was showing us what our inner earth looked like.

And so it is with you. You, too, are a traveler through this earth, sharing with everyone else not only an outer world that needs your care, but also a precious inner earth that is its reflection. You have only to look to this inner earth of yours, gently, and without haste, to discover how remarkably similar to the outer natural earth you are. She is a close relative of yours.

—JOAN SAURO
in *Whole Earth Meditation*

In New England, Frederick Buechner describes a moment of reverie when the sounds of workers making repairs on his house merged with the sounds of the world, and he came to a new insight about his life. Then, from a remote island off the northwest Pacific coast, anthropologist Richard Nelson identifies his self totally with the natural world.

The swallows, the rooster, the workmen, my stomach, all with their elusive rhythms, their harmonies and disharmonies and counterpoint, became, as I listened, the sound of my own life speaking to me. Never had I heard just such a coming together of sounds before, and it is unlikely that I will ever hear them in just the same combination again. Their music was unique and unrepeatable and beyond describing in its freshness. I have no clear idea what the sounds meant or what my life was telling me. What does the song of a swallow mean? What is the muffled sound of a hammer trying to tell? And yet as I listened to those sounds, and listened with something more than just my hearing, I was moved by their inexpressible eloquence and suggestiveness, by the sense I had that they were a music rising up out of the mystery of not just my life, but of life itself. In much the same way, that is what I mean by saying that God speaks into or out of the thick of our days.

—FREDERICK BUECHNER
in *The Sacred Journey*

There is nothing in me that is not of earth, no split instant of separateness, no particle that disunites me from the surroundings. I am no less than the earth itself. The rivers run through my veins, the winds blow in and out with my breath, the soil makes my flesh, the sun's heat smolders inside me. A sickness or injury that befalls the earth befalls me. A fouled molecule that runs through the earth runs through me. Where the earth is cleansed and nourished, its purity infuses me. The life of the earth is my life. My eyes are the earth gazing at itself.

—RICHARD NELSON
in *The Island Within*

We can be a community of purpose trying to change the world for the better.

I have often felt myself to be a point of light, connected to everyone I have ever loved or mattered to, each also being a point of light, in turn connected to those they love, so that somehow we are all part of a vast web of twinkling lights. I think that each individual light can grow brighter or dimmer over the course of a lifetime, and that whenever a light goes out on this web, it affects me. It feels as if everyone who acts compassionately, works to raise consciousness, to save the planet, to make a difference in some significant way is linked to everyone else who also does.

—JEAN SHINODA BOLEN
in *Crossing to Avalon*

Fred and I had the experience of being points of light on vacation while swimming in a shallow ocean inlet. Almost completely surrounded by mangrove trees, it was a virtual nursery for all kinds of ocean creatures, including a thick concentration of tiny bioluminescent organisms. Their light is similar to firefly light but, unlike fireflies who light up to attract the opposite sex, these bioorganisms light up when they are disturbed. Anything in the water that moves—a boat, fish, people—can bring on this light with just the slightest movement.

The scene and the sensations of that bioluminescent bay are still vivid to me: I am swimming in my own visible aura. My fingertips moving across the water are carriers of healing blue light. I raise my wet arms to the heavens and stardust runs down them. I float on the water and, spreading my legs and arms, make an angel of light. I swim breaststroke, clearing a path of light. I make a fist, open it suddenly, and light energy bursts from my hands.

I remember thinking during that swim how nice it would be if we could always see our effect on the world as clearly as I could see it then. Every action causes a reaction. All the lines of connection between my self and the world are visible. And everything is related to everything else.

The village had no rain for a long time. All the prayers and processions had been in vain; the skies remained shut tight. In the hour of its greatest need, the village turned to the Great Rainmaker. He came and asked for a hut on the edge of the village and for a five-day supply of bread and water. Then he sent the people off to their daily work. On the fourth day it rained. The people came in jubilation from their fields and workplaces and gathered in front of the rainmaker's hut to congratulate him and ask about the mystery of rainmaking. He answered them: "I can't make it rain." "But it is raining," the people said. The rainmaker explained: "When I came to your village, I saw the inner and outer disorder. I went into the hut and got myself in order. When I was in order, you, too, got in order; and when you were in order, nature got in order, and when nature got in order, it rained."

—WILLIGIS JAGER
in *Search for the Meaning of Life*

In a recent article on astrophysics I came across the beautiful and imaginative concept known as "the butterfly effect." If a butterfly winging over the fields around Crosswicks should be hurt, the effect would be felt in galaxies thousands of light years away. The interrelationship of all of Creation is sensitive in a way we are just beginning to understand. If a butterfly is hurt, we are hurt. If the bell tolls, it tolls for us.

—MADELEINE L'ENGLE
in *A Stone for a Pillow*

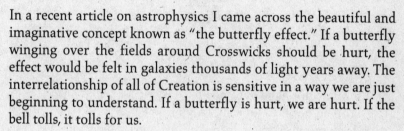

The most lasting ways to build community are by listening and by making commitments, to each other and to our animal and plant relatives.

"Listen, humans, this is our world. For hundreds of millions of years we have been evolving our ways, rich in our own wisdom. Now our days are coming to a close because of what you are doing. It is time for you to hear us."

"I am lichen. I turn rock into soil. I worked as the glaciers retreated, as other life-forms came and went. I thought nothing could stop me . . . until now. Now I am being poisoned by acid rain."

"Your pesticides are in me now. The eggshells are so fragile they break under my weight, break before my young are ready to hatch."

"Listen, humans. I am raccoon, I speak for the raccoon people. See my hand? It is like yours. On soft ground you see its imprint, and know I've passed. What marks on this world are you leaving behind you?"

The people seated in a circle are speaking extemporaneously. Stepping aside from their identification as humans, they are letting themselves be spokespersons for other life-forms. They are meeting in the Council of All Beings, a central part of the workshop they attend. These men, women, and young people have gathered in this workshop to share concerns for their planet. They have met to tell the truth about what they see happening to their world and to move beyond despair.

—JOANNA MACY
in *World as Lover, World as Self*

WILD GEESE

You do not have to be good.
You do not have to walk on your knees
for a hundred miles through the desert, repenting.
You only have to let the soft animal of your body
    love what it loves.
Tell me about despair, yours, and I will tell you mine.
Meanwhile the world goes on.
Meanwhile the sun and the clear pebbles of the rain
are moving across the landscapes,
over the prairies and the deep trees,
the mountains and the rivers.
Meanwhile the wild geese, high in the clean blue air,
are heading home again.
Whoever you are, no matter how lonely,
the world offers itself to your imagination,
calls to you like the wild geese, harsh and exciting—
over and over announcing your place
in the family of things.

—MARY OLIVER
in *Dream Work*

Heaven is my father
and earth is my mother
and even such a small creature as I
finds an intimate place in its midst.
That which extends throughout the universe
I regard as my body
and that which directs the universe,
I regard as my nature.
All people are my brothers and sisters
and all things are my companions.

—CHANG-TSAI
quoted in *The Fruitful Darkness*
by Joan Halifax

A mystical understanding of community means that nothing is ever truly "out there." Everything around us is an essential part of our being.

Oren Lyons was the first Onondagan to enter college. When he returned to his reservation for his first vacation, his uncle proposed a fishing trip on a lake. Once he had his nephew in the middle of the lake where he wanted him, he began to interrogate him. "Well, Oren," he said, "you've been to college; you must be pretty smart now from all they've been teaching you. Let me ask you a question. Who are you?" Taken aback by the question, Oren fumbled for an answer. "What do you mean, who am I? Why, I'm your nephew, of course." His uncle rejected his answer and repeated his question. Successively, the nephew ventured that he was Oren Lyons, an Onondagan, a human being, a man, a young man, all to no avail. When his uncle had reduced him to silence and he asked to be informed as to who he was, his uncle said, "Do you see that bluff over there? Oren, you *are* that bluff. And that giant pine on the other shore? Oren, you are that pine. And this water that supports our boat? You are this water."

—HUSTON SMITH
in *The World's Religions*

There is one more ring on our circle of connections. For many people, the mystical feeling of oneness with the universe includes a merging with the sacred—with the All in One. It is hard to imagine this yearning for unity being expressed any better than Rumi does it in this poem.

SAY I AM YOU

I am dust particles in sunlight.
I am the round sun.

To the bits of dust I say, *Stay.*
To the sun, *Keep moving.*

I am morning mist,
and the breathing of evening.

I am wind in the top of a grove,
and surf on the cliff.

Mast, rudder, helmsman, and keel,
I am also the coral reef they founder on.

I am a tree with a trained parrot in its branches.
Silence, thought, and voice.

The musical air coming through a flute,
a spark of a stone, a flickering

in metal. Both candle,
and the moth crazy around it.

Rose, and the nightingale
lost in the fragrance.

I am all orders of being, the circling galaxy,
the evolutionary intelligence, the lift,

and the falling away. What is,
and what isn't. You who know

Jelaluddin, You the one
in all, say who

I am. Say I
am You.

—JELALUDDIN RUMI
in *The Essential Rumi*
translated by Coleman Barks
with John Moyne, A. J. Arberry,
and Reynold Nicholson

PRACTICING SPIRITUAL LITERACY: COMMUNITY

CONVERSATIONS/JOURNAL ENTRIES

- Describe to your family and friends, or in your journal, your most satisfying experience of community. What made it so memorable?

- Make a list of the legacies that your favorite community will pass on to the next generation.

- What are the main benefits you look for in joining a community? What do you expect to give in return?

- Do you sense that you belong to a community that is not limited by time? Do you feel the presence of what in some traditions is called the "cloud of witnesses"?

- What commitment to causes has meant the most to you? What experience of community has enabled you to affirm the link between caring and commitment?

- When was the last time you projected your feelings of self-disgust, anger, and alienation on others? What have you done to try to curb your prejudices?

- Recall an incident in your life where a community you belonged to drew a line and excluded others from membership. How did you feel? What were the consequences? How did this experience influence your idealism about community?

- Much has been written lately about the impact of computers and modern communications technologies upon community life. For example, as more people work out of their homes, they are less involved in work communities and may be more involved in their neighborhoods. Through computer communications, individuals in physically isolated areas can participate in other types of communities. What has been your experience of the impact of new technologies? What do you predict will be the impact in the future?

- What have you found to be the best ways for people from different classes, religions, or ethnic traditions to learn to appreciate and understand each other?

- Do a journal exercise on "the butterfly effect." Try to imagine how one of your deeds has a reverberation in a faraway place.

- Have you ever had a mystical experience—a feeling of oneness with the universe, a transcendence of self, or a moment of deep insight? What happened? What was the spiritual message?

ACTIVITIES/PROJECTS

- With family and friends, make a drawing or a model of the ideal community where you would like to live.

- Read the book *Stone Soup* by Marcia Brown to some children. This is a story about how three soldiers taught a French village to make soup out of stones. Ask the children what ingredients they would bring to the soup pot. Then have the children read you their favorite books about communities.

- Consult with your colleagues at work about one project you could do which would be a fitting expression of civic duty.

- Hold a Council of Beings in your neighborhood. One way to get started is by putting the names of different members of your extended community—including the animals, trees, plants, and rocks—in a hat and having each participant draw a role to play. You may even want to have the drawing in advance so that people have a chance to research what their "beings" might want to say. During the council, pass a talking stick or other symbol around to signify that the speaker is not to be interrupted. Then, as a group, make a list of things you can do to address some of the issues raised by the beings.

- Rent a video about community and some of the forces which are tearing it apart. These films are highly recommended: *City of Hope, City of Joy, A Cry in the Dark, Hoosiers, Local Hero, The Long Walk Home, Matewan, The Milagro Beanfield War, The Mission,* and *The Women of Brewster Place.*

SPIRITUAL EXERCISES/RITUALS

- Create a ritual to express the life-sustaining nourishment and fellowship you derive from community. Find or make a symbol of community to give to those attending.

- St. Martin of Tours says: "All mystics come from the same country and speak the same language." Sample some readings from Sufi, Jewish, and Christian mystics.

- Extend the circle of your intercessory prayer to persons not usually included in your concerns.

- Do a mystical meditation upon your unity with all living beings on the planet.

A Day in
the Spiritual Life

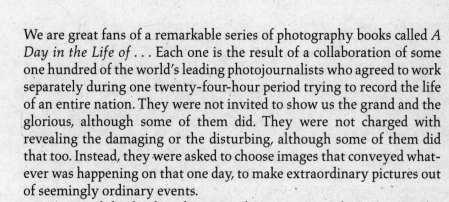

We are great fans of a remarkable series of photography books called *A Day in the Life of* . . . Each one is the result of a collaboration of some one hundred of the world's leading photojournalists who agreed to work separately during one twenty-four-hour period trying to record the life of an entire nation. They were not invited to show us the grand and the glorious, although some of them did. They were not charged with revealing the damaging or the disturbing, although some of them did that too. Instead, they were asked to choose images that conveyed whatever was happening on that one day, to make extraordinary pictures out of seemingly ordinary events.

We opened this book with a story about Auggie in the movie *Smoke*, a photographer who would have felt right at home working on one of the *A Day in the Life* projects. By focusing his camera every day on the corner where he works, he discovers the spirituality of place.

This book has been a little like Auggie's photography albums. Each chapter has provided similarly concentrated looks at different aspects of daily life. We have explored how spiritual literacy changes our perceptions of things, places, nature, animals, leisure, creativity, service, body, relationships, and community.

Now it is time to put it all together and train our newly spiritually literate lens on one twenty-four-hour period. Take one day, any day, and you can find within it a world of sacred meanings.

WAKING UP

Darkness was upon the face of the deep, and God said, "Let there be light." Darkness laps at my sleeping face like a tide, and God says,

"Let there be Buechner." Why not? Out of the primeval chaos of sleep he calls me to be a life again. . . . He calls me to be this rather than that; he calls me to be here rather than there; he calls me to be now rather than then. . . . Waking into the new day, we are all of us Adam on the morning of creation, and the world is ours to name. Out of many fragments we are called to put back together a self again.

—FREDERICK BUECHNER
in *The Alphabet of Grace*

WASHING YOUR HANDS

If you look deeply into the palm of your hand, you will see your parents and all generations of your ancestors. All of them are alive in this moment. Each is present in your body. You are the continuation of each of these people.

—THICH NHAT HANH
in *Present Moment Wonderful Moment*

GOING TO THE KITCHEN

The kitchen is alchemical,
a place where we cook—actually
and spiritually. We come to it
for nourishment and ease.
We come to it as to a center—

the heart of the house,
the heart of dwelling.
In the kitchen we are one,
linked by hunger—
actual hunger and spiritual hunger.

We go to the kitchen to be
nourished and revealed.
It is a holy place.

—GUNILLA NORRIS
in *Becoming Bread*

WAITING FOR THE WATER TO BOIL

Standing at the kitchen stove early in the morning, looking past it through an open window, I feel sleepy, unfocused, fragmented, waiting for the coffee water to boil. An impulse to pray arises in me, but the thought of God remains as vague and unfocused as I feel myself to be at that moment. I am not in the mood for words. A few months ago I was in India, and now, without consciously thinking what to do, I find myself raising my hands in front of my face and putting palms together, the way Indians do in their gesture of respect. Quickly, my emotions change. I become aware of a stir of energy throughout my body. My hands, palms still together, move downward until they are in front of my navel. I feel centered for the first time since arising, and the tree leaves outside the window begin to sparkle. During this little rite, which I have never performed before, no words pass through my consciousness. Theologically, there is either nothing or everything to say about it. Some, including myself, will call it prayer, others not. In any case, it was a short and subtle ritual of transformation.

—TOM F. DRIVER
in *The Magic of Ritual*

PICKING UP A SPOON

The simple things around you at home, all are laden with wisdom at many different levels. You have a spoon, a wooden kitchen spoon. Every time you pick it up, you could remember where you got it and when, and to fully explain that you would have to give the entire history of your life, and that of all your ancestors, because it was all the world that brought you to that shop, at that particular time, in that particular place. So every commonplace "thing" connects you to the universe. Every thing is a "souvenir," a reminder of import.

—ALICE O. HOWELL
in *The Dove in the Stone*

MAKING BREAKFAST

The woman sets the table. She watches me beat the eggs. I scramble them in a saucepan, . . . I take our plates, spoon eggs on them, we sit and eat. She and I and the kitchen have become extraordinary: we are not simply eating; we are pausing in the march to perform an act together; we are in love; and the meal offered and received is a sacrament which says: I know you will die; I am sharing food with you; it is all I can do, and it is everything.

—ANDRE DUBUS
in *Broken Vessels*

READING THE NEWSPAPER

I've never been very good at feasting on the daily newspaper. It turns bitter in my mouth. And yet, this is my world. This face of suffering I must embrace as a part of my responsibility. Part of the feast is becoming aware of the world that is mine. Part of the feast is owning this broken world as my own brokenness. I clasp the newspaper to my heart and ask once again in the stillness of the night, "What are we doing to the image of God in one another?"

—MACRINA WIEDERKEHR
in *A Tree Full of Angels*

SENDING THE CHILDREN TO SCHOOL

When I was a child, a volcano erupted unexpectedly in Iceland, burying a small town at the foot of its cone. All of the children in the town were in school at the time, and they all perished. The parents sent their sons and daughters out the door that morning, same as they always did, and never saw them again.

I remember my mother being profoundly moved by that tragedy. She always made sure that the last words we had in the morning were loving ones. That cannot always have been easy, but my memory is that she usually succeeded.

—BARBARA CAWTHORNE CRAFTON
in *The Sewing Room*

PLAYING WITH THE DOG

Everyone needs a spiritual guide: a minister, rabbi, counselor, wise friend, or therapist. My own wise friend is my dog. He has deep knowledge to impart. He makes friends easily and doesn't hold a grudge. He enjoys simple pleasures and takes each day as it comes. Like a true Zen master he eats when he's hungry and sleeps when he's tired. He's not hung up about sex. Best of all, he befriends me with an unconditional love that human beings would do well to imitate.

—GARY A. KOWALSKI
in *The Souls of Animals*

RUNNING

The person that I am is a body and a mind expressing a spirit. When I run, my entire personality participates to a greater or lesser degree. My highs, therefore, vary from a purely physical reaction to the deepest spiritual experiences. My feelings span the spectrum from simple sensual pleasure to joy, from contentment to a peace beyond understanding.

—GEORGE SHEEHAN
in *Personal Best*

SWIMMING

Water to me is a saving grace. As a child I forgot my anger at my parents or camp counselors or teachers if I went to a swimming pool, or to the lake. . . .

Water was freedom, an element in which I believed I had perfect control. Lake and pool waters were calm enough to provide that illusion. I moved through the water in a kind of ecstasy, cut away from the rules of the land, social requirements, limitations, disapproval. Water was action, more effective than prayer. When I swam I believed in God.

—DORIS GRUMBACH
in *Coming into the End Zone*

DOING CHORES

There is no more comforting sound to me than the spinning of that washer or dryer. It is the whole world spinning in there, cleansing itself and me.

As long as the washer and dryer spin, I tell myself, I am safe and those I love may choose to keep living alongside me. For there is laundry to be done and so many chores—chores of the living. There is so much to be remembered under the dust of our old contempt for cleaning up after ourselves, picking up our own socks. There is much to be swept away and shined bright and scrubbed down to its deepest, most illuminating level. Think of all the chores we have yet to do, quietly and on our knees—because home is holy.

—BRENDA PETERSON
in *Nature and Other Mothers*

PUTTING AWAY SOCKS

From the day you bring them home from the store, socks require care out of all proportion to the services they provide in return. Socks need to be put away, found, worn, washed, dried, folded or balled up, put away, worn, thrown in a corner, found, washed and dried—an endless cycle of obligation and loss. . . .

You can get metaphysical about socks if you like, pondering the grace of their design, their stubborn, catlike refusal to be team players, their bachelor-like tendencies to pair off unpredictably, and so on, but I think that may be like looking for the cosmos in a pebble: you can do it, but it takes a high level of belief.

—LAURA GREEN
in *Reinventing Home*

SITTING ON THE PORCH

From the porch one observes the simple rhythms of daily life: the neighbor setting out the garbage in the early morning, the woman from the next street who regularly walks her little dog just after suppertime, the school-age boys exercising prowess in bicycling, the elderly widow receiving a rare visit from an in-law, the business-like drivers of passing cars whose faces mirror their intent to get where they are going.

On the porch one hears the sounds that surround us—the worried chirping of jays hovering over a nest, the cries of a waking baby across the street, the approaching bell of the ice cream man's truck, distant sirens from the city, the neighborhood dogs whose resonant barks carry airborne canine conversations well over the barriers of fenced-in yards.

Seated upon the porch one finds it unnecessary to comment upon or analyze what one sees and hears. It is enough that it is. Being is not something to be taken for granted or overlooked but something to be breathed in and celebrated with sweet contentment and a grateful heart.

—WENDY WRIGHT
in *Sacred Dwelling*

GARDENING

The first flush of enthusiasm we've felt in designing and planting a new garden may give way to boredom as we settle into the routines of tending established plants. It's easy to tire of caregiving after the dedicated watchfulness required in helping young seeds and plants get started. We may mistakenly hope that things in the garden can, with some water and fertilizer, mature on their own. . . .

In fact, what may appear on the surface to be tedious physical work may, in the actual doing, be spiritually liberating. In taking time to contemplate the small—in observing the details of our gardens—we can experience life on a manageable scale.

—MARILYN BARRETT
in *Creating Eden*

WEEDING BY THE WALK

I am a naturalist at heart, with a patio for my classroom. I may not be the only student in attendance, however, for last week, as I was pulling out weeds where the walk goes by the garage, I was scolded by a squirrel who seemed to be overseeing my labors. If I continue with this task, I may get to see the baby blue jays by the compost heap learn to fly, or be around when the first autumn leaf sails onto the bricks.

This I know: There is absolutely no hope of beating the weeds, which are out there growing back this very moment.

I need to reframe this task so that my thinking fits reality and sends me outside with the proper attitude. When I step out on our patio, I'm not fighting the weeds. I'm joining them.

—LINDA WELTNER
in *No Place Like Home*

RAKING

There is an art to raking, a very fine art, one with rhythm in it, and life. On the days I do it well, the rake wakes up. Wood that came from dark dense forests seems to return to life. The water that rose up through the rings of that wood, the minerals of earth mined upward by the burrowing tree roots, all come alive. My own fragile hand touches the wood, a hand full of my own life, including that which rose each morning early to watch the sun return from the other side of the planet. Over time, these hands will smooth the rake's wooden handle down to a sheen.

Raking. It is a labor round and complete, smooth and new as an egg, and the rounding seasons of the world revolving in time and space. All things, even our own heartbeats and sweat, are in it, part of it. And that work, that watching the turning over of life, becomes a road into what is essential.

—LINDA HOGAN
in *Dwellings*

ANSWERING THE DOOR

Once you commit yourself to a place, you begin to share responsibility for what happens there. When PCBs leak into the water or dioxides into the air, it is your water and your air that is polluted. The parks, the schools, the hospitals, the government, all are yours to fret over. When kids knock at your door, requesting donations for the band or the debate team or the purchase of a limestone rhinoceros, you have to reach for your wallet. Entangle yourself in a place, and you become attached to your neighbors as to kinfolk.

—SCOTT RUSSELL SANDERS
in *Secrets of the Universe*

SHARING GOSSIP

We are interrelated in a small town, whether or not we're related by blood. We know without thinking about it who owns what car; inhabitants of a town as small as a monastery learn to recognize each other's footsteps in the hall. Story is a safety valve for people who live as intimately as that; and I would argue that gossip done well can be a holy thing. It can strengthen communal bonds. . . .

Like the desert tales that monks have used for centuries as a basis for a theology and way of life, the tales of small-town gossip are often morally instructive, illustrating the ways ordinary people survive the worst that happens to them; or, conversely, the ways in which self-pity, anger, and despair can overwhelm and destroy them. Gossip is theology translated into experience. In it we hear great stories of conversion, like the drunk who turns his or her life around, as well as stories of failure. We can see that pride really does go before a fall, and that hope is essential. We watch closely those who retire, or who lose a spouse, lest they lose interest in living. When we gossip we are also praying, not only for them but for ourselves.

—KATHLEEN NORRIS
in *Dakota*

DRIVING IN TRAFFIC

It was gorgeous traffic, it was beautiful traffic—that's what was not usual. It was a beauty to see, to hear, to smell, even to be part of. It was so dazzlingly alive it all but took my breath away. It rattled and honked and chattered with life—the people, the colors of their clothes, the marvelous hodgepodge of their faces, all of it; the taxis, the shops, the blinding sidewalks. The spring day made everybody a celebrity—blacks, whites, Hispanics, every last one of them. It made even the litter and clamor and turmoil of it a kind of miracle.

—FREDERICK BUECHNER
in *The Clown in the Belfry*

Z

ZEAL

"God wants the heart," the Talmud tells us. We are wooed and won by grace. And our response is to be aroused by life.

"Nothing great in the world has been accomplished without passion," writes the German philosopher G. W. F. Hegel. It is the fuel that moves our souls.

"The world and its beings are the spontaneous overflow of creative, imaginable energy," says Huston Smith, an authority on the history of the world's religions. And part of our mission in life is to meet and greet and mix that energy with our own.

To be aroused by life is to be spiritually literate—always on the lookout for meaning. "Love of the world," Catholic monk William McNamara notes, "does not diminish but enhances [our] dynamic, irresistible and burning love of God."

To be aroused by life is to cherish every moment and to not miss a thing. Psychiatrist Elisabeth Kubler-Ross states: "It's only when we truly know and understand that we have a limited time on earth—and that we have no way of knowing when our time is up—that we will begin to live each day to the fullest as if it was the only one we had."

To be aroused by life is to feel a kinship with other peoples. "The spiritual thirst that is latent in everybody can never come to a place of fulfillment unless people begin to think of each other as potential brothers and sisters," writes Malidoma Somé, an African medicine man.

To be aroused by life is to feel a deep connection with all else that exists. "What everyone forgets," diarist Anais Nin reminds us, "is that passion is not merely a heightened sensual fusion but a way of life which produces, as in mystics, an ecstatic awareness of the whole of life."

To be aroused by life is to honor the ties which bind us. Professor of theology Lewis B. Smedes states: "Human fellowship and sturdy joy come to us as we create and keep on re-creating our fragile human relationships making them last through the power of caring love. To dare to make and care to keep commitments, this is love."

To be aroused by life is to give of ourselves in service of the common good, to do our small bit for our extended family. "I long to accomplish a great and noble task," educator and author Helen Keller admits, "but it is my chief duty to accomplish small tasks as if they were great and noble."

To be aroused by life is to let our hearts take us where we are needed. "It is not a matter of thinking much," says sixteenth-century Spanish Carmelite nun Teresa of Avila, "so do whatever most kindles love in you."

To be aroused by life involves the wonderful realization that grace is the place where it all begins and ends. Thirteenth-century mystic Mechtild of Magdeburg gives us a beautiful image to contemplate: "The Holy Spirit is our harpist and all strings which are touched in love must sound."

Let the music of your heart play every day in every way.

ENTERING A BUILDING

We make a building beautiful when we stop for it, arrest the motion of thoughts, and linger with it, rather than merely using it. A glass tower is not unlike a computer. Both are media whose message is to increase efficiency. To spend time each day giving attention to a technical building where one works is a very unfamiliar gesture toward a thing designed to receive little attention, designed to focus attention on efficient work. The soul work here consists of defamiliarizing it, loosening the web of anesthesia.

—ROBERT SARDELLO
in *Facing the World with Soul*

TAKING CARE OF THE CAR

My station wagon is being fixed now and I hope everything comes out OK. It's good to have a car you don't worry about denting. The wagon was always the one that got left out in the rain and snow. If there was a dirty job to be done, I did it in the wagon. I saved my good car because I wanted the good car to last. I've had three good cars since I bought the wagon. The wagon, mistreatment and all, has outlasted the cars I pampered.

When I get it back, the first thing I'm going to do is give it a nice full tank of high-octane gas, some clean, fresh oil and a warm bath. I want the wagon to know that it's loved.

—ANDREW A. ROONEY
in *Not That You Asked . . .*

VISITING A FRIEND

Twice in my life I have experienced deep depression. Both times various friends tried to rescue me with well-intended encouragement and advice. . . .

In the midst of my depression I had a friend who took a different tack. Every afternoon at around four o'clock he came to me, sat me in a chair, removed my shoes, and massaged my feet. He hardly said a word, but he was there, he was with me. He was a lifeline for me, a link to the human community and thus to my own humanity. He had no need to "fix" me. He knew the meaning of compassion.

—PARKER J. PALMER
in *The Active Life*

WANDERING AROUND

There is an art to wandering. If I have a destination, a plan—an objective—I've lost the ability to find serendipity. I've become too focused, too single-minded. I am on a quest, not a ramble. I search for the Holy Grail of particularity and miss the chalice freely offered, filled full and overflowing.

—CATHY JOHNSON
in *On Becoming Lost*

COLLECTING THINGS

In my suit-jacket pocket are a couple of horse chestnuts, picked up months ago on a back street. The asphalt was littered with spiny husks and the remains of nuts that cars had run over, but in the gutter I found two burrs that were still intact, inside each a pearl of oiled and polished mahogany. . . .

. . . In whatever stratosphere of world issues I find myself, the horse chestnuts bring me back to earth.

Horse chestnuts will not work for everyone. But other grown-ups, I notice, have their equivalents: the tail feathers of a red-shouldered hawk, a glass bottle filled with beach sand, a lump of copper ore that doubles as a paperweight. Each reminds someone of a place and time when, whether they knew it or not, they had both feet firmly on the ground, a reminder that is the most subtle, and yet the strongest, form of encouragement. Horse chestnuts are my talisman. In the rarefied atmosphere of world responsibility, I find that they work a simple magic, reminding me what it is exactly that I have grown up to care for.

—ROGER B. SWAIN
in *Saving Graces*

WRITING A LETTER

Our correspondences show us where our intimacies lie. There is something very sensual about a letter. The physical contact of pen to paper, the time set aside to focus thoughts, the folding of the paper into the envelope, licking it closed, addressing it, a chosen stamp, and then the release of the letter to the mailbox—are all acts of tenderness.

And it doesn't stop there. Our correspondences have wings—paper birds that fly from my house to yours—flocks of ideas crisscrossing the country. Once opened, a connection is made. We are not alone in the world.

—TERRY TEMPEST WILLIAMS
in *Refuge*

MAKING MUSIC TAPES

For years now I've made what I call "tapes against terror" to hide me away from the noisy yak and call of the outside world. These homemade productions are dubbed Mermaid Music; sometimes I send them to friends for birthdays and feel the pleasure of playing personal disc jockey to accompany their lives too. Among my siblings, we now exchange music tapes instead of letters. It is particularly gratifying to hear my nieces and nephews singing along to my tapes, as another generation inherits our family frequency.

—BRENDA PETERSON
in *Nature and Other Mothers*

GOING TO A SPECIAL PLACE

I think everyone has a place for healing, though they do not always give it a name. As a child I didn't know that rock was my healing-rock. It is only now as I pray with these memories that I realize what was happening at that rock. The rock was the place I went when I was afraid or confused. It was a place of healing for me. It did more to soothe my soul than any confessional.

—MACRINA WIEDERKEHR
in *A Tree Full of Angels*

GOING DOWN TO THE SEA

From my mother came the idea that going down to the sea repaired the spirit. That is where she walked when she was sad or worried or lonely for my father. If she had been crying, she came back composed; if she had left angry with us, she returned in good humour. So we naturally believed that there was a cleansing, purifying effect to be had; that letting the fresh wind blow through your mind and spirits as well as your hair and clothing purged black thoughts; that contemplating the ceaseless motion of the waves calmed a raging spirit.

—ROBERT MACNEIL
in *Wordstruck*

HAVING DINNER

This is the heart of whole body eating: Be there when you eat. Achieve the fullest experience of your food. Taste it. Savor it. Pay attention to it. Rejoice in it. See how it makes your body feel. Take in all the sensations.

But don't just eat the food. Eat the ambiance. Eat the colors. Eat the aromas. Eat the conversation. Eat the company sitting next to you. Eat the entire experience. . . .

We don't just hunger for food alone. We hunger for the experience of it—the tasting, the chewing, the sensuousness, the enjoyment, the textures, the sounds, and the satisfaction.

—MARC DAVID
in *Nourishing Wisdom*

EATING PIE

The pie is religious, something from God. The only part of the meal to be eaten slowly. Huge pieces, a quarter pie per person, and between each bite a drink of coffee and when the pie is done, the fork is held sideways in the hand and swiped around the plate to get the absolute last of the juice and apple and crust.

—GARY PAULSEN
in *Clabbered Dirt, Sweet Grass*

GATHERING UP CRUMBS

Be careful with the crumbs.
Do not overlook them.

Be careful with the crumbs;
the little chances to love,

the tiny gestures, the morsels
that feed, the minims.

Take care of the crumbs;
a look, a laugh, a smile,

a teardrop, an open hand. Take care
of the crumbs. They are food also.

Do not let them fall.
Gather them. Cherish them.

—GUNILLA NORRIS
in *Becoming Bread*

WASHING DISHES

The ordinary arts we practice every day at home are of more importance to the soul than their simplicity might suggest. For example, I can't explain it, but I enjoy doing dishes. I've had an automatic dishwasher in my home for over a year, and I have never used it. What appeals to me, as I think about it, is the reverie induced by going through the ritual of washing, rinsing, and drying. Marie-Louise von Franz, the Swiss Jungian author, observes that weaving and knitting, too, are particularly good for the soul because they encourage reflection and reverie.

—THOMAS MOORE
in *Care of the Soul*

READING

I read in the hope of discovering the truth, or at least some truths. I look for truth in what some might deem strange places: novels and poems, histories and memoirs, biographies and autobiographies, letters and diaries. . . . In reading for truth, you understand, I am not seeking a full game plan, some large system that will explain the world to me, or a patent for bliss. Instead I seek clues that might explain life's oddities, that might light up the dark corners of existence a little, that might correct foolish ideas I have come to hold too dearly, that might, finally, make my own stay here on earth more interesting, if not necessarily more pleasant.

—JOSEPH EPSTEIN
in *The Middle of My Tether*

GOING TO THE MOVIES

In our recreation, as in all areas of our life, we offer our participation to God. He is there anyway. Do we imagine that when we step onto a sailboat, God stays ashore? Or that when we enter a movie, God waits on the sidewalk? Or that when we're in the heat of a tennis match, God is waiting in the church pew? We play, it is lovely, and we can revel in God in the midst of our play.

—MARILYN GUSTIN
in *You Can Know God*

EATING POPCORN

Popcorn enjoys a metaphysical bond with humanness.

Popcorn is also the world's most social food.

Consider that popcorn is the only food shared while eaten more often than it is eaten alone. Since that is so, the act of sharing brings people together, even if that togetherness is no more poignant than two greasy fingers touching and sliding off each other way down in the bottom of the bucket. True, it's not a very deep intimacy, but an intimacy nonetheless. Friends, we have to grab our moments of sharing whenever and however we can.

—JOHN V. CHERVOKAS
in *God Lives—In the Suburbs*

GOING TO A SACRED SPACE

The bedside could also be considered a sacred space where each family member begins and ends the day with prayer to God. There might also be a hermitage within the home . . .—a space in which stillness can be assured; a space to reflect, to study, or simply to be alone. This holy space could be a den, a bedroom, or a specific room in the basement maybe, which through common agreement would not be disturbed when occupied by its "hermit." Setting aside such space would itself bespeak the significance of taking time to be quiet and alone with God, and of respecting this kind of need and value for solitude in one another.

—MARY ANTHONY WAGNER
in *The Sacred World of the Christian*

TELLING A STORY

The stories people tell have a way of taking care of them. If stories come to you, care for them. And learn to give them away where they are needed. Sometimes a person needs a story more than food to stay alive. That is why we put these stories in each other's memory. This is how people care for themselves.

—BARRY LOPEZ
in *Crow and Weasel*

THROWING OUT THE GARBAGE

Garbage can smell terrible, especially rotting organic matter. But it can also become rich compost for fertilizing the garden. The fragrant rose and the stinking garbage are two sides of the same existence. Without one, the other cannot be. Everything is in transformation. The rose that wilts after six days will become a part of the garbage. After six months the garbage is transformed into a rose. When we speak of impermanence, we understand that everything is in transformation. This becomes that, and that becomes this.

—THICH NHAT HANH
in *Present Moment Wonderful Moment*

LOOKING AT THE STARS

As I write, I am thinking particularly of an evening not long ago when I was far from city lights under a sky of crystalline clarity. The earth was tented with stars, stars so numerous they appeared as a continuous fabric of light. The Milky Way flowed like a luminous river from north to south, banked with dark shoals, eddied in glittering pools. Our sister galaxy in the constellation Andromeda was visible to the naked eye, a blur of light from a trillion faraway stars. Meteors flashed like fireflies. Such skies never fail to excite the imagination. Certain constellations—Orion or Ursa Major—are perhaps the oldest surviving inventions of the human mind. The depth and beauty of the night inspired religious and philosophical speculation.

—CHET RAYMO
in *The Virgin and the Mousetrap*

TAKING OFF YOUR SHOES

Taking off your shoes is a sacred ritual. It is a hallowed moment of remembering the goodness of space and time. It is a way of celebrating the *holy ground* on which you stand. If you want to be a child of wonder cherish the truth that time and space are holy. Whether you take off your shoes symbolically or literally matters little. What is important is that you are alive to the *holy ground* on which you stand and to the *holy ground* that you are.

—MACRINA WIEDERKEHR
in *Seasons of Your Heart*

TAKING A BATH

Know thyself—this includes knowing bodies. Bathing calls forth a self-scrutiny. Certainly an hour afloat with one's own imperfect thighs, belly, and derriere, a bath familiar with one's own cellulite and flaccid fault lines, is an exercise in self-acceptance. It is hard to transcend the body in a hot bath. One sinks into one's own physical and metaphysical depths. Who knows what lurks down there? Who knows what we might plumb about ourselves?

—BRENDA PETERSON
in *Nature and Other Mothers*

TRIMMING YOUR FINGERNAILS

Your fingernails and toenails are composed of hardened skin cells. It is the same material that makes up the claws of animals and birds. Each time you trim your fingernails you are involved in primitive arms-limitation, the earliest and most basic of all disarmament.

—EDWARD HAYS
in *Prayers for a Planetary Pilgrim*

BRUSHING YOUR TEETH

Take teeth, which are so insignificant in God's layout of the human body that they're not even visible until you smile. I am committed to brushing them twice a day, not just back and forth as I was taught as a child, but one tooth at a time, in front and behind, with a vertical motion. This is no quick cleanup because company's coming. This is closer to polishing the silver every night of your life.

I always felt that brushing my teeth twice a day was religion enough, but that was before the periodontist instructed me in the ceremony of the dental floss, baptism by Water Pik, and self-flagellation with the rubber tip at the end of my toothbrush. I'm devoted to the well-being of my teeth as much as anyone. Still, I'm not prepared to take the veil for them.

—LINDA WELTNER
in *No Place Like Home*

LIGHTING A CANDLE

To light a candle by myself is one of my favorite prayers. I am not talking about reading prayers by candlelight. The very act of lighting the candle is prayer. There is the sound of striking the match, the whiff of smoke after blowing it out, the way the flame flares up and then sinks, almost goes out until a drop of melted wax gives it strength to grow to its proper size and to steady itself. All this and the darkness beyond my small circle of light is prayer. I enter into it as one enters a room. My being alone is essential to this prayer. The presence of even one other person would completely change it. Something would be lost.

—BROTHER DAVID STEINDL-RAST
in *Gratefulness, The Heart of Prayer*

CHECKING ON THE CHILDREN

It has been my habit to look at my children's feet when they are sleeping. This has helped me to cultivate an awareness of their uniqueness, their God-givenness, and to disarm myself of the posture of defensiveness and combativeness that I have created in myself. There are three different sets of feet, each perfect, each expressive of the lifestage and personality of each of my children: the blunt, babyish toes and flat arches that support a tirelessly running body, sturdy enough to use the way a rabbit uses its hind feet in defense; the slightly larger, more graceful toes and heels that are fond of practicing "ballet," feet that often remain tucked up under a frilly skirt that, when the impulse strikes, can run like the wind; the slender feet, half-child's, half-woman's, that kick off their shoes whenever they enter a room, that are alternately decorously placed in a lady-like pose or sprawled out on any and all available pieces of furniture. It is those feet that have taught me the very little I know about seeing with the eyes of love.

—WENDY WRIGHT
in *Weavings*

GOING TO BED

The heart of my house has to be my bed. If relaxation and acceptance are the warp and woof of domestic life, and if home is the place where I am most free to be myself, then my bed is the place where it all comes together. Here is where I think naked thoughts, daydream, make love, worry, plot, argue, get my back scratched, speculate, talk about growing old, and, finally, cut the mooring ties and drift out with the dream tide.

The bed, the place where we are born and die, is our primeval place . . .

—LAURA GREEN
in *Reinventing Home*

MAKING LOVE

We are neither animals nor angels. We are something else—we are humans—part spiritual and part physical, and those two parts are combined into one. A true sexuality acknowledges both these dimensions and tries to embrace them both in the act of love.

You need to accept this in yourself. Having sex is what the animals do. Achieving mystical union is what the angels do. We alone can make love, where the physical and the spiritual commingle in a single, joyous act.

—KENT NERBURN
in *Letters to My Son*

LISTENING TO DREAMS

As I began to take an interest in my dreams, I became aware for the first time in my life that God wanted to speak to me. It was during a difficult time that a friend advised me to pay attention to my dreams. I soon noticed that there was a wisdom greater than mine that spoke to me in my dreams and came to my aid.

—MORTON KELSEY
in *Dreams*

GETTING A LATE-NIGHT SNACK

This is not a group activity. It is a private religious experience. In the holy solitude of the midnight hour, you are taking communion with the spirits of bird and fruit and field. The best moments of past feasts come to mind. And it is at times like these you have no doubt that life is good, that your family, all tucked away in their beds, are royal folks, and that grace abounds. Amen.

—ROBERT FULGHUM
in *Uh-Oh*

Afterword

THE GOOD NEWS

The good news
they do not print.
The good news
we do print.
We have a special edition every moment,
and we need you to read it.
The good news is that you are alive,
that the linden tree is still there,
standing firm in the harsh Winter.
The good news is that you have wonderful eyes
to touch the blue sky.
The good news is that your child is there before you,
and your arms are available:
hugging is possible.
They only print what is wrong.
Look at each of our special editions.
We always offer the things that are not wrong.
We want you to benefit from them
and help protect them.
The dandelion is there by the sidewalk,
smiling its wondrous smile,
singing the song of eternity.
Listen! You have ears that can hear it.
Bow your head.
Listen to it.
Leave behind the world of sorrow
and preoccupation

and get free.
The latest good news
is that you can do it.
—THICH NHAT HANH
in *Call Me by My True Names*

KEY TO THE ALPHABET
OF SPIRITUAL LITERACY

ACKNOWLEDGMENTS

We were able to do this book because of the gracious support of many people. Our ideas on spiritual literacy were shaped and tested in *Values & Visions* magazine and the *Values & Visions Circles Newsletter*, the membership publications of Cultural Information Service (CIS). We are grateful to all CIS members for giving us the opportunities to apply this perspective to so many cultural resources. We especially want to thank the participants in Values & Visions Circles for their patience during our six-month sabbatical when we were finishing the book.

Carolyn Dutton has been by our sides through all the stages of *Spiritual Literacy*. She has brought the spiritual practice of attention to the critically important steps of typing and proofing the readings and the enormous task of clearing all the permissions.

Our agent, Ned Leavitt, instantly grasped the concept of *Spiritual Literacy* and, over the months, proved to be its effective advocate through a graceful combination of the spiritual practices of justice and kindness.

Leigh Haber, our editor at Scribner, sought out this book and encouraged its birth and development; she knows a lot about the spiritual practice of nurturing, and is a good exemplar of the practice of enthusiasm. Susan Moldow, our publisher, has been a strong supporter of the book from our very first discussions about it. We also have appreciated the help of others at Scribner as the manuscript came together, including Greer Kessel, Kristina Nwazota, and Angella Baker. We want to recognize the ongoing work on the book's behalf by Rosalind Lippel, Pat Eisemann, Sharon Dynak, Hilary Dunst, and Anita Halton. Interior designer Erich Hobbing, through his inspired choice of typeface and his artful balancing of the many elements of the text, has shown us that he is indeed a master in his vocation.

Nancy Burke, a colleague as a book and media editor, copyedited *Spiritual Literacy* and helped with many last minute details. We treasure her openness and zeal.

ACKNOWLEDGMENTS

We want to thank editor Elizabeth Bogner, art director Cherlynne Li, and their colleagues at Touchstone for watching over the book's transformation into a beautiful paperback. We appreciate the care and imagination they invested in this stage of the book's life.

We are indebted to the many spiritually literate writers and producers whose works are cited here. We want to recognize as well the people who brought them to our awareness—publicists and publishers' publicity departments—and who helped us bring them to you—agents and permissions' departments.

All the voices in *Spiritual Literacy* have been teachers to us, but we have been particularly inspired by Thomas Moore's writings on the practice of imagination, Thich Nhat Hanh's demonstrations of the practice of connections, Edward Hays's diverse examples of the practice of devotion, and Coleman Barks's expression, through the poetry of Rumi, of the practices of gratitude and mystery.

Many friends have made indirect contributions to this book. We thank Martina Fritsch, Marge and Paul Patterson, and Chris and Annie Flanders for providing ways and places for us to engage in the spiritual practice of play. Manny and Alex and the staff of El Parador Café have nourished our souls as well as our bodies.

Mary Ann is grateful to Marjorie Ann Allen for her encouraging words and her artful ministrations of the Ohashiatsu touch of peace. Karl Koss's interest in our work for many years has been liberating. Jerry Epstein has reminded us of the practice of being present. Debra Farrington and Phyllis Tickle have been cheerleaders for our focus on a wide range of spiritual books. Linda Hanick and Jeff Weber of Trinity Video have encouraged our explorations of everyday spirituality. The women's circle of Judson Memorial Church and the Shimoni Street Stompers have shown us the breadth and vitality of today's spiritual renaissance. We have been reminded constantly of our blessings by our dear friends Joy Carol, Ieva Graufelds, Pat Repinski, and Les Schwartz.

In our families, we first learned about the spiritual practices of listening and love. We are still enjoying these gifts from Wildred Michael, Philip Michael, Colin and Elisa Michael, Cora Louise Kevan, Harriett Brussat, Carol Hagen, Val Luljack, Laurel Sacks, and Linda Cutting. In our own home, we are buoyed by the affection and companionship of Boone and Bebb. Hard work is always good work in such company.

Finally, doing this book has reminded us again and again that, as Rumi puts it, we are the guests that the mystics talk about, and everything is for the Host. Thank you.

PERMISSIONS
AND SOURCES

Grateful acknowledgment is made for permission to reprint the following materials.

READING THE SACRED IN EVERYDAY LIFE

Selected excerpt from page 70 from *The Music of Silence* by David Steindl-Rast and Sharon Lebell. Copyright © 1995 by David Steindl-Rast, OSB, and Sharon Lebell. Reprinted by permission of HarperCollins Publishers, Inc.

Four lines from Lao-tzu in *Tao Te Ching* by Stephen Mitchell. Translation copyright © 1988 by Stephen Mitchell. Reprinted by permission of Harper-Collins Publishers, Inc., New York, and Macmillan General Books, London.

From *There Is a Season* by Joan Chittister. Copyright © 1995 by Joan Chittister. Reprinted by permission of Orbis Books, P.O. Box 308, Maryknoll, NY 10545.

From *Grace and Grit* by Ken Wilber, © 1991. Reprinted by arrangement with Shambhala Publications, Inc., 300 Massachusetts Ave., Boston, MA 02115.

Source Unknown. Quoted in *Peacemaking Day by Day*. Pax Christi, 348 East Tenth St., Erie, PA 16503.

From *Celtic Fire* by Robert Van de Weyer. Copyright © 1990 by Robert Van de Weyer. Used by permission of Doubleday, a division of Bantam Doubleday Dell Publishing Group, Inc., New York, and by Darton, Longman and Todd, Ltd., London.

From *Challenge* by Mark Link. Copyright © 1988 by Mark Link. Reprinted by permission of Tabor Publishing, Allen, Tex.

Reprinted from *Cultivating the Mind of Love: The Practice of Looking Deeply in the Mahayana Buddhist Tradition* (1996) by Thich Nhat Hanh with permission of Parallax Press, Berkeley, Calif.

THE ALPHABET OF SPIRITUAL LITERACY

THINGS

NATURE

ANIMALS

LEISURE

CREATIVITY

From *Money and the Meaning of Life* by Jacob Needleman. Copyright © 1991 by Jacob Needleman. Used by permission of Doubleday, a division of Bantam Doubleday Dell Publishing Group, Inc.

From *Secular Sanctity* by Edward Hays. Copyright © 1984 by Edward Hays. Reprinted by permission of Forest of Peace Publishing, Inc., 251 Muncie Road, Leavenworth, KS 66048.

From *Feathers on the Wind* by Edward Hays. Copyright © 1995 by Edward Hays. Reprinted by permission of Forest of Peace Publishing, Inc., 251 Muncie Road, Leavenworth, KS 66048.

From *A Big-Enough God* by Sara Maitland. Copyright © 1995 by Sara Maitland. Reprinted by permission of Henry Holt and Company, Inc., and Cassell, London.

Peter Terzick in *Of Human Hands: A Reader in the Spirituality of Work* edited by Gregory F. Augustine Pierce. Copyright © 1991 by Augsburg Fortress. Reprinted by permission of Hazel Terzick and the United Brotherhood of Carpenters.

From *A Return to Love* by Marianne Williamson. Copyright © 1992 by Marianne Williamson. Reprinted by permission of HarperCollins Publishers, Inc..

From *Love & Profit* by James A. Autry. Copyright © 1991 by James A. Autry. By permission of William Morrow & Company, Inc., and the author.

Maxine F. Dennis in *Of Human Hands* edited by Gregory F. Augustine Pierce. Copyright © 1991 by Augsburg Fortress. Used by permission of Maxine F. Dennis.

Selected excerpt from page 61 from *The Common Table* by John Cowan. Copyright © 1993 by John Cowan. Reprinted by permission of HarperCollins Publishers, Inc.

SERVICE

From *Teaching Your Children About God* by David J. Wolpe. Copyright © 1993 by David J. Wolpe. Reprinted by permission of Henry Holt and Company, Inc.

From *Roots of Buddhist Psychology* by Jack Kornfield. Dharma Seed Tape Library.

From *Some Do Care: Contemporary Lives of Moral Commitment* by Anne Colby and William Damon. Copyright © 1992 by Anne Colby and William Damon. Reprinted with permission of The Free Press, a division of Simon & Schuster.

Selected excerpt from pages 29–30 from *A Tree Full of Angels* by Macrina Wiederkehr. Copyright © 1988 by Macrina Wiederkehr. Reprinted by permission of HarperCollins Publishers, Inc.

Selected excerpt from page 174 from *Prayer: Finding the Heart's True*

BODY

RELATIONSHIPS

From *Owning Your Own Shadow* by Robert A Johnson. Copyright © 1992 by Robert A. Johnson. Reprinted by permission of HarperCollins Publishers, Inc.

Lonnie Barbach and David L. Geisinger in *Going the Distance: Secrets to Lifelong Love*. New York: Doubleday, 1991. Reprinted by permission of Doubleday, a division of Bantam Doubleday Dell Publishing Group, Inc.

From *The Trickster, Magician & Grieving Man* by Glen A. Mazis. Copyright © 1993 by Glen A. Mazis. Reprinted by permission of Bear & Company Publishing, Santa Fe, N.Mex. 87504.

Selected excerpt from pages 4–5 from *Lights of Passage* by Kathleen Wall, Ph.D., and Gary Ferguson. Copyright © 1994 by Kathleen Wall, Ph.D., and Gary Ferguson. Reprinted by permission of HarperCollins Publishers, Inc.

Excerpted from *The Art of Ritual*, copyright © 1990 by Renee Beck and Sydney Barbara Metrick. Reprinted by permission of Celestial Arts, P.O. Box 7123, Berkeley, CA 94707.

From *Breathing Lessons* by Anne Tyler. Copyright © 1988 by Anne Tyler. Reprinted by permission of Alfred A. Knopf, Inc., and Penguin Books Canada Limited.

From *Why Not Celebrate?* by Sara Wenger Shenk. Copyright © 1987 by Good Books. Used by permission. All rights reserved.

From *Intimate Play* by William Betcher, M.D., Copyright © 1987 by William Betcher. Used by permission of Viking Penguin, a division of Penguin Books USA Inc., and Brandt & Brandt Literary Agents for the author.

From *We: Understanding the Psychology of Romantic Love* by Robert A. Johnson. Copyright © 1983 by Robert A. Johnson. Reprinted by permission of HarperCollins Publishers, Inc..

From *Love's Compass: A Natural History of the Heart* by Daniel Mark Epstein. Copyright © 1990 by Daniel Mark Epstein. Reprinted by permission of Addison-Wesley Publishing Company, Inc., and the author.

From *Feathers on the Wind* by Edward Hays. Copyright © 1995 by Edward Hays. Reprinted by permission of Forest of Peace Publishing, Inc., 251 Muncie Road, Leavenworth, KS 66048.

Reprinted with the permission of the author and Scribner, a division of Simon & Schuster from *The Foreseeable Future* by Reynolds Price. Copyright © 1989, 1991 by Reynolds Price.

Selected excerpt from page 61 from *When the Heart Waits* by Sue Monk Kidd. Copyright © 1990 by Sue Monk Kidd. Reprinted by permission of HarperCollins Publishers, Inc.

From *To Taste and See* by Thomas W. Mann. Copyright © 1992 by Thomas W. Mann. Reprinted by permission of the Pilgrim Press, Cleveland, Ohio.

From *Teaching Your Children About God* by David J. Wolpe. Copyright © 1993 by David J. Wolpe. Reprinted by permission of Henry Holt and Company, Inc.

From *Embracing the Beloved* by Stephen and Ondrea Levine. Copyright © 1995 by Stephen and Ondrea Levine. Used by permission of Doubleday, a division of Bantam Doubleday Dell Publishing Group, Inc.

COMMUNITY

From *The World's Religions* by Huston Smith. Copyright © 1991 by Huston Smith. Reprinted by permission of HarperCollins Publishers, Inc..

Jelaluddin Rumi in *The Essential Rumi* translated by Coleman Barks with John Moyne, A. J. Arberry, and Reynold Nicholson. HarperSanFrancisco, 1995. Reprinted by permission of Coleman Barks.

A DAY IN THE SPIRITUAL LIFE

A Day in the Life® is a registered trademark of HarperCollins Publishers. Inc. Books in this photography series cover life in Australia, Ireland, Israel, Italy, Japan, and other countries.

From *The Alphabet of Grace* by Frederick Buechner. Copyright © 1970 by Frederick Buechner. Reprinted by permission of HarperCollins Publishers.

Reprinted from *Present Moment Wonderful Moment: Mindfulness Verses for Daily Living* (1990) by Thich Nhat Hanh with permission of Parallax Press, Berkeley, Calif.

From *Becoming Bread* by Gunilla Norris. Copyright © 1993 by Gunilla Norris. Reprinted by permission of Bell Tower, published by Harmony Books, a division of Crown Publishers, Inc.

From *The Magic of Ritual* by Tom F. Driver. Copyright © 1991 by Tom F. Driver. Reprinted by permission of HarperCollins Publishers, Inc.

From *The Dove in the Stone* by Alice O. Howell. Wheaton, Ill.: Quest Books, 1988. Reprinted by permission of the publisher.

From *Broken Vessels* by Andre Dubus. Copyright © 1991 by Andre Dubus. Reprinted by permission of David R. Godine Publisher, Inc.

Selected excerpt from page 146 from *A Tree Full of Angels* by Macrina Wiederkehr. Copyright © 1988 by Macrina Wiederkehr. Reprinted by permission of HarperCollins Publishers, Inc.

"If I Should Die Before I Wake" from *The Sewing Room* by Barbara Cawthorne Crafton. Copyright © 1993 by Barbara Cawthorne Crafton. Used by permission of Viking Penguin, a division of Penguin Books USA Inc., and the author.

From *The Souls of Animals* by Gary A. Kowalski. Walpole, N.H.: Stillpoint Publishing, 1991. Reprinted by permission of the publisher.

Reprinted from *Personal Best* © 1989 by George Sheehan. Permission granted by Rodale Press, Inc., Emmaus, PA 18098.

From *Coming into the End Zone: A Memoir* by Doris Grumbach. Copyright © 1991 by Doris Grumbach. Reprinted by permission of W. W. Norton & Company, Inc., and by Russell & Volkening as agents for the author.

From *Nature and Other Mothers* by Brenda Peterson. Copyright © 1995 by Brenda Peterson. HarperCollins, 1992; Fawcett/Columbine, 1995. Used by permission of the author.

"Socks" by Laura Green, copyright © 1991 by Laura Green, from *Reinvent-*

ing Home by Laurie Abraham et al. Used by permission of Dutton Signet, a division of Penguin Books USA Inc.

Excerpted from *Letters to My Son* by Kent Nerburn © 1994. Reprinted with permission of New World Library, Novato, CA 94949.

From *Dreams: A Way to Listen to God* by Morton Kelsey. Copyright © 1978 by The Missionary Society of St. Paul the Apostle in the State of New York. Reprinted by permission of Paulist Press.

From *Uh-Oh* by Robert Fulghum. Copyright © 1991 by Robert Fulghum. Random House, Inc.

AFTERWORD

Reprinted from *Call Me by My True Names: The Collected Poems of Thich Nhat Hanh* (1993) with permission of Parallax Press, Berkeley, Calif.

A lengthy and comprehensive effort has been made to locate all copyright holders and to clear reprint permission rights. If any acknowledgments have been omitted, or any rights overlooked, it is unintentional. If notified, the publisher will be pleased to rectify any omission in future editions of this book.

INDEX

ABOUT THE AUTHORS

Frederic and Mary Ann Brussat have been covering contemporary culture and the spiritual renaissance for three decades. They founded and codirect Cultural Information Service, a nonprofit organization. They produced a series of viewer's guides to television programs and movies, and they wrote *Values & Visions,* a magazine about resources for spiritual journeys. Currently, they are the directors of the Values & Visions Circles, an international network of small groups who use movies, videos, books, and spoken–word audios as catalysts to soul making. The authors write a newsletter and have created more than 250 Values & Visions Guides for these groups and interested individuals.

Through the Values & Visions Reviews Service, the Brussats provide book, movie, video, and spoken word audio reviews to computer Web sites, magazines, newspapers, newsletters, and radio stations. They are the editors of two books of quotations and activities, *100 Ways to Keep Your Soul Alive* and *100 More Ways to Keep Your Soul Alive.*

Frederic is a United Church of Christ clergyman with a journalism ministry. The Brussats live in New York City.

Frederic and Mary Ann have developed a workshop based on *Spiritual Literacy* and are also available for speaking engagements. For more information on the Brussats' work, write:

CIS/Values & Visions Circles
P. O. Box 786, Dept. SL
Madison Square Station
New York, NY 10159
USA